The Fascist *Persuasion* in Radical Politics

THIS BOOK WAS WRITTEN UNDER THE AUSPICES OF
THE INSTITUTE OF INTERNATIONAL STUDIES,
UNIVERSITY OF CALIFORNIA, BERKELEY.

THE
FASCIST
PERSUASION
IN RADICAL
POLITICS

by A. James Gregor

PRINCETON UNIVERSITY PRESS

PRINCETON, NEW JERSEY

Copyright © 1974 by Princeton University Press

All Rights Reserved
LCC: 73-2463
ISBN: 0-691-07556-5

Library of Congress Cataloguing in Publication data will
be found on the last printed page of this book.

This book has been composed in Linotype Caledonia

Printed in the United States of America
by Princeton University Press
Princeton, New Jersey

This Book is Dedicated to
Paula, Gloria, Ann and Lucille—

Who Shared my Youth and
my Parents With Me.

Contents

Preface

In his preface, an author has the opportunity to pursue some personal concerns, settle some debts, and deliver a brief synopsis of his work. He is generally expected to allude to some special merits possessed by his book, and to apologize for inevitable deficiencies. I should like to attempt something of all that.

First, and perhaps foremost, I should like to settle some accounts. This book is largely the product of other people's responses to my previous work. My first book, *A Survey of Marxism*, was well received by professional reviewers. One of them, whose opinion I hold in high regard, suggested that he would have liked to have had me deal with the economic constituents of classical Marxism more extensively. I think he was quite right. In order to make sense out of classical Marxism, one must reflect on Marx's extensively elaborated economic theories and relate them to Marx's social and political prognostications as well as to his normative convictions. I think Professor Alfred Meyer will find that I have attempted to accomplish just that in Chapters Two and Three.

But more than that, one of the principal reasons for the appearance of this book is the reception accorded by my third book, *The Ideology of Fascism*. While professional judgments concerning its merits ranged from the laudatory to the depreciatory, I found some reviewers terribly dismayed by several things I had attempted to accomplish. Professor Dante Germino, for instance, was concerned that I did not catalogue all the "deep scars" left by fascist regimes—that I attempted an objective reconstruction of Fascist ideology. Professor Germino, unfortunately, will find that the same disability afflicts the present discussion. I have catalogued neither fascist horrors *nor* socialist horrors—nor for that matter have I recounted the horrors perpetrated in pluralistic and liberal political systems. Only if fascist systems were uniquely guilty of inhumanity, brutality, and murder would it serve some cognitive purpose to review such considerations. Since "Marxist" systems are as guilty as fascist ones—and liberal political systems are not completely devoid of guilt—the distinction is not system specific and consequently of no specific cognitive merit. Cataloguing the moral disabilities of various political systems, particularly revolutionary regimes, is not an enterprise calculated to produce defensible distinctions. Only if one could provide a defensible distinction between the mass murder of Jews and the mass murder of kulaks or landed gentry could intelligent discussion commence.

The most modest estimate of Stalin's victims make them out to number more than six and a half million Russians. The number of "bandits" and "bad gentry" massacred by the forces of Mao Tse-tung in the first few years after the termination of hostilities in China number, by conservative estimates, no less than one to three million persons. In effect, mass murder, brutality, and violence do not uniquely distinguish any political system—they certainly do not distinguish fascist from socialist ones. As a consequence I have not taken seriously Professor Howard L. Parsons injunction that the real difference between fascist and socialist systems is "peace vs. war, humanism vs. anti-humanism. . . . communisms' . . . quest for peace and democracy, its affirmation of man's power to fulfill himself through life and not death" as against fascism's "glorification of war."

I have found such suggestions transparently silly. There are many distinctions that could be drawn between fascist and "Marxist" radicalisms. "Peace vs. war, humanism vs. anti-humanism," love vs. hate, and beauty vs. ugliness just don't happen to be among them. One might have thought that contemporary political discussions could be expected to be more sophisticated than that. The sophomoric distinction between "good guys" and "bad guys" doesn't afford us much cognitive leverage.

On the other hand, the fact that I had not discussed Castro's Cuba was looked upon by some as a serious shortcoming. I think that the absence of any discussion of Cuba in my volume on Fascism constituted, in fact, a disability. Given the main thrust of that volume, however, any discussion of so complicated a political phenomenon as the Cuban Revolution would have far exceeded its limits. In this volume I have attempted to make up for that deficiency with what I take to be an interesting and competent discussion of Castro's revolution, highlighting its affinities with generic fascism.

Needless to say, I do not anticipate that the present book will please some of my critics any more than did my antecedent volume on Fascism. Not long ago, while participating in a seminar on Fascism, I suggested that the political history and the political culture of Castro's Cuba shared certain species traits with Mussolini's Fascism. Rarely have I witnessed academic colleagues possessed of such moral outrage. Since their outrage did not permit them to articulate any counterarguments—and since Hugh Thomas, in his recent study of Cuba, has suggested the same similarities—I have permitted Chapter Seven to appear without substantive change.

Chapter Eight, devoted to the student and black variants of the "new radicalism," is largely the consequence of a series of lectures I delivered before the Seminar on the "New Left" conducted by the Foreign Service Institute in Washington, D.C. Whatever is of merit in the chapter is largely the consequence of the criticisms and suggestions of Mr. John Bowling of the Institute.

In general, the book should be much better than it is. I have profited from the contact with some of America's most gifted political analysts. Moreover, I have lived through a good part of the student movement on the Berkeley campus. My students, both inside and out of the movement have assisted me in more ways than I could recount. They have delivered astute criticism and afforded welcome support—and in general have given me a gratifying response in courses where I have tried out some of the ideas contained in the forthcoming pages.

The book attempts, in discursive outline, a reexamination

of common distinctions that most who think about things political accept without very searching criticism. In this respect most of us, in our political ascriptions, simply accept the self-avowals of radicals when they insist that they are "Marxists." In the following pages I have attempted to measure the distance that, in fact, separates today's radicals from the belief system left them by Karl Marx and Friedrich Engels—irrespective of what our radicals claim. In plotting the distance from Marx and Engels, I have, furthermore, attempted to indicate their proximities to paradigmatic Fascism.

This is obviously a preliminary attempt to reformulate a comprehensive and potentially useful classificatory schema. In its present form it is intended to be heuristic—an effort to redirect thinking concerning the mass-mobilizing and revolutionary movements of our century. Equally obvious is the fact that a more *rigorous* analysis would require a criterial characterization of "generic fascism" that I cannot, at this juncture, formulate. The treatment here, as a consequence, is nonrigorous and discursive, corresponding to the nonrigorous and discursive claims made in the course of the discussion.

For the purposes of the subsequent discussion, I will take "radicalism" to refer to any belief system that departs in any significant way from the traditional political convictions now prevailing in North America and Western Europe. This stipulative meaning of radicalism would refer to any collection of political convictions that entails an abandonment of the multiparty and compromissary parliamentary system that has characterized the "Western persuasion" for some considerable time. That such a stipulative definition provides us with an inordinately large class of radicalisms need not detain us, for our concern here will be with the class of *new* radicalisms. The new radicalism I take to refer to that contemporary form of radicalism that seeks to legitimate itself as a species of "new democracy" that can do without formal or informal opposition—and that finds the "will of the masses" articulated in a relatively specific monopolistic ideology and expressed in the will of a single man or a single hegemonic party. In this sense, Fascism, National Socialism, Bolshevism, Maoism and Castroism all belong to the class of "new radicalism"—while regimes such as those of traditional despotisms, constitutional dictatorships, or political curiosities like the Duvalier regime in Haiti would not.

Finally, writing this book has put me in debt to many people. Numbered prominently among them are colleagues such as Aaron Wildavsky, Robert Scalapino, Paul Seabury, Carl Rosberg, and Peter Sperlich. They have made my ideal of a community of scholars a reality. Among research assistants I owe more than I can repay to Mrs. Mari Malvey. Mrs. Jean McGrath and Miss Bonnie Berch prepared this manuscript for press and did far more than could legitimately be expected of them. My wife, Dorothy, aided in more ways than I could enumerate.

Above all, perhaps, I owe most to the University of California, Berkeley, itself. It has afforded me all manner of good things, but best of all it has provided me an academic home in what must surely be the best institution of higher learning in the world.

A.J.G.

Berkeley, California

The Fascist *Persuasion* in Radical Politics

CHAPTER ONE

Revolution, Radicalism, and the Twentieth Century

... When one considers both the various theories which call themselves Marxist, and the realities of the world today, it would seem that the only alternative lies in a choice between a scholastic Marxism which has nothing to do with revolution and a revolution which has nothing in common with Marxism. Never, in the course of the past century, has the name of Marx been so widely invoked; never has this name served to justify so many ideas and actions totally foreign to the genius of Marx.[1]

Stuart Schram

THE twentieth century is obviously a time of troubles. Not a year has gone by since the turn of the century that modern man has not been beset by revolutions and wars—and rumors of revolutions and wars. So traumatic has the entire experience been—so dislocating the irrepressible violence—that we have not yet succeeded in attaining an adequate understanding of what has been, and is, transpiring. We are living through a century in which one-third of mankind now finds itself involved in political systems self-characterized as "socialist," and another third in political systems that are clearly dominated by the military. The prospects for liberal and pluralistic political democracy seem dim.

For some time it was considered sophisticated to suggest that we were passing through a transitional period between the "bourgeois democratic" and the "socialist" eras. This conviction produced a disposition to read the events of the interwar years as a conflict between the forces of "historical

[1] S. R. Schram and H. Carrère d'Encausse, *Marxism in Asia* (Baltimore: Penguin, 1969), p. 112.

3

reaction" and those of historical inevitability. The Soviet Union was advertised as the "socialist vanguard"; and generic fascism, the fascism that manifested itself in southern, central, and eastern Europe during those years, was characterized as the last resistance of "bourgeois dictatorship in decay," of "monopoly" or "finance capital," or of "privilege, irrationality and hatred" against "equality, reason and brotherhood."

The defeat of the Axis powers, the embodiment of "reaction," did not, however, usher in the era of "socialism, progress and amity." The period after the conclusion of the Second World War marked the commencement of the protracted "cold war" and the tortuous conflict not only between the "bourgeois democratic" and "socialist" states but eventually between the "socialist" states themselves. The Sino-Soviet dispute confounded what used to be considered the inevitable march of history. Not only did China and the Soviet Union begin to level charges of "reactionary" and "anti-progressive" against each other, but both began to assume military postures along the long Sino-Soviet border. China denounced the Soviet Union as a reactionary and fascist regime. The Soviet Union decried the "irrationalism," the "adventurism" and the "cult of personality" that characterized the "peasant utopian" and "anti-Marxist" regime of Chairman Mao. Since the end of the Second World War the "progressive" forces in the contemporary world, the "Marxists" and "socialists," have undergone startling changes. The "socialist" and "revolutionary" powers have begun to take on characteristics that are, to say the least, singular. Only in the immediate past has it been conceivable that a "Marxist" and "humanist" radical could say: "*War* is the highest form of struggle for resolving contradictions . . . ," and "All wars that are progressive are just . . . ," "Every Communist must grasp the truth, 'Political power grows out of the barrel of a gun,'" and "[We] are advocates of the omnipotence of revolutionary war; that is good . . . it is Marxist."[2] Only in

[2] Mao Tse-tung, *Quotations from Chairman Mao Tse-tung* (Peking: Foreign Languages, 1966), pp. 58, 59, 61.

4

the immediate past has it become conceivable for a "Marxist humanist" to announce that "hatred is an element of the struggle; a relentless hatred of the enemy, impelling us over and beyond the natural limitations that man is heir to and transforming him into an effective, violent, selective and cold killing machine."[3]

The "Marxism" that has manifested itself after the termination of the Second World War has come to understand revolution in terms of underprivileged or underdeveloped countries as opposed to "privileged" or "capitalist" countries in what Lin Piao described as the rural areas of the world aligned against the cities of the world. The contest is one in which "politics is the commander, politics is the soul of everything"—and the principal tool in the conflict is the military, for "without a people's army the people have nothing."[4]

Radicalism has surely undergone a startling transmogrification. The original Marxist emphasis on economic determinants in historical development has succumbed to voluntarism and activism—and an emphasis on violence, sacrifice, and dedication. The Marxian emphasis on *internationalist* and *class* determinants has succumbed to war conducted by "*national* and *multiclass* liberation movements." The revolution Marx anticipated in the industrially most advanced communities is heralded in the most backward economic systems. The revolution that Marx had foreseen manifesting itself without violence in England, the United States, and Holland is now understood to ride in behind full-scale regular or irregular military operations. Entire societies are militarized in Marx's name, and the humanism that constituted the ethical substance of the Marxist *Weltanschauung* has given way to the invocation of hatred, bloodshed, and sustained violence in order to conjure up the good society.

The magnitude of the change that has overtaken radical-

[3] Ché Guevara, *Venceremos! The Speeches and Writings of Ché Guevara*, edited by J. Gerassi (New York: Macmillan, 1968), p. 422.

[4] Lin Piao, *Long Live the Victory of People's War* (Peking: Foreign Languages, 1968), pp. 108, 67, 57.

ism has only now become apparent. Incremental changes that within the context of an elaborate ideological corpus passed unnoticed have accumulated to the point where they can no longer be ignored. It is no longer possible to neglect the full measure of transformation. "Marxists" themselves have simply pronounced it; they have applauded the "creative developments" classical Marxism has suffered at the hands of such gifted theoreticians as Joseph Stalin, Mao Tse-tung, and Fidel Castro.

The fact is that contemporary radical thought bears remarkably little resemblance to the thought of Karl Marx and Friedrich Engels. Many of the foremost contemporary radicals who advertise themselves as "Marxists" became Marxists, in fact, *before* being exposed to the writings of Marx and/or Engels. When Mao became a "Marxist," for example, very little of the Marxist corpus had been translated into Chinese, the only language he could read. Castro, in turn, in proclaiming his "Marxism-Leninism" admitted that he had read no further than the first few chapters of the first volume of *Das Kapital*—only to throw it aside and insist that only "life" and "revolution" can make one a "true Marxist-Leninist."

In effect, the "Marxism" of contemporary radicals has become increasingly diaphanous. As more and more of the constituents of classical Marxism are jettisoned, the space vacated is filled with alternate substance.

Why this should be the case is not difficult to divine. The problems that afflict the most revolutionary of contemporary societies bear very little resemblance to the problems with which Marx and Engels occupied themselves. The first, and perhaps foremost, problem that weighs on many contemporary societies is, for instance, underdevelopment—delayed or thwarted industrial development. As a consequence of underdevelopment, a colonial heritage, inadequate population or material resources, or one or another disability, many communities suffer collective threat and serious status deprivation. The enhancement of national prestige, the mobili-

6

zation of natural and human resources in the service of that end, the insistence upon individual sacrifice in the furtherance of collective well-being, the commitment to personalist leadership and a one-party state, are features that have become more and more prominent in the thought of contemporary radicals.

These are evidently not exclusively the species traits of "left-wing" or "Marxist-Leninist" political systems. The same or similar features have appeared in the non-Marxist "socialism" of Nasser and Nkrumah, and in the "guided democracy" of Sukarno. "Radical" or "revolutionary" political systems during the second half of the twentieth century, whether "Marxist" or not, have begun to share identifiable traits that suggest they are all members of the same political genus.

Less and less frequently have contemporary radicals in the underdeveloped countries spoken, for example, of a "withering away of the state," or of "universal suffrage," or "referendum and recall"—much less of the industrial self-management and voluntary, productive communes that characterized Karl Marx's vision of the postrevolutionary society. More and more frequently the talk is of "centralized," "directed," and "planned economies," of a unitary vanguard party that "brings consciousness" to the "working masses" that gradually comes to include not only the peasantry, urban and rural "proletariat," but the "national bourgeoisie," and even "progressive gentry and nobility" as well. *Nationalism* has become the principal mobilizing strategy, and not a few contemporary radicals have entertained injunctions such as "The Fatherland or Death!" All of which makes very curious "Marxism" indeed.

Recently Mary Matossian has spoken of a class of mobilizing belief systems she identified as "ideologies of delayed industrialization," a class that includes "Marxism-Leninism, Shintoism, Italian Fascism, Kemalism, Gandhism, the current Egyptian Philosophy of the Revolution, Sun Yat-sen's Three Principles of the People, the Indonesian Pantjasila

7

and many others." Among the "many others" she suggested that Hitler's National Socialism might be included.[5] The ideologies to which she refers seem to constitute a class of mass-mobilizing belief systems generated to organize human energies behind a program of national rehabilitation, intensive development and/or aggrandizement. Where this does not necessarily mean the augmentation of per capita production in primary, secondary, and tertiary productive activities and the transfer of manpower from agricultural to industrial pursuits, it involves the expansion of special industries (armaments, for example) and/or the mobilization of human beings for protracted defense or aggression.

If radicalism, as a political persuasion, evinces a constellation of traits, those traits seem to be characteristically, but not exclusively, the response to a set of circumstances that have become increasingly commonplace in the world of the twentieth century. Most of the radical movements of our time have appeared and matured in environments best identified as those produced by delayed or thwarted industrialization. In an environment where the bulk of the population is involved in agricultural production—characteristically conducted with labor intensive methods—in which per capita productivity is low and the ratio of savings to consumption is low, one expects not only a pervasive sense of inadequacy, frustration, and free-floating hostility but a disposition to anticipate and favor change as well.

In such an environment one reads a history of humiliation. A community that remains at the level of preindustrialization, or which is only partially industrialized, finds itself suffering low competitive potential. More advanced economies "oppress" and "exploit" it. It suffers national humiliation. Such a community is manifestly disadvantaged and disposed to favor radical change.

Often, within such communities, a small nucleus of declassed intellectuals—frequently the offspring of traditional

[5] M. Matossian, in J. Kautsky, *Political Change in Underdeveloped Countries: Nationalism and Communism* (New York: Wiley, 1962), p. 253.

or interstitial elites who receive their educations in more advanced economies or whose educations make increasingly manifest the backwardness of their homeland—begins to agitate for massive change. When their homelands are destabilized by war, economic dislocation, or population pressures, such elements can act as catalyzing agents, nuclei around which dissidents collect. Under "revolutionary" circumstances, such elements and the dissidents that collect around them can effect rapid or phased change in order to begin or accelerate the process of industrial development and modernization. Industrialization and modernization are clearly perceived as necessary antecedents to obtaining a "place" in the modern world.

Since the end of the Second World War the process that carries a nation from the level of an agricultural and pre-industrial stage to that of advanced industrialization has been the object of protracted and somewhat detailed study. The works of W. W. Rostow[6] typify the literature devoted to the study of this process. It is a literature that attempts to identify the various stages of economic growth and to specify some of the preconditions and conditions governing the process.

Rostow has attempted to schematize the preconditions for what he terms "industrial take-off." One necessary precondition is "nation building," a development of a sense of political community without which resources cannot be mobilized, local industries cannot be insulated from foreign competition, and local integrity cannot be defended. Moreover, since the preconditions necessarily involve a considerable reallocation of limited resources to "social overhead"—provision of an economic infrastructure requisite to development, the construction of an adequate road and rail system, the systematic instruction in skills necessary for competent utilization of potential enterprisory and organizational talents—a whole series of dislocating po-

[6] W. W. Rostow, *The Stages of Economic Growth* (Cambridge: Cambridge University Press, 1969), *Politics and the Stages of Economic Growth* (Cambridge: Cambridge University Press, 1971).

litical decisions must be made. Potential financial and investment resources must be released from "nonproductive" uses and differentially employed. Often this entails the elimination of large incomes unproductively dissipated in the traditional or landlord sectors of the economy. This suggests extensive agrarian reform or "class" expropriation, but can be accomplished in a variety of fashions. If "take-off" is to be successful, there must be a rise in the rate of capital investment that outstrips population growth. Prior to the twentieth century, all this could have been undertaken at a relatively leisurely pace and without the massive political and social dislocations that characterize the transition between stages of economic growth in the contemporary world. Under the competitive conditions that obtain in the twentieth century, the transition from one to another level of economic maturity seems to require radical changes in social and economic conditions. If nations negotiated passage from underdevelopment to economic maturity under the auspices of "liberal" and "parliamentary" regimes in the nineteenth century, the transition in the twentieth has regularly been made under the tutelage of a "totalitarian" political system. "Modernizers," in the twentieth century, are ill-disposed toward liberalism. They are, more frequently than not, "radicals"—advocates of a strong, one-party state that is charged with a mass-mobilizing and renovating mission.

Whether the "mission" assumed by radicals in the twentieth century is to create the conditions for take-off, to direct take-off, or to drive their communities to industrial maturity and modernization, they must address themselves to a related set of problems and employ a related set of political strategies and institutions. Men must be mobilized to collective purpose. Energy must be directed and opposition suppressed. During take-off, capital must be collected to underwrite the costs of building a necessary economy infrastructure for modernization and growth. During the drive to maturity, capital must be accumulated to support industrial expansion and agricultural modernization. If foreign sources of capital are excluded by necessity or political choice, take-off and industrial maturity can only be purchased by extracting investment potential from the available net national product—that is to say, at the cost of overall consumption. Under such circumstances one would expect modernizers to attempt to control consumption so that the process of modernization and industrialization can continue as rapidly as possible. The success of such a program is governed by a variety of factors—population size, the institutions available for effective control of mass consumption, the availability of natural resources, the degree of insulation from foreign influences that may affect the disposition of the population to submit to protracted (and sometimes onerous) austerity, the availability of human talents, and the political security of the modernizing party, among the most significant.

It seems intuitively obvious that both stages, that of take-off and that of the drive to industrial maturity, have certain features in common. Under either circumstance and in the modern world, with the availability of techniques for mass communication and mass manipulation, one might well expect a "revolutionary" movement to attempt to maintain hierarchical control in order to enhance national consciousness and in order not to dissipate scarce resources in intrasystemic conflict. Furthermore, as a function of such control, one might expect a revolutionary party to manipulate information flow, excluding "foreign influences" in particular, so that its constituency will not have to suffer the awareness of competitive disadvantage. In the effort to maintain consumption at the lowest tolerable levels—in order either to produce the investment capital to fire take-off or to maintain the high investment ratio required by the drive to maturity—the revolutionary party would, moreover, be expected to attempt to generate and maintain a high level of emotional salience. The sacrifice, discipline, and commitment required by the developmental program of austerity and intensive labor would be the product of systematic and sustained exhortation and inculcation—a program frequently spoken of as instilling "revolutionary consciousness in the masses." Possessed of the appropriate consciousness, one

11

would recognize that his "proletarian" nation requires his dedication and sacrifice in order to resist the machinations of the "plutocratic" and "imperialist" powers.

In such an environment "radicalism" flourishes. But it is a radicalism which has precious little affinity with the Marxism of Karl Marx and Friedrich Engels. That Marxism, as we shall suggest, was addressed to advanced industrial systems —systems in which a class-conscious proletariat had already spontaneously emerged. The environments to which we have briefly alluded would be environments in which a self-selected minority of declassed elements would characterize themselves as "revolutionary leaders" (whether they call themselves "proletarians" or not is a matter of complete indifference) and would proceed to mobilize the "masses," or the "people" to the service of rapid industrialization. Within such a context most of the theoretical substance of classical Marxism would be irrelevant.

If such an account is plausible, it suggests that most of the radicalisms with which we are concerned are developmental and national in character. In this sense, the affinities between Mussolini's Fascism and the "socialism" of Stalin become intelligible. If both were developmental dictatorships (their relative success as such would be a function of variables other than their political similarities), we would expect them, under modern conditions, to share sustained similarities. Radicalisms which developed in environments at different stages of economic growth would share some of the similarities but perhaps not others. China, for example, is apparently at an earlier stage of economic growth than either Russia or Italy were when they suffered their revolutions. We would expect differences to distinguish the one from the others. Nonetheless, the fact that all are developmental in character, and that there are shared affinities between the stages of economic development, suggests that we should expect some sustained similarities to characterize all of them. The stages of economic growth are not discrete. Significant degrees of overlapping characterize them. Take-off and the drive to maturity both seem to require an emphatic nationalism to effect the measure of sacrifice and discipline requisite to both. Both stages feature systematic resource allocation and control. Both seem to require controlled consumption and forced savings. How much "class warfare" and "expropriation" each system will tolerate seems to be a function of the circumstances in which each revolution manifests itself. If the political system that is being revolutionized has suffered a "power deflation" as a consequence of massive military defeat (as did Russia in 1917) or protracted war (as did China in 1949), the revolution can apparently dislocate the entire prevailing social and economic structure. If the system suffers only extensive economic damage (as did Italy in 1918-1922) the freedom of action of the revolutionary and developmental elite is confined by still viable nonrevolutionary allies from the traditional as well as the industrial sectors. After the Second World War any number of possibilities were opened to nations undergoing rapid industrialization that had not been available in the interwar years. Because of the availability of material and moral assistance from the bloc of "socialist" states, or the economic aid from the "capitalist" world, we find any number of modern developmental variants—Castro's Cuba being only one of the more unusual.

We are not here concerned with anything other than the plausibility of such suggestions in attempting to understand something of the nature of the similarities shared by contemporary mass-mobilizing, radical movements. We are primarily concerned with the shared similarities in what we have called the radical persuasion—the *ideas* that animate radicalism. Any number of accounts attempt to make a case for the association of radicalism and industrial development.[7] What we are attempting to provide is a context for the discussion. The discussion proceeds on its own merits.

---

[7] A.F.K. Organski, *The Stages of Political Development* (New York: Knopf, 1965); L. Garruccio, *L'industrializzazione tra nazionalismo e rivoluzione* (Bologna: Mulino, 1969).

13

How it might be interpreted against a background of social, economic, and psychological variables is outside our focus of attention.

Even if such a schematic account seems plausible, certain anomalies suggest themselves. First of all some of the non-regime radicalisms to which we shall address ourselves have appeared in advanced industrial environments. Student radicals and Black Nationalists in the United States share some singular similarities with the Fascist persuasion and yet are the products of an advanced industrial society. But, as we shall argue, such contemporary radicalisms are, by and large, *nonviable*. They are inappropriate and have shown themselves to have a very low recruitment potential. On the other hand we do have at least one special historic instance of a mass-mobilizing radical movement that shared many affinities with Fascism, that *did* mature in an industrial environment: Hitler's National Socialism. So it would seem that some form of radicalism can make a successful appearance in a society that has transcended the stages of take-off and the drive to maturity.

In response to such a consideration, one can invoke at least two interpretative strategies: (1) National Socialism in Germany, for all its historic impact, was an anomaly, a "historic accident" unlikely to be repeated; or (2) National Socialism represents an instance of the kind of radicalism that can come to an advanced industrial community suffering not underdevelopment, per se, but protracted economic threats and massive national humiliation. The response to those threats and that humiliation might trigger a drive to increase the defensive and offensive military capabilities of the nation—a drive that shares some significant traits with the circumstances surrounding take-off and the drive to maturity. Nonetheless, however one chooses to handle the National Socialist case, the central thesis of our present discussion is not irretrievably impaired. We do not know, in any definitive sense, what produces a radical persuasion or makes it successful. We have, at best, an indication of some of the necessary conditions that seem to make societies amenable to its influence. We have no exhaustive catalogue of causal factors that produce, with predictable assurance, a political system animated by radicalism in whatever form.

The radicalisms that have made their appearance in the twentieth century all differ, in a variety of ways, among themselves. That they seem to share sustaining similarities has been common, if not universal, knowledge for some considerable time. For our purposes we shall expand on significant similarities in order to suggest a possible strategy of interpretation.

The ideologies of the new radicalisms do in fact share a number of common traits. They are all opposed to "foreign oppression" whether that oppression is "colonial," or "imperialist," or "barbarian." They all reinvoke the myths of ancient glories to animate the masses: ancient Roman grandeur for Mussolini, the civilization of China for Mao, the ancient Akan society for Nkrumah, Russian creativity for Stalin, the civilization of the Pharaohs for Nasser, Nordic superiority for Hitler. They all tend to generate a one-party political structure and a charismatic leader to act as final arbiter in intrasystemic disputes and to act as the embodiment of the nation for the mobilized masses. More and more frequently the mass-mobilizing movement is the product of the activities of displaced intellectuals, frequently exploiting the deployable energies of a youth movement for which the mass mobilizing movement acts as a carrier. The youth movements associated with Bolshevism, Fascism, National Socialism, Maoism, and Castroism constitute a significant part of the history of such movements.

It has become increasingly apparent that the traditional classificational schema in which political systems and their advocates are plotted along a unilinear continuum from the "right" to the "left" is no longer particularly informative. Whatever differences distinguish "Marxist-Leninist," "non-Marxist socialist," and "fascist" political and social systems, pervasive similarities unite them. For other analytic purposes the differences are, of course, no less important. But to attempt to understand the character of contemporary

15

radical politics—to begin to appreciate the magnitude of the changes that have overtaken the "left" in terms of political style and political culture—an account of the similarities that obtain between the Marxist "left" and the fascist "right" undercuts persistent misconceptions and conveys an important insight.

One need only review synoptic accounts of paradigmatic Fascism, the Fascism of Mussolini, to begin to appreciate the extent of the involution that has afflicted "left-wing" radicalism. Gioacchino Volpe, the official historian of Mussolini's Fascism, for example, correctly described Fascism as having originated among "elements from the left, socialists, revolutionaries, syndicalists and the lower middle classes as well as proletarians who had broken with the older parties." He spoke of Fascism as a "truculent socialism" (*un socialismo . . . molto battagliero*)—of Fascism as a radical movement that conceived violence as a legitimate lever of social change. Fascism, as he described it, was a "nondogmatic, nonconfessional and pragmatic" movement, characterized by its "youthfulness," and animated by "impulse" and "faith." As a movement it was charged with a "myth of youth" and dedicated itself to the "breaking away from the plutocratic nations" that kept Italy in a kind of economic and political vassalage—a "breaking away" that required the "development of [Italy's] forces of internal production. . . ."[8]

The Fascist emphasis on economic and political independence, on the high emotional salience in which all these efforts were to be effected, on the quasi-military organization of society through the inculcation of "moral incentives," on the "primacy of politics," on a "collectivistic" rather than a "liberal" social order, on the necessity of "revolutionary war" in order to break the trammels of the exploitative capitalist world order, on nationalism as a mobilizing strategy, all are emphases that have become more and more characteristic of *all* radical political ideologies in the second half of the twentieth century.

[8] G. Volpe, *History of the Fascist Movement* (Rome: Novissima, 1936), pp. 11, 12, 17, 18, 27, 44, 48.

The trajectory followed by Mussolini's Fascism is, in fact, instructive and interesting for a number of reasons—not the least of which is the fact that more and more "left radical" movements have increasingly taken on its ideological attributes. Recently, with some seriousness, Zbigniew Brzezinski has suggested that "recent developments in the Soviet Union seem to indicate that the highest stage of communism is fascism." Elsewhere, addressing himself to a wider range of political systems, he maintained, "[The] Communist parties in East Europe are beginning to resemble the semi-fascist nationalist movements of radical protest, reform and modernization that were beginning to gain the upper hand in East European politics prior to World War II. 'Social Fascism' rather than 'Social Democracy' seems to be the more likely future for the East European Communists."[9]

The fact is that many scholars have, for some considerable time, alluded to or attempted to explicate the pervasive similarities shared by "left" and "right wing" radicalism. Franz Borkenau, Peter Drucker, James Burnham, Ely Halevy, and Bruno Rizzi were among the first to call attention to the shared similarities. Fascists themselves, during the prewar period, recognized the affinities between Bolshevism and Fascism. Mihail Manoilescu, as a fascist theoretician, called attention to the institutional similarities shared by Fascism, National Socialism, and Stalin's "Marxist" Russia.[10] Mussolini, himself, identified Stalin's "Bolshevism" as "crypto-fascism." Trotsky, at almost the same time, spoke of the "deadly similarity" that subtended both the Fascist and the Bolshevist political phenomena.

What seems fairly clear now is that classical Marxism has gone through a singular transformation. While the First World War constituted a major watershed in its development, significant alterations in the ideological system left by Karl Marx had already been introduced as early as the turn

[9] Z. Brzezinski, "Five Years After Khrushchev," *Survey*, No. 72 (Summer 1969), p. 39; "Communications," *Dissent, 12*, 3 (Summer 1965), p. 383.

[10] M. Manoilescu, *Die einzige Partei* (Berlin: Stollberg, 1941).

17

of the century. About that time, both Lenin and Mussolini introduced modifications into classical Marxism (while they were both recognized leaders of revolutionary socialism) that were not only to transform its substance but to alter its spirit as well.

Marxism became a vehicle of revolutionary change in environments which displayed few, if any, of the preconditions Marx insisted were necessary for revolution. Neither Russia nor Italy enjoyed the "masses of class conscious proletarians" that Marxism seemed to require to make a reality of its historic vision. Neither country found itself beset with an excess of productive capacity that made the "absurdity of overproduction" one of its complaints. Both countries were largely, or in significant measure, agrarian. Both countries required industrial development, at the expense of almost incalculable collective effort, rather than socialist redistribution of surplus value. These considerations were, for all intents and purposes, transparent to Mussolini. By 1919, abandoning identification with Marxian socialism, he called for a "national syndicalism" in which all productive categories of the nation would unite to increase the per capita productivity of Italians so that Italy might effectively compete with the industrialized nations of the earth. Only gradually did Lenin come to a similar understanding about the Russia that emerged from the revolution. Only gradually did Lenin begin to speak of the necessity of introducing Prussian efficiency, an effective railway system, American universal education and expanded industrial capabilities if "Soviet" Russia were to survive. It was Stalin, of course, who inherited the task of making the Soviet Union a modern industrial nation. At that point both Fascist Italy and Stalin's Russia began to share impressive similarities. Both, for example, sought to intensify capital accumulation by restricting the consumption of the working masses—in what Trotsky called "primitive socialist accumulation."

Rapid industrialization required intensive capital outlays. The burden fell on the general population. To render the effort as painless as possible the entire machinery of the

18

state and its agencies was employed to inculcate the virtues of the "new man," "Fascist man," or "socialist man." Both systems sought to produce individuals disposed to submit to taxing discipline and self-sacrifice in order to enhance the public good as that good was conceived by the political elite. Fascists and Stalinists alike insisted on the high moral qualities displayed by their political systems as distinguished from the "materialist" capitalist systems. Mussolini characterized his state system as an "Ethical State." Stalinists never tired of characterizing their state as the most "humane," "just," and "progressive" of the modern world. In our own time Castro's Cuba characterizes itself as a "socialist state" whose citizenry is motivated by "moral" rather than "material" incentives. Mao's China is no less moralistic. There seems to be, in effect, a rough correlation between the measure of developmental needs of a community and its emphasis on the moral virtues rather than material welfare benefits.

A further similarity shared by revolutionary mass-mobilizing movements in our time is a developmental program that turns on the creation or enhancement of defense capabilities. One always seems to require an elaborate military establishment to "defend the revolution" or to realize its ends. Resource and budget allocation, protracted developmental plans, the special emphasis on select industries, the effort to enjoy essential economic self-sufficiency, are all geared to the military capabilities of the revolutionary community. The industrial development of the Soviet Union and Communist China has been largely a function of the expansion of armaments and armaments-related industries. Where revolutionary powers have neither the resources nor the population base to undertake the development of indigenous armaments manufacture, they import finished military hardware in order to maintain a competitive defense capability. In such circumstances the military elite begins to wield impressive influence. If the prewar fascist powers made such postures commonplace, the radical regimes that have come to power in China and Cuba have, after the Second World War, made the emphasis on war and the military a no less

19

common element in their doctrinal paraphernalia. If the militiaman and squadrista provided the mythic hero for the youth of Fascist Italy—and the S.S. "peasant warrior" became the prototype of the National Socialist man in Hitler's Germany—the "peasant-soldier" of the People's Liberation Army and the rural guerrilla warrior provide their analogues in Communist China and Communist Cuba.

The reactive nationalism that provides one of the preconditions for rapid industrial development is sustained and enhanced in all cases by maintaining what Mussolini called "an atmosphere of high moral tension."

Reactive nationalism is, of course, generally the consequence of a history of humiliations. Industrial development and military capability thus tend to mark the occasion for the redress of old grievances. Little is more satisfying to status-deprived peoples than victory in armed conflict. Regional conflict characterizes such situations. Since 1945, for example, there have been approximately eighty international conflicts involving the measurable loss of life and destruction of property. All but eight of those conflicts involved "Third World" participants on both sides. Developing countries attempt to generate and harness volatile energies. Those energies can be most effectively controlled by turning their hostility against outgroups. What results is conflict, the effort to redress old grievances, to fulfill "national" aspirations. Soviet Russia, before the Second World War, "restored" the "historic boundaries" of Russia. Latvia, Lithuania, Estonia disappeared and parts of Finland and Rumania were absorbed. China has "restored" its "historic" control over Tibet. Nkrumah prepared an army of "liberation" to be used not only against white South Africa but against "neocolonialist" African neighbors. Nasser and Sukarno both sought to redress "historic grievances" through military adventure. One need not seek far to find the parallel. Mussolini sought to undo the shame of the Italian army's nineteenth-century defeat at Adowa in Ethiopia. Hitler sought to "restore" Germans to their "historic" and "natural" homeland.

It would seem that strange things have transpired in the

world since the turn of the twentieth century. It seems equally clear that one does not succeed in understanding what has transpired if one continues to seek explanatory leverage in classical Marxism. One of the first victims of the turn of the century was, in fact, classical Marxism. Whatever has survived of the life work of Marx and Engels, for all its intellectual and social science significance, does not help us much in understanding the political events of our time. Classical Marxism neither constitutes an unambiguous explanatory device for understanding our time nor does it provide a mass-mobilizing belief system. Those radical movements that populate the second half of the twentieth century have very little affinity with the Marxism of Marx and Engels. By the end of the nineteenth century, classical Marxism was being extensively "reformed" at the hands of Marxists themselves. Beginning with Bakunin and Bernstein, any number of Marxist theoreticians, including V. I. Lenin and Benito Mussolini, began to divest classical Marxism of its substance. Today, precious little of the system left by Karl Marx has survived. What passes as "Marxism-Leninism" or "radicalism" is a singular product of a singular time. To begin to appreciate the magnitude of the changes that have marked the history of a belief system, one must review the original system as it found expression in the works of its cofounders. That having been accomplished, one need review, albeit briefly, a system of thought conceived, for some time, to be the very antithesis of classical Marxism—the paradigmatic Fascism of Benito Mussolini—to discover that the Marxism of "Marxism-Leninism" is a most gossamer stuff.

The radicalism of contemporary political thought is a fascinating amalgam of ideas rooted in the intellectual history of modern man. The common elements shared by its major variants have appeared and reappeared in a variety of places under a variety of circumstances. We have only begun to understand some of the conditions governing the appearance of successful radicalism, much less the conditions which produce the peculiar collection of ideas that we will here identify as the "fascist persuasion."

21

In effect, little will be said here of the social, political, and economic circumstances that give rise to "radicalism." Radicalism as a political disposition—that is to say the disposition to systematically reject the philosophical presuppositions and institutional organization that characterize the liberal and parliamentary state system—is obviously the product of a multitude of personality, social, and economic variables as yet only vaguely understood. We will not attempt to identify or trace the impact of those variables. Rather, an attempt will be made to outline the decay and transformation of a belief system. As such, no attempt will be made to provide a history of Leninism, Stalinism, or Maoism—any number of competent books accomplish just that. We will be involved in the pursuit of suggestive similarities, to the neglect of obvious (but to my mind and for our purposes, unilluminating) differences. If the treatment is at all successful, it should stimulate political analysts to reconsider the now traditional distinctions between "left" and "rightwing" radicalism and perhaps suggest some testable hypotheses about developmental dictatorships and the radicalism that is the consequence of protracted social and political crises.

In substance, this book will be an extended gloss on George Lichtheim's recent judgments concerning radical movements in the twentieth century. The burden of revolution, Lichtheim has suggested,

> is cast upon the peasantries of Asia, Africa, and Latin America, who are to take up where the industrial working class—now supposedly integrated into the system—left off. Thus nationalism is identified with socialism, the peasantry with the proletariat, anti-imperialism with anti-capitalism, until all the distinctions painfully elaborated in Marxist literature for a century are cast overboard in favor of a simple dichotomy: Western imperialism versus the starving masses of the Third World. People equipped with this kind of perspective no longer need a theory: practice grows out of populist sloganeering, as power is

22

supposed to grow from gun barrels. Populism indeed is more relevant to Third World politics than Marxism.

Maoism, as a characteristic form of modern radicalism, affirms

> the natural unity of the entire people when rallied around a truly selfless leadership imbued with the proper convictions and determined to defend the national interest against domestic and foreign enemies. This ideology . . . has nothing in common with Marxism, but it can be described as populist socialism for want of a better term.

This kind of populist and mass-mobilizing nationalism, under the aegis of a unitary party organized behind the personality of a charismatic leader, is a product of the urban intelligentsia, and is calculated to promote development and/or restore national sovereignty and dignity to economically and politically deprived communities. It is, in effect, "the intelligentsia—civilian or military, in any case urban and classless—which seizes power. . . . [and] decides whether the modernization drive shall take place under Communist, fascist, pseudo-socialist, or straightforward nationalist slogans. . . . What is not always understood is the fact that in [such circumstances] and faced with such tasks, 'Communism'—or Marxism-Leninism, to give it its official label—ceases to be a theory of anything worth being called a workers' movement. It becomes the ideology of an elitist avant-garde drawn from the intelligentsia."[11]

Tracing the involutionary process that has made classical Marxism the radicalism of our own time is what this book is all about. The tracing will be undertaken in broad outline—and must commence with a fairly accurate account of the intellectual heritage left to the modern world by Karl Marx and Friedrich Engels.

---

[11] G. Lichtheim, *Imperialism* (New York: Praeger, 1971), pp. 147, 150, 158f.

Chapter Two

The First Marxism

A NY effort to characterize the differences that separate contemporary radicalism from the system left to us by Karl Marx and Friedrich Engels is beset by problems, not the least of which involves fixing the sense of what it might mean to talk of "Marxism." Minimally, what is required is a synoptic account of what Marx and Engels themselves conceived Marxism to imply in terms of theoretical and political commitments as well as practical outcomes. When we speak of Marxism as a "theoretical system," we mean that Marxism can be identified with some reasonably specific body of theoretical commitments—major intellectual strategies and specific empirical and, perhaps, logical propositions. These, conjointly held, support prescriptive admonitions about how revolutionaries are to proceed and what they can expect as a consequence of their efforts.

Fortunately for our purposes, the last four decades have finally made the complete writings of Karl Marx and Friedrich Engels available for the first time. For almost half a century interpretations of Marxism have had to remain content with a body of materials from which significant manuscripts were missing. In the thirties the manuscripts now identified as the *Economic and Philosophic Manuscripts of 1844* made their appearance.[1] In the mid-fifties another large and hitherto unpublished block of Marx's writings became available. For the first time, an account of Marxism can be delivered that rests on the complete corpus of the texts of Marx and Engels.

The availability of new materials has produced no little consternation among established "Marxist" regimes. The Soviet Union, for example, has declaimed loud and long

[1] Cf. I. M. Zeitlin, *Marxism: A Re-Examination* (Princeton: Van Nostrand, 1967).

against the "romantic" exploitation of the early Marx manuscripts—and for a time the manuscripts were not included in the "complete" works of Marx and Engels published in East Germany. On the other hand these early manuscripts stimulated a spate of literature that "reinterpreted" Marxism in light of the new materials.

The publication of the manuscripts from Marx's maturity, the *Grundrisse der politischen Oekonomie* (*Rohentwerf*)[2]— which made their appearance in the mid-fifties—is not calculated to generate as much interest nor to produce as varied a collection of "reinterpretations," but is surely a significant addition to the Marx corpus. The *Grundrisse* derives from Marx's maturity and provides considerable evidence of the development that characterized Marx's intellectual coming-of-age.[3]

We can now document, with significant plausibility, the stages of Marx's theoretical maturation, and we can provide a reasonably full statement of the system he left as a patrimony to his intellectual and revolutionary heirs. We can now outline the complete system—we can identify some of its major shortcomings—and use it as a measure against which contemporary radicalism can be assessed. The "creativity" of the "creative developments" to which Marxism has been subjected since the turn of the century can only be measured against the system as it was left to us by Marx and Engels.

Classical Marxism is not only a complex of parts, it was also subject to development at the hands of Marx and Engels. As a consequence, one of the most convenient strategies for providing a competent outline of the entire system involves tracing its chronological stages of maturation. Armed with such an account, we can compare the belief systems of contemporary radicalism.

[2] K. Marx, *Grundrisse der Kritik der politischen Ökonomie* (Berlin: Dietz, 1953).

[3] A partial translation is available as K. Marx, *Pre-Capitalist Economic Formations*, edited by E. J. Hobsbawm (New York: International, 1965).

THE STAGES IN THE DEVELOPMENT OF CLASSICAL MARXISM

Contemporary Marx scholarship now conceives classical Marxism as having traversed several reasonably distinct chronological periods. The distinctions between the periods are relative, of course, and serve essentially didactic and heuristic purposes. There is no suggestion that such distinctions identify objective and rigorously distinct periods. The distinctions are entertained in order to focus on the particularly significant cognitive interests that governed Marx's intellectual development. Thus if one focuses on Marx's economic concepts one might, as have some scholars, divide Marx's thought into three or four relatively distinct periods: (1) 1843-1848/9, (2) 1850-1859, and (3) 1860-1883. The distinctions are predicated on the maturity, that is to say the degree of formalization, standardization, and conceptual complexity, that characterizes the use of specifically economic categories in Marx's progressive exposition and analysis. In *The Poverty of Philosophy*, for example, written during the winter of 1846-1847 and published in 1847, it seems clear that Marx had not advanced, explicitly, beyond the economic conceptions of David Ricardo.[4] Marx later indicated that the economic analysis of *The Poverty of Philosophy* contained only the "germs" of the twenty-year labor that produced the first volume of *Das Kapital* in 1867. Marx's work from 1850 until 1860, in turn, was dedicated to working out some of the germinal ideas found in the economic writings of the period between 1843 and 1849. In 1850 Marx began the analyses found in the *Grundrisse*, which concluded, in 1859, with the publication of *The Contribution to the Critique of Political Economy*. In the period after the publication of the *Critique*, Marx decided to em-

[4] K. Marx, *The Poverty of Philosophy* (Moscow: Foreign Languages, n.d.), p. 97. This is denied by D. I. Rosenberg, *Die Entwicklung der ökonomischen Lehre von Marx und Engels in den vierziger Jahren des 19. Jahrhunderts* (Berlin: Dietz, 1958), p. 304; but see W. S. Wygodski, *Die Geschichte einer grossen Entdeckung* (Berlin: Wirtschaft, 1967), pp. 29-35.

bark on a new publication, rather than attempt to resolve some of the problems that beset the *Critique*. The result was the publication of the first volume of *Das Kapital* in 1867. The remaining volumes of *Kapital* were not completed by Marx himself and fulfillment of the task remained the obligation of Engels. Volumes two and three were published only after Marx's death, in 1885 and 1894. The fourth volume was never published as such and made its appearance as *Theories of Surplus Value* long after the death of Engels.

If one concerns himself with the development of certain critical economic concepts—the labor theory of value, the conception of surplus value, the average rate of profit, and the secular decline in the rate of profit—one can distinguish with a fair degree of specificity the three periods indicated above. The periods are distinguished on the basis of the degree of conceptual sophistication that characterizes Marx's analysis. If, on the other hand, one wishes to deal with Marx's thought more comprehensively, that is to say with concepts that are not specifically economic—philosophical, sociological, and psychological concepts—one can distinguish a number of other relatively distinct periods: (1) the period from 1837 until 1844, during which Marx admitted his specific ignorance of economics and was preoccupied with more general philosophic concerns. This period ends with an increased preoccupation with economic considerations—stimulated in part by the insistence with which economic affairs imposed themselves on him because of Marx's involvement with political and social problems—and in part under the influence of Friedrich Engels, with whom Marx became associated during this period. (2) The period from 1845 through 1849 marks a period in which Marx himself indicates that he undertook a systematic and sustained "self-criticism."[5] The period began with the preparation of *The German Ideology*, a long manuscript that was not published in its entirety until 1932. Out of the "germinal ideas" that found expression in *The German Ideology*, both Marx

[5] K. Marx, *A Contribution to the Critique of Political Economy*, tr. N. I. Stone (Chicago: Kerr, 1918), pp. 13f.

27

and Engels produced the preliminary conceptual schema now identified as "historical materialism." *The Communist Manifesto* of 1848 was a condensed and stenographic statement of their views on historical development predicated, as they conceived it, on the influence of dynamic changes taking place in the economic base of society. (3) The period following the publication of the *Manifesto*, marking the decade between 1850 through 1859, was devoted essentially to the analysis of the economic foundations of historical change, and culminated in the publication of *The Contribution to the Critique of Political Economy*, the first volume of a planned series of volumes that would reveal the true basis of social change. (4) The period after the publication of the *Critique*, 1860 until Marx's death in 1883, was devoted to the standardization and formalization of the preliminary schema of 1845-1849. Marx found the *Critique* of 1859 inadequate and decided, in this final period, to begin his work anew. He sought to articulate what we would today identify, with few qualifications, as a theory of social and political dynamics—a theory of society and revolution. The periods indicated correspond to the loose distinctions between a "young Marx" (1837-1845) and a "mature Marx" (1860-1883)—with the two intervening periods (1846-1849, 1850-1859) characterized as "transitional."

Only in the mature writings do the concepts that appear in the preliminary schemata, the products of Marx's early assessments, receive anything like reasonably adequate explication. The concept of "alienation," for example, which appears so prominently in the *Manuscripts of 1844* is significantly modified by 1845—modified so extensively as to be abandoned by Marx—and by 1848 to invoke his ridicule. This is not to suggest that Marx abandoned all the cognitive content of the concept. Some of the constituent elements of "alienation" in 1844 remain central to Marx's analysis and reappear, sometimes even identified as "alienations," in the last notes that Marx was writing before his death in 1883. Similarly, the concept "labor," which appears so prominently in the *Manuscripts of 1844*, underwent an analogous transmogrification. Only in the relatively specific period between October 1857 and May 1858, for example, did Marx clarify his conceptions of the labor theory of value and the theory of surplus value. "Labor," like "alienation," thus remained central to Marx's thought, but the cognitive content of such concepts was subject to continuous reformulation. As Marx reduced the syntactical imprecision, the implications of his terminology took on more specific cognitive meaning.

If this is true of terms such as "labor" and "alienation," it is equally true of terms having high emotional salience such as "freedom" and "fulfillment"—characteristically normative expressions. While no strictly dichotomous distinction between cognitive and normative terms can be established, it is relatively clear that terms such as "labor" are essentially cognitive, while terms such as "freedom" are essentially normative. "Alienation," on the other hand, can be employed in either capacity: at times Marx renders its referent specifically descriptive, as when he refers to the "alienation" of property; at times the term is employed to refer to normative considerations, i.e. that men should not be "alienated" from their "species being."

Any effort to provide an intelligible, intelligent, and defensible interpretation of classical Marxism must recognize the *variable meanings* invoked by some of the most critical conceptual terms employed by Marx throughout his productive life. While it is true that almost all of the conceptual apparatus employed by Marx during his youth remained part of his intellectual armory, the meaning that could be reasonably accorded such concepts differs from period to period. Moreover, there are clearly instances of confusion and paradox in Marx's writings—a consideration that is not too surprising, since his literary labors covered over a forty-year period.

Marx's early writings are almost all in literary and academic language style. Only after the beginning of the second "intermediary" period (from 1850 through 1867) does his language develop to a special and more sophisticated level. During this period he made systematic efforts to produce a specifically "scientific" treatise on political economy, and his language gives every evidence of sophisticated and cognitively specific use. The use of special symbolic and propositional language becomes increasingly evident in the three available volumes of *Kapital*. Almost all the conceptual machinery of his youth is reinvoked, but the terms are stipulatively defined and housed in a relatively specific theoretical structure that delivers a set of logically integrated predictions concerning the secular decline of capitalism, cyclical crises of overproduction, concentration of capital and the subsequent reduction in the number of capitalists, the corresponding increment in the number of proletarians, the development of socialist productive relations within the "womb" of the capitalist mode of production, and the ultimate revolution which shatters the capitalist "integument." Within the context of the mature work, the normative commitment to "dealienation" and the accession to the "realm of freedom," and the "fulfillment of the self," are given relatively specific meaning.

In the immediate past Marx commentators have devoted their attention, by and large, to an interpretation of the newly discovered documents from Marx's youth. The preoccupation is healthy as long as one does not succumb to the temptation to treat the work of the "mature Marx" as a forty-year gloss on these vague and loosely written documents. The youthful writings of Marx are an essential part of the Marx corpus; but they are not the most important constituent parts of that corpus, nor are the mature works "incomprehensible" without them. The availability of Marx's youthful writings makes reconstruction of Marx's mature works more responsible—we can now fill in lacunae in the continuum from the discursive and correspondingly vague preliminary works, through the mature, partially standardized, and formalized works. Any content analysis of the works at the chronologically later end of the continuum reveals certain regularities: a decrement in the occurence of normative expressions on the one hand and an increment in the frequency of stipulatively defined expressions on the

other. In effect, the preoccupation with specifically normative issues is significantly reduced in the later works, while
the concern for standardized language becomes increasingly
emphatic. This does not mean that Marx was no longer concerned with normative issues. Marx's normative concerns
characterized his work throughout his life—the suffused
moral outrage clearly evident in his mature work is evidence
enough for that—but it is equally apparent that by 1860
Marx's moral preoccupations articulate themselves through
the medium of a relatively rigorous theory of social dynamics.[6]

To provide a responsible account of classical Marxism is
to retrace its development from the largely normative, discursive and literary efforts of the young Marx through the
various transitional periods to the mature works.[7] Each suc-
cessive period is marked by an increasingly systematic treatment of the theoretical commitments first expressed in the
early writings. The transits are marked by more sophisticated conceptual treatment of the broad and ill-defined categories invoked in the first statements of a nascent Marxism.
Marx himself was well aware of the vagueness and obscurity
which afflicted these early texts, and all of his subsequent
labor was devoted to the effort to expose and resolve the
real cognitive issues they concealed.[8]

The Normative Commitments of the Young Marx

As early as 1835 in an essay written in his final term at
the Trier Gymnasium, the adolescent Karl Marx wrote:
"Man's nature makes it possible for him to reach his fulfill-

---

[6] Cf. A. J. Gregor, *Contemporary Radical Ideologies* (New York:
Random House, 1968), Chap. 2.

[7] For a more extended account of the process of theory generation,
cf. A. J. Gregor, *An Introduction to Metapolitics* (New York: Free
Press, 1971).

[8] I have attempted a more adequate account of the processes involved in generating "ideological systems" in "Marxism and Ethics:
A Methodological Inquiry," *Philosophy and Phenomenological Research*, 28, 3 (March 1968), 368-384.

ment only by working for the perfection and welfare of his society," a judgment he never had cause to abandon. "To man," he went on, "the Deity gave a general goal, to improve mankind and himself . . . ." Marx elaborated on this theme in an essay on religion, written on the same occasion, in which he maintained that man could transcend his "egotism" only by entering completely into the larger community in Christ, in which he would find virtue and true fulfillment by answering the voice of his extended self. In effect, man would then fulfill himself in virtue by contributing to the perfection of the Christian community.[9]

By 1837, when he was nineteen years old, Karl Marx confessed to his father the profundity of the disturbance generated by his recognition of "the conflict between what is and what ought to be . . . . Setting out," he went on, "from idealism . . . I hit upon seeking the Idea in the real itself. . . . I had read fragments of Hegel's philosophy and had found its grotesque craggy melody unpleasing. I wished to dive into the ocean once again but with the definite intention of discovering our mental nature to be just as determined, concrete, and firmly established as our physical. . . ."[10]—a concern and an enterprise he was never to forsake.

Marx's doctoral dissertation, written between 1839 and 1841, contains an explication of freedom which conceives it not as "freedom *from* being (*Freiheit vom Dasein*)," but as "freedom *in* being (*Freiheit im Dasein*)"—that is to say, Marx argued that real freedom for man could only obtain in complex interactivity with co-members of a community (*Gemeinschaft*). Anything else would be a fictive freedom.[11]

[9] K. Marx, "Reflections of a Youth on Choosing an Occupation," in *Writings of the Young Marx on Philosophy and Society*, edited and translated by L. Easton and K. Guddat (Garden City, New York: Doubleday, 1967), pp. 39, 35, and "Die Vereinigung der Gläubigen mit Christo nach dem Evangelium des Johannes," Marx and Engels, *Gesamtausgabe* (Berlin: Dietz, 1927), *1*, part 2, 171f.

[10] K. Marx, "Letter to his Father," *Writings*, pp. 42, 46f.

[11] K. Marx, "The Leading Article in No. 179 of the Kölnische Zeitung," *ibid.*, p. 120, 122.

Thus, by the time he was twenty-two years old, Marx had committed himself to two interrelated themes: (1) man can fulfill himself and find freedom only through labor in a community, and (2) the tension between what is the case and what ought to be the case can be resolved in the real world, a world in which man's mental nature is "just as determined, concrete and firmly established as [his] physical."

These convictions resonate in an essay written in 1842 in which Marx articulated a notion of a society (he still spoke of it at that time as a "state") which "transforms" the "aims of the individual into universal aims," as a consequence of which the "individual [finds] his satisfaction in the life of the whole and the whole in the attitude of the individual." This was conjoined, in an essay written the following year, with the assertion that the explanation of political events could proceed most effectively, *not* from the scrutiny of the "*will*" or "*ideas*" of political actors, but by assessing "the *objective* nature of the relationships" between them and between them and society—relationships which are as independent of the will of historic agents as is their breathing. Once such objective and lawlike relationships are adequately characterized, Marx argued, one might predict a sequence of historical events "with almost the same certainty as a chemist determines under which external circumstances some substances will form a compound."[12]

There is a remarkable theme and category persistence, as well as a commitment to a relatively specific cognitive strategy, in the work of Karl Marx. He sought a solution to man's most fundamental ethical concerns in a vision of society that saw the fulfillment of the individual in terms of a harmony of individual and collective interests. In *The Communist Manifesto* of 1848 this was expressed in a paraphrase of Marx's adolescent commitment. The victory of the proletariat would produce an association of men in which the "free development of each is the condition for the free develop-

[12] Marx, "From the Defense of the Moselle Correspondent," *ibid.*, pp. 144f.

33

ment of all."[13] The reality of this "ought," this normative conviction, was to be sought in the "is," in the determinate and factual circumstances in which man finds himself. It was not man's thinking that determined the course and content of his life, but man's life that determined the course and content of his thinking. Man's "mental nature" was conceived to be "just as determined, concrete and firmly established" as his physical nature. The relationships that obtained between men were understood to be just as law-governed as the relationships that characterized the interactions in nature. In 1847 the conviction that man's social life exemplified the lawlikeness of natural events was expressed in terms of a study of "social relations of production" which develop "in conformity with . . . material productivity," which in turn produce the "principles, ideas and categories" which are the "historical and transitory products" to which men had hitherto looked for an explanation of the dynamics of human history.[14] In his maturity, in the first volume of *Kapital*, which appeared in 1867, Marx maintained that his work laid bare "the economic laws of motion of modern society," which could be studied with the same objectivity as the laws of nature.[15]

These ideas were not, of course, uniquely Karl Marx's. Even before his collaboration with Marx, Friedrich Engels insisted that in the future communist society "the interests of individuals would not conflict, but be identical. . . . Public interests would no longer differ from the interests of each individual."[16] The circumstances which would produce such a harmonious state of affairs were governed by objective laws so precise that prediction could be undertaken with all the confidence of a mathematical demonstration.[17] In his

[13] K. Marx and F. Engels, "The Communist Manifesto," *Selected Works* (Moscow: Foreign Languages, 1955), I, p. 54.

[14] K. Marx, *The Poverty of Philosophy*, p. 122.

[15] K. Marx, *Capital* (Moscow: Foreign Languages, 1954), I, 9-10.

[16] F. Engels, "Zwei Reden in Elberfeld: I," in K. Marx and F. Engels, *Werke* (Berlin: Dietz, 1957), II, 539, 542.

[17] F. Engels, *The Condition of the Working Class in England in 1845*, tr. F. K. Wischnewetzky (London: George Allen and Unwin, 1950), p. 18.

maturity, in the *Anti-Duehring* of 1878 and the *Ludwig Feuerbach*, written in 1887, Engels persisted in this account of the "objective laws" governing social dynamics which would produce the communist society in which the interests of each was fully compatible with the rational freedom of all.

This conception of "rational freedom,"[18] the conception of the ultimate harmony of interests between the individual and his community, was intrinsic, of course, to the Hegelian tradition to which Marx and Engels adhered.[19] The individual was understood to be, in some serious sense, an *ensemble* of social relations. "What is to be avoided above all," Marx insisted in 1844, "is the re-establishing of 'Society' as an abstraction *vis-à-vis* the individual. The individual *is the social being*. His life . . . is . . . an expression and confirmation of social life. Man's individual and species life are not different, however much . . . the individual is . . . more *particular* . . . ."[20] The foundation of the normative notions of "equality," "freedom," and "alienation" is to be found in this conviction of "the unity of human essence . . . the practical identity of man with man. . . ."[21] The failure to appreciate this identity is the root of the "selfishness" and "egotism" so much deplored by both Marx and Engels in their youth.[22]

"Equality" refers to the "unity of human essence," a recognition that the fundamental interests of each do not violate the fundamental interests of all. "Rational freedom" is predicated on the recognition that men share a common essence in reason. "Alienation" is the consequence of man's inability to realize that "essence" in an *actual* community. Men are driven to make recourse to a fictive realization of

[18] K. Marx, "The Leading Article . . . ," *Writings*, p. 128.

[19] Cf. A. J. Gregor, "Classical Marxism and the Totalitarian Ethic," *Journal of Value Inquiry*, 2, 1 (Spring 1968), 58-72.

[20] K. Marx, *Economic and Philosophic Manuscripts of 1844*, tr. Martin Milligan (Moscow: Foreign Languages, n.d.), pp. 104f.

[21] Karl Marx and F. Engels, *The Holy Family*, tr. R. Dixon (Moscow: Foreign Languages, 1956), p. 56.

[22] Cf. particularly, Marx, "On the Jewish Question," *Writings*, pp. 216-48, and Engels, "Outlines of a Critique of Political Economy," in Marx, *Economic and Philosophic Manuscripts*, pp. 175-209.

that community in religion and philosophy. Man, in the real world, is separated from his fellows and searches out his now lost unity in some transcendent realm, some unity above and/or beyond his real life circumstances. Rather than seeking the ideal in the real, men labor in the vagueness and vastness of thought to reaffirm their humanity—to find the semblance of humanity in religion and philosophy.

The true community for both the young Marx and the young Engels was a community (in the early writings they frequently refer to that community as the "state") bound in an organic collective unity of mutual and abiding rational interest. Such a community would be predicated on the full awareness that the nature of man is that of a "social being," a "real generic being."[23] Marx's criticism of political alienation turns on the recognition that what we call "bourgeois liberalism" invests each constituent member of society with individual sovereignty, the exalted expression of egotism and selfishness that divorces man from man, leaves him "uncivilized" and "unsocial," divested of his "actual species being." Marx argued that bourgeois liberalism conceives society an artifact of compromise between the competitive self-interests of society's constituent members. The "more ideal and profound view" with which Marx identified was that which conceives the community (or the state) predicated on the antecedence of the "whole," the "totality," the conception of society as a "great organism" in which the legal, ethical, and political freedom of the individual is realized in the *universality of reason*, the recognition that each individual, though particular, participates in a universal community of reason. Such participation transforms "raw impulse into ethical inclination" and "natural independence into spiritual freedom," the "individual finding his satisfaction in the life of the whole and the whole in the attitude of the individual."[24]

All of Marx's subsequent moral pronouncements—the doctrine that "man is the supreme being for man . . . ," "the

[23] Marx, "On the Jewish Question," *Writings*, p. 231.
[24] Marx, "The Leading Article . . . ," *ibid.*, pp. 120, 130.

highest being for man," the insistence that man is subject
to a "categorical imperative to overthrow all those conditions
in which man is abased, enslaved, abandoned, contemptible
being," to make "out of society a community of men devoted
to their supreme ends . . . ," to invoke a "radical revolution,"
a "universal human emancipation"—are comprehensible
within the context of such critical convictions about the
essential oneness of man, the "practical identity of man with
man . . . ."[25]

That individual men could find true fulfillment only in
society presupposes that a genuine *Gemeinschaft* would be
a society that was preeminently rational and whose members would exemplify reason. The life of society and the life
of its constituent members would be fully rational—and being fully rational would be governed by "laws." "Laws" are
the regularities governing social and individual life; they
govern both natural and social processes. In such a system
there is little place for idiosyncrasies such as "will" and
"ideas" that are not themselves reducible to natural or social
"laws."

While such notions constitute the substance of the philosophical or ethical communism of Marx's youth,[26] they clearly remain central to Marx's mature analysis. The realization
of "fulfillment," "equality," and "freedom," as Marx understood those normative terms, is possible only in a society in
which the ultimate interests of the individual and the community are, in a real sense, identical. And that seems to require that individual will and ideas are subject to the same
lawlike regularities that govern both nature and society.

There are, nonetheless, significant differences in Marx's
treatment of these problems at various periods. The differences are marked by clear discontinuities in the develop-

[25] Marx, "Toward the Critique of Hegel's Philosophy of Law: Introduction," *ibid.*, pp. 257, 260; "An Exchange of Letters," *ibid.*, p.
206.

[26] Cf. Editor's comments to Engel's "Outlines . . . ," in Marx, *Economic and Philosophic Manuscripts*, p. 175, n. 1. While the reference
here is to Engel's essay, the central notions entertained by Engels are
those of Marx as well.

ment of Marx's thought. He, himself, identified the year between 1844 and 1845 as a period of intense self-criticism. Years later, in referring to this period, he wrote of it as a time in which he sought to "settle accounts" with his "former philosophic conscience," a time in which he proceeded to "resolve" significant questions for himself.[27]

It seems relatively clear that Marx's first concerns were essentially normative. These concerns were not uniquely his own—he shared them with the philosophy of his time. Hegel, as had most of his predecessors and his subsequent followers in the idealist and neo-idealist tradition, preoccupied himself with the broad problem of man's "freedom." Fichte, one of Hegel's principal predecessors, indicated in a letter to Reinhold, for example, that his own philosophy was "from beginning to end only an analysis of the idea of freedom." Hegel characterized his time as one which saw the birth of the "idea of freedom," and its special problem was determining how the "political realization of freedom was to be achieved."[28]

The concerns, then, that animated Marx's efforts were common to an entire philosophic tradition—if not common to critical social and political thought since time immemorial. To be told, therefore, that Marx entertained normative commitments to the freedom, fulfillment, and self-realization of man in society is not to learn a great deal. None of these preoccupations is specifically Marxist, nor do they move us closer to explaining the cognitive character and content of Marx's thought. The motives that impel a man to undertake intellectual labors can only tangentially assist us in understanding his thought. That Marx was concerned with the realization of man's freedom and fulfillment no more committed him to revolution and socialism than the individual's

[27] K. Marx, *The Critique of Political Economy*, pp. 13f.

[28] Cf. W. T. Harris, "Preface," to J. G. Fichte, *The Science of Knowledge* (London: Truebner, 1889), p. xii; G. Hegel, *The Philosophy of History*, translated by J. Sibree (New York: Dover, 1956), p. 447; J. Ritter, *Hegel und die französiche Revolution* (Frankfurt a.M.: Suhrkamp, 1965), pp. 24f.

desire to reduce the measure of unnecessary pain in the world compels him to be a doctor or a dentist. One could, without faulting his commitments, be either or neither. He might just as well be a policeman or a research physicist. That Marx sought to realize man's potential freedom could have directed him as well toward the study of psychology as economics, might as well have made of him a "conservative" as a "revolutionary," might have made of him a monarchist rather than a socialist.

The themes found in his early writings—themes which persist throughout his productive life—are common to the political and social thought of his (if not all) time. Marx's normative ideal of "democracy" as the "true unity of the universal and the particular," in which "man's communist essence" (*das kommunistische Wesen des Menschen*) would be fulfilled, on the other hand, is an ideal that is singularly Hegelian,[29] but Hegel could hardly be identified as a socialist revolutionary.

Marx's work becomes uniquely "Marxian" when certain cognitive postures are assumed and their implications drawn out in the protracted labors left to us in the form of an intellectual patrimony that is specifically Marxist. These cognitive postures include a broad epistemological stance which Marx identified as an "inversion of Hegelianism." This "inversion" was the product of Marx's traffic with Feuerbachianism. Ludwig Feuerbach had discovered the "mystery" of Hegel—Hegel's disposition to treat the properties of things as though they had an independent and substantive existence. If the individual mind was possessed of reason, Feuerbach argued, Hegel exalted that property and reified it as a universal and transcendent "Reason." Hegel had, Feuerbach maintained, elevated a *predicate* into a *subject*. Good sense counseled a restoration of the predicate and the identification of the "true subject." The true subject for Feuerbach, as it was to be for Marx, was man. If Hegel had proceeded speculatively, Feuerbach and Marx after him were to proceed empirically. Marx was to later characterize his method

<hr />

[29] Cf. Marx, "Kritik des Hegelschen Staatsrechts," *Werke*, I, 231.

as a "profane history" of the Hegelian "categories," a method he had adopted and adapted from Feuerbach.[30]

This "reform" of the Hegelian method was not dictated by either Feuerbach's or Marx's *moral* commitments. It was the consequence of an essentially *intellectual* decision. It was conceived as resolving some of the paradox of the Hegelian system. Marx's efforts, in his critique of the Hegelian philosophy of the state written in 1843 and his critique of the Hegelian dialectic contained in the *Manuscripts of 1844*, were undertaken to resolve paradox and confusion. They were, no doubt, motivated by Marx's normative concerns, but they were advanced in compliance with, and were understood to satisfy, cognitive criteria of adequacy. Marx did not argue that his normative ideals were superior to those of Hegel—rather, he maintained that Hegel's account generated intellectual difficulties and seeming contradiction. Hegel's account was *cognitively implausible*, not *morally impaired*.

That Marx's account was essentially, if not exclusively, cognitive is evidenced by the fact that Marx was ultimately dissatisfied with his youthful attempts at reformulation. His *Manuscripts of 1844* did not resolve, to Marx's own satisfaction, some of the problems inherited from Hegel. Marx did not long remain content with his analysis as it developed through 1844. In the year between the writing of the Paris *Manuscripts* and *The German Ideology*, Marx abandoned some of the analyses now identified with the "young Marx." Where he spoke in the *Manuscripts* of "categories working themselves out" in the object world, in *The German Ideology* he was to speak of "empirical relations" giving rise to "categories" in thought. The process which characterized this epistemological reinterpretation is clearly documented in the notes which have survived from this period. The reinterpretation was not the consequence of any ethical considerations—it was the product of cognitive reappraisal. Marx's

---

[30] Cf. A. J. Gregor, "Marx, Feuerbach and the Reform of the Hegelian Dialectic," *Science and Society*, 29, 1 (Winter 1965), 66-80.

normative commitments remained constant throughout the change.

In the period immediately preceding the writing of *The German Ideology* Marx undertook a summary criticism of the Feuerbachianism that had sustained his critique of Hegel through the writing of the *Manuscripts* and *The Holy Family*. Engels indicated that the *Theses on Feuerbach* contained the "brilliant germ of the new world outlook." As we have already indicated, Marx held that the antecedent *German Ideology* had served the purpose of "self-clarification."[31]

The German Ideology contains, therefore, the preliminary statement of a specifically Marxist theory of history.[32] It was an analysis concerned with an adequate appraisal of men "as they are" and as "they ought to be," a concern that reflects Marx's persistent normative perspective. The persistence of the normative themes found in the writings from 1837 through 1844 and their recurrence in the critical texts of 1845 and 1846 indicate that Marx's normative commitments did not determine the cognitive content of his subsequent accounts. The development evidenced in those accounts is to be explained by time-specific cognitive rather than the transperiodic normative concerns.

In *The German Ideology* Marx remained convinced that the "personal freedom of the individual" as well as his "cultivation of his gifts in all directions" can take place only in a real and not an illusory community. It is only in the "real community [that] individuals obtain their freedom in and through their association."[33] The conditions governing the

[31] Engels, *Selected Works*, ii, p. 359. The theses on Feuerbach are provided in English translation as an appendix to the English translation of *The German Ideology*, tr. S. Ryazanskaya (Moscow: Progress, 1964), pp. 645-53.

[32] Without embarking on a digression that serves little purpose, the expression "theory of history" seems justified in view of the fact that Marx wrote: "We know only a single science, the science of history," a conviction that, while the passage containing it was, in fact, deleted in the finished manuscript, seems to have remained constant throughout Marx's life. *The German Ideology*, p. 28, n.

[33] *Ibid.*, pp. 91f.

historic development of community are traced in the real history of men rather than in its ideal "reflection" in the minds of men; that is to say, the tension between what is the case and what ought to be the case is resolved in the *real world,* a world in which *men's mental nature* is "just as *determined, concrete* and *firmly established* as our *physical."* These convictions are expressed by Marx as early as 1837. What has changed is the degree of precision that characterizes them. By 1845-1846 they are housed in propositions of fair specificity, generated by analyses that are essentially empirical—that abandon the neo-Hegelian search for "categories" and "logical concepts." The argument is consistently empirical, rather than analytic. While the propositions that result remain painfully vague, and the syntax which related them imprecise, the change they evidence is a cognitive rather than a normative one.

Marx's values, then, are in a real sense extrinsic to the assessment of his system. His normative commitments certainly motivated a life's labor—and the congruence of his system is the measure of the compatibility of his conclusions with his normative intentions—but the cognitive merit of his system is judged by criteria that are independent of his motives and his intentions.

The Preliminary Conceptual Schema

Karl Marx was clearly animated by an ethical impulse— he may have articulated a "primitive" ethical theory as well (what we speak of today as having metaethical interests)[34] —but for all that, he developed a scientific theory of social dynamics, a synoptic view of man in history. That "view" can be characterized with economy and considerable specificity—and it can be judged by criteria of adequacy common to the social sciences.

[34] In this regard see E. Kamenka's recent *Marxism and Ethics* (New York: St. Martin's, 1969); for my views, which are very similar to those of Kamenka, cf. "Comments on Stojanovic," in N. Lobkowicz, *Marx and the Western World* (Notre Dame: Notre Dame, 1967), pp. 172-75.

To speak of Marxism as possessing a "scientific theory of social dynamics" implies that Marxism can be understood to possess a collection of propositions, systematically related, among which are lawlike statements which permit (when conjoined with statements that identify the empirical conditions which make the lawlike statements applicable) the generation of explanations and predictions that are subject to empirical confirmation and disconfirmation. Marxism has, since its inception, pretended to retrodict, explain, and predict. Whatever recommendations Marx and his followers tendered, they were as compelling as the truth of the theory that constituted their empirical substance. If Marx and the Marxists advocated revolution it was because they understood society to be moved by empirical forces they had come to understand. If Marx and the Marxists foresaw a society in which the exploitation of man by man would cease, it was because they projected empirical trends moving toward "necessary" consequences in which exploitation would be "impossible."

After Marx completed his work on *The German Ideology* he never again couched his discussion in terms of moral imperatives. His writings remain alive with moral outrage, but he insisted that his outrage was not directed against persons but against classes. Men could not be criticized for being what their conditions made them. Marx regularly and consistently spoke of individuals as "personifications" of classes, as the products of their circumstances.[35] When he was forced by the "bourgeois sentiments" of his fellows to include characteristically moral terms such as "freedom" and "justice" in his Preamble to the Call for the Organization of the International Workingmen's Association, he informed Engels he put those expressions in the text where "they could do no harm."[36] He had, in fact, as early as the preparation of *The German Ideology* in 1845-1846 insisted that "Communists preach no morality at all."

[35] Cf. Marx's "Preface to the First German Edition," *Capital*, i, 10.
[36] Marx to Engels, Nov. 4, 1864, in *Werke*, xxxi, 15. Marx and Engels, *The German Ideology*, p. 267.

By the time he prepared the manuscript copy of *The German Ideology* Marx had worked out, to his own satisfaction, *a conceptual schema which made moral concepts, and ideology in general, a derivative product of a more fundamental and objective process.* In the years antecedent to the preparation of *The German Ideology*, Marx and Engels had developed their own views independently. Marx had, since his adolescence, sought a conception of society in which the individual would find fulfillment only through labor in communion with his fellows. He sought to support his views through a critical assessment of prevailing social and political conceptions. It is neither necessary, nor is there space available here, to pursue the gradual articulation of Marx's account. By 1843 he had developed several critical conceptions that were to be reformulated, but were nonetheless to occupy central roles, in his first serious attempt to formulate a defensible conceptual schema in 1845-1846. As early as 1843 one finds the "proletariat" assigned the specific historic task of overcoming the oppressive conditions of the contemporary world. Equally evident, however, is the absence of any theoretical infrastructure that would make this ascription much more than a pious hope. The subsequent discussions in the *Manuscripts of 1844* are more extended and more interesting, but there is ample evidence of confusion and the regular reappearance of Hegelian residues. *The Holy Family*, to which Engels contributed, is equally interesting, but remains the product of a Feuerbachian enthusiasm that Marx found, twenty years later, to be "comical."[37]

When Engels and Marx met in the summer of 1844 it was obvious to them both that they were in essential agreement concerning theoretical matters. Both agreed that "politics and the history of political development must be examined in the light of economic conditions and their evolution, not the other way about as heretofore." Engels had claimed as much in his *The Condition of the Working Class in England in 1844* and in his "Outlines of Political Economy," which

[37] Marx to Engels, Letter of April 24, 1867, *Werke*, xxxi, 290.

was published in the *Deutsch-Franzoesische Jahrbuecher*. Engels, who was far more sensitive to the influence of economic factors on historical development, probably influenced the direction of Marx's intellectual maturation—although it is clear that Marx had already anticipated some of the subsequent emphases in the Paris *Manuscripts*. When Marx and Engels met (for the second time) in Brussels in the spring of 1845, Marx, Engels informs us, "had already elaborated the main points in his materialist theory of history." They then both "set about the task of working the theory out in its manifold details."[38]

The confluence of the antecedent thought of both Marx and Engels, the special genius and application Marx brought to the effort, produced in 1845-1846 the long (and more than sometimes tedious) *The German Ideology*—an extended criticism of the Left Hegelians of the period, particularly Ludwig Feuerbach and Max Stirner. In addition, the manuscript contains the first statement of historical materialism. *The German Ideology*, the subsequent *The Poverty of Philosophy* (1847), and *The Communist Manifesto* (1848) provide an account of the conceptual schema Marx was subsequently to formalize and standardize more extensively through the next two major periods of his life (1849-1859 and 1860-1883).

The German Ideology commenced with a specific rejection of the "Hegelian method" of "mystification"; that is to say, Marx rejected the "philosophical" disposition he found prevalent among the neo-Hegelians—the disposition to undertake the analysis of contemporary problems via "categories" and "concepts." The Hegelians, Marx lamented, "comprehend everything as soon as it [is] reduced to an Hegelian logical category." His recommended corrective was a return to a reality assessment which involved "real premises from

[38] Cf. Engel's account, in *The Communist Manifesto of Karl Marx and Friedrich Engels*, edited by D. Ryazanoff (New York: Russell & Russell, 1963), pp. 8f. The complete German text of Engels' account is to be found in "Zur Geschichte des Bundes der Kommunisten," *Werke*, xxi, 206-24.

which abstraction can only be made in the imagination." In effect, Marx was continuing a cognitive strategy he had adopted as early as *The Holy Family*. In *The Holy Family* Marx had rejected the notion that there were some sort of "subsistent" logical categories. He saw general terms only as abstractions from a class of particular empirical individuals. Individual things exist, general terms are class *names*; their substantive reference is a *class* of individual objects. For this reason Marx rejected the general term "history" when it was conceived as a "person apart, a metaphysical subject of which real human individuals are but the bearers."[39] Thus, in *The German Ideology* his "first premises" for analysis are "real individuals, their activity and the material conditions under which they live . . . ." Such premises "can . . . be verified in a purely empirical way."[40]

Whatever general terms, "categories," or "concepts," are employed in the account can be, in principle, reduced to individual referents and activities between individuals and classes of individuals. Marx's strategy is that of any empirical analysis. It is essentially nominalist; i.e. general terms are in some real sense reducible to observable referents. Individual things and the relations that obtain between them have a "reality" not enjoyed by "constructs" and "theoretical terms."

This cognitive strategy is conjoined with a conviction that men are specifically distinguished from animals by their ability to *produce their means of subsistence*. Furthermore, by "producing their means of subsistence men are indirectly producing their actual material life. . . . As individuals express their life, so they are. What they are, therefore, coincides with their production, both with what they produce and with how they produce. The nature of individuals thus depends on the material conditions determining their production."

Immediately in the next paragraph Marx indicates that

[39] Marx and Engels, *The Holy Family*, p. 107.
[40] *The German Ideology*, pp. 30f.

46

material production (*die Weise der Produktion*) can be distinguished into two apparently distinctly categories: (1) the productive forces (*Produktivkraefte*) and the division of labor (*Teilung der Arbeit*), and (2) the "intercourse of individuals with one another" (*Verkehrsform*). The latter is determined (*bedingt*) by the former. The relationship between the "productive forces" and the "division of labor" is equally one of dependence. "Each new productive force," Marx maintains, "causes a further development of the division of labor," and the "various stages of development of the division of labor" produce "just so many different forms of ownership, i.e., the existing stage in the division of labor determines also the relations of individuals to one another with reference to the material, instrument, and product of labor."[41] The result is an account which can be economically expressed with the condensed proposition: "the multitude of productive forces accessible to men determines the nature of society, hence, . . . the 'history of humanity' must always be studied and treated in relation to the history of industry and exchange."[42]

The productive forces determine the division of labor, which in turn determines the "form of intercourse." These in turn determine "the production of ideas, of conceptions, of consciousness . . . ." "The phantoms formed in the human brain," Marx insisted, "are . . . necessarily, sublimates of [the] material life process. . . . Morality, religion, metaphysics, all the rest of ideology and their corresponding forms of consciousness, thus no longer retain the semblance of independence. They have no history, no development; but men, developing their material production and their material intercourse, alter, along with this their real existence, their thinking and the products of their thinking. Life is not determined by consciousness, but consciousness by life."[43]

Men, in order to "make history," must meet elemental needs of sustenance, raiment, and shelter. The "first historical act" is the satisfaction of these needs, the "production of

[41] *Ibid.*, pp. 32f.　　[42] *Ibid.*, p. 41.　　[43] *Ibid.*, pp. 37f.

material life itself." As each need is satisfied by employing some productive instrument, new needs are generated. Increased needs (*vermehrten Beduerfnisse*), satisfied by a multiplicity of productive instruments, alter the productive forces fundamental to the social system. Changes in the productive forces alter the division of labor, which in turn alters the prevailing form of intercourse and subsequently all the forms of consciousness which attend the manner of meeting the requirements of material life. "Consciousness," Marx could insist, "is, therefore, from the very beginning a social product . . . ."[44]

As long as social consciousness, the forms of intercourse (or as Marx alternately expresses the same concept, "social relations" [*gesellschaftlichen Verhaeltnisse*]), and the existing forces of production are compatible, the social system is in relative stability. When "contradiction" (*Widerspruch*) mounts between social consciousness and the manner of producing material life, "pure" theory, that is to say theology, philosophy, and ethics, undergoes significant change. They express in "idealistic, spiritual expression" the real fact that "empirical fetters" constrain the mode of production of material life. The contradiction to which Marx alludes in *The German Ideology* is the consequence of the division of labor. The division of labor "implies the contradiction between the interest of the separate individual . . . and the communal interest of all individuals who have intercourse with one another," for the "division of labor and private property are . . . identical expressions." Private property implies a distinction between individual and communal interests. As long as such a distinction obtains it is possible for "man's own deed" to become "an alien power opposed to him, which enslaves him instead of being controlled by him."

There is some considerable confusion at this point in Marx's account, but the argument seems to proceed in something like the following fashion: first and foremost, the division of labor and private property were conceived by Marx

[44] *Ibid.*, p. 42.

to be, in some sense, "identical."[45] Since the division of labor is produced by the development of the productive forces, it would seem that the development of the productive forces generates new divisions of labor which, in turn, generate altered social relations, with "private property" constituting one, if not the principal, form of social relation which necessarily undergoes alteration. To identify the division of labor and private property is a confusion, for Marx almost immediately modifies this "identification" by saying that "the division of labor implies from the outset the division of the conditions of labor, of tools and materials . . . among different owners, and thus, also, the division between capital and labor, and the different forms of property itself. The more the division of labor develops and accumulation grows, the sharper are the forms that this process of differentiation assumes."[46] Thus the division of labor *implies*, but is not *identical* with, changes in property relations. There can be a considerable time lag between the one and the other. The various forms of property, tribal property, feudal landed property, corporate movable property, local investment capital, and ultimately modern capital, unlimited in its range of application and unrestrictedly private, are the consequence of the development of the productive forces (which Marx seems to equate in several critical passages with development of the "instruments of production"[47]).

Out of the "contradiction" between the productive forces and the social relations (the instruments of production and the forms of property generated by them) a tension mounts. As productive forces develop they find the existing forms of intercourse fetters their further maturation. The possessing classes, those that profit from the prevailing form of social intercourse, paticularly where private property is fully divorced from estate capital, create the political state, that "form of organization" that provides a "mutual guarantee of their property and interests." The state takes on an "independent form," divorced from "the real interests of individ-

---

[45] *Ibid.*, p. 44.   [46] *Ibid.*, p. 82.   [47] *Ibid.*, pp. 64, 80-85.

ual and community." The state, the agency of the possessing class, advances itself as representative of the community. Since it, in reality, represents only the interests of the possessing class, it is revealed as an "illusory communal life," the caricature of the true community (*Gemeinschaft*) in which the fulfillment of each is the necessary condition for the fulfillment of all.

As the productive forces develop, the existing social relations—protected by the state—become increasingly counterproductive. The forms of intercourse, once supportive of the developing productive forces, become "no longer productive, but destructive forces." The productive forces in contemporary society are possessed as private property by individual capitalists, and consequently they face those individuals who must work for wages as "alien forces" rather than as real extensions of themselves. Private property as an institution wrests from the *majority* of the members of society the productive forces which, as extensions of themselves, provide their existence with "real-life content." Labor, which alone still links them with the alienated productive forces, becomes itself demeaning. It stunts, rather than enhances, life. Thus historical development has produced a class which "bears all the burdens of society without enjoying its advantages, which ousted from society, is forced into the most decided antagonism to all other classes; a class which forms the majority of all members of society, and *from which emanates the consciousness of the necessity of a fundamental revolution. . . .*"[48]

The singularity of the contemporary revolution is that it transcends national boundaries. The development of the productive forces had attained that level of universality that the distinction between nations becomes increasingly evanescent. Large-scale industry has created an international proletarian class "which in all nations has the same interest and with which nationality is already dead; a class which is really rid of all the old world and at the same time stands

[48] *Ibid.*, p. 85. Emphasis supplied.

pitted against it."[49] That class, the international proletariat, is destined to produce the liberating revolution—a revolution which will produce a genuine community, that community in which "personal freedom" becomes possible.

> In the previous substitutes for the community, in the State, etc., personal freedom has existed only for the individuals who developed within the relationships of the ruling class, and only insofar as they were individuals of this class. The illusory community, in which individuals have up till now combined, always took on an independent existence in relation to them, and was at the same time, since it was the combination of one class over against another, not only a completely illusory community, but a new fetter as well. In the *real* community the individuals obtain their freedom in and through their association.[50]

In *The German Ideology* there are to be found, therefore, some of the critical conceptual artifacts that have become characteristic of classical Marxism: (1) the distinction between what was later called the *superstructure* and the *economic base of society*; the first understood to include all the ideational or "ideological" products of a particular society, and the latter composed of (a) the forms of intercourse (or, as they were later characterized, "the productive relations") and (b) the productive forces (later generally referred to as the "material productive forces") with emphatic emphasis on the instruments of production as prime constituents; (2) the relationship between "ideology" (or social consciousness) and the forms of intercourse (or social relations) and the productive forces is one of dependency—that is to say ideology "reflects" or is "determined" by the "mode of material production"; (3) the form of social intercourse is in turn determined by development of the productive forces; (4) revolution is explained by the development of "contradictions" between the form of social intercourse and the development of the productive forces; (5) classes are defined in terms of property relations (or as these relations

---

[49] *Ibid.*, p. 76.   [50] *Ibid.*, pp. 91f.

are characterized in *The German Ideology*, "forms of social intercourse"); (6) all of which takes place "independent of the will and consciousness" of historic individuals and entire classes.

The entire analysis concludes with a conviction of an immanent "liberating" revolution in which the majority of contemporary manhood will rise up to overthrow the social relations predicated on private property and sustained by the state. The revolution will create the classless, stateless, international social order that Marx identifies with the universal and fully rational community in which personal freedom develops as a condition and a fulfillment of the freedom of the whole—in the unity of the particular and the universal.

The account which Marx provides in *The Poverty of Philosophy*, written in 1846-1847, restates essentially the same concepts. The same epistemological strategy is employed: Marx rejects the disposition to assess problems by reducing them to "logical categories" that work themselves out in some "subsistent logical realm."[51] The treatment of social dynamics remains the same:

> In acquiring new productive forces men change their mode of production; and in changing their mode of production, in changing the way of earning their living, they change all their social relations. The handmill gives you society with the feudal lord; the steam-mill, society with the industrial capitalist.
>
> The same men who establish their social relations in conformity with their material productivity, produce also principles, ideas and categories, in conformity with their social relations. . . . There is a continual movement of growth in productive forces, of destruction in social relations, of formation in ideas . . . .[52]

As new productive forces develop they find themselves fettered by existing social relations; "new productive forces

[51] Marx, *The Poverty of Philosophy*, pp. 117-21.
[52] *Ibid.*, pp. 122f.

[constitute] the material conditions of a new society."[53] "For the oppressed class to be able to emancipate itself it is necessary that the productive powers already acquired and the existing social relations should no longer be capable of existing side by side."[54]

The conceptual apparatus developed in *The German Ideology* and used to such devasting effect against Proudhon in *The Poverty of Philosophy* was reinvoked at the end of 1847 and the beginning of 1848 in the preparation of *The Manifesto of the Communist Party*. The "fundamental proposition" of the *Manifesto*, identified as such by Engels in 1888, was that "in every historical epoch, *the prevailing mode of economic production and exchange*, and the social organization necessarily following from it, *form the basis upon which is built up, and from which alone can be explained, the political and intellectual history of that epoch . . . ."[55]

The *Manifesto* provides an analysis of social dynamics predicated on the proposition that, since the modern bourgeoisie "cannot exist without constantly revolutionizing the instruments of production and thereby the relations of production," a transformation of society must be the predictable consequence. The "rapid improvement of all instruments of production" constitutes the foundation of the real history "of the revolt of modern productive forces against modern conditions of production, against the property relations . . . ."[56]

The class that represents the productive forces (which Marx again seems to equate with the "instruments of production") is the proletariat, which, alienated from the real content of its life because the productive foundation of communal life is the possession of an exiguous possessing class, is compelled to revolt against the established order. Just as in feudal times when the "feudal relations of property became no longer compatible with the already developed productive forces," contemporary empirical conditions demand

---

[53] *Ibid.*, p. 168.   [54] *Ibid.*, p. 196.

[55] Engels, "Preface to the English Edition of 1888," in Marx and Engels, *Selected Works*, I, 28. Emphasis supplied.

[56] Marx and Engels, "The Communist Manifesto," *ibid.*, I, 37, 38, 39.

that prevailing property relations, now fetters on production, be "burst asunder." Class antagonisms have, in the modern epoch, become increasingly simplified. Society is riven more and more emphatically into two "great hostile camps," the proletariat on the one hand representing the rapidly expanding productive forces, and the bourgeoisie, vested and entrenched advocates of the established property relations.

Under the prevailing conditions governing property in bourgeois society, the rapidly expanding productive capacity of society fails to find effective demand for its produce. There are periodic "epidemics" of overproduction (or, more accurately, underconsumption). The proletariat, stripped of any trait other than its capacity to labor, becomes an ill-paid appendage of the machine. "In proportion, therefore, as the repulsiveness of work increases, the wage decreases." Economic crises become increasingly emphatic. More and more people from the middle strata are jettisoned into the proletariat. The economies of large-scale production, the necessity of capital-intensive investment, reduce the capacity of the intermediate economic strata to survive. The proletariat increases in number while their life circumstances deteriorate. As a class they sink "deeper and deeper below the conditions of existence . . . ." The proletariat "becomes a pauper, and pauperism develops more rapidly than the population and wealth. And here it becomes evident, that the bourgeoisie is unfit any longer to be the ruling class in society. . . . It is unfit to rule because it is incompetent to assure an existence to its slave within his slavery, because it cannot help letting him sink into such a state, that it has to feed him, instead of being fed by him."

The thesis of "emiseration" (*Verelendung*) is critical to the prediction of forthcoming revolution. To talk about the "revolt of the modern productive forces against modern conditions of production" is singularly unconvincing unless the class identified with the modern productive forces can be shown to possess motives for revolution. Marx provides the motive for revolution by conjuring up the thesis of proletariat emiseration, the increasing poverty of the entire class.

In the *Manifesto* Marx insists that the average price of wage labor is the minimum wage, "i.e. that quantum of the means of subsistence, which is absolutely required to keep the laborer in bare existence as a laborer."[57] The "spontaneous class organization of the proletariat," which in *advanced capitalist countries* involves *nine-tenths of the population,* is the necessary consequence of increasingly desperate conditions.[58] The ideas which animate a social movement are the "outgrowth of conditions of . . . production," they are changed with "every change in the conditions of . . . material existence. . . . What else does the history of ideas prove, than that intellectual production changes its character in proportion as material production is changed?"[59] Because of the contemporary and unique *development of productive forces,* a class is produced which is the harbinger of a unique, universal, and liberating revolution. Because the productivity of contemporary capitalism drives it over the surface of the globe to find market outlets for its productivity, the distinction between nations is suppressed, and a universal class is created which universally opposes the international representatives of the constraining social relations. "All previous historical movements were movements of minorities, or in the interest of minorities. The proletarian movement is the self-conscious, independent movement of the immense majority, in the interests of the immense majority."[60]

The conceptual schema articulated by Marx between 1845 and 1848 draws extensively on the antecedent work of 1841 through 1844, but the schema outlined in *The German Ideology* remained relatively constant throughout the remainder of Marx's productive life. Real innovation takes place essentially in terms of more systematic economic analysis. By 1845 Marx was clearly convinced that historical explanation trafficked on the analysis of the lawlike "material conditions of life," the regularities governing the "economic basis" of the social order. "Ideas" and "will," the stuff of political con-

[57] *Ibid.,* pp. 47f.
[58] *Ibid.,* pp. 48, 62.
[59] *Ibid.,* pp. 49, 52.
[60] *Ibid.,* p. 44.

victions, were derivative products of such lawlike social and essentially economic regularities. Lacking, during this period of Marx's thought, was a relatively precise economic theory that provided an account of those lawlike regularities. The schema Marx entertained in 1845 was pretheoretical and preliminary.

In the first place, the collection of propositions which constitutes the substance of his conceptual schema is couched in terms of metaphor and analogy. In *The German Ideology* Marx spoke of "the production of ideas" as being variously "sublimates" of material life processes, as having no "semblance of independence," as "altering" with alterations in material production and material intercourse, as being "determined" by life, as being "nothing more than the ideal expression of the dominant material relationships." On the other hand, and in the same volume Marx maintained that "consciousness can sometimes appear further advanced than the contemporary empirical relationships . . . ."[61] The "productive forces" are sometimes spoken of as though the expression referred to "instruments of production," and yet at other times the instruments of production are spoken of as *part* of the productive forces; at other times he speaks of the "revolutionary class itself" as an "instrument of production," and "individuals" as themselves "instruments of production."[62] It is equally difficult to specify unequivocally what the "forms of exchange" or "social relations" might mean. Clearly both expressions involve reference to property relations, but what else is involved remains obscure. In *The Poverty of Philosophy* Marx speaks of a "proletariat" *in feudal times*, a confusion he himself subsequently recognized.[63]

Even the most orthodox commentators on this period recognize that the schema Marx developed during this period was only *preliminary* to his mature work. T. I. Oiserman refers to the relatively modest economic analysis to be found

----

[61] Marx and Engels, *The German Ideology*, p. 89.

[62] Marx, *The Poverty of Philosophy*, p. 196; *The German Ideology*, p. 80.

[63] Marx, *The Poverty of Philosophy*, p. 137.

in *The German Ideology*, the obvious implausibility of "identifying" the "division of labor" and "private property," the inadequacy of the conceptualization of the "forms of exchange."[64] Furthermore, V. S. Wygodski speaks of this period as the "prehistory" of Marx's economic theories.[65] Marx began his intensive labor in the sphere of political economy only in July 1850, and it was only between October 1857 and May 1858 that Marx produced, in its mature form, the labor theory of value, the theory of surplus value. Only thereafter did Marx develop his theory of average rate of profit and of the price of production. This work, which commenced only after Marx took up permanent residence in England, filled in the theoretical infrastructure of the preliminary conceptual schema he had articulated between 1843 and 1849. In 1880, when Marx's *The Poverty of Philosophy* was to be reissued, Marx indicated that the work written in 1847 contained only the "germ" of twenty years of labor that produced *Kapital* in 1867.[66] He went on to indicate that *The Poverty of Philosophy* and the *Manifesto* might serve as an "introduction" to *Kapital*.

That the creation of a convincing theoretical infrastructure involved so onerous an obligation was not evident to Marx at the commencement of his labors in the intermediary period between 1850 and 1859. In April 1851 he wrote Engels that he expected to be finished with the "economic crap" (*oekonomischen Scheisse*) in five weeks.[67] Engels awaited the standardization and formalization of the theory day by day. It was not to be completed in Marx's lifetime. Marx was to spend thirty-three years providing the economic infrastructure of historical materialism.

[64] T. I. Oiserman, *Die Entstehung der marxistischen Philosophie* (Berlin: Dietz, 1965), pp. 406, 412, 420, 422.

[65] Wygodski, *Die Geschichte einer grossen Entdeckung*, p. 15.

[66] K. Marx, Über Misere de la philosophie," in *Werke*, xix, 229.

[67] Marx to Engels, April 2, 1851, *Werke*, xxvii, 228.

CHAPTER THREE

Classical Marxism as a Mature System

BOTH Marx and Engels were convinced that the "contradiction" between productive forces and productive relations provided the dynamic force for revolutionary social change. Such a conviction constituted a broad knowledge claim and required some kind of public evidence to make it credible. But before such evidence could be sought out and collected, the claim itself had to be advanced in a form that would permit its implications to be drawn out.

Until Marx moved to England in 1849, the preliminary conceptual schema, the "germ" of his "world view," was couched in metaphor and simile: productive relations as "fetters" were "burst asunder," and ideas were "echoed" and "effluxed." Critical terms were only vaguely defined: what the constituents of the "productive forces" might correctly be conceived to be, what constituted the sum of "productive relations," was never made sufficiently clear to permit the generation of verification studies. The schema had evident heuristic merit. It was bold and held the promise of considerable theoretical yield; but it remained for all that a *preliminary* schema, the first important step in social science theory construction.

While the elements of Marx's "labor theory of value"— the theory that living labor was the sole and ultimate source of all commodity exchange value—were contained in Marx's article, "Labor, Price and Profit," written in 1848, his economic analysis was no more than a "mere sketch" (*eine blosse Skizze*), the *promise* of a theory.[1] Only in 1851 were the implications of the labor theory of value worked out in some detail. It was not until 1857-1858 that Marx worked out a systematic exposition of his theory of surplus value.[2]

---

[1] R. Rosdolsky, *Zur Entstehungsgeschichte des Marxschen "Kapital"* (Vienna: Europa, 1968), I, 15.

[2] D. I. Rosenberg maintains that rudiments of the theory of surplus

Only then was he prepared to deliver an account of the theoretical infrastructure of his preliminary schema and to make of his schema a theory. What resulted was the publication of Marx's *Contribution to the Critique of Political Economy* in 1859, a decade after the first formulation of his preliminary schema.

The first volume of the *Contribution* was to be the first in a series of publications on economics in which Marx intended to provide an account of his theory. He wrote Lasalle that the publication of the work would finally provide a "scientific" insight into social relations.[3] Marx fully intended (as his letters of 1859 and 1860 reveal) to complete the work and offer the remaining volumes for publication as soon as possible. It became evident almost immediately, however, that the theory was incomplete. Marx embarked on a long and detailed study of theories of surplus value. The renewed inquiry was, at least in part, motivated by two considerations: to uncover and characterize the relationship of profit to surplus value, and to develop an insight into the dynamics of capitalism that suggested that capitalism *must* produce a secular decline in the rate of profit. These ideas are to be found in outline in the *Grundrisse* of 1857-1858,[4] but they were not explicated until 1861-1863, when Marx developed his conceptions of the average rate of profit, the price of production, and the decline of the rate of profit. In 1893 Engels wrote to a Russian correspondent that Marx had worked out his theory of surplus value in the fifties, but that the implications of his insight had not been fully worked out by the time he published the *Contribution*. The *Contribution*, as we now know, was published under the pressure of Marx's expectation that a new wave of revolu-

value were to be found in *The Poverty of Philosophy*, but see Wygodski's objections. D. I. Rosenberg, *Die Entwicklung der ökonomischen Lehre von Marx und Engels in den vierziger Jahren des 19. Jahrhunderts* (Berlin: Dietz, 1958), p. 304; W. S. Wygodski, *Die Geschichte einer grossen Entdeckung* (Berlin: Wirtschaft, 1967), p. 32.

[3] Marx to Lasalle, November 12, 1858, *Werke*, xxix, 566.

[4] Marx, *Grundrisse*, pp. 648f.

tions would soon break out in Europe. With the passing of the crisis that Marx had expected to generate those revolutions, he repaired to his study once again to work out the details of his theory. He ultimately abandoned the publication of the subsequent volumes of the *Contribution*, and it was not until 1867 that the first volume of *Das Kapital* appeared, twenty years after the publication of the "germ" of his theory.

With the publication of the first volume of *Kapital*, a great puzzlement settled on reasonably sophisticated readers. Marx's preliminary formulation of his theory of value, contained in the first volume of both the *Contribution* and *Kapital*, maintained that the value of a commodity was determined by the amount of socially necessary labor time incorporated in it. Only living labor, it was argued, has the capacity of endowing things with value—a theme already suggested in Marx's early philosophic and economic manuscripts of 1844. "Labor power," the working capacity of the wage earner, is a commodity which the capitalist purchases and pays for at its own cost of production. But labor power has the capacity of creating value. The value created by labor power during the working day can be divided into two discrete components: necessary labor and surplus labor. Necessary labor is that labor necessary to sustain the worker and provide for his replacement in terms of progeny (labor's "natural price"). Whatever value his labor contributes to the production of commodities that exceeds that necessary for his maintenance and the maintenance of his class goes to the capitalist as surplus value. The worker is not cheated—his labor power is purchased at its "fair" market price—the amount of working time necessary for its reproduction, i.e. the working time necessary to create so much means of subsistence required for the maintenance of the worker and to provide for his replacement. But if such is the case, if only the amount of living labor "concretized" imparts value to a commodity, one would expect that an industry that had a low organic composition of capital, that is to say, an industry in which little fixed capital (as distinguished from variable capital, i.e. wages) is employed, would produce a higher rate of profit (more surplus value) than one in which the ratio of fixed to variable capital (e.g., more machinery and less dependence on "living" labor) was higher.[5] Yet to suggest that an industry with a high organic composition, a high ratio of fixed to variable capital, would be one with a low rate of profit seemed to contradict the simplest and most evident facts of industrial production.[6]

Engels was well aware of this apparent contradiction in the theory, and in the posthumous publication of Marx's second volume of *Kapital* he alluded to the evident consternation Marx's theory had generated among professional economists and educated laymen. The paradox remained unresolved until the publication of Marx's third volume in 1894, almost thirty years after the publication of the first volume of *Kapital*!

The second and third volumes of *Kapital* were published after Marx's death in 1883, and it was only in 1894 that Marx's system could be said to have been provided for the scrutiny of the educated public—and then only in a form that makes evident its fragmentary and incomplete character. Engels worked diligently (often to the neglect of other matters that he was more disposed to undertake) in preparing Marx's literary legacy for publication; and even after years of effort the two volumes evidently suffered for want of the master hand of their author.

For all that, the three volumes of *Kapital*, published during the lifetime of Karl Marx and Friedrich Engels (supplemented by the material now collected separately in *Theories of Surplus Value*) provide access to Marx's mature thought, the explication of the "economic basis" of social dynamics, as well as an implicit definition of such critical normative terms as "freedom" and "alienation." The original normative commitments are defined within the context of a systemati-

[5] Marx, *Contribution to the Critique of Political Economy*, Bk. 1, chap. 1.

[6] Cf. E. von Boehm-Bawerk, *Karl Marx and the Close of his System* (New York: Kelley, 1949), chaps. 1 and 2.

cally related set of propositions—a set of propositions having explanatory and predictive power—a set of propositions that provides the substance of the preliminary schema that directed Marx's systematic inquiries for almost four decades.

THE MATURE SYSTEM[7]

Marx's systematic inquiry into the dynamics of capitalist society began with a study of the commodity, an article produced not for immediate consumption but for exchange. The fact that commodities are defined in terms of exchange implied that men stand in definite social relations to each other. The commodity and the nature of commodity production were conceived as providing insight into the relationships that obtain in civil society. In itself the commodity can be analytically reduced to a complex of use value and exchange value: the former defined in terms of a thing's utility and the latter defined in terms of the proportion in which things of one sort are exchanged for things of another sort. Exchange value implies that two things can be exchanged because they possess in equal quantities something common to both. The "something common to both" we have already suggested is the common property of being products of human labor. Human labor in the abstract can be measured in terms of discrete units of socially necessary labor time. The amount of human labor (unskilled labor being conceived of as simple reductive units of skilled labor), that is socially necessary human labor (defined in terms of the average time

[7] There are any number of good, relatively simple treatments of Marxian economics that provide adequate introduction to the mature system of Marx. An elementary, but particularly lucid short treatment can be found in E. Mandel, *An Introduction to Marxist Economic Theory* (New York: Merit, 1968); for an extended treatment by the same author see *Marxist Economic Theory* (New York: Monthly Review, 1968), 2 vols. For a pedestrian treatment published in Moscow see P. Nikitin, *Fundamentals of Political Economy: Popular Course* (Moscow: Foreign Languages, n.d.). The orthodox Marxist views embodied in the Erfurt Program are explicated in K. Kautsky, *The Class Struggle* (New York: Norton, 1971), chaps. 1-3.

necessary at any specific historical period under specific technological conditions for the production of an article), required for the production of a commodity determines its natural value. The common constituent of commodities, therefore, that make them equivalents in exchange is "concretized" human labor. A given quantity of coal is equivalent to a coat because each contains equal amounts of socially necessary labor time. When the time necessary to produce one commodity changes because of technological development, its exchange value changes. The productiveness of labor determines the socially necessary labor time required in the manufacture of a commodity; therefore, changes in factors which alter the productiveness of labor affect exchange relationships.

The purchaser of labor power, employing it as a use value, has purchased labor power at its natural price. He is then free to employ it in the service of a special task: the production of value. Labor power is the only commodity that can be employed in such fashion. To understand this critical distinction between labor power as a commodity and any other commodity is the beginning, according to Marx, of a comprehension of the capitalist system. The broad and vague propositions of the early Paris manuscripts are explicated in an analysis now characterized as the "labor theory of value": all value originates in human labor measured in discrete units of time. Man's labor power, expended in the process of production, is materialized in the object of labor; it has "externalized" itself in the commodity. The "producer," who has poured himself into an object, receives as compensation for his externalization, the exchange value equivalent of labor power (i.e. the price of labor power) rather than the totality of produced value (the price of labor power plus surplus value). The laborer receives the equivalent of his means of subsistence—a claim made as early as the *Manifesto* of 1848. Because of capitalist property relations, the commodity produced, incorporating the living labor of the wage earner, is the property of another man. The worker, in externalizing himself, has created

63

something alien to himself: the object of his efforts, his "alienated self," becomes something that stands against him because it has become the property of another—the capitalist.

As Marx developed his account, the distinction between labor power and the material instruments employed in the process of production are distinguished. The former is variable capital and the latter constant capital. Only living labor has the capacity of *creating* value. The instruments of production represent only the "dead" labor of past productive efforts. Only variable capital is capable of generating increments of value; only labor power as a commodity can be employed to produce the surplus value that ultimately constitutes the source of all capitalist profit.

Dead capital, the means of production exclusive of variable capital, can only transfer units of its own intrinsic exchange value to commodities. Only labor power, as a use value, is capable of producing that increment of value above and beyond its exchange value that Marx identifies as surplus value. Given these convictions it follows, logically, that one can determine the *rate of surplus value* by dividing the surplus value (s) by the sum of variable capital (v) in the formula: s/v. If 100 units of s are produced in the realization of exchange, and the capitalist has expended 100 units of v in the process (the commodity sells for \$200, and \$100 represents s and \$100 represents v) the rate of surplus value is one hundred percent. Since the capacity of living labor to produce value will be a function of available technological and efficiency factors, the rate of surplus value will be determined by those factors. The productiveness of labor will be a function of the organic composition of capital, i.e. a relationship between constant capital (c) and the total capital outlay ($c/c+v$). The degree of exploitation of labor power by capital will reflect the organic composition of capital. Since constant capital cannot itself produce value, but only produces value as it itself is consumed as a use value by living labor, the capitalist increases the amount of surplus value produced by labor power by investing more capital in constant capital (machinery and efficiency economies). The relationship between surplus value (s) and the total capital outlay ($c+v$) is identified by Marx as the *rate of profit*, $s/(c+v)$.

The rate of profit is a function of the ratio of surplus value to total capital outlay, the degree of exploitation is a measure of the amount of surplus labor extracted from the laborer beyond that necessary for his sustenance, and the rate of surplus value is a ratio of surplus value to variable capital (i.e. wages paid).

If such an account is accepted, it would logically follow that capitalists, driven by a variety of rational considerations, would seek to increase the productivity of labor (i.e. the exploitation of labor) by introducing increased economies and more sophisticated instruments of production into the processes of production. But such efforts inevitably increase the ratio of constant to variable capital—larger expenditures on "dead" labor (in the form of machines) produce a higher organic composition of capital (c increases relative to v). The rate of surplus value increases, the degree of exploitation increases; but the overall rate of profit declines, since profit rate is a function of $s/(c+v)$. Fewer and fewer living laborers produce more and more commodities (the rate of surplus value increases), but profits, $s/(c+v)$, tend to decline.

Marx spent much of the third volume of *Kapital* answering the obvious objections raised by professional economists that, if his account were true, investment capital would simply flood those industries with a low organic composition (those industries in which capital outlay was deployed over variable rather than constant capital)—a conclusion against which there was compelling counter-evidence. Marx's resolution involved significant modifications in the simplistic account given above, but the modifications did not alter the basic tendencies his account identified. Marx conceived the process of profit generation and distribution as a complex one involving what he termed the "total social surplus value" produced by the "total capital of society," so that his analysis did not permit the determination of any particular price or value in any particular case but was understood to hold over the entire system. Marx conceived his account as macroeconomic rather than a microeconomic effort to determine specific exchange values or market prices.

The account which Marx provides in *Kapital* constitutes the theoretical infrastructure of the preliminary conceptual schema formulated from 1845 to 1849. It is the set of theoretical propositions, partially formalized and standardized in *Kapital,* from which flow the predictions proclaimed in *The German Ideology, The Poverty of Philosophy* and *The Communist Manifesto.* Lenin was quite correct to characterize "historical materialism" as a "hypothesis" until the production of *Kapital.* Only with its production did Marxism evince the species traits of a "scientific" assessment of "historical and social questions."[8]

From the theories formulated in *Kapital* two major theoretical propositions emerge: (1) the necessity of incessant technological change, and (2) the inevitability of a secular decline in the rate of profit. From these two major propositions a variety of consequences logically follow.

In *The Communist Manifesto* Marx was emphatic concerning the necessity, on the part of the bourgeoisie, of "constantly revolutionizing the instruments of production" and, he continued, "thereby the relations of production, and with them the whole relations of society." The same claim was made as early as *The German Ideology* and was repeated again in the famous introduction to *The Contribution to the Critique of Political Economy.* As the forces of production change, the relations of production undergo, of necessity, corresponding alteration. The source of change, therefore, must be found in the dynamic qualities of the productive forces. In *Kapital* this contention is provided substance by relating surplus value, the degree of exploitation, to the degree of development of the instruments of

[8] V. I. Lenin, "What the 'Friends of the People' Are," *Collected Works* (Moscow: Progress, 1960), i, p. 142.

production. Each capitalist realizes increments in surplus value by improving his capacity to exploit living labor. Each technological improvement provides the enterprising capitalist with an immediate advantage over his competitors, and each competitor is driven to introduce that innovation and seek innovations of his own if he is to survive. Whatever advantages the innovating capitalist enjoys are, at best, temporary. His competitors are compelled to innovate. Once the rate of profit becomes stabilized at the new and higher level of organic composition, each capitalist is driven to innovate further. But the necessity to constantly innovate produces a *secular* decline in the rate of profit. The proposition that capitalism must "constantly revolutionize the instruments of production" is logically related to the proposition that there is a secular and irreversible decline in the rate of profit. The two propositions are similarly related logically to the conception of value as the exclusive product of living labor.

What we find in *Kapital* is a theory, in the reasonably formal sense of the term—a collection of propositions, among them some having lawlike character, subsumptively related, conjointly having the capacity to generate explanations and predictions and subject to confirmation and disconfirmation by direct or indirect empirical test. Prior to the publication of *Kapital* Marx had entertained a number of ordinary or academic-language conceptual schemata, loose formulations that provided some leverage on understanding. Marx's original schemata were composed largely of relatively vague formulations that are almost always the preliminary to serious theory construction.

As in the case with most theory construction in the social sciences, Marx's more mature formulations were almost always severely qualified by the recognition of countertendencies. In fact the "law" of the secular decline in the rate of profit is spoken of as "the law of the falling tendency of the rate of profit," conjoined with a recognition of the influence of counteracting factors. Marx refers to a variety of such factors (a catalogue which cannot here detain us), but he insists that the *ultimate* decline in the rate of profit is predictable.

Given such theoretical commitments, an entire collection of entailed predictions result. Because of necessary innovative change, the value of labor power will decline to its least common denominator; because of innovative change, industry becomes capital intensive—heavier initial capital outlays are necessary to found an industry and to maintain one. Competition favors the large capitalist, and the peripheral entrepreneurs are jettisoned into the proletariat. Because of the high organic composition of industries in the advanced capitalist countries, capital is driven into the underdeveloped areas in the search for a higher profit rate. *The capitalist mode of production is internationalized.* The more intensive exploitation of labor will produce commodities in hitherto unimagined quantity; the search for market supplements to the internal market will drive capitalists over the world to seek outlets for their products. Because of the constant necessity to increase the rate of exploitation, capitalism periodically finds itself with swollen inventories, the involuntary accumulation of commodity capital. This is what Marx identifies as the "crisis of overproduction" (or underconsumption). Capitalist production requires complete sale of commodities at their values if profits are to be maintained. When inventories exceed effective demand there is intense competition among sellers, a decline in market prices, wages, interest rates, and a depreciation of capital values—followed by an increase in unemployment and a cessation of production. These are economic dislocations within the secular decline in the rate of profit. Each one of these crises of overproduction increases the potential for social revolution, the violent alteration in the relations of production that are now out of phase with the development of productive forces. This synoptic account outlines the theoretical infrastructure that Marx developed in order to support those preliminary statements found in his work before 1850. In the *Grundrisse* the connection is quite explicit. "The highest development of productive power together with the greatest expansion of existing wealth will coincide with depreciation of capital, degradation of the laborer. . . . These contradictions lead to explosions, cataclysms, crises. . . . At a certain point the development of productive forces constitutes a fetter (*eine Schranke*) on capital; the relations of capital a fetter to the development of the productive power of labor . . . ."[9]

Marx argued that the existence of laborers becomes increasingly precarious with the maturation of capitalism, since increments in constant capital reduce labor to its unskilled common denominator and periodic accumulations of commodity capital generate increasingly severe crises. It is predictable that capital-intensive forms of production will displace labor from the process and/or force wage rates to mere subsistence levels. While a minority of capitalists accumulate more and more capital at one pole, the producers of value become increasingly "emiserated" at the other. The numbers of capitalists decrease in inverse ratio to the extent of their holdings; the numbers of proletariat increase in inverse ratio to the standard of living. *Class struggle is the predictable consequence.* Economic in origin, synoptically referred to by Marx as the "struggle" of the productive forces against productive relations, the struggle ultimately becomes political. The ultimate, predictable consequence is revolution.

While Marx clearly refers to both relative *and* absolute decline in their standard of living. This is quite explicit in analysis, that ultimately workers must experience a *real* decline in their standard of living. This is quite explicit in *The Communist Manifesto*, where the decline in the standard of living of the proletariat is characterized in terms which deny that the capitalist can provide for the "very existence" of his wage slave. Marx felt he had revealed the economic laws which made the increasing emiseration of the proletariat under capitalism a predictable necessity.

[9] *Grundrisse*, pp. 635f.

The increasing misery of the proletariat provided the immediate motive for revolution that would overthrow the productive relations of capitalism.[10]

As the organic composition of capitalism becomes higher, the proportion of capital devoted to wages (v) becomes smaller, thereby increasing the "industrial reserve army" (unemployment increases). Although constant capital-intensive industries may stimulate some degree of labor recruitment because of the increased rate of exploitation and the temporary realization of an increased rate of surplus value, the number of workers *displaced* by technological innovation always exceeds that number *demanded* by technological innovation. The demands of high capital investment in industry, conjoined with intensive competition between capitalists, forces more and more of the peripheral bourgeoisie into the proletariat. Society becomes dichotomized into two opposed classes: the proletariat and the bourgeoisie. The proletariat increases in number while becoming increasingly miserable, and the bourgeoisie become fewer in number while those that survive become increasingly wealthy. As capitalism expands during its initial phases of development it draws the rural population into its processes. This is the consequence of a variety of factors that Marx analyzes in considerable detail. Partly because of the introduction of a money economy and the cyclical character of capitalist production, agricultural production becomes increasingly unstable. More and more rural workers are drawn into the urban centers where they swell the industrial reserve army, further aggravating the tendencies endemic to capitalist production.

This "vast majority" of men (in *The Communist Manifesto* Marx and Engels speak of nine-tenths of the population) *develop a consciousness of their class interests as a consequence of their position in the productive process.* They begin to organize, they are brought together into productive associations by the capitalists themselves, who seek to rationalize production and exploit the economies of large-

[10] Cf. A. J. Gregor, *A Survey of Marxism* (New York: Random House, 1965), pp. 175-85.

scale production. Each economic dislocation within the compass of the general decline in the rate of profit provokes increasingly organized and self-conscious resistance on the part of the proletariat until finally the sheer weight of their numbers and their clear awareness of their uniform anticapitalist interests becomes irresistible. In *The Civil War in France* Marx referred to the periodicity of the revolutionary efforts of the proletariat, initiated each time by cyclical dislocations. In 1851 Marx wrote to Freiligrath that he "was convinced that a serious revolutionary effort is impossible without an economic crisis (*Handelskrise*)."[11] In 1854 Engels warned that "economic crisis and hunger" might provoke revolution at any time.[12] In his *Class Struggles in France*, Marx even suggested an indicator of economic crisis, public and private credit, as a "thermometer" by which "the intensity of the revolution can be measured. To the same degree as they fall, the glow and generative force of the revolution rise."[13] Since credit falls with each secular decline, and the rate and extent of fall would become increasingly emphatic, Marx could predict increasing revolutionary activity. "The battle must break out again and again in ever growing dimensions, and there can be no doubts as to who will be the victor in the end—the appropriating few, or the immense working majority."[14]

In effect, the economic analysis of *Kapital* provides the theoretical basis for the general claims made as early as 1845. The four decades after the publication of *The German Ideology* were devoted to the articulation of a partially formalized and partially standardized social science theory. The theory that was ultimately produced was only partially formalized and standardized simply because there remained any number of obscurities among the collection of propositions that constituted the statemental components of the theory. One critical omission in the theory was a compelling

[11] Marx to Freiligrath, letter of December 27, 1851, *Werke*, xxvii, 597.
[12] Engels, "Der europäische Krieg," *Werke*, x, 8.
[13] Marx, "The Class Struggles in France," in *Selected Works*, i, 151.
[14] Marx, "The Civil War in France," in *ibid.*, i, 541.

account of how class consciousness is related to the economic conditions of class membership. Marx, as we have seen, frequently spoke as though class consciousness was an automatic product of "material life conditions," i.e. the conditions surrounding class membership. He spoke of social consciousness as a "reflex" or "echo" of material life conditions. The dependence on metaphor indicates serious gaps in the theory. Precisely how is class consciousness produced?

Both Marx and Engels became increasingly suspicious about the ability of material life conditions simply to "generate" the class consciousness requisite to revolution. Marx, in his maturity, indicated that the objective conditions for revolution existed in England, and yet the English proletariat had not developed the requisite class consciousness. Engels and Marx both voiced their misgivings concerning the "automaticity" of the process of developing revolutionary consciousness. In 1870 Marx confided to Kugelmann that "the English have all the material conditions necessary for a socialist revolution. What they lack is . . . the revolutionary passion."[15]

The partially formalized theory which received its most mature expression in the three volumes of *Kapital* lacks a subset of propositions linking the economic conditions that constitute the "material conditions of life" and the ideas, motives, intentions, convictions, and aspirations of historic actors. The conviction that the increasing misery of the proletariat, their mobilization in urban centers, their enurement to the discipline of labor and organization would produce the consciousness requisite to "liberating" revolution was supported, at best, by common sense generalizations about human psychology, at worst, by metaphors.

In order to expose the lacunae in any theoretical structure, contemporary social science practitioners attempt to axiomatize, to reduce the ordinary language theory to a collection of basic propositions, and, given certain rules of transformation, to generate secondary propositions (or theo-

---

[15] Marx to Kugelmann, as cited, Sidney Hook, *Towards the Understanding of Karl Marx* (New York: John Day, 1933), pp. 111f.

rems) from the basic subset. Fred Gottheil has provided a partial axiomatization of Marx's economic theory, and the partial formalization reveals the absence of any defensible generalizations that would systematically relate the economic conditions prevailing at any specific time in history and the state of mind of human participants at that specific time. The connection was simply tacitly or explicitly assumed.[16] "[I]ndividuals are dealt with only insofar as they are the personifications of economic categories, embodiments of particular class relations and class interests. My standpoint," Marx contended, "from which the evolution of the economic formation of society is viewed as a process of natural history, can less than any other make the individual responsible for relations whose creature he socially remains . . . ."[17] Engels spoke simply of socialism as a "reflex" of the tensions between the productive forces and productive relations.[18] Lenin asserted that "individual . . . consciousness must be explained from the contradiction of material life . . . ." and that "all ideas and all the various tendencies *stem* from the condition of the material forces of production."[19]

The relationship between ideas, motives, and intentions and "material life" is simply asserted and the semblance of argument provided by metaphors: ideas "stem" from material life circumstances, they "flow," or are "effluxes" or "reflexes." The fact remains that the relationship is proclaimed —the loosely formulated propositions which are characteristic of Marx's own works do not lend themselves to any possible confirmation or disconfirmation. One simply does not know how to proceed to license the claim that ideas "stem," "flow," or are "reflexes" of "social being." Moreover

[16] F. Gottheil, *Marx's Economic Predictions* (Evanston, Ill.: Northwestern University, 1966), pp. 165-68; cf. A. J. Gregor, *Contemporary Radical Ideologies* (New York: Random House, 1968), pp. 44-46.

[17] Marx, *Capital*, I, 10.

[18] Engels, *Anti-Duehring* (Moscow: Foreign Languages, 1962), p. 367.

[19] Lenin, "Karl Marx," *Collected Works*, XXI, 56f.

the relationship understood to obtain between the two "spheres" is not only vaguely characterized but at times ambiguously characterized as well. Marx spoke of social being "altering" consciousness, and at other times (sometimes in the same paragraph) as "determining" consciousness. In effect, considerable and theoretically important portions of Marx's social theories remained rudimentary, not much more sophisticated than ordinary and academic-language formulation—footholds on understanding, but hardly testable propositions about psychological dynamics.

Much of Marx's work in economic theory was extensively formalized and standardized and consequently provided explanatory and predictive leverage. In his correspondence with Engels, Marx intimated that he intended to pursue "other sciences" once he had completed his work in economic theory. His program was ambitious, and as it was he never fully completed his work in economics. To his own satisfaction he had identified and characterized the objective conditions which created the objective reality of a "class-*in*-itself" in the form of the proletariat. He only succeeded in alluding to the circumstances which produce a "class-*for*-itself," a class conscious of its solidarity and class interests. The relationship between the two conditions, one objective and the other subjective, remained obscure. Both Marx and Engels clearly understood that the connection was not simply automatic, even though in much of their writing they continued to refer to it in terms of the metaphorical language of "reflexes" and "echoes."

In the twentieth century, Soviet theoreticians attempted for some considerable time to provide the missing psycho-sociological infrastructure by interlarding "Marxist theory" with supplements borrowed from Pavlovian psychology.[20] The attempt was a notable intellectual disaster, but it indicates the recognition, now general among Marx scholars, that classical Marxism had not developed an adequate psychological theory and would provide substance for the metaphors and tropes of the preliminary conceptual schema left

[20] Gregor, *Survey*, pp. 261-73.

by classical Marxism. The issue remains a critical one not only for a general theory of historical and social dynamics and ethics, but because it creates, as we shall argue, special problems for political activism and revolutionary organization.

The Congruence of the Mature System

The work of Karl Marx, the product of four decades of intense intellectual and research activities, left a partially formalized and standardized theory as a heritage to the twentieth century. The constituents of the theory included formal as well as substantive propositional components. The formal elements included definitions, typological and classificational schemata; the substantive statemental components included restricted, low order generalizations, unrestricted lawlike generalizations and detailed descriptions among them. Conjointly held and subtending normative elements infuse the entire system with ethical implications; and Marx's accounts always betray a specifically revolutionary intention. The system can, as a consequence, be identified as "ideological," capable of generating prescriptions, proscriptions, and recommendations as well as providing the justificatory grounds for political organization and activity.

For the purposes of analysis it is necessary to recognize classical Marxism as, in part, a social science theory. Its formal elements can be measured against the adequacy criteria of contemporary logic, and its synthetic elements can be similarly measured against the adequacy criteria of contemporary empirical inquiry. Nonetheless, it becomes immediately apparent that such treatment neglects some of the most significant aspects of Marx's work. Marx was committed to normative concerns. He sought a world in which men could attain the fullness of self in an association that made the fullness of each the condition of the fullness of all; in which political power, per se, defined as the employment of force by one class to keep another in subjection, would disappear; in which the rational organization of the forces of production would reduce necessary labor time to a minimum and provide the occasion of "free" and leisure activity; in which national and class distinction would no longer isolate men from their universal humanity; in which, in effect, men would no longer be "alienated" from their full humanity.

Such a partial inventory of Marx's normative concerns identifies the extrinsic commitments that governed his intellectual and research efforts, but it does not attest to their competence. The measure of competence remains the consequence of applying standards of logical and empirical adequacy to the statemental components of Marx's social science theories. In the last analysis, Marx's injunctions, proscriptions, and recommendations have only as much force as his logical and factual assertions have truth. If men are to labor for the liberating revolution, it can only be because they can legitimately entertain a conviction in its objective, that is to say empirical, potential success and the revolution's capacity to satisfy normative aspirations. If the proletariat is the revolutionary class, it is because *historic, social,* and *economic circumstances* render it the "carrier" of a *liberating mission.* If capitalism is to be overthrown, it is only because capitalism, as a productive process, can be convincingly and objectively identified as the source of man's alienations.

No one resists the injunction that man should fulfill himself. No one defends a system that can be shown to oppress, misshape, and alienate. But unanimity of intention can obtain only when the conditions governing fulfillment are specified with some precision—only when an account is forthcoming that characterizes how oppression, misshaping, and alienation proceeds, and how it can be conceived as intrinsic to one rather than to another system.

Only if Marx's theoretical system is conceived as true, in some significant and defensible sense, can his normative injunctions have merit. Marx fully understood the requirements that motivated and directed his work. While his normative commitments remained constant throughout his life, they surfaced, in the course of his maturation, with less and less frequency. His arguments proceeded forthrightly without the ballast of moral suasion. He invoked men individually and collectively to action not because his moral insights were compelling, but because his theories were true. Capitalism would be overthrown not because it was morally defective, but because its dynamics created internal tensions which the system could not tolerate. The proletariat would rise up against capitalism not because capitalism was morally offensive, but because it was not a viable productive system—it was destined ultimately to succumb to a fatal torpor incapable of providing even the minimum subsistence for the vast majority of men. The political state would dissolve itself not because men found political domination insupportable, but because the state was, by definition, an agency of oppression that attempted to mediate irrepressible class differences borne of the very "contradictions" of the productive process itself. When the productive forces and the relations of production were fully in phase, the state, by definition, would cease to exist. Its place would be taken by the governance of things, the rational organization of the processes of production by fully enlightened men who recognized the reality of the ultimate compatibility of collective and individual interests.

The analyses to be found in *Kapital* contain the rationale that supports these convictions. The labor theory of value, contained in the first volume of *Kapital*, explicates what it means to say that men, under capitalism, project themselves into objects and then find themselves opposed by alien things of their own making. In commodity production the worker infuses value into objects—objects which, because they are the private property of another, become alien and opposed to the worker's ultimate life interests. The resolution of this alienation does not rest upon the worker's immediate grasp of what is transpiring. The process must proceed to the point where the very alienation of the worker makes the entire system inoperable. The effort on the part of the entrepreneurial class to wring forever increasing measures of value from the worker, an effort the system compels it to undertake, burdens the system with a constant revolutionizing of the instruments of production. The constant technological innovation necessitates an increasingly higher organic composition of capital, which in turn depresses the rate of profit that the system is capable of providing. The system, periodically shocked by cycles of destruction and dislocation, gradually falls into a fatal inactivity, unable to generate a minimum profit level capable of sustaining production. Having drawn the entire world into its productive processes, capitalism exhausts itself, and revolution (violent or nonviolent as the case might be) becomes the only alternative.

In 1885, two years after Marx's death, Engels summarized the process in the following fashion:

> The law which reduces the value of labor-power to the value of the necessary means of subsistence, and the other law which reduces its average price, as a rule, to the minimum of those means of subsistence, these laws act upon [the working class] with the irresistible force of an automatic engine, which crushes them between its wheels .... [The] monopoly of England is the pivot of the present social system of England. Even while that monopoly lasted, the markets could not keep pace with the increasing productivity of English manufacturers; the decennial crises were the consequence. And new markets are getting scarcer every day. . . . Capitalist production cannot stop. It must go on increasing and expanding, or it must die. Even now, the mere reduction of England's lion's share in the supply of the world's markets means stagnation, distress, excess of capital here, excess of unemployed work people there. What will it be when the increase of yearly production is brought to a complete stop?

> Here is the vulnerable place, the heel of Achilles, for capitalistic production. Its very basis is the necessity of constant expansion, and this constant expansion now be-

comes impossible. It ends in a deadlock. Every year England is brought nearer face to face with the question: either the country must go to pieces, or capitalist production must.[21]

Forty years before, in 1845, Engels had written:

But assuming that England retained the monopoly of manufactures, that its factories perpetually multiply, what must be the result? The commercial crises would continue, and grow more violent, more terrible, with the extension of industry and the multiplication of the proletariat. The proletariat would increase in geometrical proportion, in consequence of the progressive ruin of the lower middle class and the giant strides with which capital is concentrating itself in the hands of the few; and the proletariat would soon embrace the whole nation, with the exception of a few millionaires. But in this development there comes a stage at which the proletariat perceives how easily the existing power may be overthrown and then follows a revolution.[22]

The proposition that the proletariat would "perceive" with "ease" its historic mission was never abandoned. When Engels, in 1890, wrote an introduction to the German edition of *The Communist Manifesto*, he insisted that:

Marx relied entirely upon the intellectual development of the workers to ensure their final triumph. Schooled by united action and by discussion, the workers would gradually come to understand and adopt these theories. Experience gained in the ups and downs of the struggle against capitalism, in defeat even more than in victory, would teach the combatants the worthlessness of the panaceas they had hitherto advocated, and make their minds more

[21] Engels, "England in 1845 and 1885," *London Commonweal*, in *Werke*, xxi, 196.

[22] Engels, *The Condition of the Working Class in England in 1844*, pp. 295f.

receptive to a thorough understanding of the real conditions of working-class emancipation.[23]

Only a class-for-itself, created by the conditions appropriate to the creation of a class-in-itself, could produce men capable of undertaking the reorganization of society in which the fulfillment of each is the condition of the fulfillment of all. Such a community of rational agents would be one, as Marx clearly indicated in *The Civil War in France*, in which *universal suffrage* provided for the rational self-rule of the vast majority of men—an organization of society which would make *minoritarian rule impossible*, in which *hierarchical investiture would be inconceivable*, in which *referendum and recall* would insure the complete responsiveness of publicly elected officials to the will of the community.[24] The *Gemeinschaft*, which Marx in his youth saw as the only vehicle suitable to man, becomes in his maturity, a "life process of society, . . . based on the process of material production . . . by freely associated men, . . . consciously regulated by them in accordance with a settled plan,"[25] in which classes no longer exist because the very abundance of commodity production makes class distinctions dysfunctional. As early as *The German Ideology*, Marx indicated that *class distinctions were the consequence of restricted productivity* and Engels repeated that assessment in the *Anti-Duehring* of 1877 and 1878.[26]

[23] Engels, in Ryazanoff, ed., *Communist Manifesto*, pp. 266f.

[24] Marx, "The Civil War in France," *Selected Works*, I, 519-23.

[25] Marx, *Capital*, I, 79-80.

[26] In *The German Ideology* the relationship between classes and the restricted productive base of society is characterized in the following fashion: ". . . the form of community . . . must correspond to the stage of development of the productive forces they find in existence. . . ." "[If] production which these productive forces could provide was insufficient for the whole of society . . . some persons satisfied their needs at the expense of others." (pp. 90, 475). In 1847 Engels wrote: "There must always be a dominant class controlling the forces of production, and a poverty stricken oppressed class, so long as there is not enough produced not only to supply the immediate wants of all the members of society, but also to provide a surplus of products for

The preconditions for the rational association that would be the consequence of revolution included (1) a vast majority of men fully conscious of their life interests and (2) the inheritance of a productive base capable of sustaining the abolition of class differences. Since the maturation of capitalism would create the recruitment base for a revolutionary force, the revolution was inevitable. Since a mature capitalism would possess an industrial base adequate to the abolition of classes and would have produced a politically mature proletarian majority, the revolution would be the liberating historical event that Marx had foreseen in his young manhood. It would occur, as Engels indicated in 1847, as the "outcome of circumstances quite independent of the will or the guidance of particular parties or classes."[27]

The revolution would occur like a "natural event in accordance with natural laws"[28] with the vast majority of men fully conscious of their ultimate interests. The time for minoritarian revolutions, conspiratorial adventures undertaken under the leadership of "dedicated men" with "ruthless energy," capable of seizing power and then "sweeping the mass of the people into the revolution" was deemed past by Engels. Past also was a revolution that would invest such leaders with "the strictest, dictatorial centralization of all power."[29]

The revolution would occur not only in those circumstances where capitalism had produced the economic base capable of supporting a classless society but in circumstances which had produced a correlative maturation of

the increase of social capital and for the further development of the forces of production." Engels, "Principles of Communism," in Ryazanoff, ed., *Communist Manifesto*, p. 329.

[27] *Ibid.*, p. 330. But see also Marx's comments on the "necessity" of a "party" to "insure" the "triumph of socialism" and the "abolition" of classes; "Allgemeine Statuten der Internationalen Arbeiterassoziation," in I. Fetscher, *Der Marxismus: Seine Geschichte in Dokumenten* (Munich: Piper, 1965), III, p. 162.

[28] Engels to Marx, February 13, 1851, *Werke*, XXVII, 190.

[29] Engels, "Introduction to the Civil War in France," *Selected Works*, I, 482f.

social consciousness on the part of the working class itself. Only a self-conscious working class could undertake the obligations of universal suffrage and self-governance. Such a revolution would be international and would involve "all civilized countries, or at least . . . Great Britain, the United States, France and Germany, at one and the same time."[30] In *The German Ideology* this was made quite specific. Although peripheral areas might be drawn into the revolution, *the revolution must involve the most advanced industrial countries*, or socialism would not inherit the legacy of capitalist productivity.[31] Toward the end of his life, when revolutionary activity began to mount insistently in Czarist Russia, Marx was asked if revolution could commence in such an industrially backward area and he replied: "If the Russian revolution sounds the signal for a workers' revolution in the West, so that each becomes the complement of the other," then such a revolution might "serve as a starting point for a communist course of development."[32]

It was manifestly clear that a *socialist* revolution could realize itself only in circumstances where the productive forces of society had attained that level of development capable of supporting a classless society. For Marx, socialism could, in fact, only develop within the "womb" of capitalism. The institutional infrastructure of socialism would develop within capitalist property relations. The revolution need do no more than strike off the capitalist "integument." The revolution would find itself possessed of a "universal" proletarian class intellectually prepared to assume radically democratic control over the material conditions of production, a class armed with universal suffrage and the power of recall, a class to whom hierarchical investiture would be anathema. "Nothing," Marx had written, "could be more for-

[30] Engels, "Principles of Communism," Ryazanoff, ed., *Communist Manifesto*, p. 333.

[31] Marx and Engels, *The German Ideology*, pp. 46f.

[32] Marx, Introduction to the Russian edition of the "Communist Manifesto," *Selected Works*, I, 23f.

eign to the spirit of the Commune [which he, Engels and Lenin had all identified with the dictatorship of the proletariat] than to supersede universal suffrage by hierarchic investiture."[33]

Under the conditions of mature capitalism, the working class, whose interests, because of the full maturity attained by the material processes of production, had become universal, could overcome the "alienations" characteristic of antecedent modes of production. The working class could no longer be "awed" by the state, what Marx had early identified as "political power as such." The working class could no longer be confused by the religious, philosophical, and aesthetic rationalizations by which the oppressing classes kept men in subordination. Only when social consciousness attains the faculty of perceiving social relations directly, stripped of "mystical veils" manufactured by men consciously or unconsciously attempting to obscure social reality, can men come to rule themselves. Only in the circumstances which prevail in advanced capitalist society do social relations become so "transparent," so obvious that man is "compelled to face with sober senses, his real conditions of life, and his relations with his kind."[34]

Under such circumstances those ideologies which are truncated, refracted conceptions of reality—truncated and refracted because they are made to serve the life interests of a restricted social class—are dissipated. "Ideology" gives way to a "science," a true vision of reality because it is the product of the consciousness of a universal class, a class unconstrained by the necessities of subordinating members of its own species to a position of inferiority in the service of special interest. The ideology of the working class is a science because it is the vision of a universal class, a class whose universality is predicated on the universality of the fully developed mode of production which has drawn into itself all the peripheral and immature systems of production

[33] Marx, "The Civil War in France," *ibid.*, I, 521.
[34] Marx and Engels, "Communist Manifesto," *ibid.*, I, 37.

that have hitherto prevailed throughout the world and throughout man's history.[35]

Only the economic and intellectual maturity that is the fruit of the maturation of capitalism itself could produce the material basis of a classless society and the intellectual prerequisites of collective and rational self-governance that would satisfy Marx's normative intentions. Marx conceived those conditions to have been fulfilled in the advanced economies of his time. Both he and Engels had anticipated revolution in those countries that had achieved the requisite levels of development prior to the advent of the twentieth century. In those environs Marx anticipated the liberating revolution in which the state as political power would dissolve, in which men armed with universal suffrage and the power of referendum and recall would overcome political alienation, in an enlightened intellectual environment in which the false consciousness, the product of a restricted and confining economic base, no longer obtained. Engels made it quite clear that, if revolution came in the advanced countries before the peripheral or underdeveloped countries had attained the requisite levels of economic maturity, those areas would remain under the tutelage of the advanced countries until the objective conditions for liberation obtained. It was manifestly clear to Engels and Marx alike that, where social conditions were primitive, advanced social ideas could only become caricatures of themselves. In *The Communist Manifesto*, when they mocked the intellectual products of German or "true" socialism, they called attention to the fact that socialist literature could not simply be imported into Germany. The German would-be philosophers had overlooked "that French social conditions had not been imported . . . side by side with French socialist literature. Confronted with German social conditions, French socialist literature had no importance in the world of practice . . . . It necessarily assumed the aspect of idle specu-

[35] Cf. H. Lefebvre, *The Sociology of Marx* (New York: Pantheon, 1968), chap. 3; S. Avineri, *The Social and Political Thought of Karl Marx* (Cambridge: Cambridge University, 1968), chap. 2.

lation . . . ."[36] Similarly when Engels addressed himself to the revolutions that afflicted the underdeveloped countries of eastern Europe he made quite apparent what he thought of intellectuals, schooled in the advanced countries, who sought to import the ideas with which they had become infused in environments in which social conditions remained primitive. The only consequence could be the deformation of those ideas—planted in soil in which the social conditions remained inappropriate.

Classical Marxism was inextricably "Eurocentric." The liberating revolution would be the product of a politically sophisticated European proletarian class, generated by the maturity of the European economic system. The system of thought left to the revolutionaries of the twentieth century was addressed to the proletarians, and the leaders of the proletarians, of the advanced capitalist countries. The revolution they were to generate was to complete a historic process as old as man himself, the leap from necessity to freedom, the universal liberation of man.

[36] Marx, Engels, "The Communist Manifesto," *Selected Works*, I, 57f.

CHAPTER FOUR

The Twentieth Century
and the Crisis of Classical Marxism

THE advent of the twentieth century marked a critical turning point in the development of Marxism. With the death of Engels in 1895, classical Marxism entered the protracted crisis in which it remained embroiled until the outbreak of the First World War in 1914—and from which it was never to emerge. Classical Marxism disintegrated under the impact of events, and out of its elements emerged the two *revolutionary* movements that were to shape, in large part, the political, social, and intellectual history of the twentieth century. The years between the two world wars were to be dominated by two radical movements: Leninism on the one hand and Fascism on the other. Both were the direct or indirect heirs of classical Marxism. Lenin had been a leader of a faction of the Social Democratic Party of Czarist Russia; Mussolini had been one of the most prominent leaders of the left wing faction within the Socialist Party of monarchial Italy. Both men came to lead independent revolutionary movements of their own. Neither movement remained faithful to the classical Marxism left to them as a spiritual patrimony. While Lenin insisted on his orthodoxy and forever characterized his movement as "Marxist," his movement, its program, and effective policies, particularly as they found expression in the dictatorship of Joseph Stalin, were no less singular and just as questionably "Marxist" as the programs and policies of Mussolini's Fascism. Both movements were irrepressibly elitist; both led minoritarian revolutions, and both consequently conceived violence essential to the acquisition of political power; both retained that power, once seized, by monopolizing all the effective control devices afforded by contemporary technology: arms, the educational and propaganda media, and mass organizations. The one-party state became the institutional manifestation of their revolutionary success, the "exceptional leader," the *Voshd*, or the *Duce*, gave expression to special relationships understood to obtain between leaders and followers.

That classical Marxism could devolve into such systems is a phenomenon of such complexity, and yet of such significance for our time, that some attempt should be made to outline briefly but as responsibly as possible at least part of the process. Needless to say, the process is as complex as the phenomenon itself, and the account advanced here would have to be significantly qualified and amplified if the concern was to deliver an exhaustive and accurate rendering of that fateful and protracted developmental sequence. What will be attempted will be the highlighting of features of that process, focusing on two special issues around which a constellation of related issues collected: (1) the problem of the nonrevolutionary proletariat, and (2) the problem of nationalism. If the following account is at all correct, these two concerns have remained and will remain the preoccupations of radical thought throughout the twentieth century.

Classical Marxism and the Problem of Revolutionary Consciousness

The conceptual schemata of classical Marxism had made it possible for Marx enthusiasts to conceive the development of the class consciousness of the proletariat in the most simplistic fashion. If Marx, in his full maturity, could applaud a review which characterized his views as conceiving "the social movement as a process of natural history, governed by laws not only independent of human will, consciousness and intelligence, but rather, on the contrary, determining that will, consciousness and intelligence . . . ," it was fairly easy to deduce that the revolutionary class consciousness of the proletariat would be the necessary consequence of the

87

lawlike developments of the "social movement," what Marx called "tendencies working with iron necessity towards inevitable results."[1]

In 1851 Engels had written to Marx that a "revolution is nothing more than a natural phenomenon (*ein reines Naturphaenomen*) that obeys physical laws rather than the rules which govern the development of society in ordinary times. Or, to be more precise, the rules take on a more physical character during a revolution—the material force of necessity becomes more emphatic. . . . One is irresistibly drawn into the vortex."[2]

This disposition to conceive social revolution in terms of "natural laws," characteristic of Marx's thought from his youth, inured a generation of Marxists to a conviction that the revolution of the proletariat would be the consequence of the working out of natural processes—that the consciousness requisite to the revolution would be the "reflex" in the minds of men of developments in the "real base" of society, developments of productive forces straining against the fetters of productive relations. "Modern socialism," Engels insisted, "is nothing but the reflex, in thought" of a conflict between developing productive forces that "have already outgrown the capitalistic mode of using them. . . . [This] conflict between productive forces and modes of production is not a conflict engendered in the mind of men. . . . it exists in fact, objectively, outside us, independently of the will and actions even of the men that have brought it on."[3]

The bourgeoisie, according to the analysis left by Marx, are compelled, in the effort to increase the rate of surplus value, to revolutionize the forces of production. Innovative change produces concentration of capital because rapid technological development requires increasingly intensive capital outlay. Fewer and fewer capitalists survive the com-

[1] Marx, *Capital* (Moscow: Foreign Languages, 1954), I, 18; Engels, "Preface to the German Edition of 1890, Manifesto, *Selected Works*, I, 31; and Marx's "Preface to the First German Edition," *Capital*.

[2] Marx to Engels, February 13, 1851, *Werke*, XXVII, 190.

[3] Engels, *Anti-Duehring* (Moscow: Foreign Languages, 1962), p. 367.

petition. One capitalist kills many. Periodic gluts, produced by increasingly effective technological innovation, further shake out small capitalists. Industries become larger and localized in urban centers. Workers are drawn into capitalist relations, and their existence comes to depend exclusively on their ability to find employment. Extensive mechanization displaces more workers than it attracts—the reserve army of labor becomes larger and more restive. At the same time the high organic composition of industrial capital depresses overall profit rates. Capitalists are compelled to innovate and concentrate; but the necessary and inevitable consequence is a decline in the general level of profit, a suppression of the very motive of capitalist production. "The rate of profit is the motive power of capitalist production . . . ," and its decline marks a decline in the vitality of the entire social system.[4] The system must ultimately sink into a fatal torpor. Its immediate by-products are saturation in investment potential, an absolute increment in functionally superfluous population, and the inability of the system to distribute effectively its commodities—a circumstance determined by "the antagonistic conditions of distribution, which reduce the consumption of the bulk of society to a minimum varying within more or less narrow limits."[5]

Within the system, beset by internal contradictions which must inevitably produce its demise, the "first sprouts" of a new social order of "associated laborers" make their appearance. The proletariat undertakes "cooperative factories," and the credit system of capitalism itself gradually transforms capitalist private enterprises into capitalist stock companies. "The capitalist stock companies, as much as the cooperative factories, should be considered as transitional forms from the capitalist mode of production to the associated one."[6]

Marx's analysis not only attributed an admirable auto-

---

[4] Marx, *Capital*, III, 245-54.

[5] "[A] rift must continually ensue between the limited dimensions of consumption under capitalism and a production which forever tends to exceed this immanent barrier." *Ibid.*, p. 251; cf. p. 239.

[6] *Ibid.*, p. 431.

maticity to the economic process itself, but it clearly seemed to argue that the development of a revolutionary class consciousness by the agents of history, the proletariat, would be a no less automatic by-product of that specifically economic process itself. Engels insisted that "the growing perception that existing social institutions are unreasonable and unjust, that reason has become unreason and right wrong, is only proof that, in the modes of production and exchange, changes have silently taken place with which the social order, adapted to earlier economic conditions, is no longer in keeping. From this it also follows that the means of getting rid of the incongruities that have been brought to light must also be present, in a more or less developed condition, within the changed modes of production themselves . . . . From this point of view the final causes of all social changes and political revolutions are to be sought, not in men's brains, not in man's better insight into eternal truth and justice, but in changes in the modes of production and exchange."[7]

Given the collection of propositions that constitutes the cognitive constituents of the doctrine, Engels could only argue that any expression of revolutionary sentiment must "reflect" changes in the economic base of society. Conversely, if one knew the nature of those changes one could, theoretically, argue that the appearance of revolutionary sentiments would be inevitable. Since the most consistently elaborated constituents of Marxism were precisely those subsets of propositions devoted to economic theory, the predictions implicit and explicit in the theory provided the foundation for predictions concerning the inevitable manifestation of that working-class consciousness requisite to the socialist revolution.

The forty-year labor that occupied Karl Marx was devoted to an economic theory which predicted the inevitable demise of capitalism as a social system. Since, as Engels insisted, politics could be "completely absorbed" by economics,[8] the revolutionary consciousness of the proletariat could be conceived as an inevitable result of a "natural" and

[7] Engels, *Anti-Duehring*, p. 365.   [8] *Ibid.*, p. 354.

"lawlike" process. Marx himself had earlier maintained, "The question is not what this or that proletarian, or even the whole of the proletariat at the moment *considers* as its aim. The question is *what the proletariat is*, and what, consequent on that *being*, it will be compelled to do. Its aim and historical action is irrevocably and obviously demonstrated in its own life situation as well as the whole organization of bourgeois society today."[9]

With some considerable variations both Marx and Engels remained faithful to this conception until the end of their lives. Engels did admit that his "youthful ardor" had induced him to predict imminent social revolution in England in 1845 and that subsequently he had been compelled to modify his analysis; he realized that England's "industrial monopoly" had, in fact, to a "certain extent" improved the conditions of the British working class.[10] He had written to Marx in 1858 that England had managed to produce a "bourgeoisified" proletariat—a proletariat with a bourgeois social consciousness.[11] In 1868 he lamented that in the elections the proletariat, "tag, rag and bobtail," had succumbed to the blandishments of the "official parties."[12] Marx himself identified a disposition on the part of the proletariat to act, at times, "like sheep"—even in England where the objective conditions for social revolution were most mature.

The fact is that the relationship between the "material conditions of life" and "consciousness" is one of the most obscure in the entire body of Marxist theory. As has already been suggested, Marx most frequently characterized the relationship in terms of metaphor, with expressions such as "sublimate," "reflex," and "reflection" doing the service of serious theoretical formulations. To speak of "ideas" or "consciousness" as "sublimates" of "material life conditions" gives us very little leverage on a serious comprehension of the

[9] K. Marx and F. Engels, *The Holy Family*, p. 53.
[10] Engels, The 1892 Preface to *The Condition of the Working Class*, pp. xi, xvii.
[11] Engels to Marx, October 7, 1858, *Werke*, XXIX, 358.
[12] Engels to Marx, November 18, 1868, *Werke*, XXXII, 207.

relationship obtaining between two very vaguely defined categories.

Even if one could make some serious sense out of the metaphors which characterized the relationship, neither Marx nor Engels ever attempted to apply *time qualifiers* to any of their formulations. How long, for example, does it take for "consciousness" to come to "reflect" the "economic base"? In the now famous preface to *The Critique of Political Economy*, Marx maintained that the "ideological superstructure" of any social system only *more or less rapidly* comes to conform, "reflect," or "correspond" to the economic base. How more or less rapidly the process is completed is left to conjecture and would obviously vary as a consequence of an indeterminate number of contingent and situation specific circumstances.

Marx had only partially formalized and standardized his system of thought. The most extensively formalized and standardized portions were those devoted to the economic dynamics of capitalist society. How the economic mode of production ultimately came to "reflect" itself in the consciousness of men was left couched in the variable and vague language of ordinary discourse. Any number of mutually incompatible but equally plausible constructions could be placed upon his broad, abstract, and operationally obscure statements.

There seems to be little doubt that Marx conceived the relationship between the economic base and the ideological superstructure in terms of a dependency relationship, with "material" factors having causal priority. The *direction* of change is fairly obvious. Material life circumstances *determine* ideological processes; but questions concerning precisely what might be numbered among the ideological elements and whether all such elements "reflect" the economic base with the same faithfulness, how rapidly they can be expected to so faithfully correspond, and whether such "reflections" can be understood to affect, in turn, the economic base, are nowhere clearly answered in the Marx corpus. Is the relationship between the economic base and the ideological superstructure deterministic, necessary, sufficient, sequential, and irreversible—or is the relationship probabilistic, contingent, coextensive, and reversible? There are almost as many answers to such questions as there are Marxists; and almost all of them propose equally plausible interpretations. Interpretations still compete for place almost one hundred years after the death of Marx. As late as 1951 Joseph Stalin himself introduced a major reinterpretation of the putative relation between life circumstances and ideas by insisting that language and grammar (and, by implication, logic) were *not* part of the ideological superstructure and consequently did not "reflect" the economic base. Marx's dichotomy has been replaced (at least in the Soviet Union) by a trichotomous division, and the relationships between the parts remain obscure.[13]

For the immediate successors of Marx and Engels, men who were actively concerned with organizing the saving revolution, the question was not academic. Does the proletariat *automatically* develop the consciousness requisite to revolution and to socialism? Or is the process more complex, more dependent, specifically, on human intervention?

Both Marx and Engels were aware, by the time of their deaths, that the proletariat had not developed the consciousness that would make a revolution and sustain a socialist society. As late as 1892 Engels insisted that the English trade union movement had failed to develop the political sense required of revolutionaries. He put his hopes in the development of organizations among the "unskilled"—those who did not enjoy the advantages of protection and privilege possible during England's monopoly of mature industrial production. He felt assured that the unskilled, bringing "virgin minds" to the class struggle, would manifest, ultimately, the requisite consciousness.[14] Similarly, Marx tolerated the Prou-

[13] Cf. A. J. Gregor, *A Survey of Marxism* (New York: Random House, 1965), chap. 4; G. Leff, *The Tyranny of Concepts* (London: Merlin, 1961), pp. 128-43.

[14] Engels, The 1892 Preface to *Conditions of the Working Class*, pp. xviiif.

dhonist and Bakuninist fancies of the members of the First International because he was convinced that, ultimately, true working class consciousness would prevail. *The Communist Manifesto* had maintained that the class interests of the proletariat were becoming increasingly uniform, that the spread of capitalism carried in its wake the material basis for a homogeneous class consciousness. *If* the collection of propositions Marx entertained concerning the generation of human consciousness were true—and *if* his analysis of the dynamics of capitalist production were equally true—proletarian consciousness must be, ultimately, the final outcome of irreversible economic processes which are intrinsic to modern industrial society.

Neither Marx nor Engels ever despaired. The ultimate result of the historic process which began with man's first efforts to produce his means of subsistence must ultimately produce the proletarian revolution. What troubled Marxists after the death of Engels was: what are revolutionary Marxists to do in the interim?

From 1848 until their deaths both Marx and Engels expected revolution to destroy capitalism within the immediate future. Marx labored hard and long to finish *The Communist Manifesto* of 1848 in anticipation of the *imminent* "workers' revolution." The revolution which occurred was not very much of a revolution and it was clearly not a workers' " revolution. Subsequently, Marx rushed to complete his *Critique of Political Economy* before the outbreak of a revolution he anticipated in 1859-1860. There was no revolution, much less a workers' revolution. Throughout the remainder of their lives both Marx and Engels anticipated revolution. They went to their deaths still awaiting its advent.

By the time of Engels' death it had become increasingly obvious to Marxists that something was amiss somewhere. Europe was possessed of a substantially nonrevolutionary proletariat. The "revolution" in Paris in 1871, which Marx made into something of a legend, was, he clearly recognized, little more than an adventure and not much of a revolution.

Where there was much revolutionary talk, among the French and Italian workers, Marxism as "scientific socialism" had the least influence. Where Marxism exercised the most influence, within the German Social Democratic Party, the proletariat was apparently least disposed to revolution. Engels, in one of his last major pieces of work, seemed to legitimatize the parliamentary disposition of the German proletarian party. He spoke of the changed circumstances governing revolution, of the logistics problems revolutionaries would face when opposed by modern armies, of the strategic problems of fighting in the cities; and he waxed eloquent over the electoral successes of the German workers who were politically organized.[15] Marx, himself, had in fact maintained, as early as 1872, that socialism might come to England, the United States, and perhaps Holland without violent revolution.[16]

In effect, classical Marxism as it was received by the followers of Marx and Engels at the end of the nineteenth century was not a body of thought capable of providing clear and uneqivocal guides to political action. It failed to provide such a guide at least in part because as a body of thought it contained any number of propositions that were, in and of themselves and within the collection of propositions that made up "scientific" Marxism, vague and ambiguous. The portions of Marxist thought most consistently elaborated were those which provided some predictive leverage on the development of capitalism as an *economic system*, but that portion could be used for organizational, strategic, and tactical planning only if the collection of theoretical propositions devoted to the development of human consciousness was equally well articulated. Every assertion Marx advanced concerning the economic system of advanced capitalism could be true, and, unless the propositions concerning the origin, nature, and transformation of

[15] Engels, Introduction of 1895 to K. Marx, "The Class Struggles in France," *Selected Works*, I, 118-38.

[16] Marx, as cited S. Avineri, *The Social and Political Thought of Karl Marx* (New York: Cambridge University, 1968), pp. 215f.

collective human psychology were equally true (by implication at least as equally well formalized and standardized), revolutionaries could derive but few specific implications for organization and conduct.

There is, in fact, little in the Marx corpus that could pass as a *theory* of individual or collective human psychology. There is certainly none to be found in either the works of Marx or Engels. Since the death of the founders of classical Marxism any number of attempts have been made by Marxists to fill the interstices of the body of thought left by them. Until fairly recently, as has been indicated, the reflex psychology of Ivan P. Pavlov was conceived by Soviet Marxists as providing the necessary theoretical adjunct to Marxism; but the effort has not been notably successful and remains peculiar to a particular period in the history of Soviet Marxism.

At the turn of the century the lacuna in the theoretical structure of classical Marxism provoked significant efforts at reinterpretation, supplementation, and reassessment in the effort to discover in Marxism a reasonably specific guide to revolutionary conduct.

The Dilemma of the Nonrevolutionary Proletariat

The death of Engels saw the immediate manifestation of a variety of "revisionist" tendencies, variable interpretations of some significant aspects of classical Marxism—all of which were to transform the system, in one way or another, into something other than that which Marx had left to his spiritual heirs.

The one revision that invoked the most immediate and heated response was that of Eduard Bernstein. Bernstein was one of the most respected of the Marxist theoreticians of the German Social Democratic Party. He was a confidante of Engels and of Karl Kautsky. Engels trusted him so implicitly that he made him his literary executor. Nonetheless, almost immediately upon the death of Engels, Bernstein published a series of articles that culminated in the appearance, in 1898, of *Die Voraussetzungen des Sozialismus*, a searching and wide-ranging criticism of the theoretical system of classical Marxism.[17]

Bernstein's criticisms are important and interesting for a variety of reasons, but for the sake of exposition they are noteworthy because they focused on a fact that had been common knowledge for some considerable period of time: German Social Democracy had been, and remained, characteristically legalist and parliamentary—the German proletariat, and its revolutionary party, was lamentably nonrevolutionary.[18]

Bernstein was intellectually disturbed by the discrepancy between social democratic protestations of revolutionary fervor and its legalistic and reformist behaviors.[19] If classical Marxism were true, the proletariat should have become increasingly revolutionary. All the indices, however, indicated that the German proletariat was essentially reformist rather than revolutionary. If Marx had correctly divined the dynamics of capitalist society—and if the consciousness of men was a reflex of their material life conditions—the proletariat should have become, or should be becoming, increasingly revolutionary. In their more sober moments none of the leaders of social democracy in Germany believed this to be the case.

These considerations had troubled Bernstein even before the death of Engels. By 1896 Bernstein was prepared to enter into dialogue with other Marxist theoreticians to resolve the apparent paradox of the nonrevolutionary proletariat. Bernstein insisted that if Marxism pretended to scientific

---

[17] The *Voraussetzungen* has been translated into English as *Evolutionary Socialism*, tr. E. C. Harvey (New York: Schocken, 1961). Unfortunately, the English edition does not contain Bernstein's criticism of Marx's use of the Hegelian dialectic and Marx's "Blanquist bias." All references will be to the English edition unless otherwise indicated.

[18] In this regard see W. Sombart's contemporary work: *Sozialismus und soziale Bewegung im neunzehnten Jahrhundert* (Jena: Fischer, 1897), pp. 36-39.

[19] For a discussion of Bernstein's intellectual development and social concepts see P. Gay, *The Dilemma of Democratic Socialism* (New York: Collier, 1962).

competence its defenders must resolve the problem: either Marx's anticipations of economic developments in the capitalist world were in some respect incorrect, or the proletariat did not simply reflect processes acting themselves out in the economic base, or both. Bernstein, in fact, considered all possibilities. He argued that (1) classical Marxism advanced a deterministic thesis with respect to collective human psychology that was extremely difficult to defend (a) because it was intuitively implausible, and (b) because it was poorly formulated, articulated as it was in terms of broad "principles" and unqualified generalizations. He further argued that (2) the economic analysis of classical Marxism, (a) the labor theory of value, (b) the conception of the secular fall in the rate of profit, (c) the notion of the real or relative emiseration of the proletariat, and (d) the inevitable collapse of the capitalist mode of production, were all theoretical artifacts that were subject to extensive reservation and significant qualification.

Bernstein argued that classical Marxism was a partially axiomatized theoretical system possessed of "chief" or "basic" propositions which, in its pure (rather than the applied) formulations, permitted the derivation of implied theorems, propositions whose range and scope were correspondingly restricted. When the theory was applied to the object world, a finite, but indeterminate number of qualifications, local conditions, would have to be supplied. Bernstein insisted that both Marx and Engels had, in significant instances, supplied those qualifiers and suggested the implicit restrictions on their formulae. Although Marx had argued, in "pure theory," that society is, or would be, dichotomized into *two* contending classes, yet in his detailed treatment of empirical circumstances, i.e. in his study of England and France, he admitted the existence of a *variety* of classes and social strata. Not only did Marx admit that the conception of a dichotomized society was an abstract characterization, but whenever he employed class analysis to interpret events, the relationship between class and class consciousness was far from the simple "reflex" suggested by the theory. In pursuing an analysis, Marx insisted that "in France, the petty bourgeois does what normally the industrial bourgeois would have to do; the worker does what normally would be the task of the petty bourgeois; and the task of the worker, who accomplishes that? No one."[20] Concerning England, Marx spoke of "an *infinite fragmentation* of interests and rank created by the social division of labor among laborers, capitalists and landlords."[21]

Scientific theories, when they are to be employed for empirical purposes, require a statement of conditions governing their application. The scientists articulating a law will generally append a *ceteris paribus* clause—an "all things being equal" qualifier—to indicate that the law is understood to be operable only under a certain range of circumstances. In the case of classical Marxism, given its broad range and scope, it is extremely difficult to specify what those conditions might be. Marx (more so than Engels) was generally careful to characterize the "laws" with which he dealt as "tendencies"—and throughout *Kapital* some of the "countertendencies" were reasonably well characterized. Both Marx and Engels cautioned against the disposition on the part of their followers to simply apply the "chief propositions" of their theory without a careful inventory of the qualifiers that were applicable and the conditions under which any historic tendency works itself out.

Bernstein's analysis of classical Marxism was broad-gauged and penetrating. The bulk of his criticisms need not detain us. The criticism around which a generation of Marxists was to argue was the role of "ideological" or "ethical" factors in the determination of collective conduct. Bernstein insisted that "it cannot be denied that Marx and Engels originally assigned to the non-economic factors a much less influence on the evolution of society, a much less power of modifying by their action the conditions of production, than in their later writings." Whatever the case, Bernstein continued, "the point of economic development attained today

[20] Marx, "The Class Struggles in France," *Selected Works*, I, 211.
[21] Marx, *Capital*, III, 863. Emphasis supplied.

leaves the ideological, and especially the ethical, factors greater space for independent activity than was formerly the case.[22]

Bernstein objected to the determinism implicit, and sometimes explicit, in the formulations of classical Marxism. Around this issue a number of arguments were to collect. Almost immediately after Bernstein published his critique, Ludwig Woltmann followed it with an account of classical Marxism that developed essentially the same themes. Woltmann spoke of the "dialectical schema" of classical Marxism, formulated in terms of broad and general principles that conceived "social development in terms of a natural process in which economic causes and laws (*technische-oekonomische Ursachen und Gesetze*) proceeded with inevitable necessity and determined the intentions and ideas of human consciousness."[23] He also indicated that the schema itself was extensively modified when Marx and Engels sought to apply it to any historic situation. Moreover, the logic of even the pure schema was impaired by some of Marx's own formulations. If Marx's schema distinguished between an economic base, composed of material productive forces and a determinate set of relations identified as productive relations, and an ideological superstructure ultimately determined by that base, Marx's insistence that "of all the productive forces the most significant productive force is the working class itself" hopelessly confounded the logic of the putative relationship. If the proletariat itself constitutes part of the productive forces—and the productive forces determine the ideological structure of society—are the intentions and ideas, the consciousness, of the proletariat *dependent* or *independent* variables in the process? Does the consciousness of the proletariat *determine* the historic process, and revolution as a specific and fundamental aspect of that process; or is the consciousness of the proletariat *determined* by

[22] Bernstein, *Evolutionary Socialism*, pp. 11, 15.

[23] L. Woltmann, *Der historische Materialismus* (Düsseldorf: Michels, 1900), p. 416.

some specific subset of independent variables in the economic base?

These questions were to create intolerable tensions within the structure of classical Marxism. Bernstein and the "revisionists" served only to focus attention on them; but it was inevitable that they would ultimately have to be faced if men seek to govern their conduct by some rational assessment of real possibilities.

Until these issues were made the subject of public inquiry, Marxists were content simply to reiterate what were understood to be "orthodox" formulations. This disposition was evident in the work of Georgi Plekhanov, one of the principal theoreticians of Russian social democracy. In 1898, in his essay on the role of consciousness in history, Plekhanov had argued that human action in history could best be conceived as the consequence not of "free will," but of a "dialectical necessity." Human action was best understood as an "inevitable link in the chain of inevitable events." To illustrate his point Plekhanov maintained that the Marxist "serves as an instrument of . . . necessity and cannot help doing so, owing to his social status and to his mentality and temperament, which are created by his status. This too," he went on, "is an aspect of necessity. Since his social status has imbued him with this character and no other, he not only serves as an instrument of necessity and cannot help doing so, but he passionately desires, and cannot help desiring, to do so." Plekhanov conceived that human action is "free" only when it "is identical with necessity—it is necessity transformed into freedom."[24]

Plekhanov's account is an interesting effort to explicate some of the concepts of classical Marxism. For our purpose it is interesting to recognize their existence and to relate them to the kinds of problems that were being considered at the turn of the century. Plekhanov defended the kind of "dialectical determinism" that was considered "orthodox"

[24] G. Plekhanov, *The Role of the Individual in History* (New York: International, 1940), p. 17.

101

among Russian Marxists. V. I. Lenin, under the influence of Plekhanov, initially accepted a similar interpretation. He insisted that Marx's analysis provided an account of "the origin of man's social ideas themselves," an account which conceived the "course of ideas" as "dependent" "on the course of things"—the only account "compatible with scientific psychology." Lenin went on to indicate that Marxism not only "proves" the necessity of the present order of things but also "proves the necessity of another order which must inevitably grow out of the preceding one regardless of whether men believe in it or not, whether they are conscious of it or not. *Marx treats the social movement as a process of natural history, governed by laws not only independent of human will, consciousness and intentions, but rather, on the contrary, determining the will, consciousness and intentions of men.*" He went on to conclude that "if the conscious element plays so subordinate a part in the history of civilization, it is self-evident that a critique whose subject is civilization, can least of all take as its basis any form of, or any result of, consciousness."[25]

These were conceptions entertained by "orthodox" Marxism at the close of the nineteenth century—at about the time that Bernstein was advancing his first criticisms. In Italy, in 1896, Antonio Labriola insisted that Marx's account gave "theoretic expression" to the objective "necessity of the new social revolution" which was "more or less explicit in the *instinctive* consciousness of the proletariat and in its passionate and *spontaneous* movements . . . ."[26] Similar construals of the nature of social revolution could be culled from the literature of the period. By the turn of the century, however, such interpretations could no longer be made with the easy confidence that had hitherto characterized them. Both Benedetto Croce and Giovanni Gentile argued that classical Marxism had left its adherents only "formulae" and "general

[25] V. I. Lenin, "What the 'Friends of the People' Are," *Collected Works*, I, 137f., 166. Emphasis supplied.

[26] A. Labriola, *Essays on the Materialistic Conception of History*, tr. C. H. Kerr (Chicago: Kerr, 1903), p. 29. Emphasis supplied.

aphorisms" that failed to specify how economic determinants manifested themselves through the agency of human will and consciousness. Both Croce and Gentile insisted that if Marxism wished to move from "theory" to political action it would be necessary for Marxists to engage "moral sentiments and human enthusiasm."[27]

During the period between the turn of the century and the commencement of the First World War, these were the questions that generated the most insistent problems for thinking Marxists. For Max Adler the "question of the relationship between the material and the ideational (*die Ideellen*), the question of how the two enter into relationship," constituted the "fundamental problem (*das Grundproblem*) of the materialist conception of history." The followers of Josef Dietzgen, in turn and with equal emphasis, insisted that classical Marxism had provided only the "schematic outlines" (*skizzenhaft entworfene Formel*) of a theory of will and consciousness, and of psychology in general.[28]

In France, during this same period, Georges Sorel raised objections to the entire notion that political convictions were, in some intelligible sense, the *products* of economic circumstances. The uncritical use of metaphors, what Sorel impuned as "word plays," concealed the poverty of the intellectual apparatus of the conceptual schema with which the followers of Marx attempted to interpret contemporary history. Marx, Sorel maintained, has provided "schematizations"; neither he nor Engels had formulated a "precise and detailed exposition of their ideas," particularly with respect to human motivation and consciousness. As a conseqence a rigorously scientific theory of social revolution cannot be

[27] Cf. G. Gentile, "La filosofia di Marx," in *I fondamenti della filosofia del diritto* (Florence: Sansoni, 1955), pp. 183f., 190; B. Croce, *Materialismo storico ed economia marxistica* (Bari: Laterza, 1921), pp. 27f.

[28] Cf. M. Adler, *Marxistische Probleme*, 5th ed. (Berlin: Vorwärts, 1922), p. 1; the original edition was published in 1913; E. Untermann, *Die logischen Mängel des engeren Marxismus* (Munich: Verlag der dietzgenschen Philosophie, 1910), p. 616.

found in their works; nor do their lucubrations offer a guide to contemporary political conduct.[29]

Sorel argued that, even if Bernstein's criticisms of Marxian economics were confirmed, the failure of Marx's predictions concerning the economic system had no direct relevance on the *mobilization* and *organization* of revolutionary forces in capitalist society. Sorel insisted upon an all but complete disjuncture between human motives, the organization of masses, and the economic substructure of society.

It is evident that by 1905 Marxism was undergoing an incubation that portended significant changes. Bernstein had attempted a reassessment of classical Marxism in order to explain the nonrevolutionary disposition of the proletariat. Until Bernstein articulated his criticism, committed revolutionaries such as Labriola, Plekhanov, and Lenin were content simply to reiterate formulas about the "necessary" and "spontaneous" development of revolutionary consciousness. With the advent of Bernstein's criticisms, revolutionaries could opt for at least one of two immediate strategies, they could reject Bernstein's criticisms out of hand and retain the familiar formulae, or they could (as did Sorel) accept Bernstein's criticisms and deny that the relationship between economic variables and human consciousness and will was one of dependency. Sorel simply insisted that men are motivated to revolution by considerations that are substantially independent of economic determinants.

The first alternative became increasingly difficult to defend. During the first decade of the twentieth century, it became evident that the proletariat of the advanced capitalist countries was lamentably nonrevolutionary. Revolutionary Marxists began to reinterpret classical Marxism. In France, Russia, Italy, and Germany, radical and intransigent

[29] Sorel's assessment is found throughout his work, but perhaps the most relevant and specific comments can be found in G. Sorel, *Les polémiques pour l'interprétation du Marxisme* (Paris: Giard & Brière, 1900), "La necessità e il fatalismo nel marxismo," in *Saggi di critica del Marxismo* (Milan: Sandron, 1903), pp. 59-94.

revolutionaries produced interpretations of Marxism that preserved and/or enhanced its revolutionary character at the price of reformulating some of its theoretical elements. For our purposes the developments in Russia and Italy are most significant. In Russia the intransigents collected around Lenin and constituted themselves the Bolshevik faction within the Social Democratic Party. In Italy a faction, identified as the "radical left," collected around a young revolutionary socialist who, under the influence of Sorelian syndicalism, construed Marxism as a voluntaristic and elitist revolutionary credo. By 1912 that faction was characterized as the most intransigent and radical within the Socialist Party. Its leader, after the party congress at Reggio Emilia in 1912, was twenty-nine-year-old Benito Mussolini.

Perhaps the most significant feature of these developments, for the restricted purposes of our account, was that the reformulations entertained by Lenin and Mussolini shared a number of critical similarities.

Lenin had originally accepted Plekhanov's deterministic interpretation of classical Marxism.[30] Lenin simply reiterated that the primary agency of social development and revolutionary change was the material life processes of society and the "fact that the workers became united, welded together and organized" in the struggle for a social society was "a derivative and secondary phenomenon."[31] But by 1900 Lenin recognized that the working class movement, isolated from the leadership of revolutionary Marxists, would be irredeemably "petit bourgeois." By the end of 1901 Lenin insisted that a revolution required the intercession of a critical revolutionary elite. He spoke of a conspiratorial cadre of "ideologists" who would precede the "spontaneous" mass movement—who would "point out the road" it was to follow. He

[30] For explicit references to Plekhanov's views and Lenin's acceptance, cf. A. J. Gregor, *Contemporary Radical Ideologies* (New York: Random House, 1968), pp. 65-68.

[31] Lenin, "What the 'Friends of the People' Are," *Collected Works*, I, 185, 177.

105

spoke of "elevating" the working class to the consciousness of its historic mission.[32] He spoke of the necessity of a "vanguard organization," self-selected and self-purifying, that would provide the necessary leadership for a Marxist revolution. He insisted that "the history of all countries" indicated that the proletariat, without the intercession of declassed bourgeois ideologists, is capable of developing only "trade-union consciousness," that is to say the proletariat is capable, by its own efforts, of developing only a petit bourgeois consciousness. The proletarian consciousness, necessary for the social revolution, could only be brought to the working class from without, by the self-selected vanguard of revolutionary Marxists.[33]

Classical Marxism had, on a variety of occasions, insisted that revolutionary leadership and party organization constituted at best a substitutable variable in the development of social revolution. Engels, as early as 1847, had insisted that revolution was a "natural phenomenon" that proceeded with or without leadership or a party organization.[34] *Nowhere did classical Marxism explicitly entertain the conviction that a revolutionary party and revolutionary leadership was either the necessary or sufficient condition of revolution.* The revolution was rendered necessary—the consequence of natural laws—by the very processes of capitalist production.

Lenin, after 1900, opted for an interpretation of Marxism that made the role of a revolutionary vanguard *essential*, a nonsubstitutable condition, to the revolutionary process. That essential revolutionary vanguard was composed of declassed bourgeois intellectuals who were capable of correctly anticipating events because of their superior theoretical insight. They addressed themselves to the real and ultimate, if still unconscious, will of the masses. They could *anticipate* history.

At precisely the same time, independent of developments

[32] Lenin, "A Talk with the Defenders of Economism," *ibid.*, v, 316.
[33] Lenin, "What is to Be Done?" *ibid.*, v, 374f., 383f.
[34] F. Engels, "The Foundations of Communism," in Ryazanov, ed., *Communist Manifesto*, pp. 330.

in Czarist Russia, the radical syndicalist wing of the Italian socialist movement developed a remarkably similar conception of social revolution. Under the influence of Sorel, Italian syndicalists argued that revolution could only be the consequence of an impulse imparted to the proletariat by a self-selected vanguard.

Men such as Arturo Labriola, A. O. Olivetti, and Sergio Panunzio represented the radical wing of the socialist movement. Under the influence of a sociological tradition that had begun to manifest itself during the last quarter of the nineteenth century, the syndicalists offered reinterpretations of classical Marxism that emphasized the role of *motivation* and mass *organization* in revolutionary struggle.[35] Lenin had, in fact, denied that there was a direct determinate relationship between economic variables, class membership, and revolutionary consciousness. Lenin had argued that proletarian circumstances produced only petit bourgeois consciousness and that, under unspecified conditions, membership in the bourgeoisie was capable of producing in select members of that class a "proletarian and revolutionary consciousness." The Italian syndicalists did little more than make the disjuncture between class membership and class consciousness more explicit. The Italian syndicalists, like Lenin's Bolsheviks, denied that class consciousness would be the spontaneous product of class membership. Both the Italian syndicalists and the Bolsheviks argued that the critical element in the development of revolutionary consciousness was the intercession of a vanguard elite possessed of special moral and intellectual qualities that licensed their leadership roles. As early as 1904, under the influence of Italian and French syndicalism, Mussolini insisted that the socialist revolution would be "initiated by a minority," a "proletarian elite," a "socialist vanguard."[36]

[35] For a discussion of the elements that entered into Italian syndicalism cf. A. J. Gregor, *The Ideology of Fascism* (New York: Free Press, 1969), chap. 2.

[36] B. Mussolini, "Pagine rivoluzionarie: 'Le parole d'un rivoltoso'," *Opera omnia* (Florence: La fenice, 1951), I, 51; and "Interne alla

Both the Bolsheviks and the Italian syndicalists and socialist radicals considered themselves "Marxists." Neither felt
that their reformulations constituted significant departures
from classical Marxism. In certain respects the syndicalists
were more explicit in their reassessments. Lenin, for example, continued to maintain that his interpretation of Marxism
was the only correct interpretation; Italian syndicalists recognized that classical Marxism was a loose theoretical structure which permitted a variety of equally plausible interpretations.[37] Mussolini admitted as much, and he maintained
that radical socialists chose to interpret Marxism voluntaris-
tically, recognizing the role of will, conviction, and dedication in the revolutionary struggle. He insisted, furthermore,
that the very slackness of the theoretical system of classical
Marxism permitted such interpretations. Like Woltmann,
Mussolini indicated that if one chose to construe classical
Marxism as a quasi-deductive system in which consciousness
is interpreted as a necessary product of processes in the material base of society—with material productive forces determining productive relations, and productive forces and productive relations the determinants which produce social
consciousness—one must face the fact that Marx himself
had identified the working class, itself, as the most powerful
productive force. If the working class is the most powerful
instrument of production, and instruments of production are
material forces, the deductive relations between economic
base and social consciousness are hopelessly confounded.[38]

In retrospect, it is quite evident that classical Marxism
was suffering fateful changes. Lenin's reinterpretation of
Marxism, his commitment to a declassed bourgeois revolutionary vanguard that would bring revolutionary conscious-

notte del 4 Agosto," *ibid.*, I, 61; cf. A. O. Olivetti, "I sindacalisti e la
elite," in *Sindacalisti Italiani*, ed. R. Melis (Rome: Volpe, 1964), pp.
191-93.

[37] This is particularly true of Sorel, but is equally true of Italian
syndicalists; cf., A. O. Olivetti, *Questioni contemporanee* (Naples:
Partenopea, 1913), p. 19.

[38] B. Mussolini, "Evoluzione sociale e lotta di classe," *Opera*, II, 31.

ness to the proletariat, was resisted by the bulk of thinking socialists. Even Rosa Luxemburg, as radical and as revolutionary as Lenin, rejected his reformulation as "elitist" and "non-Marxist."[39] The Italian syndicalists, Mussolini among them, simply maintained that classical Marxism could be legitimately and plausibly interpreted in a variety of ways. They chose the most "revolutionary" and "radical" interpretation; and their interpretation was remarkably similar to that entertained by Lenin's Bolsheviks. Both the Bolsheviks and the radical socialists of Italy conceived revolution as an eminently political affair; they became increasingly concerned with motivational and organizational matters. Rosa Luxemburg insisted that Lenin conceived revolution as "commencing from the top," informing the irresolute consciousness of the masses.[40] The Italian syndicalists and radical socialists became no less increasingly preoccupied with questions of mobilization and organization, with the specific function of strategic revolutionary elites. The syndicalists conceived the revolution as the consequence of the intercession of special organizations of revolutionary elites, the working class syndicates capable, at critical junctures, of invoking a general strike. The Bolsheviks conceived the revolution as a consequence of the intercession of strategic revolutionary elites organized in a party of "a new type," an elite cadre, highly centralized and hierarchically constituted, that would constitute the nucleus around which the masses would collect.

By 1910 Mussolini had abandoned the syndicalists and had opted for an interpretation of revolution very similar to that advanced by the Russian Bolsheviks. He conceived revolution as the consequence of the activity of a small minority of dedicated revolutionaries capable of activating the inert masses. By 1910 Mussolini had opted for a party of

[39] R. Luxemburg, *The Russian Revolution and Leninism or Marxism* (Ann Arbor: University of Michigan, 1961), pp. 81-108.

[40] Cf. C. Elliott, "Lenin, Rosa Luxemburg and the Dilemma of the Non-Revolutionary Proletariat," *Midwest Journal of Political Science*, 9, 4 (November 1965), 327-38.

"a new type," a hierarchically constituted, elitist party, capable of mobilizing the masses to revolutionary purpose.[41]

By 1914 the most revolutionary elements of the various European Marxist movements had wrought significant changes in the loose structure of classical Marxism. Both the Bolsheviks under Lenin and the Italian radical socialists under Mussolini came to construe revolution as the consequence of the influence of mobilizational and organizational, i.e. specifically political, factors. Both entertained, implicitly or explicitly, a relatively specific theory of motivation and organization not to be found in classical Marxism. Both denied that revolutionary consciousness is the automatic consequence of processes in the economic base of society. Both had little confidence in the ability of the masses to develop spontaneously the consciousness requisite to the social revolution. Both had little, if any, confidence in "majority opinions." Both were convinced that leadership required special qualities.

Lenin's elitism was probably rooted in the Russian literature with which he had become familiar, particularly Nicholas Chernyshevsky's *What is to Be Done?* Chernyshevsky had foreseen the necessity of "strong personalities" that would impose their will upon the course of events and infuse revolutionary purpose upon the "chaotic movement of the masses." When Lenin articulated his elitist conception of revolutionary socialism, he chose *What is to Be Done?* as the title of his exposition.[42]

Mussolini's elitism was rooted in the Italian literature of the period including that of Alfredo Oriani, *La rivolta ideale*, who had called for "select individuals" possessed of "special gifts" to "develop the ideas that form the essence of a people," ideas capable of leading the masses to fulfillment.

Classical Marxism was sufficiently porous to permit reinterpretations as extensive as those of Lenin and Mussolini.

[41] For more adequate documentation of Mussolini's development, see Gregor, *The Ideology of Fascism*, chap. 3.

[42] Cf. Gregor, *A Survey of Marxism*, pp. 217-19.

While both had opponents within the ranks of revolutionary socialists, both were recognized as Marxists. Both rose to leadership within the ranks of socialist parties as knowledgeable Marxists. Both were recognized as factionalists and sectarians—but Marxists nonetheless.

By 1910, thus, the most significant revisions to classical Marxism turned on the issues of revolutionary consciousness and the organizational strategy of the revolution. The Bolsheviks, the French syndicalists, and the radical socialists that gradually collected behind Mussolini, all conceived revolution as a consequence of elitist initiative, with masses mobilized behind a self-selected cadre of revolutionaries. French and Italian syndicalism long entertained anarchistic elements; but a considerable number of syndicalists in Italy had followed Mussolini back into the Socialist Party to constitute themselves its radical wing. Both Lenin and Mussolini came to reject the anarchism and the narrow economic focus of syndicalism and gradually formulated a notion of mass mobilization for revolution through the agency of a radical party "of a new type."

The reformulations of Marxism that occupied revolutionary Marxists through the first decade of the twentieth century attempted to unpack the implications of Marx's account of social consciousness and its putative relationship to the economic base. Not only was this question of the role of will and consciousness in social development of prime strategic importance, but it was also a question which Marx had dealt with only tangentially. Marx had, of course, left Marxists some general propositions concerning the conceived relationship between ideational and material elements, but the accounts were loose enough to permit a variety of mutually exclusive, but equally plausible interpretations.

NATIONALISM AND ORTHODOX MARXISM

Those Marxists who remained "revolutionary" during this period had, with some notable exceptions, simply rejected Bernstein's criticism of Marxist economics. Among the revolutionaries only Sorel accepted the criticisms directed against Marx's economic analyses—he accepted them because he was convinced that revolution is made by men animated by a vision of the future, a "myth," rather than by any determinate economic development. Lenin and Mussolini, however, continued to insist on the substantial integrity of Marx's economic system. Only the crisis of the First World War provoked major departures. While those departures introduced fundamental changes in Marx's economic analyses, and had already been anticipated by the work of Rudolf Hilferding, Rosa Luxemburg, and Nikolai Bukharin, it was the irrepressible manifestation of proletarian nationalism that invoked them. The outbreak of the First World War saw the immediate disintegration of proletarian internationalism and the reemergence of nationalism. Some of the most "orthodox" of Marxists, Karl Kautsky, Georgi Plekhanov, and Gustave Hervé among them, opted to support their respective nations in the conflict that began with the assassination at Sarajevo.

Marxist "orthodoxy" had argued that nationalism, as a consequence of the international character of capitalism, was necessarily moribund. As early as 1845 and 1848, Marx had insisted that nationalism could no longer influence the proletariat. Industrial capitalism had succeeded in defining class interests with such specificity and with such urgent consequences that the proletariat could no longer be conceived as being moved by nationalist appeals. In 1845 Engels wrote that "the proletarians are in the great majority already by nature without national prejudices, and their whole education and movement is essentially humanitarian, anti-national."[43] Marx seemed to be equally definitive. He insisted, as early as *The German Ideology*, that not only was nationalism no longer an influence among the proletariat, but its advocates were found only among the bourgeoisie.[44] Such convictions, conjoined with explicit statements found in the

[43] F. Engels, "Das Fest der Nationen in London," *Werke*, vi, 614.
[44] Marx and Engels, *The German Ideology*, pp. 76f.

Manifesto and supported by an economic analysis that saw the economic developments of the nineteenth century creating, inevitably, an *international* proletarian class, produced among Marxist theoreticians a disposition to deny *any* revolutionary role to nationalist sentiments. The proletarian class had no fatherland. The proletarian revolution was to be an international uprising against the capitalist mode of production and would produce a "universal emancipation."

If the dilemma of the nonrevolutionary proletarian induced significant reinterpretations of classical Marxism, the issue of proletarian nationalism was to generate changes so extensive that it can be said that classical Marxism ceased to be a viable revolutionary ideology with the advent of the First World War.

MARX AND ENGELS ON NATIONALISM

Neither Marx nor Engels conceived nationalism as having any *independent* historical and social significance. Nationalist sentiment was a derivative of more fundamental processes in the economic base of society. Nationalism, per se, for both Marx and Engels, was a singularly bourgeois artifact—the product of a bourgeois disposition, at a particular stage of history, to create a viable internal market for their manufactured goods. With the decline of feudalism, the manufacturing and industrial bourgeoisie found themselves in need of a sufficiently broad internal market to absorb their increasing productivity. They required relative freedom of movement within that market area for the transportation of goods, resources, and services. What resulted, as a consequence, was the creation of national states. But since the bourgeois must forever revolutionize the instruments of production—revolutions which ultimately mature in greater productivity—capitalism is forever driven to exceed the absorptive capacity of the internal market it has created for itself. The super-profits that attend innovation, the economies of rationalized and large-scale production, all conspire to drive

113

the bourgeoisie beyond the limits of the nation state for investment and marketing opportunities. Ultimately, the entire world is involved in the frenetic capitalist process. That involvement produces a class which, in the terms used by Marx and Engels in *The German Ideology*, has "absolutely no national interests": the proletariat.

The theoretical formulations are rather simple. Predicated on certain convictions concerning the generation of collective consciousness, and having analyzed the principal species traits of capitalism, the founders of classical Marxism felt confident in their judgment that the working class had no national interests.

Nonetheless, there remained a number of problems. Both Marx and Engels knew that capitalist expansion was accomplished by military adventures in the underdeveloped parts of the world. The tempo of colonialist incursions increased throughout the nineteenth century. Even within Europe the more aggressive industrial powers were pressing against the less developed. Both Marx and Engels were forced to address themselves to the question of the steady expansion of the industrially advanced nations: England's inroads into Asia and Africa; France's incursions into North Africa; the annexation of vast territories in the western part of North America by the United States—not to speak of the pressure directed by industrial Germany against the Slavs of southeastern Europe.

Because of their analysis, both Marx and Engels produced a relatively consistent interpretation of these phenomena: such aggressions were, for the most part, "progressive." They responded to the "logic of history."

It is perfectly clear, of course, that Marx found the *methods* employed by the English, for example, in subduing India and China morally objectionable; but it is equally clear that he felt such conquests to be historically necessary. The ultimate victory of socialism could only be the consequence of the prior universalization of the capitalist mode of production. Colonialism, therefore, could only be the brutal but necessary antecedent to the universalization of capitalism and the ultimate emancipation of man.[45]

Marx was convinced that the industrial capitalists were compelled by the circumstances inherent in their mode of production to serve the purposes of world history. His locutions about the lawlike character of historical change, its inevitability, its "logic," convey the import of such an orientation. While the British exploit India, or China, for their own immediate interests, he argued, they actually serve the ultimate cause of world revolution. In his account of "The Future Results of British Rule in India," Marx maintained that England had "a double mission in India: one destructive and the other regenerating—the annihilation of old Asiatic society, and laying of the material foundation of Western society in Asia."[46] In 1853 Marx insisted that British colonialism in Asia had produced "the only social revolution ever heard of in Asia," and that, in the last analysis, "she was the unconscious tool of history in bringing about . . . revolution."[47]

A similar analysis was offered with respect to western colonialism in China and Africa. Colonialism, however abhorrent, was a necessary progressive step in preparing the preconditions for the socialist revolution. In 1848 Engels offered a revealing account of the French suppression of the Bedouin rebellion in Algeria. "Upon the whole," Engels maintained, "it is, in our opinion, very fortunate that the Arabian chief has been taken. The struggle of the Bedouins was a hopeless one, and though the manner in which brutal soldiers, like Bugeaud, have carried on the war is highly blameable, the conquest of Algeria is an important and fortunate fact for the progress of civilization. . . . After all, the modern bourgeois, with civilization, industry, order, and

---

[45] Cf. the Introduction to S. Avineri, *Karl Marx on Colonialism and Modernization* (Garden City: Doubleday, 1968), pp. 1-28.

[46] Marx, "The Future Results of British Rule in India," in Avineri, *ibid.*, p. 125.

[47] Marx, "The British Rule in India," *ibid.*, pp. 88, 89.

115

at least relative enlightenment following him, is preferable to the feudal lord or to the marauding robber, with the barbarian state of society to which they belong."[48]

Engels' judgments about the seizure of the Mexican territories in the western part of the North American continent were the same: American expansion served the "interests of civilization" by wresting California "from the lazy Mexicans who did not know what to do with it." The "energetic Yankees . . . increased the medium of circulation, . . . concentrated in a few years a heavy population and an extensive trade on the most suitable part of the Pacific Coast, . . . built great cities, . . . opened up steamship lines. . . . Because of this the 'independence' of a few Spanish Californians and Texans may be injured, but what do they count compared to such world historic events?" He went on to argue, "When it is a question of the existence, of the free development of all the resources of great nations, then . . . sentimentalities . . . will decide nothing." It is a matter of "trade, industry and profitable methods of agriculture, . . . [the] level of social development of the individual peoples, . . . [the] influence of the more highly developed nation on the undeveloped one." Engels conceived it to be inevitable that the more highly developed industrial nation would bind "tiny, crippled, powerless little nations together in a great Empire, and thereby [enable] them to take part in an historical development which, if left to themselves, would [remain] entirely foreign to them! To be sure such a thing is not carried through without forcibly crushing many a delicate little national flower. But without force and without an iron ruthlessness nothing is accomplished in history . . . ."[49]

Throughout his life Engels never altered his judgments concerning the historic role of advanced nations. His judgments about the historical significance of the Slav nations

[48] Engels, "French Rule in Algeria," *ibid.*, p. 44.

[49] F. Engels, "Democratic Panslavism," in *The Russian Menace to Europe*, ed. P. W. Blackstock and B. F. Hoselitz (Glencoe: Free Press, 1952), pp. 71, 74, 75, 76.

116

of southeastern Europe were emphatic. He regularly, and throughout his life, referred to them as "phthisical bodies," as "dying" or "retrograde" peoples, destined only to be absorbed by the "mighty Germans," to remain, at best, as "ethnographic monuments without political significance" within the German Empire.[50]

Engels mocked the entire strategy of national liberation when the "cry of sympathy and love for all the suppressed nationalities" was raised in the Europe of his time. He insisted that such "romantic exultation" could only create real obstacles to truly revolutionary emancipation. Where peoples of "two completely different levels of civilization" confront each other, Engels insisted that the more developed has the historic right to dominion. It is a question, he argued, "of the level of social development of the individual peoples." Engels was seemingly convinced that most national liberation movements could not be, in any sense, "progressive." He saw such movements fostered by factions that were "democratic because of their education acquired abroad," but which could only fail since the social circumstances in which such factions sought to generate revolution were "retarded" and offered "no or merely imaginary points of contact" for serious democratic developments. Both Marx and Engels insisted that, where the economic base of society was incapable of production in sufficient quantity to maintain a society if not in affluence at least in adequacy, a class-riven, i.e. a nondemocratic, society was an inevitability. They insisted, both in 1845 and in the *Anti-Duehring* of 1878, that *any society which rests on a restricted economic base must necessarily be a class society, possessed of an exploiting and an exploited class.*[51]

Wherever Marx or Engels supported national liberation

[50] F. Engels, "Po und Rhein," *Werke*, XIII, 267; cf. also, Engels, "Hungary and Panslavism," and "Democratic Panslavism," in Blackstock and Hoselitz, eds., *The Russian Menace to Europe.*

[51] Marx and Engels, *The German Ideology*, pp. 475f.; Engels, *Anti-Duehring*, pp. 386f. See Chap. 3, note 26, above.

movements it was always because they conceived such movements as "progressive," in terms of the revolutionary strategy of the proletariat. They supported Polish nationalism because they felt that the weakening of Russia was essential to the development of Europe. They supported Irish nationalism because they felt it essential to the weakening of the English ruling class.

Nationalism, in effect, was to be employed to serve either (1) the progressive development of the forces of production, and/or (2) the weakening of reactionary forces or dominant classes. Needless to say the criteria employed to determine when nationalism in the form of European colonialism was to be construed as "progressive," and when nationalism in the form of "national liberation movements" undermining the dominance of reactionary nations or classes was to be characterized as "progressive," were never specifically formulated. It is clear, however, that both Marx and Engels opposed any general principle of national liberation, and, further, that they were committed, in general, to the notion of a "progressive" role for European colonialism.

The Problem of "Proletarian" Nationalism

These were the convictions Marx and Engels left to their followers in the twentieth century. Their central judgments were painfully specific: European colonialism was, in general, progressive. They apparently had no occasion to consider the counterargument that perhaps colonialism might have *retarded* economic development in those areas brought under colonialist domination. But whatever the case, conjoined with this conviction was their support for some nationalist movements—movements they conceived as, in some sense, progressive. In effect, considerable confusion surrounded the interpretation of nationalism. While it was clear that nationalism, in general, was considered, by classical Marxism, an anachronism, the very complexity of the issues that surrounded the political phenomenon left Marxists no little confused.

118

Once again it was Bernstein who brought the confusion to public attention. In his *Voraussetzungen*, he addressed himself specifically to the issue of "proletarian nationalism." Is there any sense in which it might be said that the proletariat possessed a national identity, a national interest? Since Bernstein rejected any imminent catastrophic collapse of capitalism, he argued that it was quite evident that the proletariat *had* an interest in their national community. Bernstein insisted that the working class that has a voice, no matter how faint, in the deliberations concerning its national community has an interest in that community. Its interests range over the education and the health and security of not only itself but its children as well. Moreover, in an echo of the convictions of Marx and Engels, Bernstein argued that the more advanced nations of the world had not only a right, but an obligation, to undertake colonial enterprises. "The higher civilization ultimately can claim a higher right."[52] He admitted that it was difficult to "fix the boundary where the advocacy of the interests of one's nation ceases to be just and to pass into pseudo-patriotism," but he held it to be just as pernicious to fail to make any distinction.

The fact is that in the first years of the twentieth century classical Marxism was incapable of dealing with the issue of nationalism in any coherent fashion. The orthodox and the revolutionary elements of social democracy prided themselves on their "internationalism" and their rejection of nationalism. But any scrutiny of the literature of the period indicates that there was more slogan than substance to such protestations. At various times leading members of German Social Democracy had made plain that they were not indifferent to the national interests of the Fatherland.[53] In France, while a "left-wing bloc" made vociferous declamations of international solidarity, the syndicalists were forced to admit, as early as 1902, that the "masses" were "chauvinistic." Ultimately, Sorel was to make common cause with

[52] Bernstein, *Evolutionary Socialism*, pp. 178f.
[53] Cf. H. B. Davis, *Nationalism and Socialism* (New York: Monthly Review, 1967), chaps. 4 and 5.

French nationalism. In England, not only did the Social Democratic Federation, founded by H. M. Hyndman, defend England's colonial policy but Hyndman became such an ardent advocate of British naval supremacy that he was finally expelled from the Federation. In Italy Antonio Labriola supported Italy's expansionist policies in the Mediterranean, and the most radical of the syndicalists supported the Libyan War of 1911-1912.

Nonetheless, the most vociferous of the radicals continued to advocate an uncompromising internationalism. In 1903 Lenin insisted that "class antagonisms" had relegated "national questions far into the background"—that Marxism was committed to "struggle against any and every appearance of nationalism among the working masses."[54] At about the same time Mussolini was insisting that the logic of class obligations required that the proletariat "reject the Fatherland." He contended that "the proletariat must never again spill its precious blood for the Moloch of patriotism. . . . The national flag is for us a rag to be planted on the dunghill. There are only two nations in the world: that of the exploited and the other of the exploiters."[55]

The Second International met regularly to announce its opposition to international war; it announced "revolutionary resistance" to war and advocated a variety of antiwar strategies ranging from the withholding of war credits through parliamentary maneuver to a general strike on the occasion of a declaration of war.

Clearly, the "nationality question" was an unresolved problem for theoretical Marxism. Classical Marxism left nothing that could be seriously advanced as a "theory" of nationality. Horace Davis (who is by no means unsympathetic to Marx's efforts) has maintained that "it is not even clear that Marx intended any theory of the nation at all. . . .

[54] Lenin, "The National Question in our Program," *Collected Works*, vi, 459f.; Davis, *Nationalism and Socialism*, p. 199.

[55] Mussolini, "L'attuale momento politico e partiti politici in Italia," and "Il contradditorio di Voltre," in *Opera*, iii, 288, 137.

Before modern Marxism could cope seriously with the problem of nationalism, it had to rework this part of Marx's theory completely."[56]

In 1907 Otto Bauer admitted that the question of nationalism was of critical importance for socialism. His *Die Nationalitaetenfrage und die Sozialdemokratie*[57] was the first systematic attempt to deal with the issues of nationalism in a responsible and Marxist fashion. The volume generated an acrimonious response, which continued until the outbreak of the First World War and beyond. Kautsky, for example, objected to Bauer's emphasis on nationalism as a relatively independent determinant in international affairs and insisted upon the efficacy of the "international impulse" among the proletarian masses.[58] Joseph Stalin and V. I. Lenin, in turn, both resisted Bauer's account, indicating that there was implicit in his analysis a suggestion that national communities were interclass associations with proletarians and bourgeoisie sharing common features of a "national character." As early as 1904 Stalin had insisted upon a consistently international organization of the working class, emphasizing the destruction of national distinctions "and the amalgamation of the workers irrespective of nationality in united proletarian organizations."[59]

The First World War intruded into these deliberations. Under its impact classical Marxism shattered into two mass-mobilizing revolutionary movements that were to dominate the remainder of the twentieth century: Fascism on the one hand and Bolshevism on the other.

[56] Davis, *Nationalism and Socialism*, pp. 7, 9.

[57] O. Bauer, *Die Nationalitaetenfrage und die Sozialdemokratie* (Vienna: Ignaz Brand, 1907).

[58] K. Kautsky, "Nationalität und Internationalität," *Neue Zeit*, xxvi Supplement, Bd. 1 (January 18, 1908), p. 35.

[59] Cf. Bauer, *Die Nationalitätenfrage*, p. 4, n. 1; cf. M. D. Kammari, *The Development by J. V. Stalin of the Marxist-Leninist Theory of the National Question* (Moscow: Foreign Languages, 1951), p. 10.

THE BOLSHEVIK SOLUTION[60]

Lenin, as we have suggested, had early opted for an elitist interpretation of classical Marxism. Until the turn of the century he had clearly subscribed to what was then the orthodox interpretation. He conceived political developments to be the by-product of processes fundamental to society. He conceived revolutionary consciousness to be a function of the maturation of economic forces. By the turn of the century, however, he had significantly modified his position and argued that the proletariat, left to its own devices, would remain forever venal, dedicated to its immediate rather than its ultimate economic interests—to reformism in its meanest form rather than social revolution. Although he regularly waxed eloquent about the proletariat, it was quite clear that he never expected it, as a class, to develop the consciousness requisite to the revolution of the twentieth century. Revolutionary consciousness could only be brought to the proletariat through the agency of an exiguous minority of declassed bourgeois intellectuals.[61] These declassed revolutionary leaders were self-selected and dedicated men, dominated by a vision of the future which licensed their leadership.

Lenin's reinterpretation of Marxism was resisted by a variety of knowledgeable Marxists including such intransigent revolutionaries as Rosa Luxemburg.[62] Lenin, nonetheless, persisted and continued to identify himself as a Marxist. His strategy was to insist, even though his position was clearly a minoritarian posture within the ranks of official

[60] I have provided only minimum documentation for this section. Documentation can be found in Gregor, *A Survey of Marxism*, chap. 6, and *Contemporary Radical Ideologies*, chap. 3. There are a number of good accounts of Lenin's ideological development; cf. A. G. Meyer, *Leninism* (New York: Praeger, 1962), and A. B. Ulam, *Lenin and the Bolsheviks* (London: Secker & Warburg, 1966).

[61] Cf. J. E. Connor's introduction to *Lenin: On Politics and Revolution* (New York: Pegasus, 1968), pp. xi-xxvii.

[62] Vide R. Luxemburg, *The Russian Revolution and Leninism or Marxism*.

socialism, that his was the *only* legitimate Marxist interpretation of revolution.

With the advent of the First World War Lenin had to face a still more urgent issue: the problem of proletarian nationalism. The war revealed the masses of the proletariat opting for international conflict rather than evincing international working class solidarity. At first Lenin refused to acknowledge what was evident fact; but soon he was compelled to come to grips with the issue.

Unlike Mussolini, Lenin resolved the problem of proletarian nationalism by denying that the proletariat was nationalistic. He interpreted proletarian defections as a surface manifestation of a special form of working class corruption —the seductive influence of a small coterie of "aristocrats of labor," false leaders of the proletariat who self-served the special interests of monopoly capital in the era of imperialism. What Lenin did was to "creatively develop" classical Marxism in the effort to explain the anomaly of proletarian nationalism. The result was the Leninist theory of imperialism.

The fact is that a "theory of imperialism" is not to be found in the works of either Marx or Engels. This is not to say that various threads of Marx's arguments could not be employed to fashion a conception of imperialism relevant to the international politics of Lenin's time. The events that attended the First World War compelled Lenin to just such a task.

The notion that capitalism was inherently dynamic and expansive was explicit in Marx's account. Recurrent innovation generated increments in production that produced inventory surpluses that capitalism sought to reduce by acquiring market supplements throughout the world. This was quite clear to Marx, who recognized that, while India had been acquired in the eighteenth century and had been a source of raw materials and simple tribute, it had gradually become a market supplement for industrial products. The countries that had attained an advanced level of industrial development found themselves compelled to exploit underdeveloped countries as sources of supply and/or as market adjuncts to the internal markets already available to capitalism. Merchant capitalism had exploited underdeveloped portions of the globe as a source of precious metals in a process of "primitive capitalist accumulation" upon which industrial development was based. Industrial capital exploited the same areas in the effort to reduce its inventories and thereby to maintain enhanced profit levels.

Marx had further argued that the high organic composition that characterized advanced capitalism, the anarchic competition between producers and the uneven development of enterprise, gradually produced vast accumulations of capital, monopoly in production, and a concentration of investment capital which ultimately sought investment opportunities abroad.

Marx had intended to develop his economic theories in a volume devoted specifically to the world system. He never completed that work, and what was left to the Marxism of the twentieth century were the elements of an analysis that might be elaborated into an explanatory and predictive theory of imperialism. There is, as a consequence, no "orthodox," or "authoritative" Marxist theory of imperialism. There is a variety of interpretations based on Marxist elements which have been advanced by a variety of authors.[63]

Curiously enough one of the first efforts to develop a theory of imperialism was that delivered by J. A. Hobson in *Imperialism: A Study*, first published in 1902, which influenced both socialist and nonsocialist currents of thought. Hobson was not a Marxist—Lenin identified him as a "bourgeois social reformer"—and yet he was to provide the impetus for a "Marxist" theory of imperialism.[64] For Hobson the motive force of imperialism originated in the necessity

[63] Cf. T. Kemp, *Theories of Imperialism* (London: Dobson, 1967), p. 23; E. Germain, "The Marxist Theory of Imperialism and its Critics," in *Two Essays on Imperialism* (New York: Young Socialist Alliance, 1967).

[64] B. Semmel, *Imperialism and Social Reform* (London: Doubleday, 1960), pp. 14, 16.

of advanced capitalism to find investment opportunities and market supplements for its enterprise. In the search for investment and market outlets, advanced capitalism marshals its military establishment and exploits preexisting forces of nationalism and collective self-interest. According to Hobson, in an analysis very similar to that of Marx, the productive capacity of capitalist industry tended to outstrip the capacity of the internal market to absorb it profitably and more capital accumulated than could find remunerative investment within the national community.

Hobson's account is important for our purposes for two principal reasons: (1) Hobson denied that the introduction of capitalist interests in underdeveloped areas of the world would necessarily introduce "civilization" into those regions[65]—an assumption which both Marx and Engels seemed to have entertained until their deaths; and (2) Hobson was convinced that imperialism was capable of harnessing the support of the majority of people in the exploiting nation by trafficking on public sentiments, moral effusions, "masked words," and verbal tricks.[66] In effect, Hobson not only morally condemned imperialism (something Marx had already done), but he denied that the "civilized" powers, the industrialized nations, did, in fact, further the economic development of the colonized territories. Furthermore, Hobson made it clear that the entire population of the exploiting power, irrespective of class origin and social status, might consciously or unconsciously serve the interests of imperialism. The masses of the most advanced nations on earth might be moved, by suasive language and political manipulation, to serve the interests of an economically dominant minority.

Rosa Luxemburg's *The Accumulation of Capital,* which appeared in 1913, shared many features with Hobson's analysis. Taking her point of departure from Marx's analysis of expanding capitalist reproduction in the posthumously pub-

[65] Cf. J. A. Hobson, *Imperialism: A Study* (Ann Arbor: University of Michigan, 1967), part II, chap. 4.

[66] *Ibid.,* part II, chap. 3.

lished second volume of *Kapital*, Luxemburg insisted that capitalism was inherently incapable of "monetizing" its surplus value, i.e. finding effective demand for its commodity production, without extending itself outside the confines of capitalism itself.[67] The fundamental problem that dogs the "aggregate capitalist" (as distinct from the individual entrepreneur) is the search for effective purchasers for his steadily increasing productivity. In this she was developing a central theme already prominent in the work of Marx himself: the "fundamental contradiction" of industrial capitalism arises out of capitalism's intrinsic dynamic properties. Capitalism must constantly expand its commodity production—which requires, in turn, commensurate increases in effective demand. At the same time, capitalism compensates labor only at the level of the necessary means of subsistence. The inevitable result is that capitalism cannot profitably empty its inventories.[68]

While the specifics of Luxemburg's analysis need not detain us, it is important to note that she focused on an aspect of the politics of imperialism that was to become increasingly significant in the mass-mobilizing strategies employed by revolutionary Marxist parties. Luxemburg indicated that capitalism, as it had matured after Marx's death, had developed features which Marx could not have anticipated. One of those features, to which she referred at the conclusion of her analysis, was capitalism's control of "a press whose function is to mould so-called 'public opinion.' . . . All other attempts to expand markets and set up operational bases for capital largely depend on historical, social and political factors beyond the control of capital, whereas production for militarism represents a province whose regular and progressive expansion seems primarily determined by capital

[67] R. Luxemburg, *The Accumulation of Capital*, tr. A. F. Schwarzchild (London: Routledge and Kegan Paul, 1951), pp. 131, 133, 143, 145.

[68] Cf. Luxemburg's quote from Marx's *Theorien über den Mehrwert*, in *ibid.*, p. 218, n. 4.

itself. . . . Capitalism is the first mode of production with the weapon of propaganda . . . ."[69]

Luxemburg repeated a theme that was prominent in Hobson's work and which implicitly conflicted with Marx's conception of the increasing political maturity of the proletariat under the advanced conditions of capitalism: capitalism was capable, by careful manipulation of the media of information, of inculcating a "bourgeois consciousness" in the proletariat. Luxemburg clearly conceived the induced "false consciousness" as falling away under the impact of a "string of political and social disasters and convulsions, and . . . punctuated by periodical economic catastrophes or crises." Under the impact of such catastrophes, the "true consciousness" of the revolutionary proletariat would be restored. Luxemburg, in effect, attempted to retain the vision of a necessary revolution, predicated on the inevitable catastrophe of capitalism as a mode of production. Important for our purposes is the recognition that the proletariat could be seduced from its historic mission, at least for significant periods of time, by controlled propaganda and capitalist blandishments. The conviction, conjoined with Lenin's elitism, produced a fateful compound: Bolshevism.

When Lenin undertook his analysis of imperialism in 1916 he had the antecedent analyses of Hobson, Hilferding, Luxemburg, and Nikolai Bukharin at his disposal. He used their accounts not only to explain to his own satisfaction some of the contemporary features of capitalism, but to account for the massive defection of the working class from proletarian internationalism.

The specifics of Lenin's account are not here our principal concern. What is of concern is Lenin's analysis of the role of "bribed labor leaders and the upper stratum of the labor aristocracy" who "live in more or less petty-bourgeois conditions of life" and become the "principal social . . . prop of the bourgeoisie." They constitute the "real agents of the

69 *Ibid.*, pp. 466, 467.

bourgeoisie in the labor movement, the labor lieutenants of the capitalist class, real channels of reformism and chauvinism. . . . Not the slightest progress," Lenin insisted, "can be made toward the solution of the practical problems of the Communist movement and of the impending social revolution unless the economic roots of this phenomenon are understood and unless its political and sociological significance is appreciated."[70]

Lenin maintained that imperialism provided advanced capitalism, the industrial system enjoyed by a minority of "world marauder nations," with "super-profits" which permitted the bourgeoisie to suborn a thin stratum of the working class. This stratum, a labor aristocracy (to whose existence Engels had already alluded), led the working class into a "wholesale betrayal of socialism." It was this "aristocracy," this "social prop of the bourgeoisie," that had provoked the proletarian nationalism that found expression in the war hysteria of 1914. Imperialism permitted capitalist enterprise to maintain wages and living standards at a generally higher level than would have been the case without the adjuncts supplied by dependent areas. Moreover, these material concerns were supplemented by "ideological currents"—nationalism, racism, and political reaction—purveyed by the suborned labor leaders.

Lenin had, by the turn of the century, seriously questioned the assumption that the proletariat would automatically develop a rational awareness of its historic class interests, a revolutionary consciousness that was a reflex of its economic conditions. Lenin had argued that the proletariat could not develop "an independent ideology" and that what the revolution required was a vanguard party, an exiguous minority of men, capable of distinguishing the ultimate interests of the masses from those specific sets of interests of local and contingent character.

Once Lenin had opted for such an interpretation of revolutionary mobilization and organization, it became increas-

[70] V. I. Lenin, *Imperialism: The Highest Stage of Capitalism* (New York: International, 1939), pp. 12ff.

ingly evident that revolution could be made in underdeveloped countries embarrassed by a lack of proletarians. Having identified the ultimate interests of the proletariat, the class of the future, the *revolutionary elite*, could *mobilize masses, of whatever class provenience*, to the standards of the "socialist revolution," even if that revolution was in a backward country. At first Lenin characterized such revolutions as "completing the tasks of the industrial bourgeoisie" in the effort to accommodate them in the schema inherited from classical Marxism. He expected such revolutions to "spark" the conflagrations of revolution in the advanced industrial nations, so that "socialism" would inherit the industrial base which Marx and Engels insisted would be necessary for the effective attainment of human "emancipation." The classical Marxist strictures about the consequences of inheriting a restricted productive base were too fresh in his mind to permit Lenin to argue that any revolution in an underdeveloped country could lead to any form of "socialism" that would eliminate class differences and provide for each "according to his needs."

What is significant for our purposes is Lenin's recognition that mass mobilization required tapping responses which were not simply the spontaneous reflexes of economic processes. The revolutionary elite must "instill" revolutionary sentiment in the masses (now no longer the proletariat alone)—all, of course, in the name of the world historical proletariat. But by this time the expression "proletariat" refers to a quasi-Hegelian category, no longer to an economic class. The "proletariat" lives in the inner recesses of the consciousness of the revolutionary elite—the declassed bourgeois intellectuals who foresee the future. They alone speak to the ultimate interests of the proletariat, an interest which the proletariat in the advanced countries cannot appreciate and which the masses of the underdeveloped countries are as yet unprepared to recognize.

What resulted from these modifications of classical Marxism is now history. As long as Lenin, in his *State and Revolution*, imagined that the socialist revolution was on the immediate agenda, he spoke of everyone employed at "work-ingmen's wages," he spoke of referendum and recall, of universal suffrage, of workers' ownership and management. When Stalin opted, after the death of Lenin, to "build socialism in one country," it became obvious that such strategies could not conceivably be entertained. The attacks on the "bourgeoisie" and the "bureaucracy" ceased, and almost the entire "bureaucratic bourgeoisie" was transferred as a strategic functional elite into the "socialist system" with wages sometimes twenty times that of "simple workingmen's wages."[71] Notions of referendum and recall were totally abandoned; a parody of universal suffrage was introduced, with all effective control passing not only out of the hands of the "people" but out of the hands of the Communist Party itself, into the control of the "exceptional leader," the "universal genius," Joseph Stalin. Labor unions and associations of peasants ceased to be agencies for the defense of working class interests and became state agencies for the implementation of state policies. The principal preoccupation of the entire tutelary, enterprisory and control agencies of the state turned on the accumulation and allocation of resources, both human and natural, in the service of increased production and the defense of "socialism" against external and internal enemies. Ultimately the cry became the defense of the socialist *nation* against capitalist *nations*, and "Mother Russia" began to figure more and more prominently in the accounts of "proletarian" responsibility.

Commencing with the period 1921 through 1925 characterized as that of "reconstruction," while Lenin was still alive, the propaganda emphasis upon national symbols became increasingly insistent. Condensed language, political symbolism, increasingly exploited national sentiments. After the defeat of Trotsky, the commitment to the development of "socialism in one country" reinforced the Bolshevik disposition to use nationalist strategies in mobilizing the

[71] Cf. J. R. Azrael, *Managerial Power and Soviet Politics* (Cambridge: Harvard, 1966).

masses. By 1934, the Red Army was no longer swearing allegiance to the "international proletariat" but to the "Socialist Fatherland." At the same time the Soviet Union began to be regularly characterized as "our Great Fatherland." By 1936, references to the population of the Soviet Union were made in terms of "the working people" and the "whole working people" rather than to distinguishable classes and strata —signaling an effort on the part of the unitary party to produce a single-minded, single-purposed community in the service of national development. By 1937 "faithfulness to the Fatherland" had become a special virtue in the Soviet Union.

The features of "socialist" nationalism became increasingly evident up to, and through, the "Great Patriotic War" of 1939-1945. The population of Soviet Russia became the "free, powerful, talented Soviet people, the people of heroes, the people of creators." The blandishments, the collective flattery, and the mobilizing appeals were directed toward a politically defined population, the "people," the common denominator of all nationalisms—rather than to any class or productive category.[72]

In effect, what had transpired in the Soviet Union was a further, and rapid, involution of the modified classical Marxism that Lenin had bequeathed. Stalin opted to create a nationalistic and developmental dictatorship in a marginally developed country, employing the inherited rationale of an internationalistic revolutionary movement which had originally proccupied itself all but exclusively with the advanced capitalist countries. Stalin's accomplishment was not consummated without the massive resistance on the part of the Bolshevik cadre that had led the forces of revolution in 1917. In the course of accomplishing his purpose Stalin sacrificed almost every member of Lenin's Bolshevik leadership—and decimated the Communist Party itself in the process.

To accomplish the task he set for himself, Stalin was com-

---

[72] Cf. S. Yakobson and H. D. Lasswell, "Trend: May Day Slogans in Soviet Russia," in H. D. Lasswell et al., *Language of Politics* (Cambridge, Mass.: MIT, 1966), pp. 233-97.

pelled to create an imposing state machinery, a hierarchically organized and bureaucratically controlled apparatus charged with the enterprisory, tutelary, and pedagogical responsibilities that were the functional analogues of those assumed by the Fascist state. The structural similarities shared by the Fascist and Stalinist states did not escape the attention of Marxists and non-Marxists alike. Among the Trotskyites the phenomenon of "non-Marxist bureaucratic collectivism" was seen represented in the state system of both Mussolini's Italy and Stalin's Russia. Trotsky's acknowledgment of the "deadly parallels" displayed by Fascism and Stalinism either found expression in or reflected the analysis of an Italian Marxist, Bruno Rizzi. In two books, *Dove va l'U.R.S.S.?* and *La Bureaucratisation du Monde*, Rizzi catalogued the functional equivalency of the Fascist and the Soviet political systems.[73]

Rizzi argued that developments after the First World War had revealed a political system unanticipated by classical Marxism: a "bureaucratic collectivism" that found expression in the "socialism" of the Soviet Union and the "workers' state" of Fascist Italy.[74] This judgment was either echoed or anticipated by a number of political commentators, historians, and sociologists, Fascist and non-Fascist, Marxist and non-Marxist alike.[75] By 1938 Mussolini could confidently assert that, "in the face of the total collapse of the system [bequeathed] by Lenin, Stalin has covertly transformed himself into a Fascist."[76] Years later, Rizzi as a Trotskyite Marxist, lamented, "that which Fascism consciously sought, we involuntarily constructed."[77]

By the time the Bolshevik revolution matured into a viable political system, classical Marxism had been transformed into a legitimizing rationale for a developmental and autar-

[73] B. Rizzi, *Dove va l'U.R.S.S.?* (Milan: La Prora, 1938), and *La Bureaucratisation du Monde* (Paris: Rivière, 1939).

[74] B. Rizzi, *La lezione dello Stalinismo* (Rome: Opere nuove, 1962).

[75] Gregor, *Ideology of Fascism*, pp. 332f., 345ff.

[76] Mussolini, "Atto quinto finora," *Opera*, xxix, p. 63.

[77] Rizzi, *Lezione*, p. 38.

chic nationalism, energized by a self-selected and self-per-
petuating leadership that wielded the complex apparatus of
a bureaucratic state in the service of human and natural
resource mobilization, allocation, and control. Lenin's conception of imperialism had licensed revolution in underdeveloped portions of the globe; his recognition that the
proletariat of the advanced nations could be suborned by
material advantage and propaganda supplied the rationale
for conceiving the world divided into "capitalist nations"
and "socialist nations"—the functional analogue, as we shall
argue, of Fascism's distinction between "plutocratic" and
"proletarian" nations. Lenin's concept of the "vanguard
party" shared the species traits of Mussolini's "vanguard
elite"; and Lenin's "democratic centrism" had little to distinguish it from Mussolini's "organized, centralized and authoritarian democracy." Lenin had taken a crucial step in di-
vorcing the "socialist" revolution from the class conscious
proletariat and in making the vanguard party the necessary
and nonsubstitutable variable in the complex of factors productive of revolution. The party assumed the responsibility
of mobilizing the "working masses" and the "people" in the
service of the "proletarian" revolution. In an underdeveloped
country notable in its signal lack of proletarians, Lenin led
a party of declassed intellectuals on a revolutionary adventure that ultimately culminated in a developmental, autarchic, hierarchically controlled dictatorship of an exiguous
minority—who invoked, ultimately, all the energy of the
Russian *people*, the peasantry, the bourgeois intelligentsia,
the urban working class—and domesticated the established
church, strategic and functional elites, and the military. The
Leninism of Lenin and Stalin was not simply an exploitation
of the vagueness, ambiguity, and incompleteness of classical
Marxism; it was a conscious or unconscious adaptation of a
political ideology fashioned to provide the rationale for revolution in industrially advanced economies to the demands
of a developmental dictatorship in a marginally developed
economy.

Similar adaptations are evident in the "communism" of

underdeveloped countries. Little of classical Marxism's theoretical structure is suitable to the clear purpose of such contemporary "Marxist" parties. Classical Marxism has been transformed from a "proletarian" and libertarian into a modernizing and authoritarian movement. In the course of this transformation the transmogrified Marxism of Stalin created the functional analogue of the Fascist state: (1) the imposition of an official and specific ideology and an attendant official art, philosophy, literature, and science; (2) the dominance of a unitary and hierarchically organized political party, (3) the ultimate and decisive control by a charismatic or pseudocharismatic leader possessed of "universal genius" and/or "infallible intuition," (4) bureaucratic control over the economy, the media of communication, and the instruments of control and coercion, (5) an infrastructure of associations, youth groups, communes, cooperatives, nurseries, women's clubs, and class and category agencies that act as transmission belts for official policy, and (6) the consequent extensive erosion of private life.

It now seems relatively clear that classical Marxism went into eclipse with the advent of the First World War. It has lived a shadow existence in the sectarian and devotional Marxist parties of the industrially advanced Western nations. Where mass-mobilizing, "revolutionary Marxists" have come to power, and remained in power sufficiently long to create a viable political system, what they have generally succeeded in creating is a reasonable analogue of the Fascist state.

The Eclipse of Classical Marxism

Karl Marx delivered a mature ideology to his contemporaries. For the purposes of this discussion a mature ideology is a belief system composed minimally of (1) a partially standardized and formalized social science theory that has explanatory and predictive pretensions, and (2) a reasonably specific collection of argued normative commitments. These constituents, conjointly entertained, permit the issuance of proscriptions, prescriptions, and recommendations. A congruent ideology is one in which the normative components remain consonant with the descriptive and logical elements that constitute the social science component of the ideology. What this means, for the sake of our discussion, is that a normative commitment to "equality" would not be "consonant" with a social science commitment to the descriptive inequality of men—unless the ideologist is prepared to supplement the discussion with an auxiliary argument that would characterize the equality he advocates as "ethical," "moral," "metaphysical," or what have you, i.e. that the equality he seeks is specifically nondescriptive.

The relevance this has for the transformation of classical Marxism into a rationale for a totalitarian state is reasonably apparent. Marx advocated freedom and individual fulfillment as normative ideals. He conceived the "dictatorship of the proletariat" as one in which universal suffrage, referendum and recall, and a restricted mandate forever protected a political constituency from the threat of hierarchical investiture. Marx clearly imagined that such political institutions would be the by-product of the sophistication of the "vast majority" of men having become class conscious proletarians. The creation of this vast majority of proletarians would be the responsibility of the "working out of the laws of capitalist society." If the laws fail to "work out"—if Marxist theoreticians introduce modifications of those putative laws—the congruence of the ideology is threatened. Because of the vagueness, ambiguity, and incompleteness of Marx's social theories, Marxists such as Lenin and Mussolini introduced extensive modifications into the set of propositions understood to constitute the content of "Marxist" theory. Both modified the concept of the relationship between "objective" and "subjective" conditions, that is to say that, while classical Marxism consistently held that class consciousness was somehow the necessary consequence of class conditions, both Lenin and Mussolini were explicitly to deny the contention. Both Lenin and Mussolini insisted that class consciousness could only result as a consequence of the intercession of a vanguard elite. Classical Marxism insisted that the socialist revolution must be "universal," that any system predicated on a restricted productive base must necessarily produce a class-riven society. Both Stalin and Mussolini maintained that revolution can come to underdeveloped economies that were to remain, for the foreseeable future, national in character.

The insinuation of such substantive changes into the body of classical Marxism created the internal tensions between normative commitment and factual judgment that could be characterized as *prima facie* incongruity. Marx had descriptively characterized freedom and fulfillment in terms, at least, of majoritarian rule, the disappearance of the repressive apparatus of the state, the voluntary association of productive communes, increased leisure time for productive workers, and the transcendence of national, ethnic, and racial identifications. The society Stalin produced displayed none of these features—and yet Stalin insisted on his Marxist integrity.

The fact is that classical Marxism had failed to anticipate those very developments that were to characterize the twentieth century. For this reason contemporary Marxists speak of "creative developments" in "Marxist" theory—to better respond to the challenges of our time. Lenin, Stalin, and, as we shall suggest, Mao and Castro have undertaken similar, and as extensive, "creative developments." Each such "development" is evidence of a failure in prediction, and each "development" is evidence of the porosity of the original theory. But if normative prescription is the logical consequence of conjointly holding a specific set of normative and social science propositions to be true, any change in the constituents of the set must necessarily produce a change in the prescriptions held. If the descriptive propositions held to be true are modified, then ideological congruence can be preserved by redefining some of the normative terms. What was once conceived to be descriptive of "freedom" becomes now "anarcho-syndicalist" and "anarchistic" "disorders." What was once conceived as "fulfillment" becomes "counterrevolutionary." The vocabulary remains relatively constant but the cognitive content and normative implications are transmogrified.

Soviet Marxists continue to pay ritual obeisance to the theoretical system of classical Marxism. *Kapital* is published and republished; and yet it does not influence decision making with respect to economic or political policy. Cost accounting, industrial planning and management, wage determination and price fixing are undertaken just as though Marx had never written a word. Nor can it be said that the extensively formalized theory found in *Kapital* influences internal political behavior or foreign policy deliberations in the Soviet Union. *Kapital*, the entire fabric of classical Marxism, has become a sort of legitimizing mythology for Soviet leaders. Its function is no longer cognitive—to explain and predict—to afford leverage on strategy and tactics for a revolutionary proletarian party. Its function is to legitimize one-party rule. As such, the truth or falsity of its constituent parts taken severally or collectively is of little importance.

Contemporary "Marxist" revolutionaries no longer read those works which Marx conceived as representing his system in its most mature form. While Lenin could still insist that it was *Kapital* that made Marxism a science, Castro can candidly admit that he has read no more than some one or two hundred pages of the thousands of pages in *Kapital*. It is doubtful if Mao Tse-tung has read *any* of *Kapital*; certainly there is little definitive evidence in his writings of any such exposure.

Mussolini early abandoned the reading of the works of classical Marxism in his effort to construct a revolutionary, mass-mobilizing party and to direct the internal and external affairs of state. He jettisoned classical Marxism and generated his own rationale and his own legitimizing myths. His was an explicit rationale and a charter myth for a totalitarian state. That Stalin should have created the analogue of that state is not, in itself, singular. That he should have employed Marxism as its rationale is. That much of what passes as "radical" thought in our own time ventilates

137

themes, emphases, and arguments more akin to those found in Fascism than any to be found in the corpus of classical Marxism is more unusual still.

Before a plausible review of such developments can be undertaken, a brief and necessarily schematic characterization of the "Fascist persuasion" must be attempted. That will be the task of the next chapter.

CHAPTER FIVE

The Fascist Persuasion:
Prototypic New Radicalism

PARADIGMATIC Fascism, the Fascism of Benito Mussolini, is perhaps the least understood political movement of the twentieth century. Ranging from Benedetto Croce's rather quaint assessment of Fascism as a peculiar "moral disease," through the orthodox Marxist characterization of Fascism as the "terroristic tool of finance capital," to the more sophisticated analyses suggested by contemporary social and political science, interpretations of Fascism are often mutually exclusive, almost always tendentious, and rarely intellectually satisfying.[1] It is doubtful whether an entirely satisfying account will be forthcoming in the immediate future. Most of our present interpretations, for one thing, rest on severely circumscribed data. Much of the archival material that might reveal relationships between labor organizations, industrial elites, political influentials, and the Fascist Party hierarchy either has been destroyed or is inaccessible. Much of the data we have from official sources during the Fascist period are of doubtful value. Short of some of the contemporary work of Renzo De Felice, we do not even have an adequate descriptive record of the entire political phenomenon.[2]

[1] Cf. B. Croce, *Per la nuova vita dell'Italia* (Naples: Ricciardi, 1944), pp. 13-20, 50-57; J. M. Cammett, "Communist Theories of Fascism, 1920-1935," *Science and Society, 31,* 2 (Spring, 1967); W. W. Rostow, *The Stages of Economic Development* (New York: Cambridge, 1960), *Politics and the Stages of Economic Growth* (Cambridge: Cambridge University, 1971); A.F.K. Organski, *The Stages of Political Development* (New York: Knopf, 1967); L. Garruccio, *L'industrializzazione tra nazionalismo e rivoluzione* (Bologna: Mulino, 1969).

[2] R. De Felice, *Mussolini il rivoluzionario* (Turin: Einaudi, 1965); *Mussolini il fascista* (Turin: Einaudi, 1966), Vol. 1; *Mussolini il*

Fascism was, of course, the product of a number of factors—most of which fall outside our purview. Our attention, here, will focus on the attempt on the part of a number of intransigent Italian radicals to resolve the urgent theoretical and practical problems they had inherited from classical Marxism—an attempt in which Benito Mussolini participated and which, in significant measure, produced the rationale of Fascism.

We have suggested that the two most urgent problems Marx and Engels left to their heirs were (1) the matter of the nonrevolutionary proletariat, and (2) the entire issue of nationalism and its role in the revolutionary mobilization of men. Both problems turned on one or more critical concerns unanticipated or unresolved in the relatively well-standardized theoretical system developed by Marx.

The men who were to become the ideologues of Fascism, from Mussolini to any number of lesser lights, consciously responded to just those problems. As we shall indicate, Mussolini was schooled among syndicalists and Marxists to whom the problems of mass motivation and nationalism were urgent practical, strategic, and ultimately theoretical problems. Mussolini, under the influence of the syndicalists, early opted for an interpretation of mass mobilization and organization that conceived men, collectively, as mobilized by other than exclusively rational economic concerns. Long before he was alienated from the official socialism of his time, Mussolini attempted to resolve the tactical, strategic, and theoretical problems he, as a revolutionary, had inherited from classical Marxism. After the turn of the century those problems were familiar to all thinking Marxists. Mussolini's response to them was a response common to any number of other radicals of his time. Revolutionary syndicalists began to assume postures that distinguished them from more orthodox Marxists. Those postures were to be shared not only by the revolutionary nationalism that began to organize itself in Italy during the first decade of this

fascista (Turin: Einaudi, 1968), Vol. 2; and *Le interpretazioni del fascismo* (Bari: Laterza, 1969).

century, but ultimately by Fascism as well. All became concerned with mobilizing men to revolutionary purpose.

It was Fascism's early preoccupation with the psychosocial factors involved in the process—its conceptions of mass motivation and organization—that made it possible for the earliest Fascism to make common cause with the most radical youth movement of the period: F. T. Marinetti's Futurists. That Fascism could accommodate the Futurists is extremely interesting for a number of reasons. First of all it suggests the ease with which mass-mobilizing movements can, to their own ends, effectively exploit youth movements. Second, it was Futurism that provided Fascism with a special political "style." Third, the political style identified with Futurism could be employed only by a political elite that entertained certain convictions about the nonrationality of mass man, about the historic responsibility of a self-selected cadre of professional revolutionaries and about the political opportunities that awaited a hierarchically organized mass movement.

Classical Marxism seemed unable to provide a competent explanation for the failure of the proletariat to discharge its revolutionary obligation. A number of revolutionary Marxists, including Georges Sorel and Roberto Michels, had begun to insist that Marxism would have to be supplemented with more adequate assessments of human motivation and organization if the problems of the nonrevolutionary proletariat and, ultimately, the influence of nationalism on the political mobilization of men were to be satisfactorily managed.

The turn of the century found Marxists in all the major European countries attempting to resolve the problems inherited from Marx and Engels. In Italy, Marxists and revolutionary syndicalists became immersed in the works of Vilfredo Pareto, Gaetano Mosca, and Gustave Le Bon. They sought generalizations about men in society—generalizations, for instance, addressed to the influence of ideas and "charismatic leaders" upon the "masses." They sought answers that they had not found in the works of Marx and

Engels. Gradually, the assimilation of propositions culled from the psychological and sociological literature of the period helped transform Italian radicalism. Italian radicalism began to take on a political character unknown to classical Marxism and unknown to the orthodox Marxism of the first decade of the twentieth century.

The collection of propositions that was to alter the complexion of Italian radicalism derived from a variety of sources. But more important than the sources was the impact effected by their assimilation. The recognition that men, the proletariat no less than any other, were subject to influences that could only be characterized as nonrational at one and the same time explained the absence of a revolutionary proletariat and suggested a mass-mobilizing strategy that might create revolutionary dispositions. During this period, any number of Marxists began to conceive revolution (given suitable conditions) to be, in significant measure, the product of a special style in mass mobilization. As early as 1902 Mussolini was to be counted among them. Thus, more than a decade before the organization of the first Fascist squads, Mussolini had assimilated convictions that made the adoption of a singular political style a real possibility. It was the *content* of what was to become Fascist convictions that made the adoption of Futurist *style* a high order probability.

THE ANTICIPATIONS OF FASCISM

Fascism, as a system of thought—as a reasonably coherent collection of convictions about men in association—was in large measure a response to problems left unresolved by classical Marxism. While Fascist commentators never tired of alluding to a general catalogue of "protofascist" ideas available as early as the first years of the nineteenth century, it has become increasingly obvious that the *substance* of Fascist thought derives from relatively specific sociological and philosophical traditions that manifested themselves, largely in response to the system of thought left by Marx and Engels, during the last quarter of the nineteenth century and the first decade of the twentieth. The sociological tradition that provided Fascist ideologues with certain critical conceptual categories, analytic strategies, theoretical and descriptive claims, is that now identified, principally, with Vilfredo Pareto, Gaetano Mosca, and Roberto Michels, all of whom addressed themselves to the problems which afflicted classical Marxism. More specifically, the substance of that sociological tradition surfaced in the thought of Georges Sorel, whose writings, as a "critical" and "radical" Marxist, worked a major influence on the principal ideologues of Fascism.

Almost every Fascist account, even the most incompetent, identified Fascist political and social ideas with the sociological tradition which included Pareto, Mosca, and Sorel.[3] Enzio Maria Olivetti, in one of the first mature statements of Fascist ideology, traced the substantive elements of Fascist doctrine to the "anti-individualist sociological tradition" popular in antebellum Italy—a clear allusion to the tradition with which we are concerned.[4] Perhaps the most convincing way of documenting the impact of the ideas given currency by Pareto, Mosca, and Sorel is to trace something of their influence on the thought of Benito Mussolini, who left, for all intents and purposes, a public record of that impact in a series of articles, pamphlets, and reviews written between 1903 and 1914, while he still identified himself as a revolutionary Marxist.

As early as 1903 (when he was but twenty) Mussolini expressed the conviction that "sentiments are the dynamic motives of human actions," and that one of the cardinal

[3] This is as true for the closing years of the regime as it was at the commencement. Cf. Sergio Panunzio, *Che cos'è il fascismo* (Milan: Alpes, 1924), p. 77; A. C. Puchetti, *Il fascismo scientifico* (Turin: Bocca, 1926); Carlo Costamagna, *Dottrina del fascismo*, 2nd ed. (Turin: Utet, 1940); Sergio Panunzio, *Teoria generale dello stato fascista*, 2nd ed. (Padua: CEDAM, 1939), p. 13, n. 1; Aldo Bertelè, *Aspetti ideologici del fascismo* (Turin: Druetto, 1930), chaps. 2 and 3.

[4] E. M. Olivetti, *Sindacalismo nazionale* (Milan: Monanni, 1927), p. 95.

sentiments moving men to act was a "sentiment of solidarity."[5] Mussolini realized that such a conviction was a scandal among the advocates of a "positivistic" Marxism, for positivists seemed ill-disposed to recognize the historic role of sentiment in the processes that produce social change. Mussolini was to insist, with Pareto, Michels, and Sorel, that revolution involved not only the calculation of the material interests of men and classes but an invocation of sentiment as well. Like Pareto, Michels, and Sorel, Mussolini became convinced that the problem of the nonrevolutionary proletariat was to be resolved by employing a specific mobilizing and organizing strategy.

It is impossible, given the surviving information, to document the precise source of Mussolini's convictions concerning the "sentiment of solidarity" and its role in mass mobilization. We do know that Mussolini had, by 1903, already read Gustave Le Bon's *Psychology of Crowds*, in which group sentiment and the psychological properties of "masses" and "crowds" were utilized to explain collective behaviors. Mussolini indicated that he had been "enormously impressed" by Le Bon's book.[6] We also know that Pareto had also undertaken to explain mass behaviors by employing "sentiment" and a collective disposition toward "solidarity" in his "An Application of Sociological Theories," which appeared in 1901, and in his *Socialist Systems*, which appeared in 1902.[7] Both Le Bon and Pareto were occupied with the explanation of mass behavior—mass mobilization being one of their central concerns. Both analyzed socialism in general and Marxism in particular in this context. Both criticized

[5] B. Mussolini, "Ne l'attesa," in *Opera omnia* (hereafter referred to as *Opera*. Florence: La fenice, 1951), i, 41.

[6] "I have read all the works of Gustave Le Bon and I don't know how many times I have reread the *Psychology of Crowds*. It is a major work to which, even today, I frequently return." Mussolini, "Il progresso e la scienza," *Opera*, xxii, 156; cf. Mussolini, *My Autobiography* (London, Paternoster, 1936), pp. 25, 36.

[7] Cf. V. Pareto, "Un applicazione di teoria sociologiche," translated as *The Rise and Fall of Elites* (Introduction by H. L. Zetterberg. Totowa: Bedminster, 1968).

Marxists for not appreciating the impact of "paralogical" or "sentimental" determinants in the behavior of human groups. Many Marxists were, in fact, raising the same objections. In France and Italy the syndicalists were among the most articulate. It seems clear that Mussolini, still a radical Marxist, had begun to assimilate such analyses and, through the influence of men such as Pareto, Michels, and Sorel, had begun to modify the Marxism to which he was committed in order to accommodate the new insights.

By 1904 Mussolini was addressing himself to a "proletarian elite," a conscious and aggressive minority that was to serve as a vanguard of the revolution. Mussolini was clearly convinced, as were Pareto and Michels, that revolutions are "initiated" by vanguard elites—elites that serve to mobilize the sentiments of masses in the service of the revolution. Elites, Mussolini insisted, by exploiting sentiments of solidarity, marshaled individuals into "communities of consanguinity, of territory, of economic interest and intellectual affinity," to become the motive force of social change. Revolutions become a social reality when individual men can be so mobilized. The young Mussolini did not hesitate to identify such convictions as a "new conception of socialism, one profoundly 'aristocratic.' "[8]

These ideas were shared by any number of radical syndicalists and Marxists with whom Mussolini interacted. The ideas can all be traced to the sociological tradition that included Pareto as one of its principal spokesmen. In October 1904, Mussolini specifically referred to Pareto's *Socialist Systems* as the source of his convictions.[9] In April 1908, he specifically identified Pareto's "theory of elites" as the "most ingenious sociological conception of modern times."[10]

In effect, and by the time he was twenty-five, Mussolini had committed himself to a number of substantive propositions about the nature of man and of men in association. He explicitly rejected the "contractual theory" of society which

[8] Mussolini, "La crisi risolutiva," *Opera*, I, 70.
[9] Mussolini, " 'L'individuel et le social,' " *Opera*, I, 73-75.
[10] Mussolini, "Intermezzo polemico," *Opera*, I, 128.

145

conceived men as individuals coming together to create rationally a rule-governed association. He insisted that men were social by intrinsic disposition and that they interacted in association because that association was sustained by an animating "moral order," articulated by directive elites, and accepted by passive majorities. A minority of men, an elite, was gifted with the capacity to mobilize the "torpid consciousness" of the majority to respond to their "true" interests.[11] Socialists were enjoined to constitute themselves "a vigilant and combative vanguard, in order to compel the masses never to lose sight of their ideal goals."[12]

In 1909 Mussolini reviewed a number of books and pamphlets written by men in the sociological tradition with which we are concerned. One of those books was *Cooperation* by Roberto Michels, who at that time still identified himself as a "revolutionary socialist." Michels, a student of Pareto, Mosca, and Sorel, gave expression to a conviction with which Mussolini had already identified: "modern economic man exists only insofar as he is a member of an aggregate"—a conviction which Mussolini insisted "demolished that individualism which has been now reduced to a theory entertained only by *litterateurs* on holiday." Man, Mussolini held (taking his point of departure from Michels' tract), was a natural denizen of a collective—a collective animated by a sentiment of in-group solidarity and out-group enmity.[13] These were, again, convictions articulated in the sociological tradition of Pareto and Mosca.

It seems reasonably clear that all these ideas had, for Mussolini, significant implications for political conduct. Mussolini maintained: (1) that individuals are creatures of both reason and sentiment and that for purposes of organization both aspects must be accorded their due significance; (2) that to satisfy material and/or sentimental concerns individuals must function as constituent parts of a self-con-

[11] Cf. Mussolini, "L'attuale momento politico," *Opera*, i, 120.
[12] Mussolini, "Al lavoro!" *Opera*, iii, 6.
[13] Mussolini, "Fra libri e riviste," *Opera*, ii, 248f.

146

scious community; (3) that such communities are moved to action by minorities capable of setting into motion "torpid" or "indifferent" masses.

Some of the further, if informal, implications of such notions include a disposition to conceive parliamentary maneuvering or the pursuit of exclusive economic interests as neither the sole nor most important strategies for a revolutionary movement. Both such strategies appeal to pervasive material interests and restricted rational concerns, but fail to tap reservoirs of psychic energy generally characterized as "ideal" or "sentimental." Absent from such political strategies is a technique for creating a "psychological unity that reinforces the will and directs energies"—a sensitive and broad pedagogical and mobilizing task involving not only intellectual cultivation but "paralogical" invocations—what Mussolini was, thereafter, forever to refer to as "myths."[14] Mussolini clearly sought techniques that would "create new personalities, new values, *homines novi*"—results that could not be realized through parliamentary tactics and appeals to exclusively economic interests.[15] A truly competent revolutionary persuasion must be composed of ideal, as well as practical and doctrinal constituents.[16] To mobilize masses in the service of ideal ends, the appeal to episodic, albeit real, interests can never be sufficient. What is required is a sustained recognition that one moral order must intransigently oppose itself to another. Parliamentarianism and economism are tactics suitable to an *intra*systemic struggle; the preparation for revolution requires the girding for *inter*systemic conflict—a conflict between integral communities, total systems in competition. It was within this context that Mussolini republished Sorel's small piece on "The Apology for Violence" in *La Lima* of June 1908.[17]

Mussolini's early objections to parliamentarianism in gen-

---

[14] Cf. Mussolini, " '*La Voce*,' " *Opera*, II, 55.

[15] Mussolini, "La teoria sindacalista," *Opera*, II, 125.

[16] Mussolini, "Socialismo e socialisti," *Opera*, I, 142.

[17] Mussolini, "Per finire," *Opera*, I, 147-49.

eral and socialism's seeming fascination with electioneering[18] were rooted in a sociological tradition that conceived men moved, in substantial part, by paralogical or nonrational sentiments—that conceived viable associations animated, in significant measure, by quasi-religious dispositions of discipline and sacrifice. Only if masses were organized by "resolute and audacious nuclei," capable of inspiring reason with faith, could the revolution, calculated to produce a new breed of man, make its appearance.[19] Mussolini's evident approval of Sorel's work turned on the preoccupation with individual and collective motivation shared by both men. Sorel, Mussolini maintained, was concerned with making political actors out of what would otherwise be historical "onlookers." What Sorel provided, again according to Mussolini's account, was a theory of individual and collective motivation missing from classical Marxism. Sorel made plain that what we speak of today as "grand alternatives" succeed only insofar as they become "animating myths" for the masses. Historic myths are those symbolic and linguistic artifacts that elites, leading responsive masses, employ to reshape political and social commitments. As effective instruments, myths serve to define the moral universe in which men, individually and collectively, must operate. Men, as active moral agents, are necessarily members of an association which shares a sustaining sense of solidarity. Outside that association are out-groups against which in-group solidarity defines and articulates itself. The ultimate test and the ultimate measure of group cohesion and survival potential is the readiness to suffer and employ violence. Violence is a moral therapeutic insofar as it compels the agent prepared to suffer and employ it to make clear his commitments.

Violence, in this context, was not, as it was for classical Marxism, a perhaps necessary evil; it was, in significant respects, a positive good. It defines with precision the char-

[18] Cf. for example, Mussolini, "Il socialismo degli avvocati," *Opera*, III, 122-24, "Vecchiaia," *Opera*, III, 130f.

[19] Mussolini, "La nostra propaganda," *Opera*, III, 26.

acter and scope of the revolutionary's obligations. Violence not only "generates new energies," but "new moral values, new men who approximate in character the heroes of antiquity."[20] Violence becomes an agency of moral perfection for creatures for whom social and political activity is a result of the intersection of material, intellectual, moral, and sentimental concerns. Revolution was no longer conceived of as a spontaneous reflex of the "economic base" of society.

All these convictions—bruited by Mussolini before he was thirty years of age and while he still identified himself as a Marxist attempting to resolve problems of applied revolution—are clearly anticipations of some of the critical substantive constituents of the belief system that was to become Fascism. As convictions, they were in no small measure the consequence of attempting to resolve the problem of the nonrevolutionary dispositions of the proletariat. Like Lenin, Mussolini was to conceive the revolution to be the consequence of the intercession of a self-selected minority of radical leaders organized as the directive elite of a vanguard party. To make revolution, the proletariat required leaders armed with "theoretical consciousness." Without such leadership the proletariat would languish.

Throughout this period, and until 1914, Mussolini associated the mass disposition to identify with some community of solidarity with *class membership*. Mussolini's anti-individualistic and solidaristic convictions were *association specific*. The specific associations to which individuals gave their allegiance were *classes*. Mussolini remained a Marxist all throughout this period and was so recognized by his peers and by the party that had elected him to leadership. Mussolini, like Lenin, had attempted to explain the proletarian indispositon to make revolution—to resolve the problem of the nonrevolutionary proletariat. The common contemporary claim that the young Mussolini was ignorant of Marxist theory is belied by the overwhelming weight of evidence

[20] Mussolini, "Lo sciopero generale e la violenza," *Opera*, II, 168.

available.[21] Mussolini was, in fact, a Marxist, as orthodox as any during the period.

"Orthodoxy," of course, has variable meaning, but it generally refers to a disposition to adhere to a body of doctrine. The less well-defined that doctrine, the wider the range of permissible behavior that can count as "orthodox." "Orthodoxy" was, as a consequence and during the period under consideration, broadly construed. A large number of social theorists during the period who identified themselves as Sorelian "syndicalists" were considered and considered themselves nonetheless "Marxist." In general, they grappled with the same problems and shared the same collection of weighted judgments we have identified in the thought of the young Mussolini. They were just as disposed as he to appeal to Pareto, Mosca, and Michels to support their anti-individualist and elitist convictions. They, like Mussolini, conjoined these convictions with invocations to the "proletariat." They, like he, were anti-clerical, anti-Christian, anti-militaristic, anti-bourgeois, anti-capitalist, anti-statist, and anti-nationalist. They, like he, had identified the principal object of allegiance in the contemporary world as class membership; all their Marxist postures followed this identification by necessary implication.

For Mussolini, throughout this period and until the traumatic crisis of the First World War, the only conceivable association that could claim ultimate allegiance for politically conscious men was *class* membership. Mussolini, during this perod, conceived the associations in intersystemic competition to be *classes*. He spoke, for example, of socialists recognizing "only two nations in the world: that of the exploited and that of the exploiters."[22] His political strategy and tactics, his assumption of moral and social obligations, were a consequence of that supplementary and ancillary identification. He identified the object of his loyalty as an economic association, a class. The church, the state, the

[21] I have reviewed some of the evidence in Gregor, *The Ideology of Fascism*, pp. 95-105.

[22] Mussolini, "Il contradittorio di Voltre," *Opera*, III, 137.

monarchy, and the organized military were all institutions organized in support of his class enemies. The irrepressible conflict he anticipated was explicitly a conflict between classes; the moral violence he advocated was directed against the bourgeoisie organized as a class. Mussolini construed any appeal to interests more general than those of class to be stratagems designed to gull the working class into serving the economic, social, and political interests of the exploiting class.[23] When the syndicalists, Sorel among them, began to identify the nation as a conceivable object of loyalty, Mussolini was quick to condemn them as having betrayed their responsibilities to the proletariat as a class.

In retrospect it is clear that, theoretically speaking, the selection of one rather than another primary association was a *contingent*, rather than a necessary, choice. The convictions which Mussolini harbored in his effort to explain the nonrevolutionary disposition of the proletariat required only the recognition that men were, by nature, members of well-articulated associations struggling for existence and welfare in a highly competitive world. Marxists (of whatever special persuasion) as well as a number of other revolutionaries were all equally well aware of that. Marxists and nationalists, for example, distinguished themselves, not in terms of the analysis of the nature of men in association, but in terms of the associations they selected as worthy of men's primary loyalty. There was nothing in the analysis of man as a group animal, sustained by the influence of group-building elites, that required the selection of *class* as the association of primary allegiance. Marxists, at that time, had opted for class identification because they were convinced that all available evidence indicated that economic associations, identified as "proletarian" and "bourgeois" classes, made up the roster of the principal historic actors in the world. Nationalism was simply rejected as a serious alternative.

Others, however, had come to different conclusions. Dur-

[23] Mussolini, "Nazionalismo," *Opera*, III, 280f.; "L'attuale momento politico e partiti politici in Italia," *Opera*, III, 287f.

151

ing this period in Italy, nationalists had begun to organize themselves politically. The arguments they mounted revealed the same collection of basic substantive commitments entertained by the young Mussolini. The relationship was so clear that as early as 1909 Georges Sorel—so important in the genesis of those social and political beliefs we have associated with the young Mussolini—identified Enrico Corradini, one of the principal founders and theoreticians of Italian Nationalism, as a "remarkably intelligent" man who realized "very well the value" of his own, Sorel's, ideas.[24] Corradini did, in fact, speak (as did Sorel and Pareto) of man as an essentially social animal, a member of an organized and disciplined aggregate of "similars." He spoke of that disposition to associate as the consequence of an "instinct of association," that revealed itself in sustained in-group solidarity and out-group enmity—with groups competing for both material and nonmaterial welfare.[25] Corradini spoke of group-sustaining interests in terms of economic benefits, ethnic provenience, geographic origins, and cultural affinities.[26] The competition that ensued between groups provided occasion for the ultimate test of group viability: intergroup violence. Corradini, like Sorel and Mussolini, understood the test of force as a moral challenge. The readiness to suffer and inflict suffering in the service of the community was the *prima facie* evidence of serious commitment; all other-regarding responsibilities held a place in a descending order of obligations. In war men reveal themselves as conscientious moral agents. Men, under such ultimate challenge, were no longer spectators in the moral universe, but participants. Corradini, like Sorel and Mussolini, conceived of no more compelling test.[27]

Marxists and Nationalists alike thus shared a good deal

[24] As cited, J. Meisel, *The Genesis of Georges Sorel* (Ann Arbor: Wahr, 1951), p. 219.

[25] E. Corradini, *L'ombra della vita* (Naples: Ricciardi, 1908), p. 287.

[26] Cf. Corradini, *Discorsi politici* (Florence: Vallecchi, 1923), pp. 36f., 61ff., 106f., 126.

[27] For a full statement of this collection of commitments, cf. "Il

of common intellectual baggage. The relationships between intellectual spokesmen for these ideas were complex but evident. Among Corradini's immediate associates, for example, was Scipio Sighele, whose volume *La folla delinquente* anticipated the work of Le Bon by several years. Their ideas were so kindred that Sighele insisted that Le Bon had plagiarized. Pareto had, in the course of his *Sistemi*, cited both the work of Sighele and Le Bon, and it is clear that their ideas contributed to Pareto's own account.[28] Any reasonably careful analysis of the complex of ideas found in the works of Pareto, Sorel, Le Bon, Sighele, and Corradini reveals a relatively sustained similarity. By the advent of the First World War, representatives of the sociological tradition of Pareto, Mosca, and Michels, the syndicalist and Marxist persuasion of Sorel, and the nationalist persuasion of Corradini, Sighele, and Alfredo Rocco, were making effortless transit between each other's ideas.[29]

The problem of the nonrevolutionary proletariat, bequeathed to the radicalism of the twentieth century by nineteenth-century Marxism, was resolved in Italy by making recourse to a sociological tradition that conceived men, as social animals, moved by paralogical and sentimental appeals. The tradition produced convictions that were found compatible not only by radical Marxists but by Nationalists and student revolutionaries as well. Out of the effort to address themselves to the problem of mass mobilization and mass organization, a number of Marxists in Italy began to entertain convictions that were to reduce the gap between themselves, nationalists, and student radicals as well. Those convictions were to resurface after the First World War as fundamental to the rationale of Fascism.

Immediately prior to the First World War, there developed in Italy a student movement that was to bequeath to

manifesto di 'Politica,' " in F. Gaeta, ed., *La stampa nazionalista* (Rocca San Casciano: Cappelli, 1965), pp. 9-22.

[28] V. Pareto, *I sistemi socialisti* (Turin: UTET, 1954), pp. 58, 83, 521, 523.

[29] I have provided a more extensive account of the cognitive affinities in Gregor, *Ideology of Fascism*, chap. 2.

Fascism much of what was later to be identified as its "style." It is not necessary here to attempt a rigorous specification of the distinction between style and content. "Style" is used to refer to a constellation of behavioral dispositions —a readiness to respond in a relatively characteristic manner to stimuli, a disposition to assume certain postures, employ certain locutions, and have regular recourse to an identifiable collection of overt strategies in interacting with others.

That there was a more or less specific "Fascist style" seems to be generally accepted among commentators on the Fascist phenomenon. Ernst Nolte, for example, speaks of a Fascist style in terms of "the unshackling of primitive instincts, the denial of reason, the spellbinding of the senses by pageantry and parades," conjoined with a commitment to the " 'leadership principle,' the desire for a 'new world,' the love of power and the dramatic appeal of youth, elite-consciousness and mass influence, revolutionary ardor and veneration of tradition."[30]

Such a collection of traits clearly refers to political style rather than content. Fascists entertained such a style, but also advanced a rationale in its support and characterized their proposed "new world" as coherently as most of their competitors for political power. The political style entertained by Fascism was, by and large, inherited from the Futurists. The relationship between Futurist style and Fascist content was symbiotic; ultimately the two merged into the Fascist persuasion—the union of style and content that constitutes an instructive expression of modern radicalism —a political persuasion that may very well have been prototypic of the new radicalism.

ANTICIPATIONS OF FASCIST STYLE

During the period in which Mussolini was attempting to resolve the problems of mass mobilization and revolutionary

[30] E. Nolte, *The Three Faces of Fascism* (New York: Holt, Rinehart and Winston, 1966), pp. 20, 456.

leadership, a rather improbable student movement collected itself around the equally improbable F. T. Marinetti. The movement led by Marinetti, the Futurist movement, originated with the "Futurist Manifesto," written in 1909. It was originally an avant-garde movement composed of members who characterized themselves as aggressive, audacious, violent, and "under thirty." They were committed to the vehement rejection of the past, and to a rejection of the corrupt present—a rejection of professorial mummery, of museums and archives, of ancient ruins and "art treasures," and of "business as usual." The Futurists exulted in the fact that they were all under thirty years of age; and, should any of them ever reach forty, they advised "younger and more relevant [*piu validi*] men to throw [them] into waste paper receptacles like useless manuscripts!"[31]

The publication of the Futurist *Manifesto* marked the official commencement of a violent youth movement composed all but exclusively of intellectuals, artists, bon vivants, eccentrics, poseurs, and students—almost all from reasonably affluent middle-class families. As for the *Manifesto* itself, it has been characterized as reading like "nothing more than the ravings of a maniac, the incoherent and inconsequential denunciation of tradition by a man who knew neither the significance of culture nor its relation to present day life."[32] It was, in fact, filled with hyperbolic speech, condensed imagery, and unrestricted and unqualified condemnation. In effect, the *Manifesto* was the creature of Marinetti himself.

Marinetti identified himself as a "lunatic" (*un pazzo*), for he held that lunatics alone could serve as a salutary counterweight to the "funereal capitalist and bourgeois rationality" that dominated the Italian peninsula. He was a

[31] F. T. Marinetti, "Fondazione e Manifesto del Futurismo," *Teoria e invenzione futurista* (Verona: Mondadori, 1968), p. 12. For an English translation of the "Manifesto," vide J. Joll, *Three Intellectuals in Politics* (New York: Harper, 1960), pp. 179-184.

[32] R. T. Clough, *Futurism: The Story of a Modern Art Movement* (New York: Wisdom Library, 1961), p. 11.

"youthful madman" allied with "lions," "tigers," and "panthers" to rejuvenate a presenile and corrupt people. To shatter the constraints inherited from the past, the Futurists sought to make men once again "audacious poets," to reinvoke myths, to combat "all the intellectual and moral tyrannies" that tradition has imposed, to seek out the "impossible" and the "absurd" as the only commendable course for the "most youthful and the best" of their generation.[33]

To accomplish their purpose, to generate revolutionary ardor in an apathetic public, the Futurists mounted "actions" such as throwing 800,000 leaflets from the clocktower of San Marco proclaiming Venice to be a "sinkhole," a "sewer," a "putrescent city," filled with "stinking canals" and "leprous and crumbling buildings." In the effort to mobilize revolutionary sentiment, the Futurists advocated the destruction of the city's gondolas, for which Venice was famous, as the "playthings of cretins." Marinetti followed the "action" at the clocktower with a speech alive with invective and provocation during which bedlam was invoked; blows were exchanged, and the Futurists engaged the "Pastists" in running fistfights, exchanges of catcalls and vituperation.

The Futurists sought to accomplish a bizarre "theater in the streets," systematic provocations that would compel the slack, flaccid, and passive population of Italy to take up sides, a polarization that would clearly define the moral universe into two mutually exclusive groups. By 1915 such strategies had been fixed into a scenario that would be repeated countless times throughout the peninsula. The Futurists characterized themselves as "a revolutionary vanguard," possessed of a "new and total" world view—a vanguard committed to "youth, force, and originality at any cost" opposed to everything "professorial, old and slow." They were the "purveyors of destruction in order to recreate." They exalted "instinct," "force and courage." They welcomed opposition as a technique for "elevating the pub-

[33] Cf. Marinetti, "Uccidiamo il Chiaro di Luna!" and the Preface to G. P. Oucini's *Revolverate*, contained in *Teoria*, pp. 13-30.

lic to a higher comprehension of life." Every issue was conceived as an occasion to polarize the political environment—in parliament, in local councils, and in the streets—into irredeemably opposed factions.[34] In such fashion the Futurists imagined that they would provide the revolutionary sentiment missing during the first decade of the twentieth century.

Between 1909 and 1915, at which time the Futurists identified themselves as a political movement, they advocated a "liberating revolution" in the arts. They advocated "caprice" against everything "consecrated by time." They rejected representation in art and advocated a "carnival of fantasy," a recourse to "imagination" and a "hatred of intelligence" that would "transform all the human senses."[35] They advocated the abandonment of syntax and punctuation in literature, for they conceived rule governance as confining "free initiative." Art was to become action, sensation. Ultimately Marinetti, himself, was to characterize the style that found expression in such behaviors as "tactilism," a kind of "action-art, a defense of youth against all senility, the glorification of the innovating genius, illogical and insane . . . ." This liberating program would reduce all the artificialities that divide human beings; it would "destroy the distance and the barriers that separate men in love and friendship. One must provide for the fullness and the ample beauty of these two essential manifestations of life: Love and Friendship."[36]

In the service of such ends the Futurists challenged students to abandon the schools and academies and seek a greater understanding of life in "free study," to "transcend every social convention" and make "licit every spontaneity." If students were ill-disposed to abandon formal education,

[34] Marinetti, "In quest'anno futurista," *Teoria*, pp. 282-89.

[35] Cf. "La Pittura Futurista: Manifesto tecnico," in L. Scrivo, *Sintesi del futurismo* (Rome: Bulzoni, 1968), pp. 12-14; "Manifesto tecnico della letteratura futurista," in *Teoria*, p. 47; C. D. Carra, "La pittura dei suoni, rumori e odori," in *Sintesi*, pp. 80f.

[36] Marinetti, "Il tattilismo," *Teoria*, pp. 135-37.

they should exploit every occasion while pursuing that education to "act with spontaneity," "to shave or to undertake gymnastic exercises," for example, while their professors lectured.[37]

Giovanni Papini, making common cause with the Futurists in 1913, gave revealing expression to the style to which the movement was committed. He indicated that he had come to "howl with the wolves and laugh with the lunatics [*coi pazzi*]." He spoke of formal education as a "perdition," and admitted that he sought to "cast out everything" he had accumulated in institutions of higher learning. He sought to take up sides with the "fools" against the "learned"; to take up arms with those who are prepared to fight (*quello che hanno fatto a cazzotti*) against those content simply to contemplate. He always found pleasure "in breaking the windows and testicles" of the "bourgeoisie, the bureaucrats and the academicians." Almost everything he said, in fact, was a calculated affront to the "average" Italian. He lampooned the church and Italy's past and referred, characteristically, to the "Altar of the Fatherland," the monument to Victor Emmanuel II and the unification of the nation, as an "enormous, white, and luxurious urinal."[38]

Every element in the scenario—speech patterns, gestures, dress, posture—was a studied provocation. Futurists advocated "anti-neutral" clothing which was "aggressive, dynamic, simple and comfortable, joyful, iridescent, colorful (violet, red, green, yellow, orange, and vermilion), asymmetrical and variable."[39] Futurist speech and literature was to be characterized by "freedom," the abandonment of funded conventions, asyntactical, innocent of punctuation, articulated through "broad analogies," "alive with contradictions"—for life itself was a mass of contradictions and could find true expression only in contradictions.[40] Futurists

[37] F. Azari, "Vita simultanea futurista," in Scrivo, *Sintesi*, pp. 184f.

[38] G. Papini, "Contro Roma e contro Benedetto Croce," in Scrivo, *Sintesi*, pp. 65ff.

[39] G. Balla, "Il vestito antineutrale," in *ibid.*, pp. 107f.

[40] Cf. Marinetti, "Discorso futurista agli Inglesi," in *Teoria*, pp. 240-244.

"systematically despised every form of obedience, of docil-
ity, of imitation. . . . every habitual and hypocritical for-
malism."[41]

Their rallying cry was directed specifically to "the young,
who are the most alive among those alive"—those who could
reinvoke that revolutionary impulse toward "individual liberty" stultified by everything old and traditional. The "grand
hope" of Futurism was that "all authority, all rights and all
power be brutally wrenched from the dead and the moribund and given over to youth between the ages of twenty
and forty." Only "the young, the natural foes of books,
friends of personal experience . . . cultivators of their own
will, enflamed by the fire of their own inspiration, armed
with . . . savage instinct, intuition, astuteness, and temerity"
could contend with the oppressive accumulation of tradition
and established convention.[42]

When the Futurists tried to convey their ideas in any
coherent fashion, what was revealed was an abiding irrationalism. Futurists simply denied that rationality, as it had
been traditionally understood and as it found expression in
standard science, could deliver itself of truth. When Bruno
Corra and his colleagues wrote a "manifesto" of "Futurist
science," they not only advocated the destruction of all
schools and laboratories—plants essential to the development, storage and transmission of scientific information—
but denounced "pedantry, methodology, precision, [and]
accuracy" as fatal to any true creativity. The Futurists deplored the "prejudices" of "patient research, of seriousness
and calculation," and advocated a "new set of values," which
exhorted the student to abandon the patrimony of accumulated information to seek knowledge independently, "here
and there, through chaotic and profoundly irregular study."
This was to create a science which was to be "audaciously
exploratory, essentially sensory, vibrant, influenced by re-

[41] Marinetti, "Discorsi ai triestini," and "Discorsi futuristi agli Inglesi," in *ibid.*, pp. 212, 242; and "L'immaginazione senza fili," *ibid.*,
pp. 64-66.
[42] Marinetti, "Contro i professori," in *ibid.*, pp. 265, 263.

mote intuitions, fragmentary, contradictory . . . ," a science that was to be couched in ordinary language, free of the complicated locutions of standard science. Science was no longer to be "methodical, ordered and lumbering, but capricious, filled with turns and leaps, stormy, and continually unhinged by new intuitions. One must feel a horror of standardization and the obsession with exactitude."[43]

This was the style manifest in Futurist postures. It is legitimately characterized as a *noncognitive style* because the postures assumed were not advanced as argued beliefs. The pronouncements fired into the intellectual environment of pre-World War I Italy were simply that: pronouncements. Futurists were apparently working off intrapsychic tension and/or attempting to mobilize revolutionary sentiment rather than articulating a belief system.

Other than their mobilizing strategy, there were recurrent themes in the writings of the Futurists, particularly in the work of Marinetti. The Futurists were nationalists—their program platform was "the enhancement and grandeur of Italy." They were also machine fetishists. The advent of machines, of "diverse forms of communication, transportation and information," was conceived as exercising a "decisive influence" on the human psyche. Man was being transformed. The machine was not only a symbol of a new human sensibility but a means by which man could be liberated from "tedious and stultifying labor." The Futurists were advocates of a "liberating revolution" more comprehensive than any sought by anarchists. "The anarchists," Marinetti contended, "content themselves with attacks on the political, juridical and economic extensions of the social order while we wish to achieve far more. We wish to destroy the deepest roots of that order, those planted in the brain of man . . . , for the existing social order is absolutely decadent, reactionary, inefficient, stupid and often criminal. It is, therefore, to be abolished as quickly as possible."[44]

[43] B. Corra et al., "La scienza futurista," in Scrivo, *Sintesi*, pp. 152f.
[44] Marinetti, "Governo tecnico senza paralamento, senza senato e con un Eccitatoria," in *Teoria*, p. 360; and "Il cittadino eroico, l'aboli-

The Futurists saw the influences of that institutional corruption everywhere. The most pernicious effect of the prevalence of a "decadent, reactionary, inefficient, stupid and often criminal" order was that it succeeded in warping all the human sensibilities. The "majority" of men was irretrievably corrupt. The Futurists were compelled to struggle against them. Their cry was "Down with sedentary majorities!"[45] Their appeal was to those least corrupted—the youth of Italy, "those between twenty and thirty years of age"— the students of the peninsula.[46]

Because Futurists believed the vast majority of men to be corrupted, revolutionary change could only be the consequence of minority initiative. Futurism began as a struggle against sedentary majorities that dominated the world of art; in its struggle it "militarized" artists—they were to be "warriors" in a "war of liberation." The entire vocabulary of armed conflict came to characterize their utterances—truculence and intemperance their personal postures. Ultimately the vocabulary of violence, the enflamed language of conflict, characterized all their judgments concerning art, politics, and society. When the First World War erupted in 1914 the Futurists were not unexpectedly among the first to advocate Italy's entry on the side of the Allied powers. They conceived the war as a saving therapy for a corrupt, enfeebled, clerical, bureaucratized, and reactionary Italy. War would liberate instincts, multiply aggressions, invoke collective heroism, dissipate the quietism, the petty business mentality and the archeological preoccupations of the majority of Italians.

The termination of hostilities saw, in turn, the organization of Futurist political associations, the *Fasci futuristi*. The announced intentions of these "super-violent" political groups included the creation of "a free democracy [*una libera democrazia*]" in a strong and independent Italy, in

zione delle polizie e le scuole di coraggio," *ibid.*, p. 383. See also "La guerra, sola igiene del mondo," *ibid.*, p. 249.

[45] Marinetti, "Discorso ai Triestini," *ibid.*, pp. 212f., 214.

[46] Marinetti, "Prime battaglie futuriste," *ibid.*, p. 202.

which all forms of oppression, the police, the judiciary, and military conscription would be abolished. The Futurists' objective was a system generative of maximum liberty, maximum productivity, and maximum well-being for all Italians. This would require the abolition of parliament (that repository of majoritarian "good sense") and the substitution of a technical committee of competents composed of thirty or forty young men.[47] Only the young are capable of those flashes of improvisation that are to take the place of elephantine reason and complex bureaucracies.[48] The young constitute a "military revolutionary" force mobilized for a war against all that is traditional, anti-humanistic and anti-futuristic.

Futurism anticipated a war of the "poets against the critics, of instincts against the cultivated, of genial students against pedantic professors, of those who improvise against those who calculate."[49] It was to be a war against family life as it was then constituted, against parliamentary government, against organized religion, against a money economy, against the existence of organized forces of repression such as the police and magistrature, against the distinction between capital and labor. It was to be an attack against matrimony as a form of private property. The Futurists advocated not only the abolition of real property but the abolition of proprietary relationships between men and women. Marriage was no more than "legal prostitution." Monogamy, in fact, was a form of barbarism sustained only by the safety valve of adultery. Women should be released from that servitude, provided equality of education and opportunity, and no longer made uniquely responsible for the education and care of children and the drudgery of household chores. By means of facile divorce, Futurists aspired to liberate women to "participate fully in the life of the nation," thereby

[47] Marinetti, "Un movimento artistico crea un Partito Politico," *ibid.*, pp. 301-303.

[48] Marinetti, "Ideologia sfasciate dalla conflagrazione," *ibid.*, p. 306.

[49] Marinetti, "Crollo di filosofi e storici, sibille a rovescio," *ibid.*, p. 316.

to undermine the legal and social substructure of marriage and female servitude. The Futurists advocated *l'amore libero* and anticipated a period in which sexual promiscuity would be prevalent, repressed libidinal energies released, and with that release women would liberate their intellects from ages of confinement and servility. The result would be a community bound by "sincere solidarity," a liberated sensuality devoid of crippling sentimentality—and sex innocent of the fiction of "eternal union."[50]

By 1919 the *Fasci futuristi* catalogued their political demands: they were "anti-imperialists," resisting the attempted hegemony of some nations over others. They were opposed to "the Papacy, parliament, marriage, military conscription, gerontocracy, property, absentee landlordism, and every form of anti-productive parasitism and stagnant wealth."[51] Futurist nationalism thus distinguished itself from "the reactionary and conservative nationalism of the bourgeoisie." The national community was understood to be an "extension of the individual"; it represents "the maximum extension of the generosity of the individual." It was to be a national community of men, sharing common interests, living in voluntary and "decentralized" association and opposed to "the pretensions of bourgeois nations." Those sated, "anti-humanistic" nations, represented by executives of business interests, seek to maintain the status quo by suppressing vital and revolutionary peoples.[52]

The Futurists thus advocated an anti-bureaucratic, anti-gerontocratic, anti-imperialist, anti-capitalist, and decentralized political system. They inveighed against "bureaucratic elephantiasis" and against the prejudices that favored "old age." "It is evident," Marinetti maintained, "that be-

[50] Marinetti, "Idee-muri da sfondare," "Contro il matrimonio," and "Orgoglio italiano rivoluzionario e libero amore," *ibid.*, pp. 317, 319f., 321, 323, 327.

[51] Marinetti, "Orgoglio italiano . . . ," *ibid.*, p. 322; cf. "La Democrazia futurista," *ibid.*, p. 329.

[52] Marinetti, "Patriottismo futurista," and "Pacifismo e Società delle Nazioni carabiniera," *ibid.*, pp. 336f., 339f., 342.

tween thirty and forty the largest part of humankind suffers
a kind of spiritual involution . . . that produces 'prudence'
(that is to say chronic anxiety), 'calculation' (that is, inde-
cision, the lack of initiative and decisiveness), and 'sobriety'
(the adoration of the mean, the middle of the road, and a
horror of any type of innovation)."[53] As a consequence, the
government proposed by the Futurists would be composed
of a committee of technically competent youths not yet
thirty years of age, elected by universal suffrage with equal
participation of all Italian citizens, male or female.[54] Representatives of the various productive categories, agricultural, industrial, and labor syndicates, would take the place
of a parliament composed largely of lawyers, charlatans, and
do-nothings.

The Futurists maintained that property, as it was then
constituted, had not the semblance of justification. Property,
Marinetti argued, possessed value only as a social product,
and its possession could only be legitimated by virtue of its
social utility. For the enhancement of collective well-being,
the Futurists insisted that the resources of the peninsula be
rigorously and systematically exploited, Italy's industrial development intensified, illiteracy abolished, and extensive
land reclamations undertaken. To this purpose the conjec-
tural "rights of property" were to be subordinated. The profits of those who had amassed wealth during the First World
War were to be sequestered to provide capital for intensive
industrialization. There was to be a gradual nationalization
of the arable land, with a progressive taxation on inherited
wealth leading to ultimate expropriation. Vast public works
were conceived, provisions made for the disabled and enfeebled, the old and the destitute. Taxation was to be direct
and progressive. All of this in a system which provided the
right to strike, to associate, to organize, and to publish.
Court costs were to be met by the state, and judges were to

[53] Marinetti, "Contro l'immonda anzianità, la burocrazia, per il
decentramento," *ibid.*, p. 349.
[54] Marinetti, "Governo tecnico. . . ," *ibid.*, p. 357f.

be popularly elected officials. A minimum wage was to be established; the working day reduced to eight hours; equal conditions were to apply to both male and female workers, and provisions made for the defense of consumer interests.[55]

As Futurism sought recruits for political action it began to generate its own content. It was clearly anarchic in principle and anti-rational in disposition. Marinetti insisted that "mankind moves irresistibly toward anarchy . . . toward total liberation of the individual." That liberation, he proclaimed, could only be the consequence of violence. Men had become so devoid of humanity, so debased by the meanest materialism (*l'astuzia sfruttatrice*), the tyranny of money, bureaucratic obstruction, police constraints, and stultifying rationality, that only "with violence could justice be restored."

In effect, immediately below the surface of seeming content, Futurist style remained constant. The Futurists exalted instinct, intuition, enthusiasm, fantasy, and novelty at the expense of reasoned calculation and weighted judgment. They continued, until and through 1919, to "recognize the necessity of accepting both in ourselves and in our environment coexistence of the most contradictory elements."[56] They conceived of themselves, as artists, as preeminently disinterested and objective, gifted with youthful vitality and sure instinct, as an elite ("All power to the revolutionary artists!") capable of invoking the enthusiasm of the masses against an absolutely corrupt "system." The masses would respond not to reason, but to the "aesthetics of violence and blood . . . to the propaganda of courage and daily heroism." The Futurists were enflamed with a vision of a "new world," an "anarchistic paradise of absolute liberty," which they opposed to a "completely debased system" afflicted with the

[55] Marinetti, "Sintesi della concezione di Mazzini sulla proprietà e la sua trasformazione," and "Denaro ai combattenti!" *ibid.*, pp. 368, 374-380.

[56] Marinetti, "Il cittadino eroico, l'abolizione delle polizie e le scuole di coraggio," *ibid.*, p. 390.

"cancer of bureaucracy" and mired in the "mud of business interests" (Marinetti was an irrepressible advocate of grand metaphors). The appeal to instinct, fantasy, and intuition, a celebration of illogicality, the tolerance of contradiction in thought and speech, the exploitation of inflated and hyperbolic language, the suasive use of symbol and gesture, histrionics rather than argument, violence rather than negotiation, a disposition to dichotomize and polarize the political environment—all came to characterize Futurist style. Whatever content the Futurists advertised for recruitment purposes was to remain forever subsidiary and peripheral to its noncognitive style.

It is clear that the mobilizing strategy of Futurism was predicated on a now familiar set of rather commonplace judgments: (1) men in general were, as a consequence of inurement to direct and indirect bourgeois indoctrination, incapable of manifesting the revolutionary spirit required by the age; (2) only a select elite among men is fully capable of acting in the best and ultimate interests of all mankind; (3) in order to mobilize the active minority necessary for systemic social change, the revolutionary elite was compelled to employ provocation of every conceivable sort—and ultimately to make appeal to violence.

As we have suggested, revolutionary Marxists of a variety of persuasions had come to judgments sufficiently similar by 1914 that the rapprochement between radical syndicalists and Futurists as early as the Italian war in Libya was observed without too much consternation. Revolutionary syndicalists had accepted Sorel and Pareto without demur in the effort to resolve the difficulties left them by Marx and Engels. They were faced with practical and theoretical problems of such magnitude, problems for which Marx and Engels had left no solution, that the Italian radicals of the first quarter of our century sought recourse in a variety of sources that have only now returned to favor among our radicals. In Italy, classical Marxism was undergoing a fateful transformation.

166

THE ADVENT OF FASCISM

Between 1900 and 1914 radical thought in Italy began to display a portentous consistency. Marxist radicals, Nationalists, and Futurists began to entertain a collection of propositions about men in association, about the factors that move men to undertake revolutionary enterprise, and about the role of leadership in social change. The differences between them turned, by and large, on the issue of *which* human associations should be invested with primary loyalty. For Marxists and syndicalists, in general, the object of primary loyalty was the "proletarian *class*." For Nationalists and Futurists the critical object of allegiance was the *nation*. Marxists and syndicalists, by and large, accepted the prevailing socialist conviction that nationalism was a bourgeois affliction. Men were obliged to defend class interests and pursue a revolution that would be fought along class lines.

With the outbreak of the First World War the issue of the relationship between socialism and nationalism became critical. Prior to that time Marxists consistently maintained, irrespective of Bernstein's disclaimers, that national sentiment was no more than a bourgeois snare—designed to gull the working class to serve capitalists' interests. The Second International, throughout the first decade and a half of the twentieth century, met regularly to announce its internationalist orientation. The world, for socialist orthodoxy, remained divided between the oppressed and the oppressors, the international proletariat and the international bourgeoisie. The talk was of an "international brotherhood of workingmen," united against the depredations of an "international capitalist cabal." The conflict that was to herald the advent of the New World was to be a conflict of classes, not of nations. Men were to be mobilized by their class interests rather than any alternative collection of interests.

The First World War revealed, to thinking socialists, how fragile such contentions actually were. Throughout Europe masses of men were caught up in a war fever that found expression in the cry for war uttered by mobs of working-men in Berlin, Vienna, and Paris. Both Lenin and Mussolini were stupefied by the display. Lenin refused to believe that the parliamentary contingent of the Social Democratic Party of Germany had voted, almost to the man, for the Kaiser's war credits or that the German proletariat was volunteering for war service. Mussolini found himself similarly incapable of understanding what was transpiring. As war broke out over Europe, the Socialist Party of Italy took an official stand on absolute neutrality. The war was a "brigands' war," a war between capitalists. The proletariat would not shed its blood for the capitalist class. Mussolini took part in the party's deliberations—but we have compelling evidence that he was beset by almost intolerable personal doubts about the party's stand. The socialists had long proclaimed that the proletariat could never be compelled to take up arms in the service of the bourgeois nation. Throughout Europe, however, the proletariat was doing precisely what socialist theoreticians had insisted was impossible. The world, which orthodox socialism had insisted was historically stratified between the exploited and the exploiters, revealed itself to be vertically segmented into national communities composed of men of a variety of classes all mobilized to what they conceived to be a common defense.

From those fateful days in the late summer of 1914 until January 1915, Mussolini struggled to make sense of the events that had overtaken socialism. Under the impact of national loyalties, European socialism began rapidly to disintegrate. In France, Germany, and Russia, socialists were volunteering for military service. In Italy, an entire wing of the radical syndicalists, typified by Filippo Corridoni, opted for war in the service of the nation. Mussolini, as an activist, felt increasingly confined and impotent by the party commitment to "absolute neutrality" in the face of catastrophic conflict that had enveloped the continent. On October 18, 1914, in the columns of *Avanti!*, Mussolini called for a review of the socialist commitment to "absolute neutrality." He reminded the party that "national problems exist even for socialists," and then proceeded to catalogue some of the most impressive instances that involved them. He alluded to the Polish revolutionary socialist party that entertained a program of national liberation; to the Belgian and French socialists who had abandoned the doctrinaire notion that the proletariat has nothing national to defend and who had, as a consequence, volunteered to resist the German invaders; and finally, to the Italian socialists who responded to the voice of Italians within the borders of Austria-Hungary—and concluded that the socialists who refused to recognize the reality of the problem of national sentiment were "blind and dogmatic."[57]

Mussolini's call for reassessment of the party's position on the war was the immediate cause of his resignation as editor of *Avanti!* and his subsequent expulsion from the party itself. Following his resignation and expulsion, Mussolini committed himself to Italy's intervention in the rapidly expanding conflict. The recriminations that followed were tortured. Party representatives raised strident objections to Mussolini's postures, and Mussolini responded in kind. In the course of the discussions it became quite evident that Mussolini had begun to maintain that there was a legitimate point of view concerning the war that was "national," and that the war issue could not be reduced to the interests of the bourgeoisie versus the interests of the proletariat. Mussolini denied that there was a single and unambiguous "class" position vis-à-vis the war. He insisted that there were at least two manifestly distinct orientations among and within the bourgeois and proletarian elements in Italy. There were proletarians who had passed into the interventionist camp, and there were capitalists opposed to the war. Class categories, in effect, were inadequate analytic concepts for sorting out what was transpiring in the course of the crisis.[58] The notion of the "nation" began to loom larger and larger in his delibera-

[57] Mussolini, "Dalla neutralità assoluta alla neutralità attiva ed operante," *Opera*, vi, 400f.

[58] Cf. Mussolini, "Le ragioni del dissidio e le dimissioni," and "La neutralità socialista," in *Opera*, vi, 409-412, 420f.

tions. Finally, on November 10 and 11, 1914, Mussolini addressed an assembly of the Milanese section of the Socialist Party and affirmed that

> the root of the psychological difficulty that afflicted socialists was to be found in their failure to examine national problems. The Socialist International never effectively occupied itself with such issues—and as a consequence the International was dead, overcome by events. . . . We must see whether there is any basis of conciliation between the nation, which remains an historic reality, and class, which is a living reality. It is certain that the nation represents a stage of human development that we have not, as yet, transcended. . . . The sentiment of nationality exists. It cannot be denied. The anti-patriotism of old has dissipated itself . . . .[59]

While Mussolini denied that he had marshaled himself into the ranks of the nationalists, he was clearly attempting to accommodate the concept "nation" into his system of beliefs. He continued to speak of the nation as a historic and psychological reality and asked whether "internationalism remains an absolutely necessary element of socialism, or whether the socialism of tomorrow might not occupy itself in finding conceptions that might integrate [the reality of] both nation and class."[60]

Events had seemed to provoke Mussolini to a reexamination of his personal convictions. Until the crisis of 1914 he had been content to identify *class* as the primary object of loyalty for all revolutionaries. The unanticipated and unprecedented events of 1914 seemed to disconfirm his conviction that the material and sentimental interests that invoked the allegiance of masses of men led to their organization into classes. The notion that men were committed to an international class rather than a national community

[59] Mussolini, "La situazione internationale e l'atteggiamento del partito," *Opera*, vi, 427f.

[60] Mussolini, "Mussolini riconferma la sua avversione alla neutralità" *Opera*, vi, 431.

seemed to be belied by the behavior of Germans, Frenchmen, Englishmen, Austrians, and Russians. The most active, resolute, and aggressive men seemed to have been animated by *national* rather than *class* sentiments. Belgians, Germans, and Frenchmen seemed to argue that the war involved their material, sentimental, and psychological interests with an intensity which had never attended the theoretical "class war." Invasion and military defeat, occupation and the excision of territory, would work against the concrete material interests of all men, whatever their class provenience. The cry of co-nationals, confined in territories occupied by powers alien in tradition and culture, found resonance in the emotions of men of all classes. Years later Mussolini was to maintain that the war had taught revolutionaries that an international class could hardly serve as the primary object of loyalty for men. The "international working class" was simply too large, shapeless, and meaningless a candidate community to serve as that association with which men could identify and in which men could define themselves.[61]

Interventionism provided the watershed for all the currents that were ultimately to reconstitute themselves as Fascism. As Mussolini abandoned a simple class analysis of historic and political events, and the concept "nation" began to figure more and more prominently in his analyses, the distance that separated him from the Nationalists began to diminish significantly. Both Mussolini and the Nationalists shared common convictions concerning the nature of man in association. Both conceived men moved by real and ideal motives, with masses responding mimetically to mobilization strategies employed by aggressive and intransigent elites. Both conceived moral regeneration of individuals and masses to be a function of protracted and exacerbated conflict. Both dichotomized the world into in-groups and out-groups in real and potential struggle. Both opposed the "sedentary and pusillanimous bourgeoisie." What had separated them in the past—their respective primary objects of

[61] Mussolini, *My Autobiography*, p. 46.

loyalty—no longer stood between them. While Mussolini could vituperate against Corradini as late as March of 1918, by 1919 Nationalists were joining Fascist squads and Fascists had inscribed themselves members of Corradini's Nationalist Party. By 1923 Corradini's Nationalists merged with triumphant Fascism—and Corradini could dedicate the published collection of his speeches to "Benito Mussolini, the Duce of victorious Italy."

More interesting perhaps, for the purposes of exposition, is that during these same years Marinetti's Futurists became more and more intimately involved in the development of Fascism. They brought an inimitable style to the collection of ideas that were to constitute the substance of Fascism. Since Mussolini was convinced that history was made by resolute minorities activating the elemental energies of the masses, Futurist style, the histrionics and choreography of the streets, could readily become a fundamental organizing and mobilizing instrument in the Fascist armarium. By 1923, when Corradini could correctly characterize Fascism as the first self-conscious revolutionary, mass-mobilizing party,[62] the mobilization was undertaken with the strategies brought to Fascism by the Futurists.

The Futurists had been ardent interventionists, and many had passed into the ranks of the *Arditi*, the shock-troops of the Italian army. Many of the Futurists had served on perilous missions with the *Arditi* and had returned to civilian life possessed of their country's highest decorations as well as an irrepressible conviction that they had all the qualities to serve as a resolute revolutionary elite in the new Italy that was to rise out of the ashes of the First World War. When Mussolini organized the postwar Fascist movement, Marinetti and his Futurists were prominent among the leadership as well as the rank and file. The Futurists and *Arditi* brought to Fascism the principal trappings that were to subsequently identify the movement. They brought the Black Shirt and the battle cries. They brought the posturing and

[62] Corradini, *Discorsi*, p. 13.

the gestures, the slogans and the street locutions, that so endeared Fascism to the crowds.

Years later Benedetto Croce was to insist that Fascism was, in fact, a variant of Futurism—a clear exaggeration—but, with equal clarity, a judgment that contained an element of truth, which Fascist and non-Fascist commentators were quick to acknowledge. Recently Renzo De Felice maintained that the Futurists had infused a "new spirit" into the political activity of the Italian postwar period.[63] A perspicacious contemporary, Giuseppe Prezzolini, had earlier indicated as much.[64] Fascists themselves recognized that Futurism had provided the "sentimental and temperamental" adjuncts that gave Fascism its public character, but they correctly argued that Fascism's *content* found its origins in other sources.[65]

Futurism had materially assisted Fascism in resolving one of the principal problems that weighed upon prewar socialism—the problem of how to explain the nonrevolutionary character of the proletariat. Orthodox socialism had never succeeded in energizing, mobilizing, and effectively organizing the masses that were beginning to collect in the standard metropolitan areas of Europe. Futurism, on the other hand, harbored an intuitive appreciation of the psychology of displaced and restive masses. The termination of the First World War had created, in the urban centers of northern Italy, a reservoir of mobilizable masses. The war had stopped the flow of emigrants from Italy and had drawn inordinate numbers out of the countryside and thrown demobilized soldiers among them. All these combustible elements were to be found available in the urban centers of northern Italy. All these groups found themselves trapped in an environment that began, immediately upon the end of hostilities, to suffer massive economic dislocation. The Italian *lire*, measured in gold units, collapsed. Inflation swept

[63] R. De Felice, *Mussolini il rivoluzionario* (Turin: Einaudi, 1965), pp. 475-82; cf. Joll, *Three Intellectuals in Politics*, pp. 176-78.

[64] G. Prezzolini, *Fascism* (London: Methuen, 1926), pp. 84ff.

[65] Bertelè, *Aspetti ideologici*, pp. 45f., n. 10.

away savings and security. Unemployment was pandemic. In 1919 there were almost nineteen hundred work stoppages that involved over a million and a half participants. The high hopes invoked by politicians during the war years were faulted.

Many of the returning war veterans who collected in the cities were displaced and unemployable intellectuals. Italy suffered a supersaturation of dissident and classless intellectuals who had disproportionately borne the burden of war service. The socialists, in what was perhaps their most strategic failure of the immediate postwar years, rejected any rapprochement with the returning soldiers. Angelo Tasca, years later, was to denounce the intransigent socialist position on the issue of attempting to accommodate returning war veterans.[66]

The survivors of the "generation of the front," those men that Mussolini called the "aristocracy of the trenches," the "warrior intellectuals," were to provide the critical and effective Fascist cadre so absent from the postwar socialist ranks.[67] Their effectiveness was not just a consequence of the endemic elitist disposition that seems to characterize intellectuals of any nationality, nor was it simply their facility with symbol manipulation. They adopted the political style developed by the Futurists. Masses could and were mobilized. The large membership collected by the Socialist and Popular parties after the war dissolved before the aggressive Fascist movement in the critical years 1921 and 1922. The Fascists were effective not in the least because they were infused with Futurist style and street tactics. The style and tactics were appropriate to a cadre composed largely of declassed intellectuals. The rank and file could be composed of disillusioned lumpenproletarian, proletarian and petit bourgeois elements—the former alienated by the revo-

[66] A. Tasca, *Nascita e avento del fascismo* (Florence: La nuova Italia, 1950), pp. 518f.

[67] Cf. R. Michels' commentary on the role of returning war veterans and intellectuals, *Sozialismus und Faschismus in Italien* (Munich: Meyer & Jensen, 1925), ii, pp. 253ff.

lutionary talk of socialism and its ineffective political action and the latter composed of a threatened petit bourgeoisie suffering downward mobility, diminishing resources, declining job opportunities, and the indifference of an unresponsive and insecure government.

The Fascists could mobilize these elements because they had an efficient cadre and a collection of slogans calculated to invoke common national sentiments. They promised aggressive action to dissident proletarians who had seen the internationalist socialists bungle every opportunity afforded them for making revolution. They promised security and dignity to threatened artisans, shopkeepers, and civil servants. And they promised a general defense of *all* classes, the propertied and the propertyless, in an environment that gave every evidence of disintegrating into total disorder.

In June 1923, the Executive Committee of the Communist International, in attempting to analyze the events that had overtaken Italian socialism, recognized that Fascism had managed to mobilize the "small and middle bourgeoisie . . . the small landed peasantry . . . the intellectuals [as well as] many proletarian elements who, looking for and demanding action, [felt] dissatisfied with the behavior of all political parties."[68] In fact, in their less tendentious moments Communists were prepared to admit that Fascism had in fact won a significant "political and ideological victory over the labor movement."[69] The political victory was at least in part the consequence of the adoption of the Futurist political style. But that adoption was, in itself, at least in part the consequence of Fascism's ideological convictions, convictions which Mussolini harbored as early as 1904. Fascism was prepared to invoke the mass-mobilizing style of Futurism because Fascists entertained certain convictions about men in association, about the mimetism and suggestibility

[68] As cited in Cammett, "Communist Theories of Fascism, 1920-1935," p. 151.

[69] Clara Zetkin, "Der Kampf gegen den Faschismus," in E. Nolte, ed., *Theorien ueber den Faschismus* (Berlin: Kiepenheuer & Witsch, 1967), p. 99.

of crowds, about the energizing motives governing collective behavior. All of these convictions were drawn from the sociological tradition of which Pareto was perhaps the foremost spokesman—and these were convictions shared by syndicalists, nationalists, and radical socialists of Mussolini's stamp. But Fascism's ideological victory was also a consequence of its synthesis of nationalist and syndicalist content —a special combination of elements that had, and has, singular significance for Europe and, in our own time, the world. Once Mussolini had transferred his loyalty from the proletarian class to the Italian nation, his belief system underwent a transformation which ultimately revealed the shape of mature Fascist ideology. It was with the specific content that collected around Mussolini's core convictions that Fascism won its victory in 1922.

Having committed himself to intervention in 1914, Mussolini was prepared to grant that the Italian nation had legitimate interests independent of the interests of any constituent class or population category. There was a real general interest that found overt expression in the disposition of men of all walks of life, and all economic origins, to sacrifice in its defense. By the end of the First World War Mussolini was prepared to articulate the conviction that Italy, as an integral unity including all classes and all categories of persons, was as disadvantaged as the proletarian class ever conceived itself to be. Italy was, in fact, a "proletarian nation." The entire nation, faced by the impostures and imperialisms of "bourgeois" or "plutocratic" nations, found itself denied sustenance and place.[70] Mussolini, in effect, was bruiting an idea that had been given common currency by Corradini as early as 1910.[71]

As a "proletarian" nation, every element of the Italian population became heir to all the sentiments that Marxists had so long labored to inject into the intellectual climate of the peninsula. All Italians, irrespective of class or origin, could aspire to the future promised exclusively to the pro-

[70] Mussolini, "Atto di nascita del fascismo," *Opera*, xii, 323.
[71] Corradini, "Principii di nazionalismo," *Discorsi*, pp. 92f.

letarian class by the more "orthodox" socialists. More than that, a "proletarian" Italy could make effective recourse to traditional loyalties and ingrained habits of its entire population. One could sacrifice himself for his country without suffering the conflict of loyalties that proved to be the Nemesis of European socialists. The identification of the entire nation as "proletarian" forged the linchpin of a system of beliefs that the Fascists baptized "national syndicalism"— a synthesis anticipated by Michels and Sorel, and Corradini as well. Fascism had resolved for itself the problem of "proletarian" nationalism.

Once the *entire* nation was characterized as disadvantaged, "proletarian," Fascists could treat the integral community as an effective productive unit. Italy as a whole was an exploited community, just as socialists had insisted the workers had been exploited. Italy was exploited by "plutocratic" nations that used every "bourgeois" device to deny the nation its equitable share of the world's resources— "plutocratic" nations that had exploited every economic and diplomatic stratagem to defend their advantage. Italy, like the proletarian class of yore, had been denied its "place in the sun." In giving credence to such convictions, *all* Italians could give themselves over to the defense of the fatherland in order to defeat oppression and exploitation—to their collective mutual advantage and in the pursuit of justice. These were to become the constant and most successful mobilizing themes of Fascist propaganda. As early as 1914 the young Dino Grandi, who was to serve among the highest echelons of Fascism's elite, insisted that the future of the world would be dominated by "a class struggle between nations"—a conflict between "capitalist" and "proletarian nations."[72]

Both explicit and implicit in such an orientation were two programmatic themes that were equally recurrent and insistent in Fascist ideology: (1) the collaboration of all "productive classes" in the defense of the "proletarian" father-

---

[72] D. Grandi, *Giovani* (Bologna: Zanichelli, 1941), pp. 39, 41f.

177

land in the service of (2) the maximum development of the nation's productive capacities. Pareto, long before the First World War, had argued that the problems that faced most nations of the world were problems of *production* rather than socialist problems of *distribution*. As early as 1919 Mussolini insisted that the class interests that divided Italians must be superseded by a more substantial and more pervasive interest: the need to increase the productive capacity of the "proletarian" fatherland.[73] In the documents that constitute the charter of the Fascist movement, Mussolini identified for Fascists but two unalterable programmatic commitments: one, the maintenance and expansion of the nation's productive capacity and the other, the defense of the nation.[74] Sustained and incremental production required an intense collaboration of all productive elements in the national community. All the productive forces of the nation were to be marshaled in what Sergio Panunzio early called a "grand army" suffused with a "grand discipline" under the aegis of a youthful and dynamic elitist "hierarchy."[75] That maximization of production would provide the sinews for national defense.

Within the context of these convictions, all of Mussolini's ideas began to take on a special coherence. The surface features of Fascism began to take on substance. The *nation* was the association of primary loyalty to which men could give their allegiance. The out-groups against which the Italian in-group defined itself were advantaged nations, fat with "plutocratic" privilege. The constellation of obligations assumed by members of the association included disciplined and devoted labor in the service of increased national productivity. The ultimate test of loyalty was a readiness to serve the nation in times of international conflict. The national community was suffused by a sense of high moral tension out of which the "New Man" could be regenerated. That instrumental moral tension was to be sustained by

[73] Mussolini, "Rettifiche di tiro," *Opera*, xii, 250.
[74] Mussolini, "Atto di nascita del fascismo," *Opera*, xii, 325.
[75] S. Panunzio, *Che cos'è il fascismo*, p. 16.

what Fascists called "choreography, ceremony and ritual." Nationalist, syndicalist, and Futurist elements were at once fused into the ideology of Fascism.

All that remained was to leaven the entire substance with that final constituent: Fascism's conception of the state. Given the enterprisory, pedagogical, and tutelary functions of the revolutionary and national elite, the need for an organizing agency to superintend the entire process became obvious. By 1921 after considerable soul-searching and conflict (that revealed itself in the issuance of a number of mutually exclusive and contradictory postures), Mussolini explicitly adopted Giovanni Gentile's neo-idealist convictions concerning the state.[76] Roberto Farinacci (who was to serve as general secretary of the Fascist Party) refers explicitly to the decision to adopt Gentile's conception of the "ethical" and "totalitarian" state in his history of the period.[77]

Gentile had early identified himself with the interventionists, and his association with the Nationalists (irrespective of his considerable reservations) indicated a commonality of views. Ultimately, Gentile's convictions concerning the nature and function of the state became critical to the justificatory arguments of the Fascist regime. His ideas were sufficiently acceptable to the Nationalists that the Fascist state, with its hierarchical and authoritarian features, could pass as the fulfillment of *either* Nationalist or neo-idealist convictions. In any event, it was clear to Mussolini that once Fascism had assumed the collection of obligations entailed in the productionist and developmental intentions incorporated in the Fascist program, a strong and highly centralized state became a requirement. With that recognition, Fascist ideology was substantially complete. Once so fashioned it immediately became evident that almost all of classical Marxism's theoretical substance was irrelevant to the problems that faced Italy as a "proletarian" nation. Fascism had

[76] Cf. for example, Mussolini, "Il programma fascista," *Opera*, xvii, 219, 221.

[77] R. Farinacci, *Storia della rivoluzione fascista* (Cremona: Cremona nuova, 1937), iii, 230-62, particularly p. 256.

explicitly abandoned classical Marxism in the effort to re-solve the problems of the nonrevolutionary proletariat and the historic role of nationalism.

Fascist ideology became the rationale for a mass-mobiliz-ing, developmental dictatorship. It arose in a nation suffer-ing retarded industrial development. Italy had only begun its industrial development when the First World War threw the entire system into protracted crisis. Fascism undertook to resume that development in a drive toward industrial maturity. Given the circumstances in which it found itself, and the resources at its disposal, Fascism sought to accel-erate the capital accumulation necessary for industrial ex-pansion by suppressing labor unrest, controlling consump-tion, and intensively organizing industrial and managerial elements (a process that had already begun in prewar Italy). The major burden of the entire program fell, as it seems inevitably to fall in all developing nations, on the working classes. The state administered a developmental program largely articulated by private industrial and mana-gerial associations always under the threatening superin-tendence of the unitary (and increasingly dictatorial) party. The Fascists made it clear that they had no intention of nationalizing private property as long as that property was effectively administered; and the party and its leadership were to be the ultimate arbiters of what constituted effec-tive administration. The profit rates of industry were to be maintained at as high a level as possible. Capitalists were not expected to squirrel away profits, but were given every incentive to reinvest in industrial expansion. To accelerate capital accumulation, wages and nonproductive consump-tion were to be held at the lowest tolerable levels. Econ-omists will continue to argue how effective those policies were, and political analysts will continue to argue whether there were any alternatives open to the Fascists, but it is reasonably clear that Fascist ideology served this overall strategy. In the process Italy developed a modern infra-structure for modernization; road and rail systems were expanded, agricultural yield increased, and a defensive and aggressive capability of sufficient magnitude developed that gave the more advanced nations of Europe considerable pause.

Any number of commentators have highlighted these features of the regime. Peter Drucker, in the early thirties, alluded to what he termed the "noneconomic" policies of Fascism. Fascism's primary preoccupation, Drucker suggested, seemed to be "to keep the machinery of industrial production in good working order." The working classes were provided "noneconomic" benefits in order to permit increased investment in capital goods. Reduced consumption and high profit levels were strategies for creating capital for accelerated industrial investment. Drucker conceived "consumption management" to be the "secret" of totalitarian economic policy. If it was, it is clearly a perfectly rational economic strategy for a community undertaking a drive for industrial maturity.[78] The economy goes into phased development without the dislocations that would attend a "revolution" that exterminates or alienates strategic managerial or enterprisory talents or "redistributes" scarce welfare benefits. The Fascist strategy was to make the propertied classes become the vehicle for the transmission of accumulated capital into developing industries. Heavy industry was favored at the expense of smaller, relatively noneconomic

[78] P. Drucker, *The End of Economic Man* (New York: Harper, 1969), chap. 6, particularly pp. 156f. Cf. Paul Einzig's positive assessment of the Fascist developmental program, *The Economic Foundations of Fascism* (London: Macmillan, 1933), chap. 6 and passim. Compare in this context, S. Lombardini, "Italian Fascism and the Economy," in S. J. Woolf, ed., *The Nature of Fascism* (New York: Random House, 1969), 152-64, particularly pp. 156f., and W. G. Welk, *Fascist Economic Policy* (Cambridge: Harvard University, 1938). A Fascist account of the first eight years of Fascist rule is available in A. S. Benni, "Lo sviluppo industriale dell'Italia fascista," in *Lo stato Mussoliniano e le realizzazioni del fascismo nella nazione* (Rome: "La Rassegna Italiana," 1930); cf. the aggregate statistics in A. Maddison, *Economic Growth in the West* (New York: 20th Century, 1964).

units, and the process was conducted under the surveillance of the party. Ideally, managerial and enterprisory elites were to be governed by the political hierarchy; but we know, as a matter of fact, that in many instances such strategic groups have enough autonomy and political leverage to defend themselves from any such developmental regime. Nonetheless, the specific aspirations of the Fascist state *were* totalitarian—and were calculated to control both labor and capital—and its overall policy was geared to the rapid industrialization of the peninsula.[79]

James Burnham has left us an account of Fascism that conceives it to have been a "managerial ideology,"[80] an ideology calculated to enhance the expansion and viability of industry as an integrated, disciplined, and rationalized national enterprise. In such an ideology there is emphasis on "saving," "work," and "discipline." Managerial ideologies are, in effect, animated by a work and sacrifice ethic—as one might well expect in a society going through the process of intensive and intensified capital production and accumulation. Labor organizations are domesticated and disciplined to state purpose; and noneconomic social benefits ("moral incentives") are substituted for "wasteful" consumption of capital in the form of commodities. We might add that the work ethic of Fascism not only served to restrict consumption in the service of capital accumulation but provided the energy for labor intensive enterprises required in developing nations. The "voluntary" labor donated by domesticated labor organizations, for example, was a cost-free supplement to economic development. One works without material compensation for one's fatherland and the future of the nation in its entirety. One is subject to "moral incentives."

[79] This is the context in which books such as D. Guerin, *Fascism and Big Business* (New York: Pioneer, 1939) and E. Rossi, *Padroni del vapore e fascismo* (Bari: Laterza, 1966) might well be read. For a sober account of the relationship between the Fascist and the industrial hierarchies of Italy, cf. R. Sarti, *Fascism and the Industrial Leadership in Italy, 1919-1940* (Berkeley: University of California, 1971).

[80] J. Burnham, *The Managerial Revolution* (New York: Day, 1941).

Fascism and Developmental Dictatorship

If Fascist ideology was essentially if not exclusively a rationale for a mass-mobilizing, developmental dictatorship, its contemporary perceptions of the Soviet Union provide some interesting reflexive insights. Those perceptions tell us something about Fascists and their ideology—and perhaps offer some heuristic suggestions about a modern "neofascism."

While it is common knowledge that Fascism wore the mantle of an intransigent "anti-Bolshevism," it is less well known that serious Fascist ideologues entertained a rather subtle interpretation of the ideology that animated the Soviet experiment. By the mid-thirties serious Fascist literature was filled with articles devoted to the analysis of the Soviet experience. Characteristic of that literature was a distinction between various forms of "anti-Bolshevism." Fascists recognized the prevalence of a "reactionary anti-Bolshevism," an anti-Bolshevism of the threatened bourgeoisie who, after the deluge, sought a return to the laissez-faire liberalism of the past. Fascists refused to identify with such anti-Bolshevisms, and they lamented the disposition of some Europeans to identify Fascism with it.[81] Fascists argued that their anti-Bolshevism did not harken back to a restoration of prewar capitalism. They insisted that their anti-Bolshevism was a consequence of their recognition that the Soviets had misconstrued the challenge of the contemporary world. The Soviets continued to mouth internationalist, anti-statist, and "proletarian" slogans when the self-evident features of their regime attested to their abandonment of the entire substance of classical Marxism. Fascists indicated, with considerable satisfaction, that the internal policies of the Stalinist regime had "involuted" the classical Marxism of Marx and Engels and had "dialectically" transformed the anarchosyndicalist and anti-statist ideas of Lenin to produce a "political formula that galvanizes the Russian people in the service of

[81] F. M. Pacces, "Antibolscevismo e antibolscevismi vari," *Critica fascista*, 15, 17 (July 1, 1937), 289.

industrial development—to nationalist purpose."[82] Stalinist formulae further provided for a restabilization of the family as the primary nucleus of a strong and centralized state; it made the state the central enterprisory and tutelary agency of the nation, and the nation was defended by military forces for whom the "defense of the socialist motherland" was a primary obligation. Gone was the frenetic anti-religious, anti-militarist, anti-nationalist bias of the "revolutionary socialism" that had been the mortal enemy of Fascism.[83] Even in the discussions generated by this analysis, the disclaimers by Fascist discussants turned solely on what such internal developments meant for *international* relations. The most critical counterarguments contained clear recognition that Fascists generally agreed that Stalin's reforms of 1935 and 1936 had "dialectically thrown overboard the principles in whose name" the Russian revolution had been conducted— and that "Marxist-Leninist principles" had been transformed into their " 'contraries,' that is to say, the ideas that provide body and substance to the Fascism of Mussolini."[84]

This kind of analysis had been countenanced by Mussolini himself. As early as 1933 Mussolini favorably reviewed Renzo Bertoni's *Il trionfo del fascismo nell'U.R.S.S.*, and suggested that the only viable course Russia could, in fact, follow was "an abandonment of Marx and an application of the principles of Fascism."[85] In 1934, in the principal journal of the Fascist Party, M. Ardemagni could correspondingly maintain that "in the course of its development the Russian revolution has gradually given evidence of fully abandoning Marxist postulates and of a gradual, if surreptitious, acceptance of certain fundamental political principles that char-

[82] A. Nasti, "L'Italia, il bolscevismo, la Russia," *Critica fascista*, 15, 10 (March 15, 1937), 162.

[83] B. Ricci, "Il 'fascismo' di Stalin," *Critica fascista*, 15, 18 (July 15, 1937), 317-19.

[84] T. Napolitano, "Il 'fascismo' di Stalin ovvero l'U.R.S.S. e noi," *Critica fascista*, 15, 23 (October 1, 1937), 397.

[85] Mussolini, "Segnalazione," *Opera*, xxvi, 84.

acterize Fascism."[86] By 1938 Mussolini could, with considerable irony, identify Stalin as "a crypto-fascist."[87]

Sergio Panunzio, in a definitive study of Fascist ideology, published in a revised edition as late as 1939, indicated that while prewar socialism had been anti-state and anti-national, distributionistic, and singularly "proletarian" in guise—and anarchic in disposition—the state system that had evolved in the Soviet Union under Stalin had begun to take on more and more of the features of paradigmatic Fascism.[88] As early as 1925 Panunzio had indicated that "Fascism and Bolshevism were phenomena that shared critical similarities."[89] He indicated that the Soviets had given every indication of having created an armed and authoritarian, anti-liberal state that had mobilized and disciplined masses to the service of intensive internal development. The state, possessing hierarchical and juridical preeminence, generated and allocated resources, articulated and administered interests, and assumed paramount pedagogical and tutelary functions.

This kind of analysis was not restricted to Fascists by any means. Trotsky spoke of the fateful similarities shared by Fascism and Stalinism; and both Prezzolini and Rudolfo Mondolfo, as early as 1925, remarked on the shared attributes that characterized the two revolutionary regimes.[90] The similarities include an intense nationalism, the instauration of an authoritarian and anti-liberal state under a "charismatic leader" activating "masses" that included all "sound" and "productive" population elements, a domestication of

[86] M. Ardemagni, "Deviazioni Russe verso il fascismo," *Gerarchia*, 15 (July 1934), 571.

[87] Mussolini, "Atto quinto finora," *Opera*, xxix, 63.

[88] Panunzio, *Teoria generale*, pp. 5f., 8-10.

[89] Panunzio, *Lo stato fascista* (Bologna: Cappelli, 1925), pp. 145ff.

[90] L. Trotsky, *The Revolution Betrayed*, tr. Max Eastman (New York: Doubleday, 1937), p. 278; G. Prezzolini, "Ideologia e sentimento," and R. Mondolfo, "Il fascismo in Italia," in R. De Felice, *Il fascismo e i partiti politici Italiani* (Rocca San Casciano: Cappelli, 1966), pp. 522f., 549. Cf. also B. Rizzi. *La lezione dello stalinismo* (Rome: Opere nuove, 1962).

labor unions, and authoritarian control of the means of production by an enterprisory and managerial bureaucracy enjoying differential income and differential access to the levers of power. All of this took place within the confines of a political system dominated by a unitary party monopolizing the institutions of interest articulation and interest aggregation. Control over the means of communication and the prevalence of special means of social surveillance completed the picture of analogous political systems. The ultimate intentions of both were the creation of a modern and self-sufficient industrial system—economic autarchy that insured political and economic independence for what had been an underdeveloped national community. All that, coupled with instances of territorial aggression, provided a compelling picture of systemic symmetry. Drucker simply characterized the process by saying that "Russia has . . . been forced to adopt one purely totalitarian and fascist principle after the other," and Burnham could identify Bolshevism as one of the generic class of "managerial ideologies."[91] In 1936 Elie Halevy simply proceeded to "define" Bolshevism as one form of "fascism."[92] In our own time Bruno Rizzi, as a revolutionary socialist, could only lament that ". . . that which Fascism consciously sought, [the Soviet Union] involuntarily constructed."[93]

Contemporary scholarship has produced an enormous literature around the concept "totalitarianism" and, whatever its cognitive merit, it does document the pervasive similarities between various forms of dictatorial and developmental dictatorships that took shape in the interwar years. This is not the place to review that literature.[94] What would seem

[91] Drucker, *The End of Economic Man*, p. 246.

[92] E. Halevy, *The Era of Tyrannies* (New York: Doubleday, 1965), p. 278.

[93] Rizzi, *La lezione dello stalinismo*, p. 38.

[94] Among the most important are C. J. Friedrich and Z. K. Brzezinski, *Totalitarian Dictatorship and Autocracy* (New York: Praeger, 1956); H. Buchheim, *Totalitäre Herrschaft* (Munich: Kösel, 1962); W. Kornhauser, *The Politics of Mass Society* (New York: Free Press, 1959); E. Lederer, *State of the Masses* (New York: Fertig, 1967); B.

more suggestive is to consider briefly its most recent development, that which conceives totalitarian systems to be a functional artifact of national communities in the process of rapid, if phased, development. The work of Ludovico Garruccio, for example, is devoted to an account of Fascism which characterizes it as an ideology of national development, variants of which can appear most readily in environments suffering delayed or thwarted development or protracted social, political, or economic deprivation.[95] In the same context George Lichtheim has recently suggested that the "Marxism-Leninism" of contemporary revolutionary movements is little more than a rationale for accelerated national development. That rationale, coined by declassed intellectuals, could equally well be couched in fascist or socialist locutions.[96] The political system that grows out of such developmental ideologies has a now familiar constellation of characteristics: it is an "anti-imperialist" nationalism—a struggle of "proletarian" nations against "plutocratic" nations. It advocates a national union of "all productive classes," including the "national bourgeoisie" and perhaps the "honest gentry" against all "anti-national, anti-popular, and capitalist" foes in the pursuit of national sovereignty and independence. In order to attain those ends, the masses and their hitherto autonomous organizations are mobilized into paramilitary and military hierarchies under the predominance of the unitary party dominated by the charismatic leader. At its best such a system produces a forced rate of industrialization, more often than not at the expense of the urban proletariat and the rural peasantry.[97] The strategic elements, the managerial and enterprisory elite, enjoy in

Seidel and S. Jenkner, eds., *Wege der Totalitarismus-Forschung* (Darmstadt: Wissenschaftliche Buchgesellschaft, 1968).

[95] Cf. Garruccio, *L'industralizzazione tra nazionalismo e rivoluzione*; "Le tre età del fascismo," *Il Mulino, 213* (January-February 1971), 53-73.

[96] G. Lichtheim, *Imperialism* (New York: Praeger, 1971), pp. 158f.

[97] Cf. for example, W. W. Rostow, *The Stages of Economic Growth* (London: Cambridge University, 1969), pp. 47, 161 passim.

varying measure and to varying degrees, social, economic, and political advantage. The sustaining morality of the system is a work and sacrifice ethic, and the normative model of man is that of the "warrior-worker," the "warrior-peasant" or perhaps the "warrior-intellectual." In the process whole categories of citizens may be destroyed or exiled. The unitary party and authoritarian (and increasingly personalist) rule is sustained by regular "purges" which "purify" the revolutionary integrity of the movement. External intransigence and perhaps armed aggression seem to be a function of the success of the developmental drive and increased military capability. The "just and revolutionary war" can become the ultimate challenge for the "new man."

All of this suggests how irrelevant all of the theoretic substance of classical Marxism has, in fact, become. While such developmental dictatorships may continue to invoke Marxist language, it has become increasingly clear that Fascism's frank abandonment of the substance of classical Marxism anticipated its surreptitious suppression at the hands of "revolutionary" Marxists. We are left with the distinct impression that perhaps Marx was not, after all, the prophet of our time. Perhaps in a curious, but not totally incomprehensible sense, Mussolini was.

Chapter Six

The New Radicalism:
The Asian Variant

Anyone who can bring himself to affirm that a [social-ist] revolution is easier to carry out somewhere specifi-cally because such a land is innocent not only of a prole-tariat but a bourgeoisie as well, proves thereby that he still hasn't learned the ABC of socialism.[1]

Friedrich Engels (1875)

O NE of the most curious features that characterizes po-litical thinking in the years after the Second World War is the indisposition on the part of commentators, analysts, advocates, detractors, and practitioners to recognize that a spectacular transformation had settled down over "Marxist" and "radical" thought—a transformation of substance that was little less than a secular and political counterpart of what the faithful think takes place in the transubstantiation of the Holy Eucharist. "Marxist" and "radical" thought has been gradually divested of its specifically classical Marxist components to become a highly transmogrified "Marxism" identified as "Marxism-Leninism," a Marxism "creatively developed" first by Lenin, then by Stalin, and in the imme-diate present, by Mao Tse-tung. Literally all of what could legitimately pass as Marxist "theory," the partially formalized economic theory of *Kapital* and its entailments—the labor theory of value, the theory of surplus value and the average rate of profit, the conception of the secular decline in profit, the increasing severity of economic crises, the interstitial development of socialism within the integument of the ad-vanced industrial system of the West, the polarization of social elements into a "vast majority" of proletarians and an exiguous number of capitalists who had concentrated

[1] F. Engels, "Soziales aus Russland," *Werke*, xviii, 557.

economic power in their hands—became largely irrelevant to twentieth-century Marxists and radicals and were unobtrusively jettisoned. The vacated space was filled with a far different content.

To gauge the extent to which the classical Marxist elements were abandoned, or extensively modified, one need but rehearse those analyses tendered by Lenin before he embarked upon his "creative development" of Marxism. In 1894 Lenin could argue that Marxism "proves" that "one order" of society must "necessarily" and "inevitably grow out of the preceding one regardless of whether men believe in it or not, whether they are conscious of it or not." The "conscious element" plays, Lenin insisted at that time, only a "subordinate . . . part in the history of civilization . . . ." In support of this analysis Lenin quoted an early letter (1843) by Marx which maintained that "consciousness is a thing which the world *must* acquire, whether it likes it or not."[2] As late as 1905 Lenin was arguing that it was a "truism" that "politics" must be "subordinated to economics," since "Marxism teaches us that a certain stage of its development a society which is based on commodity production and has commercial intercourse with civilized capitalist nations must inevitably take the road of capitalism. Marxism has irrevocably broken with the Narodnik and anarchist gibberish that Russia, for instance, can bypass capitalist development, escape from capitalism, or skip it in some way other than that of the class struggle, on the basis and within the framework of this same capitalism."[3]

Lenin seemed clearly committed to a notion that men's "consciousness" was epiphenomenal. Marx and Engels had maintained that it was not a question of what this or that proletariat, or what the whole of the proletariat, *thought* it ought to do, but rather a question of what the proletariat as a class will be, by economic and historic circumstances,

[2] V. I. Lenin, "What the 'Friends of the People' Are," *Collected Works*, I, 166, 185.

[3] Lenin, "Two Tactics of Social-Democracy in the Democratic Revolution," *ibid.*, IX, 41, 49.

compelled to do. Only such necessity could provide the grounds for anticipating an inevitable socialist revolution. Before 1900 Lenin seemed to accept this sort of account with but few reservations. Up to at least 1905 he seemed equally committed to the notion that Russia would go through certain preordained phases of socioeconomic development: the capitalist phase with its attendant bourgeois democratic phase—and only then, a subsequent socialist phase.

For all that, Lenin had begun to argue, as early as 1900 and certainly by 1902, that "consciousness" might not, as a matter of fact, arise *spontaneously* among the proletariat—that "consciousness" was something brought to the "revolutionary class" from "without," through the medium of a politically organized, self-selected cadre of professional revolutionaries. Moreover, by the time of the October Revolution, Lenin was already toying with the idea that socialism might come to industrially backward Russia, with its minority of proletarians and its peripheral bourgeois class, as a consequence of armed revolution—that, in effect, Russia might move directly into the "socialist phase" even before the "bourgeois phase" had consolidated itself.[4]

The transformation begun with Lenin matured into the bureaucratic collectivism, the state socialism, of Stalin, in which the influence of the socioeconomic "objective conditions" on historical development were "reduced to a minimum," and the part played by political and economic "organizations and their leaders" was understood to be "decisive" and "exceptional."[5] Why this should have been the case is not difficult to appreciate. Stalin had assumed the obligation of "creating socialism in one country"—a country which enjoyed only marginal industrial development. As a

[4] For an extended discussion of the process of involution of Lenin's social and political thought, cf. A. G. Meyer, *Leninism* (New York: Praeger, 1957); A. J. Gregor, *A Survey of Marxism* (New York: Random House, 1965), chap. 6.

[5] J. V. Stalin, "Report to the Seventeenth Congress of the C.P.S.U. (B.) on the Work of the Central Committee," *Problems of Leninism* (Moscow: Foreign Languages, 1953), p. 644.

consequence "socialism" in the Soviet Union came to mean the creation of an elaborate state structure, more imposing, by Stalin's admission, than any other form of government in history.[6] That state apparatus was created as a centralized agency of control governing the rapid industrialization of a backward economy—to provide the industrial base for socialism which classical Marxism maintained would be *inherited* by the revolution. Classical Marxism had insisted that socialism could only arise in an advanced economy, for any social system based on a restricted industrial base must necessarily be exploitative—characterized by oppressive class distinctions.

What the Bolshevik revolution had *promised* was a form of modified anarchism, implied in the commitments of mature classical Marxism. The first Soviet constitutional documents, the decrees on workers' control, on referendum and recall, all promised the widest scope for regional autonomy, popular initiative, and control; and whatever economic and political coordination was necessary was to be the result of voluntary and spontaneous cooperation of democratically elected regional councils. What the Bolshevik revolution ultimately *delivered*, however, was an elaborate bureaucracy composed of politically appointed incumbents, appendages of the party, a party which in turn fell increasingly under the domination of the "exceptional leader," Joseph Stalin.[7]

"Socialism" had come to an "unripe" economy. Marx had spoken of socialism developing within the "womb" of the old order, in the form of joint stock companies, producers' and consumers' cooperatives and workingmen's associations. He conceived of socialism as having only the problem of distribution to resolve. Capitalism, Marx argued, was afflicted with problems of maldistribution, overproduction or

[6] J. V. Stalin, "Political Report of the Central Committee to the Sixteenth Congress of the C.P.S.U. (B.)," *Works* (Moscow: Foreign Languages, 1955), xii, 380f., "The 15th Congress of the C.P.S.U. (B.)," *Works*, x, 327.

[7] For a more detailed account of this involution, cf. A. B. Ulam, *The Unfinished Revolution* (New York: Random House, 1964), chaps. 5 and 6.

underconsumption. These were concerns that could be resolved by the anarchistic democracy that Marx identified with the "dictatorship of the proletariat."

Lenin's revolution brought the Bolsheviks to power in an underdeveloped economy. The problems to be resolved were not problems of abundance and maldistribution, but problems of incredible scarcity and nonexistent productive capacity. What Russia required, Lenin very rapidly learned, was not a referendum and recall democracy and a voluntary association of communes, but a hierarchically controlled network of agencies that would insure distribution of those minimal necessities that were available while permitting the accumulation of capital for intensive investment. What resulted was an elaborate system of controls radiating from an authoritarian center. The development of these agencies of resource mobilization and allocation, of control over the means of information and communication, of planning, defense, and coercion, generated what thinking Marxists could not fail to recognize as an analogue of paradigmatic Fascism. As has been indicated, Bruno Rizzi had insisted as early as 1938 and again in 1962, that "Stalinism [took on] a regressive course, generating a species of red fascism identical in its superstructural and choreographic features [with its Fasist model]."[8] Franz Borkenau insisted that Fascism and Stalinism, as political systems, shared critical attributes insofar as both were organized efforts designed to drive their respective economies to maturity. Borkenau argued that it was Fascism's "historic mission" to industrialize the Italian peninsula, which had so long languished in agrarian torpor.[9] Stalinism accomplished the same task in economically backward Russia.

Academics such as Erich Fromm and Wilhelm Reich in-

[8] B. Rizzi, La lezione dello stalinismo (Rome: Opere nuove, 1962), p. 46.

[9] F. Borkenau, "Zur Soziologie des Faschismus," in E. Nolte, ed., Theorien über den Faschismus (Berlin: Kiepenheuer & Witsch, 1967), pp. 178f., and 164f.; cf. also Borkenau, World Communism (Ann Arbor: University of Michigan, 1962), p. 423.

sisted that Fascism and Stalinism were "perfect analogues" of each other.[10] If we grant that the obligations assumed by the two regimes were similar in character, and that both were animated by the elitist and voluntarist convictions we have briefly rehearsed, one would expect that the surface features displayed by both would share significant similarities. The "fateful similarities" people such as Trotsky were prepared to identify in the Fascist and Stalinist phenomena grew out of the economic tasks each faced and their common strategies. The fact that "primitive accumulation" in the service of the drive to maturity was accomplished through "class collaboration" in the one case, and through "class struggle" in the other, does not seem to have particular historic, economic, or political significance. Roland Sarti has recently argued that Fascism in Italy had developed a control structure that gave the party more influence over the national economy than any other system short of that in the Soviet Union.[11] By the end of 1943 Mussolini was attempting to socialize the entire Italian economy.[12] Given that Fascism acceded to power in an environment in which the traditional elites remained viable and securely entrenched—circumstances with which neither Lenin nor Stalin had to contend—the processes involved in pursuing economic maturity were different. The results, given the differences in resource potential, geographic position, and the population base, were substantially the same. By the early forties both countries achieved economic maturity.

Both Stalinism and paradigmatic Fascism were nationalistic developmental dictatorships, mass-based political movements under the tutelary guidance of a unitary party and the charismatic or pseudocharismatic leadership of a "unique" and "exceptional" leader. The legitimizing ration-

[10] W. Reich, *The Mass Psychology of Fascism* (New York: Orgone, 1946), pp. 237f., 241, 256f., 261, 280; E. Fromm, *Escape from Freedom* (New York: Avon, 1965), pp. 300f.

[11] R. Sarti, *Fascism and the Industrial Leadership in Italy, 1919-1940* (Berkeley: University of California, 1971), p. 124.

[12] Cf. Gregor, *Ideology of Fascism* (New York: Free Press, 1969), chap. 7.

ale for the political system was a relatively specific ideology whose doctrine was inculcated through an elaborate network of capillary agencies, youth groups, labor organizations, women's groups, farmers' associations, and entrepreneurial or bureaucratic syndicates. The purity of doctrine was insulated by a variety of controls ranging from overt violence and censorship to moral suasion. The entire apparatus of the state was, in effect, pressed into the service of party purpose—and party purpose was, in the last analysis, interpreted by the "inspired" leader. For both systems, the lines of contest were drawn between "proletarian" and "plutocratic," "bourgeois" or "capitalist" *nations*. In effect, neither system exploited classical Marxist distinctions between economically defined *classes*. In the "classless" Soviet Union, wage differentials, access to strategic functions and power, the relationship between individuals and groups of individuals to the productive base of society, were all neglected, and the entire population, whether bureaucrats, party functionaries, managers, skilled workers, unskilled workers, agricultural laborers, were "socialists" in a "socialist fatherland." Only *politically* defined opponents were harried—"Trotskyite terrorists," "wreckers" and "saboteurs." *Political* motives generated class and category harassments. At one time peasants were exploited through the medium of forced "donations" to the Soviet state; at other times workers' organizations or managerial personnel were domesticated to insure that specifically proletarian (or managerial) economic interests would not undermine the developmental programs of the regime. Autonomous labor organizations were domesticated in the Soviet Union at about the same time they were being domesticated in Fascist Italy. Far, far fewer Communist Party leaders died in Mussolini's prisons, in fact, than died in Stalin's purges. Fewer "non-Leninist" social revolutionaries, social democrats, and classical Marxists suffered privation in Fascist Italy than in Stalin's Russia.

The transformation of classical Marxism into Stalinism during the interwar years is now generally acknowledged. The revolution which was to be the spontaneous uprising of the vast majority of men turned proletarian by the very laws of economic dynamics—a revolution that would simultaneously sweep through all the advanced capitalist countries—became a minoritarian revolution led by a vanguard party controlled by a self-selected intellectual elite, in a single industrially backward country. The revolution that was to produce the "leap from necessity into freedom," that was to substitute the "governance of men" with the "administration of things," that was to see the withering away of the state—did, in fact, produce the most elaborate state apparatus in history, with hierarchically selected bureaucrats and administrators governing both men and things. The revolution that was to be the product of the class consciousness of the proletarian makers of history was construed as the consequence of the infusion of "consciousness" brought "from without" by the vanguard elite, with the masses providing "elemental energy" and "spontaneity." The "universal" revolution became increasingly national. Even after the Second World War provided the "Marxist" revolutionaries with "fraternal socialist states," national boundaries were assiduously maintained, national sovereignty defended (whenever and wherever possible) until the gradual relaxation of Soviet control permitted the several "socialist" states to choose "national roads" to "communism."

Throughout this process more and more of the theoretical writings of Marx and Engels became irrelevant. The most extensively formalized elements of the Marxist legacy, the economic theories contained in *Kapital*, are simply without significance in the context of developmental dictatorships— in marginally developed economies making the transit to industrial maturity. Only few socialist revolutionaries have suggested that Marx's theories concerning the determination of value, surplus profit, the average rate of profit, the crises of overproduction, and the secular decline in the rate of profit as a consequence of the high organic composition of capital have any relevance whatsoever for any twentieth-century "socialist" economy. None of this has been shown to be of any service in the intranational determination of wages, the development of economic planning, the fixing of prices, the allocation of resources in any "socialist" state, or commodity exchange between "socialist" states.

The fact is that Marxism has been employed by radicals in the twentieth century to fill in the interstices of a political system that could only be identified as "Marxist" out of courtesy to the enthusiasm of its advocates. The principal revolutionary leaders of the twentieth century have been Marxists (if to be a "Marxist" means to commit oneself to the essential theoretical rationale of classical Marxism) in name only. The revolutions they made, the strategies they employed, the postures they assumed, and the states they created and ruled have had precious little Marxism about them. The most immediate evidence for such a judgment is that men such as Lenin, Mussolini, and Mao Tse-tung while self-characterized as "Marxists" had early espoused systems of thought whose content bore precious little affinity to Marxism.

THE LEADERS AND THE LED: THE REVOLUTIONARY STRATEGY OF THE NEW RADICALISM

A common curiosity attends the intellectual development of some of the most prominent of the "radicals" of the twentieth century: they all acknowledged an indebtedness to a non-Marxist source or sources for the principal constituents of the world-view they ultimately espoused. While none of them could be identified with the thought of one such antecedent, all admitted one source as being *primus inter pares*. For Lenin that source was the work of N. G. Chernyshevsky; for Mussolini it was the work of Alfredo Oriani; and for Mao it was the work of Li Ta-chao.

If we recall that one of the principal difficulties of classical Marxism as a theoretical system was its inability to explain the persistence of a nonrevolutionary proletariat, one can appreciate why Marxists would ultimately seek supplemental recourse in non-Marxist sources. We now have considerable persuasive evidence that all three men, Lenin, Mussolini, and Mao, sought such supplements in the indigenous literature available to them, and in a form compatible with their native dispositions. All committed themselves, more early than late, to a form of political and revolutionary elitism unknown to classical Marxism—but capable of providing not only an explanation for the missing revolutionary proletariat but a rationale for a vanguard party of a new type. The selection of just such a theoretical adjunct to classical Marxism carried a number of implications: (1) the emphasis on politics, rather than economics; (2) the primacy of leadership, hierarchy, organization, and mass-mobilization, rather than spontaneity; (3) the priority of "subjective" rather than "objective" conditions for the making of revolution and the creation of a "socialist state." Where Marx and Engels were convinced that "politics was reduced to economics," the new radicals were to insist on the preeminence of politics. Where Marx and Engels were to speak of a "necessary revolution" "with or without political leaders or a political party," the new radicals were to insist that "without exceptional leadership and without the party there would be no revolution." Where Marx and Engels were to insist on the "maturation" of "economic conditions," the new radicals were to insist that "the subjective creates the objective." Where Marx and Engels insisted that "socialism" would inherit the advanced industry of the capitalist state already fat with the elements of the new order, the new radicals were to contend that the revolution, the party and its inspired leadership would create "socialism" by producing a "new breed of men" in a marginally industrialized, or essentially agrarian or even a "semi-feudal and semi-colonial" environment.

This involution followed a process remarkably similar in the case of Lenin and Mussolini—and Mao as well. All three found many of the ideas that were to transform classical Marxism bruited in non-Marxist works. Their fascination with those ideas remained steadfast throughout their political careers and contributed much to the content of the radicalism of our time.

Lenin left ample testimony of his fascination with the work of N. G. Chernyshevsky (1828-1889). After the execution of his brother, Alexander, for revolutionary activity, Lenin reread Chernyshevsky's novel *What Is to Be Done?* Alexander had especially favored Chernyshevsky's book, and the adolescent Lenin apparently turned to it to discover the meaning of his brother's sacrifice. Lenin later recounted to Nikolai Valentinov that he had read Chernyshevsky's novel not once, but many times, devoting "not several days, but several weeks" to the effort.[13] He insisted that he had read Chernyshevsky "with pencil in hand," taking notes and writing summaries. Krupskaya, Lenin's wife, indicated that Lenin "reread" Chernyshevsky's novel "many times"—that he was "particularly fond" of him and kept several pictures of Chernyshevsky in his album while he was in Siberia.[14]

Lenin, himself, insisted that "before my acquaintance with the works of Marx, Engels and Plekhanov, it was Chernyshevsky who exerted the main overwhelming revolutionary influence on me—an influence which began with *What Is to Be Done?* . . . He [Chernyshevsky] showed what the revolutionary must be like, what his rules must be, how he must go about attaining his goals, and by what methods and means he can bring about their realization."[15] In effect, Chernyshevsky had (to use Lenin's own revealing characterization) "plowed him [Lenin] over."

Lenin read *What Is to Be Done?* in 1887, when he was seventeen years old. Its influence was to remain with him throughout his active political life. Although classical Marxism was to overlard that influence between 1893 (when Lenin wrote his first "Marxist" tracts) and the turn of the century when "Leninism" made its first rudimentary appearance, Chernyshevsky's contribution to Leninism became palpable with the publication of Lenin's own *What Is to Be*

---

[13] N. Valentinov, *The Early Years of Lenin* (Ann Arbor: The University of Michigan, 1969), p. 136.

[14] N. K. Krupskaya, *Lenin* (Moscow: Foreign Languages, 1959), pp. 40, 503.

[15] Valentinov, *The Early Years of Lenin*, p. 196.

Done? in 1902. The title is in itself suggestive of that fact. The essay's principal thesis was that the "proletarian masses" would remain inevitably inert without the intercession of a self-selected, declassed elite of professional revolutionaries, who would bring to them the saving vision of a new world.

The content of Lenin's *What Is to Be Done?* is too well known to require repetition here. It marked only the first of the major departures from classical Marxism that were to distinguish Leninism from classical Marxism—and it laid the foundations of the Stalinist, and the current, Soviet Regime.

Lenin was aware that his *What Is to Be Done?* marked a critical juncture in the development of twentieth-century "Marxism." Not only was the content of the tract to guide him throughout the decade and a half from its publication until the October Revolution but it was calculated to distinguish two sorts of "Marxism"—an activist, voluntarist, and elitist version from one that was more "orthodox" spontaneous, objectivist, and democratic. Throughout 1903 Lenin anxiously awaited support from members of the Social Democratic Party for his interpretation.

Between 1893 and the turn of the century Lenin had committed himself to the orthodox conviction that revolution would come with the necessity of natural law, that the proletarian masses would respond automatically and rationally to changes in the economic base of contemporary society. With the publication of *What Is to Be Done?* Lenin was to argue that "socialist consciousness cannot exist among the workers. *This can be introduced only from without.* The history of all countries shows that *by its unaided efforts* the working class can only develop trade-union consciousness, that is to say, a conviction of the necessity to form trade unions, struggle with employers, obtain from the government this or that law required by the workers, and so on . . . ." In effect, history would make the workers inevitably "bourgeois," rather than revolutionary. "Without," Lenin maintained, "the 'dozen' tried and talented leaders . . . pro-

200

fessionally trained, schooled by long experience, and working in perfect harmony, no class in modern society can wage a determined struggle."[16]

Lenin realized that his views would be stigmatized as "anti-democratic" and "anti-Marxist" by the Marxists of his time. He nonetheless insisted that the revolution required the leadership of "talented" men, a self-selected hierarchy of professional revolutionaries, who would bring revolutionary consciousness to the elementary energies of the masses. These men were exiguous in number (such men, Lenin maintained, are not born by the hundreds) and required an association so constituted as to permit them to control centrally "all the threads" of organization. While Lenin's enthusiasm for the "workers" waxed and waned over the years of struggle, one conviction remained constant: The revolutionary party must not be subject to the will of the "majority." "The Party," he insisted in 1917, "could not be guided by the temper of the masses because [that temper] was changeable and incalculable . . . ."[17]

All these were transliterations of themes found in the work of Chernyshevsky. Chernyshevsky had argued that the "new world" had as its harbingers "new men," "austere, practical and cold men," that have only just begun to appear in the midst of the "antediluvians" of the mid-nineteenth century. Chernyshevsky saw these "new men" as "exceptions" to whom all men of the old stamp will "in a very few years" appeal with the "cry, 'Save Us!' and, whatever they say will then be done by all."

Chernyshevsky admitted that he had "a very poor opinion of the public," that the general public was, in fact, "intellectually impotent"—a public which, without the special men making their appearance in anticipation of the "golden age," would "stifle" and "suffocate." So much depended on

[16] Lenin, "What Is to Be Done?" *Collected Works*, v, 375, 382f., 461.

[17] Lenin, "Meeting of the Central Committee of the R.S.D.L.P. (B.), October 16, 1917," *ibid.*, xxvi, 191.

these "new men," so few in number. "They are," Chernyshevsky insisted, "the best among the best, they are the movers of the movers, they are the salt of the salt of the earth."[18]

For Chernyshevsky the world was divided among the "new men" and the "antediluvians." The "new men" possessed a special will and an irrepressible determination that was at least in part a natural endowment. But whatever their source, that will and that determination marked the difference between victory and defeat in the coming conflict between the "new generation" and the old. For Chernyshevsky, that will and that determination constituted "causes" which "govern all historical phenomena." In the case of the forthcoming social upheaval the "new men" were—with that will and that determination—to invoke the energies of the masses. As Chernyshevsky conceived the invocation in *What Is to Be Done?* it was to be a relatively simple process. "Men," Chernyshevsky maintained, "drag themselves along in a beaten track simply because they have been told to do so; but tell them in a very loud voice to take another road, and, though they will not hear you at first, they will soon throw themselves in the new path with the same spirit."[19]

This was the supplement Chernyshevsky provided for classical Marxism. If the problem of the missing revolutionary proletariat prompted Bernstein to undertake a revision of Marxism, Lenin's attempt to solve the problem included no fewer revisions, and his modifications of the theoretical structure left by Marx and Engels was no less compromising. Revolution, Lenin argued, in effect and in fact, was too serious a matter to be left to the proletariat. It was to be the responsibility of a small self-selected vanguard cadre of declassed bourgeois intellectuals—"new men" who would channel the elemental energies of the masses—energies that would otherwise remain "changeable and incalculable."[20]

[18] N. G. Chernyshevsky, *What Is to Be Done?* tr. Benjamin Tucker (New York: Random House, 1961), pp. 13, 81, 174f., 11-13, 24, 86, 241.

[19] *Ibid.*, pp. 302, 229, 292f., 41.

[20] For a synoptic discussion of the implications of Lenin's "What

While Lenin was composing *What Is to Be Done?*, Mussolini, thirteen years his junior but already a radical socialist, was formulating his own conception of a vanguard revolutionary party led by a small minority of "men of a new type."

As early as 1903 (when he was twenty years old), Mussolini was formulating theses to supplement the theoretical infrastructure of the Classical Marxism with which he identified. As we have seen, he had already read Gustave Le Bon's *Psychologie des foules*; he was familiar with the critical work of Georges Sorel; and by 1902 he had probably read Vilfredo Pareto's *Les systèmes socialistes*.[21] Thus, by the time he reached first maturity and while he still emphatically characterized himself as a Marxist, and was so characterized by his peers in the Socialist Party, Mussolini was prepared to reduce the slack in the theoretical formulations of Marx and Engels by supplements provided in part by non-Marxist sources.

In retrospect, therefore, it is not surprising that the young Mussolini should have found Alfredo Oriani's *La rivolta ideale* "magnificent."[22] There is no way to fix with precision the date when Mussolini read Oriani's book. The book was written between May and September in 1906 and was first published in 1907. Mussolini's first reference to it appears in an article published in May 1909. Thus it cannot be argued that Mussolini's political thought was *formed* in the crucible of Oriani's work; it would be more appropriate to suggest that Mussolini used Oriani as a suitable vehicle for that thought. Nonetheless, Oriani's book provided the occasion for a more explicit statement of Mussolini's position; and years later, when Mussolini edited a collection of Oriani's works, he insisted that he had been "nourished" on the pages of *La rivolta ideale* and that he considered Oriani a "precursor of

---

Is to Be Done?", cf. A. B. Ulam, *Lenin and the Bolsheviks* (London: Secker & Warburg, 1966), pp. 176-80.

[21] For a more detailed discussion of Mussolini's development during this period, cf. Gregor, *The Ideology of Fascism*, chap. 3.

[22] Mussolini, "La teoria sindacalista," *Opera*, II, 128.

Fascism."[23] In 1939, in the plenitude of his power, Mussolini visited the home of Oriani and requested to see the manuscript copy of *La rivolta ideale*, which he "examined with great tenderness, exclaiming, 'These must be preserved with great care.' "[24]

Mussolini had, by 1909, joined irrepressible elitist convictions to his Marxist persuasion. Those convictions were couched in the idiom found in Oriani's *La rivolta ideale*. For Oriani each "epoch has but one purpose, the development of the human character." That development proceeds through the influence of an "aristocracy" that gives voice to the inarticulate revolutionary strivings of the masses. That aristocracy is a "revolutionary vanguard"—a vanguard in which the elemental instincts and the anonymous power of the multitude finds expression.[25] "An aristocracy is either the select of a nation or it is nothing. The most advanced constitute an innovating vanguard . . . a general staff [whose command] is legitimized and justified by their assumption of full responsibility. . . . It is necessary to recognize that the emancipation of the multitude requires that the multitude sees its liberty prefigured in the moral and intellectual aristocracy."[26]

Oriani's elite, his "messengers of the future"—whom Mussolini would call "new men"—were men whose superiority was at least in part the consequence of natural endowment, men who were disdainful of the counting of votes or the counting of money as strategies suitable in the determination of truth or in the assignment of responsibilities.[27] Oriani's "new men," like those of Chernyshevsky, were obliged to inform and invoke the energies of the masses, if necessary without pity and with violence.[28]

Mussolini insisted that Oriani had identified the obliga-

[23] Mussolini, "Alfredo Oriani," *ibid.*, xx, 245.

[24] Mussolini, "All Corporazione dei cereali," *ibid.*, xxix, 299f., n.

[25] A. Oriani, *La rivolta ideale* (Bologna: Cappelli, 1943), pp. 7, 29, 33, 37; cf. *ibid.*, pp. 370f.

[26] *Ibid.*, pp. 44, 93.   [27] *Ibid.*, pp. 285f.   [28] *Ibid.*, p. 36.

tions of the epoch—the creation of a "new man" suitable for a "new age." It was the task of radical Marxists to create such "new men." That the masses had been ill-disposed to revolution was a result of the fact that revolutionaries have "all but completely ignored mass psychology and have, as a consequence, been inept agitators."[29] As early as 1903, Mussolini anticipated the necessity of introducing a collection of psychological generalizations to supplement classical Marxism. Under the influence of Le Bon, Pareto, and Oriani this insight developed into a conception of the relationship between restive masses possessed of elemental energies and a directive vanguard elite composed of "new men" capable of leading the multitude. Mussolini had generated his own response to the question of the missing revolutionary proletariat. His response was not significantly different from that made by Lenin at approximately the same time.

Both Lenin and Mussolini introduced voluntarist and elitist elements into what had been classical Marxism—to produce the first moves in the direction of that radical persuasion that was to characterize revolutionary political thought in the twentieth century.

During the period in which both Lenin and Mussolini were adapting Marxism to the requirements of their individual circumstances, Li Ta-chao in China was pursuing a course that would take him from the neo-Confucianism of his youth to the activist, voluntarist, and elitist Marxism of his early maturity. Li was to have special significance in the revolutionary history of China—his thought was to exercise an abiding influence over that of Mao Tse-tung.[30]

Li Ta-chao was a Chinese nationalist—a voluntarist, influenced by Henri Bergson's notions of "free-will"—who, in adopting Marxism as a political perspective in 1919, "refused . . . to renounce his faith in the ability of conscious,

[29] Mussolini, "La teoria sindacalista," *Opera*, ii, 128.
[30] Cf. E. Snow, *Red Star Over China* (New York: Grove Press, 1961), p. 157; and S. Schram, *The Political Thought of Mao Tse-tung* (New York: Praeger, 1969), pp. 28f.

active men to remake society in accordance with their wills."

In May 1919 Li wrote a lengthy article, "My Marxist Views," in which he outlined a summary of some of the major theses of orthodox classical Marxism. The one feature of Marxism concerning which Li entertained the most reservations was the determinism that seemed to attend the materialist conception of history. The interpretation he chose is now identified explicitly with the later Engels, in which elements of the economic base of society interact in a complex, reversible, and interdependency relationship with those of the "ideological superstructure." "[Li Ta-chao] left no doubt that he found wholly unpalatable the Marxist de-emphasis on the role of ethical and spiritual factors in history."[31]

For Li those factors were determinants in the class struggle—a struggle between the propertied and the propertyless. Such a class struggle would be the medium for China's moral regeneration. The position he assumed was very similar to that assumed by Mussolini about a decade earlier. Mussolini had insisted that Marxism must be given a voluntaristic and activistic interpretation. As early as 1909 Mussolini insisted that radical Marxists, if they were serious revolutionaries, must espouse a "philosophy of action." He maintained that the laws governing the economic development of society acted and interacted with the "willed activity of man, determined and determined in turn . . . ." Radical Marxism could not reject "economic necessity," nor could it deny the impact of "ethical consciousness."[32] The change that had taken place becomes manifest when we compare these postures with that of Lenin in 1895: Lenin, at that time (before Bernstein's criticisms had become commonplace and before Chernyshevsky's influence had resurfaced) maintained that "One therefore cannot deny the justice of Sombart's remark that 'in Marxism itself there is not a grain of ethics from beginning to end'; theoretically, it subordinates the 'ethical stand-

---

[31] M. Meisner, *Li Ta-chao and the Origins of Chinese Marxism* (Cambridge: Harvard University, 1967), pp. 125, 93.

[32] Cf. Gregor, *Ideology of Fascism*, pp. 120-31.

point' to the 'principle of causality'; in practice it reduces it to the class struggle."[33]

By the first decade of the twentieth century, radicals, among whom Lenin was numbered, were supplementing classical Marxism with "ethical adjuncts" that found expression in "willed activity" on the part of "revolutionary intellectuals" who would invoke the energies of the masses in the service of revolution. In effect, radicals sought to provide the psychological generalizations and the ethical commitments that would make Marxism a guide to revolutionary conduct, and provide specialized functions for a revolutionary elite—a "socialist" vanguard. The thought of both Lenin and Mussolini had followed the same trajectory. Li's thought, quite independently, pursued the same course. He repeated arguments that had common currency among European radicals: "the [European] Marxist socialist parties, because of their belief in a fatalistic theory, proposed nothing, undertook no activities, and only waited for the natural maturation of the productive forces, until today the socialist parties of the various [European] countries have entered a period of great crisis. This can be said to be a defect left by Marx's materialist conception of history."[34] Mussolini tendered essentially the same analysis of the passivity of socialist parties and the proletariat of Europe: "Socialism, out of an addiction to economic determinism, subordinated men to inscrutable laws which were cognitively obscure but to which they had to submit." In essence, historical determinism as it was generally interpreted made men historical spectators rather than participants in the drama of history. Lenin, in turn, objected to the thesis of "spontaneity," the view that political events follow in the train of economic development. He insisted that a political elite functioned as an essential and nonsubstitutable determinant in revolutionary success—without which revolution was impossible.

Mussolini and Li recognized that their voluntaristic and

[33] Lenin, "The Economic Content of Narodism and the Criticism of It in Mr. Struve's Book," *Collected Works*, I, 420f.

[34] Meisner, *Li Ta-chao*, p. 127.

activistic interpretation of Marxism was either one of several equally plausible interpretations of, or a supplement to, Marx's views. Lenin, on the other hand, insisted that his was the *only* legitimate interpretation. Nonetheless, in the interpretations of Lenin, Mussolini, and Li, there was a significant change of emphasis in radical thought; and classical Marxism began its transformation. Neither Lenin, Mussolini, nor Li saw "revolutionary consciousness" as a property of the proletariat in itself (as Marx did), nor as a derivative product of the maturation of social forces (as was the case in classical Marxism), but rather an attribute conveyed to "masses" of men (not necessarily proletarian in their majority) via a self-selected vanguard elite.

The disassociation of revolutionary or class consciousness from a specifically defined class—making a minority of declassed intellectuals its agents—makes revolution possible in any environment, no matter how socially or economically retarded. The price one pays for increasing the range of the "relevance" and "significance" of Marxism, for making it a strategy for revolution in *any* social, economic, and political environment, is to empty it of much of its specific content.

Marx clearly saw revolution as the consequence of the maturity of economic forces that not only produced the intolerable tensions of advanced capitalism but also educated the vast majority of men, as proletarians, to their political and historical responsibilities. The proletariat, as a class in and for itself, inheriting the industrial capacity of advanced capitalism, could usher in the rational, free, and harmonious social order Marx foresaw. With the suppression of a small coterie of capitalists who had concentrated all economic power in their own hands, the "dictatorship of the proletariat" was essentially a democratic government based on universal suffrage, referendum, and recall and assiduously defending itself against hierarchical investiture.

Once revolutionary or class consciousness is conceived to be the possession of an elite, capable of bringing that consciousness not only to the passive proletariat but to subproletarian or nonproletarian masses, all coherence is gone. Both Lenin and Mussolini realized that they were operating in relatively backward economic environments. While both spoke of "proletarian" revolutions, they recognized that the majority of the working masses that provided the recruitment bases for their political organizations was nonproletarian. The entire notion of class struggle began to take on singular characteristics. For Lenin a select number of declassed bourgeois intellectuals became the repository of "proletarian revolutionary consciousness," the proletarians became afflicted with "bourgeois consciousness," while the bourgeoisie supports "feudalism." The relationships became so complicated that Lenin, by 1905, could argue that the "victory of the *bourgeois revolution*" is the responsibility of the "*proletariat* and the *peasantry!*"

During the first quarter of the twentieth century the answer to the dilemma of the nonrevolutionary proletariat was provided by the thesis that revolution is the consequence of the intercession of a self-selected vanguard elite. Without that elite, revolution would be impossible. The resolution of the dilemma was the same for Lenin and Mussolini as it was for Li Ta-chao. The problem left by Marx and Engels was resolved—but only at the expense of much of the substance of classical Marxism.

For Li Ta-chao the reinterpretation of Marxism meant that proletarian consciousness could develop in an environment completely innocent of proletarians. The nonproletarian intellectuals could be the vehicle for "socialist and revolutionary consciousness." Li's conviction that such "consciousness" could be conveyed implied that the intelligentsia not only was capable of but was charged with the responsibility for bringing it to the masses of China. As early as 1920 the expression "revolutionary vanguard" appeared in his writings, and its referent was the "intelligentsia." "A faith in the ability of 'self-conscious' intellectuals to fashion reality in accordance with their ideas and wills was an integral part of Li's pre-Marxian world view, and this faith was reflected

209

in the voluntaristic interpretation of Marxism he had arrived at . . . ."[35]

Voluntarism and activism, conjoined with an insistent elitism, was to generate enormous tensions within the structure of classical Marxism. Classical Marxism's most consistent characterization of human action conceived it as the reflex response of a determinate social class to objective social and economic circumstances. The radicals of the twentieth century have conceived collective human action as the consequence of an invocation issued by a self-selected revolutionary elite. The elite derives from all and any class; and the masses that respond are of any and all class provenience. If the existence of a vanguard party becomes the necessary, if not the sufficient, condition for revolution, "objective conditions" diminish in corresponding measure and significance. Thus, in 1934 Stalin could report to the central agencies of the party that since ". . . the strength and prestige of our Party, state, economic, and all other organizations, and of their leaders have grown to an unprecedented degree . . . their work now determines everything, or nearly everything. There can be no justification for references to so-called objective conditions. . . . [The] *part played by so-called objective conditions has been reduced to a minimum; whereas the part played by our organizations and their leaders has become decisive, exceptional.*"[36] Stalinists were to argue that under "socialism" progressive development, social, economic, and political, is "determined by the socialist consciousness of the masses, *by the degree to which the ideas and the slogans of the Communist Party are disseminated among the masses . . . .*"[37]

The Fascist analogues are obvious. By 1929 Fascists were

[35] Meisner, *Li Ta-chao*, pp. 202f.

[36] Stalin, "Report to the Seventeenth Congress of the C.P.S.U. (B.)," *Problems of Leninism*, p. 644. Emphasis supplied.

[37] F. V. Konstantinov, *The Role of Socialist Consciousness in the Development of Soviet Society* (Moscow: Foreign Languages, 1951), p. 30. Emphasis supplied.

prepared to identify the party with the very vital functions of the nation. "There is not a sector of life which does not fall under the purview of the Party. The influence exercised by the National Fascist Party is, through a variety of means, universal. It has entered . . . into all the economic, social and welfare institutions. . . . The Party . . . is the critical and dynamic element of the Regime . . . ."[38] As a consequence Fascists could dismiss "objective conditions" because, even if a nation necessarily operates within the confines of "external economic and political difficulties, these can be neutralized by its own defensive and constructive energies . . . embodied in the actions of the Party and its organizations."[39]

The party, to effect its will, employed its monopoly over the means of communication to instill in the populace the appropriate "attitudes." Fascist Italy became famous (or infamous as the case might be) for its "propaganda days," its wall slogans—the entire choreography of mass manipulation.

But more striking than the obvious parallels in organization, strategy, and justificatory rationale that came to characterize mass-mobilizing radical regimes was their ultimate generation of that phenomenon now identified as the "cult of personality"—so remote from any foundation in classical Marxism, but so natural a consequence of a sustained and systematic commitment to voluntarism, activism, and elitism.

To conceive the will and determination of a minority to be significant factors in history and revolution, suggests that some men, perhaps one man, are uniquely possessed of epochal qualities. Conspiratorial organizations, political movements with chiliastic and messianic convictions, tend to require some restricted body of men, or ideally some one man, to make decisions with dispatch, to resolve conflict

[38] *Il Partito Nazionale Fascista* (Partito Nazionale Fascista. Rome, Libreria dello stato, 1936), pp. 45f.

[39] C. Quaglio, *Orientatmenti della rivoluzione fascista* (Lucca: L'Artiglio, 1937), pp. 199f.

within the organization, to banish the heretical, to assign responsibility, and to reward accomplishment. Without viable institutions for the expression of popular opinion, for the public exchange of information, elitist systems seem to require some ultimate legitimizing authority—an authority which, because it is the source of legitimacy, the final arbiter in disputes, a canonical guide to conduct, becomes exalted.

The Soviet Union produced its "infallible genius" in the "Great Stalin." On February 4, 1935, the Leningrad *Krasnaya gazeta* published the following:

> All our love, our faith, our strength, our heart, our heroism, our life—all is for you, take it, great Stalin, everything is yours, leader of the great homeland. Command your sons, they can move in the air and under the earth, in the water and in the stratosphere. People of all times and nations will call your name the most magnificent, wisest and most beautiful. Your name is written on every factory and machine, on every piece of ground, in every heart. When my beloved wife gives me a child, the first word I shall teach him will be: Stalin.

In 1950 the Academy of Sciences of the U.S.S.R. and the Academy of Medical Sciences of the U.S.S.R. adopted a resolution, which said, in part,

> You [Stalin], as a pre-eminent scientist, produce works which are without equal in the history of progressive science. Your work *Concerning Marxism in Linguistics* is a model of genuine creative science, a supreme example of how science should be developed and advanced. It has created a revolution in linguistics, it has ushered in a new era in Soviet science generally. You, Comrade Stalin, pose and creatively solve most vital problems of Marxist-Leninist theory. The powerful light of your genius illumines the road to Communism. We, like all Soviet people, are proud and infinitely happy that world progress and advanced science are headed by you, dear Joseph Vissarionovich. Long live our beloved teacher and leader, the glory of

laboring humanity, the pride and banner of progressive science—our great Stalin.[40]

The exaltation of the Leader in Fascist Italy reveals the same pattern. In 1941 Luigi Fontanelli could ask: "Who laid the foundations of the Fascist Corporative State consecrating the 'human dignity' of labor? Who, affirming to the end of capitalism, proclaimed to the world the indispensability of the new Fascist State and of a 'more elevated social justice'? Who has given Italy its place in the sun, conquering an empire in seven months? All these questions which refer to the most glorious pages of the history of the new Italy, have as an answer one name only . . . Duce!" Ottavio Dinale, in 1934, could insist that "Mussolini . . . is the warrior and the leader, the genius and the bringer of order, the zealot and pragmatist, journalist and soldier of the trenches, the orator and writer, polemicist and politician, the man, who in sacrifice, in affirmation, in risk, in battle, in victory, in intransigence against the enemy, [possesses] a human generosity of supernatural order. [He] is the living, swift, dynamic and sustaining omnipresence that invokes dedication, generates self-sacrifice, attracts the young, arms the hero, strengthens the martyr, mobilizes a squad or an entire people, harnesses destiny, dominates adversity, seizes victory, transcends time and space: the Hero." Moreover, it is the "thought of Mussolini [*il pensiero Mussoliniano*]" that "illuminates" all things, that provides the "flashes of motive ideas" that directs the Revolution, overcomes obstacles and makes Fascism invincible.[41]

The elitism that characterized the doctrinal and organizational rationale of China's radicals has produced the Asiatic analogue of the cult of personality. If class conscious-

[40] As quoted in R. Payne, *The Rise and Fall of Stalin* (New York: Simon and Schuster, 1965), p. 646, and *Scientific Session on the Physiological Teachings of Academician I. P. Pavlov* (Moscow: Foreign Languages, 1951), pp. 6f.

[41] L. Fontanelli, *Sentimento della rivoluzione* (Rome: U.E.S.I., 1941), pp. 14f.; O. Dinale, *La rivoluzione che vince* (Rome: Campitelli, 1934), pp. 116.

ness for classical Marxism was the product, in whatever sense, of material conditions of life, class consciousness for China's "Marxists" is "the result of being nurtured on Mao Tse-tung's thought."[42] As early as 1928 Mao had suggested that he could "proletarianize" his guerrilla army, composed largely of agricultural vagrants, by intensifying "their political training so as to effect a qualitative change in [them]."[43] By the end of the sixties all that was necessary to fathom the intricacies of "proletarian politics" was the rote learning of the "principles" of the "thought of Mao Tse-tung."

That the potential for such a development was implicit in the Asian variant of contemporary radical thought is evident in Mao's criticism, in 1930, of Lin Piao (who has since learned better), for "over-estimating the importance of objective forces and under-estimating the importance of subjective forces."[44] Such contentions have become relatively commonplace in the literature of Chinese "Marxism." "Men, we are told, are not the slaves of objective reality. Provided only that men's consciousness be in conformity with the objective laws of the development of things, the subjective activity of the popular masses can manifest itself in full measure, overcome all difficulties, create the necessary conditions, and carry forward the revolution. In this sense, *the subjective creates the objective.*"[45] Such convictions have been condensed into Maoist aphorisms of the following sort: "External causes are the condition of change and internal causes are the basis of change, and . . . external causes become operative through internal causes."[46]

The principal "internal cause" is the "grasping" of the thought of Mao Tse-tung. "Once Mao Tse-tung's thought is

[42] *Mao Tse-tung's Thought is the Invincible Weapon* (Peking: Foreign Languages, 1968), p. 3.

[43] Schram, *Political Thought*, p. 269.

[44] As quoted in Schram's introduction to *Quotations from Chairman Mao Tse-tung* (New York: Bantam, 1967), p. x.

[45] Schram's introduction to *Political Thought*, pp. 135f. Emphasis supplied.

[46] *Mao Tse-tung's Thought is the Invincible Weapon*, p. 41.

grasped by the broad masses," Lin Piao informs us, "it becomes an inexhaustible source of strength and a spiritual
atom bomb of infinite power." Elsewhere we are told that

> The technical capabilities of a naval ship are limited and
> can be worked out with computers, but the power of men
> armed with Mao Tse-tung's thought is incalculable. . . .
> Although for the time being our equipment is not yet as
> good as the enemy's we have the thought of Mao Tse-tung
> as our invincible "magic weapon," with which we are sure
> to perform miracles. . . . The courage of our proletarian
> revolutionary fighters has its source in the great thought
> of Mao Tse-tung. . . . Mao Tse-tung's thought is the un-
> setting red sun.

The "great thought of Mao Tse-tung" is a "brilliant light,"
from which the "proletariat" must "at no time and in no circumstances . . . depart in the slightest . . . ."[47]

It has become quite clear that Maoism has taken on features that make it singular even within a family of singulari-
ties. That it has ceased, in a substantial sense, to be Marxist
is acknowledged by its protagonists. In 1945 Liu Shao-chi
reported that not only was Mao Tse-tung "the greatest revolutionary and statesman in Chinese history, but also its
greatest theoretician and scientist." He went on to indicate
that in "the theoretical field, [Mao] was boldly creative, dis-
carding certain specific Marxist principles and conclusions
that were obsolete or incompatible with the concrete conditions in China, and replacing them with new principles and
new conclusions that are compatible with China's new historical conditions." In 1966 Lin Piao, then Mao's new suc-
cessor-designate, indicated that while Mao "is the greatest
Marxist-Leninist of our era," he has "developed Marxism-

---

[47] Lin Piao, Foreword to the Second Edition, *Quotations from
Chairman Mao Tse-tung*, p. xxx; *The Whole Country Should Become
a Great School of Mao Tse-tung's Thought* (Peking: Foreign Languages, 1966), p. 17; *Mao Tse-tung's Thought is the Invincible Weapon*, pp. 2, 10, 32, 73.

Leninism with genius, creatively and comprehensively and has brought it *to a higher and completely new stage*."[48]

Not only has Mao "creatively developed" Marxism, but he has completely inverted what used to be conceived as the relationship between consciousness and social being. As part of the "Great Proletarian Cultural Revolution," Wang Tao-ming has revealed that the fact that one's objective social life has been peasant or working class, that one has been "revolutionary" since childhood, having been brought up in "the new society," having received "the Party's education," does not in any way qualify one as a "proletarian." The only way in which one can become a true proletarian is to have one's "consciousness remolded" by "purifying" oneself in the "thought of Mao Tse-tung." One "must resist all kinds of non-proletarian ideas"—and "permeate his thinking with Chairman Mao's teaching . . . ." For Mao has indicated that without his thought there are no "proletarians." "In the building of a socialist society, *everybody* needs remolding . . . ." The individual must realize that "just like the tender seedling which cannot grow without sunshine, [he] cannot make an iota of progress without learning from Mao Tse-tung's thought . . . . It is entirely due to Mao Tse-tung's thought that [one has] been able to grow at all. Mao Tse-tung's thought is the unsetting red sun in [one's] heart and [one] will forever [remain] a seedling which cannot do without the sunshine even for a single moment."[49]

THE NEW RADICALISM AND NATIONALISM

The very emphasis upon the decisive roles of "subjective" variables, "will," "determination," and "leadership," as determinants of behavior suggests that contemporary radicals have been more than just indifferently concerned with some-

[48] Liu Shao-chi, *On the Party* (Peking: Foreign Languages, 1951), pp. 33f.; Lin Piao, Foreword to the Second Edition, *Quotations*, p. xxix.

[49] Wang Tao-ming, "To Remold my World Outlook with Mao Tse-tung's Thought," in *Mao Tse-tung's Thought is the Invincible Weapon*, pp. 56-80.

thing not found in classical Marxism—a viable conception of individual and collective motivation. Contemporary radical movements employ elite-directed mass-mobilizing strategies. The conviction that the proletariat would automatically organize itself into a mass-based revolutionary movement has long since been abandoned. A critical and nonsubstitutable variable in the organization of the "masses" is the vanguard party under the leadership of exceptional leaders.

Having resolved the problem of how masses are mobilized, contemporary radicals did not simply intuit the population base upon which mobilization strategies were to be employed. Since radical leaders have more frequently than not found themselves, since the turn of the century, operating in environments that enjoy precious few proletarians, the immediate suggestion that they mobilize proletarians had little to recommend it. A much more promising candidate for mobilizing efforts is the "people." But the "people" have always provided the recruitment base for *nationalism* rather than *international socialism.* To address oneself to the "people" is to abandon, for all intents and purposes, "class," the seemingly proper recruitment base for Marxists.

As we have seen, Mussolini had been among the first Marxists explicitly to recognize the critical mobilizing function of nationalist sentiment in recruiting masses to revolutionary and developmental purpose. But in recognizing that function he was also prepared to recognize, with a candor uncommon among radicals, that he had undertaken significant departures from classical Marxism. Mussolini adopted elitist mobilizing strategies conjoined with the invocation of nationalist sentiment in order to recruit the masses necessary for his revolution. The strategy and the invocation were embodied in the Fascist conception of Italy as a "proletarian nation" in competition with the world "plutocracies." What has often been neglected, or suppressed, is the affinity shared by this specifically Fascist conception (which can be traced back to the writings of Corradini in 1909) and its obvious analogues in the thought of radicals who continue, to this day, to identify themselves as "Marxists."

217

Li Ta-chao, for example, even after his conversion to "Marxism," at about the same time he was articulating his conception of the historic role of the intellectual vanguard in 1920, expressed the conviction that China, in its substantial entirety, was a "proletarian nation." Li argued that the entire Chinese *people*, rather than any constituent class, suffered under the depredations of world capitalism. He maintained that "in the world economy of today China really stands in the position of the world proletariat," and, as a consequence, the revolutionary struggle between the "workers" and "capitalism" took on the form of international struggle between "worker, or proletarian nations" against "capitalist or exploiter nations." One does not have to be particularly sophisticated to recognize that if China was considered to be, in its essential entirety, a proletarian nation, Marx's historical materialism could be employed to justify a political belief system that was at once not only voluntaristic and elitist but *nationalist* as well.

Lenin had, of course, already provided the first intimations of such a rationale for a "Marxist" nationalism. Lenin's *Imperialism* provided a conception of international economic relations that made underdeveloped nations the special prey of the advanced capitalist countries—a circumstance which rendered the underdeveloped areas more immediately susceptible to revolutionary agitation. Lenin conceived the capitalist exploitation of the underdeveloped and marginally developed countries as providing the "superprofits" with which the bourgeoisie of the advanced industrial powers suborned the leaders of their own working class—making the leaders, and through their leaders the proletariat of the advanced countries, "social chauvinists." This was essentially the thesis argued, a year before Lenin wrote *Imperialism*, by N. I. Bukharin in his *Imperialism and World Economy*. Bukharin was particularly explicit about the relationship between agrarian and industrially advanced nations.

Bukharin insisted that classical Marxism had concerned itself essentially with the social division of labor within the confines of "national" economic systems. He argued that revolutionary attention should be given to the *international* division of labor, which transcends that of the "national economy." Karl Marx had never succeeded in producing the volume dedicated to world economy. It was incumbent upon twentieth-century radicals to produce it.

Bukharin suggested that the world was divided between "industrial nations," which enjoy enormous advantage, and "agrarian nations," afflicted with competitive disadvantage. "The difference," Bukharin argued, "between the 'city' and the 'countryside' . . . which at one time obtained within the confines to the national economy, is now reproduced in a much larger context. From this point of view entire nations, that is to say industrialized nations, manifest themselves as 'metropolitan areas,' while the agrarian regions serve as the 'countryside.' "[50]

In effect, the world was divided into *nations* enjoying different competitive positions. Lin Piao's recent characterization of the world as divided between "North America and Western Europe" as "the cities of the world," and "Asia, Africa and Latin America" as the "rural areas of the world" is simply a restatement of that account.[51] Both Bukharin's and Lin Piao's formulations share remarkable similarities with those bruited by pre-Fascist nationalists in Italy and Fascist theoreticians throughout the period of the Fascist regime. Not only, as we have seen, did Corradini insist that Italy was a "proletarian nation"—disadvantaged in international competition with "plutocratic nations"—but Fascist theorists articulated the distinction between "industrial nations" and "agricultural nations" made by Bukharin and Lin. G. De Florentiis, as a Fascist economist, maintained that the international division of labor had put nations specialized in agricultural production in a position of singular competitive disadvantage. Nations that have industrialized abandon agri-

---

[50] N. I. Bukharin, *L'economia mondiale e l'imperialismo* (Rome: Samona e Savelli, 1966), pp. 98f., 103.

[51] Lin Piao, *Long Live the Victory of People's War!* (Peking: Foreign Languages, 1968), p. 108.

culture to the poorer nations. The agrarian nations, he argued, become increasingly dependent on the advanced nations—and the prevailing system of international exchange insures that "the rich nations become richer while the poor nations become poorer"—to create an economic and ultimately political hegemony by the industrialized states over dependent, that is to say, agrarian, nations.[52] This analysis and the strategy it generated were to displace the "class war" from intrasocietal confines to international competition—in what the Fascists called "the class struggle between nations."[53] It was to put a premium on *national* development, to offset the disadvantages which attend underdevelopment.

Bukharin, like Lenin after him, maintained that the advanced capitalist nations exploited the underdeveloped areas of the globe in order to garner "superprofits" which could, in turn, be used in part to suborn the leadership of the working class. Without leadership the working class became, as Lenin had early suggested, "inevitably bourgeois." The revolutionary consciousness of the proletariat of the advanced capitalist countries is deflected by bribing a select stratum of the working class, and an "accommodation" between the classes takes place (at the time Bukharin insisted that the accommodation could only be of limited duration). As long as that accommodation obtains, the "class struggle" is transposed to the national plane. Substantially *all* the classes in the advanced country become "capitalist"—and substantially *all* those in the underdeveloped environment become "proletarian."

The thesis of "proletarian *nations*" as opposed to "bourgeois *nations*" permitted twentieth-century radicals to employ Marxist phraseology in the service of *national* revolution, and to explain the nonrevolutionary character of the proletariat of the advanced industrial nations.

By 1925 Stalin's thesis of "socialism in one country" had

[52] G. De Florentiis, *Le materie prime e l'Italia* (Milan: Bompiani, 1936), pp. 14-16.
[53] V. Gayda, *L'economia di domani* (Rome: Giornale d'Italia, 1941), p. 28.

transformed Marxism into a form of revolutionary, developmental, and manifestly nationalist dictatorship. Once revolutionary or proletarian consciousness becomes detached from an identifiable class base—and becomes the possession of a vanguard elite from whatever class—any and all classes can serve the "socialist" nation in its competition against the "imperialist" or "plutocratic" nations. Just as the proletarians of the advanced industrial nations are deflected from their purpose because of the characteristics of world economics, "patriotic" elements of whatever class provenience can further "proletarian" interests in underdeveloped countries.

It was not only the Fascists who made a distinction between the "productive" or "national" bourgeoisie and the "parasitic" or "anti-national" bourgeoisie—revolutionary roles defined by political criteria—Soviet "socialists" and Chinese "communists" have similarly and regularly distinguished between the merits of various social classes not in terms of some Marxist distinction, but in terms of their service to the "socialist fatherland." Thus Liu Shao-chi (when he was still in favor) could argue that the "proletarian" Communist Party of China had been the leader and organizer of the "anti-imperialist national united front of the Chinese people, embracing workers, peasants, intellectuals, the petit bourgeoisie, the national bourgeoisie and even the progressive gentry." Anyone, in effect and as a consequence, of whatever class origin can become the vehicle or the agent of "proletarian consciousness." This has found expression in the following manner: "When their class interests are encroached upon by the imperialists through national oppression, the national bourgeoisie and even certain patriotic kings, princes and aristocrats of an oppressed nationality may sometimes fight against national oppression together with the broad masses of working people of their own nationality."[54] The argument is a familiar one. It gained common currency in the works of Enrico

[54] Liu Shao-chi, *Internationalism and Nationalism* (Peking: Foreign Languages Press, 1951), p. 8.

221

Corradini and passed into Fascist theoretical accounts after the First World War.

Fascists early denied that there was any organic connection between class origins and revolutionary consciousness. Radical Marxists have come to admit as much. Fascists early insisted that the most significant competition in the twentieth century took place between nations, proletarian versus plutocratic nations, rather than between social classes. Again, radical Marxists have come to admit as much.

This is not to suggest that Fascists, any more than "Marxists," denied the existence of a variant of the class struggle within the confines of the nation. Fascists forever waged campaigns against "bourgeois thought" as that thought manifested itself in whatever class, functional strata, or population category. Such campaigns, however, were waged against *politically defined* opponents—opponents that could be of whatever objective class origin—for opponents possessed of "bourgeois mentality" were to be found in working class associations, business institutes, and even the ranks of the party itself. In contemporary "socialist" environments the situation is very much the same. "Capitalists"—those afflicted with "bourgeois" dispositions or who "take the capitalist road"—can be found everywhere: in workers' and farmers' groups, among intellectuals, and in the very highest echelons of the party itself.

Among radical thinkers the relationship between the revolutionary party, the revolutionary vanguard, and the proletariat—conceived in any Marxist sense—has become singularly insubstantial. Not only can the "Marxist" revolution be made without proletarian support, but the radical's appeal is candidly made to "all classes, parties, groups, organizations, and individuals"—including as we have suggested the "national bourgeoisie" and, in the Chinese case, even the "landed gentry," "patriotic kings, princes or aristocrats." Revolutionary consciousness, detached from an objective social base and the possession of a self-selected elite of any class origin, can be infused into any social class, stratum, or category. "From the Marxist emphasis on the working class we have, via Lenin's reliance on the party, now arrived at a party, independent of all classes and representing none, seeking a base for the realization of its own ambitions in any class where it can find support."[55]

The ambitions of the contemporary revolutionary vanguard party reduce themselves essentially to two: national independence in the face of an imposing external opposition and rapid industrialization to support that independence. In 1945 Mao identified the tasks that faced his revolution in the following manner: "Today, two big mountains lie like a dead weight on the Chinese People. One is imperialism, the other is feudalism."[56] To remove that weight Asian radicals have been prepared to entertain collaboration with any population element. Liu Shao-chi, for example, in addressing himself to China's "national bourgeoisie" in 1949 indicated that

> As Communists we consider that you are exploiting your workers, but we realize that, at the present stage of China's economic development, such exploitation is unavoidable and even socially useful. What we want is for you to go ahead and develop production as fast as possible and we will do what we can to help you . . . . If you do a really good job in developing your business, and train your children to be first class technical experts, you will be the obvious people to put in charge of the nationalized enterprise and you may find that you earn more as managers of a socialized enterprise than as owners.[57]

Li Ta-chao had early provided so slack an interpretation of the "internal class struggle" that whenever it served China's national and/or modernizing purpose he could ad-

[55] Cf. J. Kautsky, *Communism and the Politics of Development* (New York: Wiley, 1968), p. 21; cf. chap. 1.

[56] Mao Tse-tung, "The Foolish Old Man Who Removed the Mountains," *Selected Works* (Peking: Foreign Language, 1962), III, 322; cf. "The Chinese Revolution and the Chinese Communist Party," *ibid.*, II, 315, "New Democratic Constitutional Government," *ibid.*, II, 407.

[57] Quoted by M. Lindsay, in O. B. van der Sprenkel, ed., *New China: Three Views* (London: Turnstile, 1950), p. 139.

vocate the promotion of internal class harmony to defeat an external enemy or foster economic growth—a strategy faithfully followed by Mao throughout the long struggle against Japan and subsequently against underdevelopment. The characteristic internal opponents of the "Marxists" of China were the "compradores," who represented foreign interests and who were as a consequence prepared to compromise China's sovereign independence, and the "evil gentry," who represented the traditional social order which made rapid industrialization and modernization impossible. Every other class, stratum, and population component was at one time or another recruited for the "revolutionary" cause. Li had himself, early in the autumn of 1922, become the first Communist to join the Kuomintang in a forlorn effort to provide for the unity of all Chinese. It had been clear to Li that the "workers" of China were not oppressed by an indigenous class of "capitalists" but by "foreign exploitation." *Imperialism* was China's enemy, and as a consequence the recruitment of revolutionary forces could include *any* "anti-imperialist" elements. Li, like the revolutionary party he founded, was disposed to see the entire population of oppressed and exploited China as the recruitment base for the revolution—the natural demographic resource for all nationalist movements. The "class struggle" has come to mean, for modern radicals, a struggle of "emerging nations against the imperialists";[58] the critical protagonists are nations, not classes—an insight available to Fascists long before it became part of the stock-in-trade of "Marxist" radicals.

Considerations of this order led Robert Daniels to insist that "Chinese communism has not fought anything resembling a class war. It has become instead a movement to discipline and renegerate the nation as a whole. The Chinese Communists . . . profess to lead 'the people' against 'the

[58] F. Schurmann, *Ideology and Organization in Communist China* (Berkeley: University of California, 1968), p. 42.

lackeys of imperialism,' whose status is defined not by their social standing but by their political attitude."[59]

Chalmers Johnson has made a compelling case for interpreting the success of the Chinese communist movement as a special consequence of the exploitation of peasant nationalism.[60] As long as the Communist Party's strategy, before 1937, was specifically class-orientated, the party enjoyed but little success. Only with the Japanese invasion of China, and the mass mobilization of the peasantry in the effort to resist Japanese oppression, did the party begin to enjoy the successes which ultimately brought it to power. Its success was impressively correlated with its invocation of nationalist sentiment. China's peasantry was spontaneously mobilized against a particularly inept and brutal foreign enemy. The communists identified themselves as palladins of national interest. During the protracted war of resistance against the Japanese, the party systematically suppressed any suggestion of a "class struggle"; its propaganda was devoted solely to the theme of "national salvation."

Just as the First World War provided the reactive mass base for Italian nationalism from which Fascism was to profit, the Japanese invasion of China created the environment in which the nationalism of the radical intelligentsia, the nationalism of men such as Li and Mao, could find a mass-recruitment opportunity.

Unlike the nationalism of Soviet Marxism, which gradually resurfaced during the interwar years, the nationalism of Mao Tse-tung has been, with varying degrees of emphasis, a constant feature of his thought. Stuart Schram has argued that, while Lenin provided arguments that could be used to support a "Marxist" nationalism, Lenin remained discomfited by the appearance of national sentiments among the "international" proletariat. Mao, on the other hand, has

[59] R. V. Daniels, "The Chinese Revolution in Russian Perspective," *World Politics*, 13, 2 (January 1961), 218.

[60] C. A. Johnson, *Peasant Nationalism and Communist Power* (Palo Alto: Stanford, 1962).

225

never been embarrassed by Chinese nationalism. "Lenin," Schram has maintained, "was a European primarily interested in world revolution, who regarded the very existence of national differences as a misfortune, though as a realist he was quite prepared to compromise with nationalism if in this way he could harness the revolutionary energies of the colonial countries to his larger goal. Mao, on the other hand, is an Asian for whom nationalism is not a necessary evil but an authentic value in itself."[61]

While it might plausibly be argued that Stalin's nationalism—the great Russian chauvinism that characterized his rule—was an instance of *Realpolitik*, Mao's nationalism seems to be an expression of a genuine sentiment. In 1919, at about the same time that Mussolini discovered the special qualities of the Italian people, Mao was maintaining that "our Chinese people possess great intrinsic energy. The more profound the oppression, the greater its resistance . . . ." Thirty years later he could insist that "The Chinese have always been a great, courageous and industrious people. It was only in modern times that they have fallen behind, and this was due solely to the oppression and exploitation of foreign imperialism and the domestic reactionary government."[62]

Mussolini had discovered that the Italian people possessed similar attributes. He also recognized that if "the proletariat is identified with the 'people' . . . class dilates into 'nation.' "[63] The consequence is nationalism couched in the idiom of an international class struggle.

That Mussolini's insight was perceptive is indicated by the creative development of Marxism-Leninism in the Soviet Union where a "new historical phenomenon" has been recognized: the "state of the whole people." The "Marxists" of the Soviet Union no longer pretend that their party represents a class, nor their government a definable class interest. Their party is a "Party of the whole people," and their

---

[61] Schram, *The Political Thought of Mao Tse-tung*, p. 135.

[62] As translated in *ibid.*, pp. 163, 167.

[63] Mussolini, "Lotta politica e lotta di classe," *Opera*, VI, 279.

government a "government of the whole people." Irrespective of differential income, differential access to political power and social prestige, differential economic mobility, and assignment of privilege and responsibility, there are no "classes" in the Soviet Union. There is only the "people" and the "Socialist Fatherland."

F. Burlatsky, as a Soviet "Marxist," has maintained that "It is not too much to say that the idea of a state of the whole people is one of the most sparkling scientific discoveries of Marxist-Leninist thought in our time . . . . The state that had once served one class, gradually came to represent all society and became a vehicle of its will, its interests, its ideals and goals."[64] Needless to say this "sparkling scientific discovery" is surprisingly similar to the Fascist conception of the state that embodies the will of the nation and serves the nation in its entirety rather than any constituent class, social stratum, or productive category.

There is little doubt that Mao's China will produce its analogue of the "all-people's state." The elements of the notion have been in currency in China since the time of the "united front" against the Japanese and the "new democracy" with its union of "all progressive classes." The conjunction of elitism and nationalism makes such a development all but inevitable. The sustaining rationale of elitism provides that some aggregate of men find its interests embodied in the will of a vanguard party—that the vanguard party find its will embodied in the will of the party leadership—and that the will of the party leadership find its will embodied in the will of the exceptional leader. Marx had provided that the aggregate of men whose interests are embodied in a party constitutes the "vast majority" of the population—further, that that "vast majority" be an objectively defined class, the proletariat. The proletariat as a class has interests that are homogeneous by virtue of the fact that the proletarians have been leveled to one common interest by the development of contemporary industry. The party

[64] F. Burlatsky, *The State and Communism* (Moscow: Progress, n.d.), p. 5.

that would represent that interest was a party of proletarians. The party interest and the class interests were the same. In *The Communist Manifesto* Marx could simply maintain that the interests of the Communist Party and those of the working class were identical.

If, on the other hand, the men who find their interests embodied in the will of the vanguard party are not of some identifiable social class and are not all equally possessed of the same abiding interests, the conception that the will of the party embodies the interests of the "people" becomes increasingly implausible. If it is true, as Schram suggests, that Mao conceives "himself as the incarnation of the will of the masses," several problems immediately suggest themselves. How plausible is it to maintain that the "masses" have one specific and specifiable collection of mutually compatible interests that can all be incarnated in Mao's will? To talk of the "masses" is to obscure the fact that the population of China is composed of a variety of socioeconomic classes, productive categories, functional strata, age groups, and nationalities. It is not immediately self-evident that any leader, no matter how exceptional, could incarnate all those interests, all at the same time, without intolerable tension.

Parties and leaders that pretend to embody the interest and will of the "masses" and/or the "people" operate under the assumption that because a single general term is applied to a complex whole that complex whole must, in all its constituent parts, share some common element—some common interest that the party or the leader can incarnate. For classical Marxism this problem did not arise. For Marx the development of industry would reduce all proletarian interests to a constellation of common denominators. Since interests were common, one man or an exiguous group of men could represent the interests of all. The aggregate of men with common interests was a class, the proletariat. The party and its leadership were simply the most theoretically articulate segments of the class.

With the development of contemporary radicalism, the classical Marxist rationale, which provided a reasonably convincing case for the homogeneity of interests between the class and its leadership, was faulted by the conviction that revolution could arise in environments where there were few if any proletarians and the "proletarian party" would represent the interests, not of a reasonably well-defined class, but of the "masses," or the "people." At that juncture the form of elitism we have been here considering is enjoined *not*, in fact, *to embody* the will of the masses, but *to instill* a common will in the masses. The common will represented in the party is an artifact of the party's monopoly over the means of communication and control. The party defines what the interests of the masses might be. At times the party's logic is so obscure that it is spoken of as "contradictory," or baptized as "dialectical." This is as true of Fascists as it is of "Marxists."

The more emphatically and transparently nationalistic contemporary revolutionaries become, the more difficult it becomes to convincingly characterize the relationship between the exceptional leader, his party, and the mobilized masses. The problems that develop are of no small consequence. A number of the more singular features of radical regimes becomes more comprehensible considered in this context. One of those features is the disposition on the part of radical regimes to employ the party purge as a political device.

The Leaders and Their Party

The relationship between the revolutionary leader and his party could hardly be exhaustively treated within the confines of this survey. However, it seems reasonably clear that once the revolutionary vanguard party begins to conceive itself as embodying or incarnating the interests of divergent social classes, or perhaps whole nations, there will be any number of conflicting interpretations of what those interests might be. Since the revolutionary party has committed itself to a conviction that the vanguard party is the handmaiden of history and that the masses possess no more than "elemental energy" or "immediate interest," rather than "revolutionary consciousness" or an awareness of their "ultimate interests," the *party* must interpret that revolutionary consciousness and that ultimate interest. There are fewer and fewer objective indices of what a correct interpretation might be. One must more and more frequently make a judgment based on "insight," "genius," "intuition," or the "dialectic." More and more frequently conflict within the party surfaces to thwart unanimity. Lenin spent no small measure of time exposing "deviationists." Mussolini regularly sought to isolate those "bourgeois" elements that had insinuated themselves into the party. Mao has faced no small problem in organizing his party behind his interpretation of what the interests of the Chinese people might be.

Ultimately the "revolution" becomes identified with a body of thought rather than any objective indices. That body of thought at once legitimizes the elitist exercise of authority and provides a programmatic guide to conduct as well. Ultimately only the thought of the leader can resolve the conflicts that regularly and predictably arise when the party attempts to embody the interests of so disparate a collection of men as the population of a nation of millions of inhabitants.

Mussolini was the first of the radicals to insist that his party embodied the interests of the "people." As a consequence, his efforts to solve the problem of how the interests of the "people" were to be defined are instructive.

Fascism arose quite spontaneously in various parts of Italy. While Mussolini insisted that the Fascist elite informed the masses, and consequently constituted their representatives, it became quite obvious that the elite, the party leadership itself, entertained a variety of mutually exclusive interpretations of what the interests of the people might be. While Mussolini was recognized as the "exceptional leader" of the party even before the seizure of power, he was by no means in absolute control of the party apparatus.[65] Local leaders such as Dino Grandi and Roberto Fari-

[65] For a discussion of the circumstances surrounding the early party

nacci brought what was essentially a personal following into the party. Between 1921 and 1925, for three years after the Fascist seizure of power, local leaders (*Ras*, as they were called) remained local *condottieri*, in effective control of the allegiance of local Fascist groups. Each local leader, given the logic of the Fascist rationale, could claim that he represented the interests of the people; and there was no objective way to discriminate between such claims. As a consequence Fascist rule was anything but coherent or monolithic. Mussolini's will was thwarted in a variety of ways. Behind a facade of compliance it was painfully obvious that Mussolini's control was, at best, partial.

A variety of identifiable interests made their influence manifest during the first years of Fascist rule. Mussolini found himself faced not only with regional anarchy but with special and parochial interests within the party, which made his rule difficult. The immediate problems centered on the independent local leaders of Fascist squads. Mussolini had attempted their control for three years after coming to power, but his efforts were, in significant measure, fruitless. When the socialist deputy Giacomo Matteotti was murdered the entire regime was threatened. The party was not unified in the face of increasing opposition. For six months the Fascist government verged on collapse. The "revolution" could not survive without some central authority that would identify its "interests." Fascism would not survive with conflicting interpretations of what the collective interest might be.

At the beginning of 1925 Mussolini decided that the situation was intolerable, and he insisted that if the regime was to survive then the party must be "adapted" (*inquadrato*) to the requirements of the regime. By 1926 Mussolini was prepared to move against those local leaders of his own party, particularly Farinacci, who were creating centrifugal currents in the political system. Roberto Farinacci was secretary of the National Fascist Party and leader of the Cre-

---

and its relationship to Mussolini, see M. Rocca, *Come il fascismo divenne una dittatura* (Milan: Librarie Italiane, 1952).

mona Fascists. Mussolini's decision to domesticate the local leaders meant the suppression of Farinacci and a massive reorganization of the party itself. Farinacci was eased out of his position and Augusto Turati assumed the role of party secretary.

In April 1926 Mussolini announced to the newly chosen leadership of the party that the party must be disciplined, that contentious and disorderly Fascists would no longer be tolerated, and he explicitly stated that "the leader [*capo*] of the Fascist government is also the leader of the revolution."[66] In February 1927 Mussolini prepared a memorandum to Turati which in part indicated his firm resolve that "the ship [of state] will have *one* pilot—the entire crew cannot so serve." The party was to be disciplined in order that it might constitute a "civil militia" under, in effect, hierarchical dominance.[67]

In the course of domesticating the party, Mussolini had dissident *Fascist* publications suppressed, regional leaders banished, and recalcitrants purged from the party itself. Mussolini lamented that the trouble with revolutions was that, after they are successful, the revolutionaries remain. In the first six months of Turati's incumbency seven thousand four hundred members (including five deputies of the *Camera*) of the party were expelled. The "purge" (*epurazione*) was undertaken "with energy," upon the authority of the Grand Council of Fascism. In the following year two thousand "leaders" of the party and thirty thousand "members" were expelled. The total of those expelled from the party during the first three years of Turati's incumbency was probably between fifty-five and sixty thousand. At the same time "young Fascists," the youth of Italy that had had five years of Fascist indoctrination, was incorporated into the party. As a consequence of "domestication," the party

[66] Mussolini, "Se Avanzo, Seguittemi; se Indietreggio, Uccidetemi; se Muoio, Vendicatemi," *Opera*, xxii, 107-10.

[67] For a discussion of this period, cf. R. De Felice, *Mussolini il fascista: l'organizzazione dello Stato fascista* (Turin: Einaudi, 1968), pp. 176-90.

was not only structurally transformed, but its age and social composition were significantly altered. Mussolini had accomplished the dismemberment of the revolutionary organization that had brought him to power. From that point on, the "purified" party was a passive agent in the hands of the "exceptional leader," and the cult of personality was the predictable consequence.[68] After this period the adulation of Mussolini became an irrepressible and constant feature of the political scenario of Fascist Italy.

Mussolini's domestication of the party—with its tacit and sometimes explicit condemnation of those leaders and members of the rank and file that actually made the revolution—was accomplished with a minimum of violence. Mussolini's purpose was express; his directives to the party explicit. The party was to be transformed into an agency of government, and that government was to be embodied in Mussolini and Mussolini alone. The new statutes of the party institutionalized the hierarchical structure Mussolini imposed upon it. The party throughout the remaining history of the regime was a transmission channel through which the "will and purpose" of the Duce was "effected among the masses." Throughout the period the deliberative agencies of the party met less and less frequently as Mussolini assumed more and more of the responsibilities of control decisions.

Years later Sergio Panunzio, as a Fascist theorist, was not far wrong when he described the process of domestication suffered by the revolutionary party.

The Fascist party, insofar as it is a revolutionary party, creates the state and the state created by the party rests upon that party as on a pedestal. From the dynamic point of view, politically, historically, ideally, the party is prior and contains the state. It is the state in formation . . . . From the static point of view, the logico-juridical, formal and doctrinal, the state is everything, and the party comes

[68] Cf. the collection of speeches made by Augusto Turati, appointed by Mussolini to head the Fascist Party, A. Turati, *Una rivoluzione e un capo* (Rome: Littorio, 1927).

after the state, it is a part, an organ of the state . . . . One passes from the Party-State to the State-Party.[69]

The distinction is hardly one between the dynamic and the static or between the political and historical and the logico-juridical and doctrinal. The distinction is a temporal one between the revolutionary party, which serves to seize power and create a new state system, and the domesticated party, which serves as a control agency of the dictatorship as the embodiment of the new state.

In the Fascist environment the process of domestication was undertaken and concluded with a minimum amount of violence. The similar process in the Soviet Union, under Stalin's directives, cost the lives of hundreds of thousands, if not millions of Russians. Irrespective of the quantitative and qualitative magnitude of the differences which attended the process, the process was, nonetheless, the domestication of the revolutionary party. In the process Joseph Stalin dishonored and degraded, and in far too many cases put to death, almost the entire leadership of the revolutionary Bolsheviks. Precious few of the Bolshevik leaders, the collaborators of Lenin, the makers of the October Revolution, were spared in the destruction of the revolutionary Communist Party that we now identify with the "Great Purge." Stalin all but destroyed an entire revolutionary socialist leadership class. He dissolved all nonstate Marxist associations, suppressed their publications, censored their tracts. He went so far, in one instance, as to dissolve the Marx-Engels Institute and deport its founder and director, D. Riazanov, the editor of the first complete collection of Marx's works.

We know now that at least as early as 1932 Stalin contemplated the domestication of the Communist Party. Particularly between 1936 and 1938, Stalin succeeded in decimating the leadership of the revolutionary party. Not only were Lenin's immediate collaborators, men of the caliber of

[69] S. Panunzio, *Teoria generale dello Stato fascista* (Padua: CEDAM, 1939), p. 568.

Trotsky and Bukharin, identified as "political degenerates," "saboteurs and wreckers" and hounded out of the party and in many cases shot, but the ranks of the less well-known cadre were barbarously winnowed. Of the 139 members and candidates elected at the Seventeenth Party Congess in 1934, 98, or about 70 percent were arrested and/or shot or simply perished in Stalin's concentration and labor camps. Along with Lenin's collaborators at the time of the October Revolution—men such as Zinoviev, Kamenev, and Radek—the majority of the upper echelons of the Party was swept into the maelstrom. The lower echelons were not neglected. Of the total of 1,966 voting and nonvoting delegates to the Seventeenth Party Congress of 1934, no less than 1,108, or more than 50 percent, were arrested on charges of counterrevolutionary crimes.[70] Nor did the domestication of the party neglect the rank and file membership. In the course of 1933, over 800,000 party members were expelled. In 1934 another 340,000 were similarly expelled. By 1938 it is estimated that 36 percent of the party had been purged. In some cases 64 percent of the local party organization was expelled—in what could be only called an excess of zeal.

At the same time that the party was purging itself of "politically degenerate" elements, it was recruiting new membership among the young and among the new class of "Red directors," the strategic managerial and technical elite. What resulted was a domesticated party, one that could operate as an extension of the state—as a control agency for Stalin. As a result of the purge the party became not only considerably younger in composition but significantly different in social character. The party was "restocked" with persons who had been educated by the "revolutionary system" or who had investments in it in terms of institutional roles or new status acquired with the post-Leninist expansion of Russian industry and its attendant bureaucracy. The new members drawn into the party to replace those purged

[70] For an account of Stalin's Party purge, cf. L. Shapiro, *The Communist Party of the Soviet Union* (New York: Random House, 1960), chap. 22.

had investments in the established system. The predictable consequence was that during this period *Pravda* could announce that Stalin was the "genius of the new world, the wisest man of the epoch, the great leader of communism." The adulation of the "leader" became standard currency in party literature and speech.

The elitist systems that have been our concern seem to evince a disposition toward centralized and hierarchical control that, at one stage or another, and under one or another set of unique circumstances, results in the domestication of the revolutionary party and the instauration of a charismatic or pseudocharismatic leader.

While it is still too early to deliver a convincing analysis of the character and implications of China's "Great Proletarian Cultural Revolution," it has already displayed enough features to indicate that one of its principal effects has been the domestication of the Chinese Communist Party and the elevation of Mao Tse-tung to a special place in the twentieth-century's pantheon of revolutionary leaders.

It would be impossible, here, to provide an adequate background to the events that exploded in 1966, but it is clear that the period immediately following China's abortive "Great Leap Forward" was a time of considerable intra-party factional strife during which threats to Mao's leadership mounted. In 1958 Mao was, in fact, compelled to resign his post as Chairman of the Republic in order, according to the official explanation, to "pursue his theoretical work." Liu Shao-chi assumed the presidency of the National People's Congress in April 1959 and was reelected in January 1965 in what appeared to be a grooming for succession. The criticisms of Mao's "revolutionary romanticism," in fact, resulted in Mao's finding himself in a minority position within the party, with Liu Shao-chi and Teng Hsiao-ping (general secretary of the party) aligned against him. The men that ultimately came to be identified as those "Party men in authority who are taking the capitalist road" included luminaries such as Liu and Teng who had been leaders of the Communist Party for a generation and were of no less stature in their revolutionary movement than Trotsky, Bukharin, Zinoviev, and Kamenev had been in theirs, and Alfredo Farinacci, Dino Grandi, and Italo Balbo had been in theirs. All these men had been architects of their respective revolutions and among the most trusted immediate subordinates of the leader. Nonetheless, all suffered in the process that domesticated the revolutionary party.

No less has befallen the leaders of the Chinese revolutionary party. Mao's immediate subordinates in the party were to become "monsters," "ghosts," and "degenerates" in the course of the "Great Cultural Revolution." Chou Yang, the deputy director of the party's propaganda department was denounced by *Red Flag* as a "political thief, an anti-Party conspirator and a counterrevolutionary revisionist" who "in the light pretended to be a human being, but in the shade was a monster." Lu Ting-yi, head of the party's propaganda department and minister of culture, was summarily dismissed from both posts as a "black monster." Liu Shao-chi, long considered Mao's heir apparent, a hero of the legendary two-decade struggle to bring communism to China, author of what had been a standard work on the "cultivation" of communists, was denounced as a "veteran opportunist," a "bourgeois revisionist" who "wants to practice capitalism in China" and who "shamelessly emasculates the very soul of Marxism-Leninism." Teng Hsiao-ping was so humiliated by Mao's "revolutionaries" that he attempted suicide. Peng Chen, mayor of Peking and first secretary of the city's Communist Party, was denounced as a traitor plotting a coup against Mao; Po I-po, deputy premier and chairman of the State Economic Commission, was identified as an "anti-Party, anti-socialist element."[71]

[71] Cf. *Betrayal of Proletarian Dictatorship is the Heart of the Book on Self-Cultivation* (The editorial Departments of *Red Flag* and *People's Daily*. Peking: Foreign Languages, 1967); *A Great Historic Document* (Editorial Departments of *Red Flag* and *People's Daily*. Peking: Foreign Languages, 1967); *The Great Socialist Cultural Revolution in China* (A series of pamphlets numbered 1 through 10. Peking: Foreign Languages, 1966-1967).

The Great Cultural Revolution has accomplished more than the simple degradation of former functional and strategic elites of the revolutionary party. It has, in effect, "swept away almost an entire layer of leading Party cadres"; it "may turn out to be the greatest purge China has experienced since the triumph of Communism."[72] For over two years—from 1966 through 1968—the party apparatus was under powerful and unremitting attack. The attack came not from within the party itself, as was the case in Mussolini's Italy or even Stalin's Russia, but from specially created extra-party attack agencies organized and invoked by Mao and his cohorts. Although the party numbered, by the best estimates, a total membership of approximately fifty million persons, twenty million of them in the party itself and thirty million in its auxiliary organizations, Mao chose to invoke a new extra-party organization, the Red Guard, to attack the party apparatus at all levels. The Red Guard was composed largely of adolescents between the ages of thirteen and sixteen years of age. About thirty percent of its membership was made up of high middle-school students between the ages of sixteen and twenty. Together the two groups constituted about ninety percent of the membership of the Red Guard. Only approximately ten percent of the membership were university students. Mao's attack agency, in this case, was composed almost exclusively of the very young who had been educated by the system, had no previous political experience, and did not possess any "Marxist" sophistication.

In August 1966 the Central Committee of the Communist Party issued a directive that charged the Red Guard with carrying out a purge of those "Party officials in positions of authority that were taking the capitalist road."[73] At approximately the same time Mao received members of the Red

[72] Schurmann, *Ideology and Organization*, p. 517, and F. Schurmann, "The Attack of the Cultural Revolution on Ideology and Organization," in Ping-ti Ho and Tang Tsou, eds., *China in Crisis* (Chicago: University of Chicago, 1968), p. 511.

[73] *Decision of the Central Committee of the Chinese Communist Party Concerning the Great Proletarian Cultural Revolution, August 8, 1966* (Peking: Foreign Languages Press, 1966).

Guard and acknowledged his approval by donning the red arm band that identified them. On August 20 the Red Guard units began demonstrations in Peking (where Mao's position was particularly weak) in order to root out the party "bourgeoisie and revisionist elements." Wall posters announced that forty thousand "reactionaries" had been expelled from urban areas and that over sixteen thousand people had been arrested as a consequence of exposure by the Red Guard during August and September. On the night of December 4, 1966, Peng Chen was dragged from his bed and arrested by Red Guards and then displayed before a rally of one hundred thousand Red Guards in a Peking stadium. In January 1967 a special mass meeting of the Red Guards was organized to denounce Kang Sheng, a member of the party secretariat who had prior to that time been listed as seventh in the party hierarchy.

The Red Guard attacks were by no means restricted to the higher echelons of the party. In Fukien, Red Guards were reported to have stormed and sacked party offices in Foochow. In Hopei, Red Guards caused the death of several members of the party's cadre. In Kiangsu, Red Guards occupied the Communist Party headquarters. In Shensi, the secretary of the provincial Communist Party was paraded through Sian as a "black bandit." Thus not only have many, if not the bulk, of the leadership of the revolutionary party come under direct attack, but the purge has affected provincial and local party organizations.

In city after city, party secretaries have been paraded around the streets with dunce caps on their heads. Teenage students have taken the lead in attacking men of long records of service to the cause. Though in the early weeks of the Red Guard movement old men and Hong Kong types were beaten up; it is clear by now that the real thrust [was] against the party bosses, high and low. Army men and government officials have also been attacked but as influential members of the party, not as military professionals or bureaucrats.[74]

[74] Schurmann, "Attack of the Cultural Revolution," p. 542.

At the same time almost all the party's publications were suppressed. Only *Red Flag* and the *Liberation Army Daily* were not affected. The fact that the official publication of the People's Liberation Army, China's armed forces, was not affected had far-reaching implications. Wherever difficulties developed in the struggle between the Red Guard and the party, the army interceded. In fact some of the principal pronouncements concerning the Great Cultural Revolution have been issued by China's military—and the head of the People's Liberation Army, Lin Piao assumed the role of Mao's second in command. As early as June 1966, the military announced that *its* power constituted "the foundation of the dictatorship of the proletariat."[75] The role of the military in domesticating the revolutionary party became so obvious that Soviet commentators characterized the Great Cultural Revolution as an attack by the army on the organs of the Communist Party and the state.[76] Thus in the urban areas, particularly in the educational institutions, the Red Guard succeeded in wresting power from the party apparatus, while the "people's army" managed to wrest control from the party in the rural areas.

The control exercised by the Red Guards and the army was assisted by an extra-party organization of adults, the Revolutionary Rebels, who supplemented the urban activities of the Red Guards. At the same time it was announced that the All-China Trade Union Federation was to be reorganized in order to displace the "capitalist elements" and those who had taken the "revisionist road"—and its newspaper *Workers' Daily* was to be suppressed—an organization of "Red Rebels," or "Revolutionary Rebels," was officially charged with assuming the responsibilities of the Federation, and the *Workers' Daily* was to be reconstituted and restaffed as *its* organ. The resistance to the Revolutionary Rebels was apparently wide-spread, and for a period

[75] K. Mehnert, *Maos zweite Revolution* (Stuttgart: DVA, 1966), p. 14.

[76] Cf. Schurmann, *Ideology and Organization*, p. 533, n. 1.

240

it appeared as though China was on the verge of civil war. The Rebels claimed to have seized power from the provincial party authorities in Shansi, Kweichow and Shensi, Kwangtung, Kiangsi, Anhwei, Peking, Heilungkiang, Shantung, Fukien, and Kansu. In some of the urban areas, particularly Shanghai, the struggle was bitter and involved extensive fighting. At critical junctures the army intervened to weigh the balance in favor of Maoist forces.

By mid-1967 it was clear that the outcome of the Great Cultural Revolution depended less on the activities of school children and the "big character posters" with which they placarded the urban areas than with the effectiveness of the army. In July 1967 two of Mao's close collaborators were held captive by the commander of Wuhan district, and it was reported that hundreds of Maoists had been massacred. By the *end* of 1967 it was reported that China was almost entirely under military control. The intermittent fighting that had broken out between workers, peasants, members of the party and their opponents in the Red Guards, the Revolutionary Rebels and the militia was brought under control only by the massive intervention of the military.

Disorder had apparently become so far reaching and so threatening in its implications that the Maoists attempted to negotiate a stable coalition of "proletarian forces," including the army, the Red Guards and Revolutionary Rebels and the surviving "Maoist" elements of the party, that might restore a control structure to carry the nation through an ill-defined "transitional period." The Cultural Revolution was candidly described as a "seizure of power," and the "three in one" coalition a temporary device for holding power, once seized, through a "transitional period" until "completely new organizational forms of political power" could be created.[77]

---

[77] Cf. B. Luckin, "Students and the Chinese Cultural Revolution," in Tariq Ali, *The New Revolutionaries* (New York: William Morrow, 1969), pp. 115-30; "Great Alliance of All Revolutionary Forces to

Whatever else it accomplished, and whatever else motivated it, the Great Cultural Revolution domesticated the party to the control of the one exceptional leader or his agents. Although the youthful Red Guards originally identified themselves as "anti-authoritarian" and "anti-bureaucratic," it has recently been proclaimed that "Mao Tse-tung's thought" should be employed as a "weapon to correct such erroneous tendencies as . . . excessive decentralization, the disregard of organizational discipline, ultra-democracy, liberalism, subjectivism and individualism . . . ." It is abundantly clear that the "spontaneous" revolutionary enthusiasm of the masses (mostly the very young) has been carefully manipulated in the service of the Maoist vision of China. They were employed to dismantle the elaborate party structure that had controlled China since the military victory of 1949. In its place Mao, or those who speak in his name, will assume control as undisputed authority. It seems equally clear that he, or they, will construct a control infrastructure suitable to effect his or their will. For all the talk of "democracy"—constructed along the lines of the Paris Commune with its universal suffrage and referendum and recall—indulged in by Mao's youthful enthusiasts, there is little evidence that the new transitional "revolutionary" committees are any less hierarchical and bureaucratic than the party apparatus that they helped destroy. What has changed is the hierarchical control, which in the old system was far from perfect. After the massive purge of the Great Cultural Revolution it is reasonably certain that the new party which will emerge will be a pliant capillary agency for the transmission of the will of the leadership.

That this can be said with some confidence is a consequence of the fact that "Mao's thought" has been elevated to the status of the ultimate arbiter between "proletarian" and "bourgeoisie." The terms no longer refer to objective social categories nor to historical or economic roles. They

Seize Power," in K. H. Fan, ed., *The Chinese Cultural Revolution: Selected Documents* (New York: Grove Press, 1968), pp. 239-58; *A Great Historical Document* (Peking: Foreign Languages, 1967).

refer all but exclusively to the political loyalty and political attitudes of the individuals or groups that constitute the active population of China. As Joan Robinson has indicated: "Class is defined by state of mind, and the state of mind is revealed in conduct." While the *talk* of the Great Cultural Revolution employs class terms, its *practice* clearly indicates that its purpose is to *foster, control, and direct political loyalties* rather than *employ Marxist categories* in analyzing contemporary social issues. The "great proletarian cultural revolution," we are told, "is an extremely acute and complicated class struggle, a great revolution to *remold the souls of people and promote the revolutionization of people's thinking . . . .*" "Proletarian politics" simply means following the dictates of "Mao Tse-tung's thought"—however that reveals itself in the directives of the leaders of China. Only the "thought" of Mao is the "invincible ideological weapon" which provides the "most reliable and fundamental guarantee for the prevention of revisionism and a capitalist restoration . . . ."[78]

What this seems to imply is a political system in which absolute power resides in the hands of the exceptional leader, or his immediate agents, who no longer must suffer the interference of men who have long been established as functionaries of the revolutionary party. Having destroyed the party, the exceptional leader faces "masses" to be schooled in his "thought." In 1958 Mao spoke of the Chinese people in the following fashion:

Apart from their other characteristics, China's 600 million people have two remarkable peculiarities: they are, first of all, poor, and secondly blank. That may seem like a bad thing. But it is really a good thing. Poor people want change, want to do things, want revolution. A clean sheet of paper has no blotches, and so the newest and most

[78] J. Robinson, *The Cultural Revolution in China* (Baltimore: Penguin, 1969), p. 15; Wang Li et al., *The Dictatorship of the Proletariat and the Great Proletarian Cultural Revolution* (Peking: Foreign Languages, 1967), pp. 7, 16.

beautiful words can be written on it, the newest and most beautiful pictures can be painted on it.[79]

The intimation is fairly obvious. The Chinese people provide the material out of which the artist builds his masterpiece. The allusion is fairly commonplace among exceptional leaders when they refer to the "masses." Mussolini was fond of the same metaphor. In the weeks before the March on Rome, for example, he insisted that Fascism had "need of the masses, as an artist has need of raw material to fashion his masterpiece."[80]

The Great Cultural Revolution has succeeded in providing Mao direct and unrestricted access to the "blank" raw materials for the exercise of his "creative" will. The voluntarism that characterized Mao's thought since his instruction under the tutelage of Li Ta-chao has come to fruition in the creation of a political system dominated by the will of the exceptional leader, whose "thought" is "invincible," the "most scientific," the "most revolutionary."

Whatever function the party served in the past, it will no longer obstruct the exercise of the will of the leadership. For all its talk of "democracy," "anti-bureaucracy," and "anti-authoritarianism," all the evidence indicates that the prevailing Maoist sentiment will permit precious little "anti-Maoist" thought to find expression in the post-Cultural Revolution China. Since the beginning of 1968 there have been intimations that the present Chinese leadership is attempting to rebuild the party after the Maoist image—and that there has been a cessation of all Red Guard publications. As Franz Schurmann has suggested, "centralism is again returning." The difference is, of course, that the machinery of political control, of resource direction and allocation, will be exclusively in the hands of Mao Tse-tung and/or those who speak in his name. Kuo Mo-jo rejoices that "today [in China, we]

[79] As quoted, R. J. Lifton, *Revolutionary Immortality: Mao Tse-tung and the Chinese Cultural Revolution* (New York: Random House, 1968), p. 96.

[80] Mussolini, "L'azione e la dottrina fascista dinnanzi alle necessità storiche della nazione," *Opera*, xviii, 360.

see that the invincible thought of Mao Tse-tung has become the unified thinking of China's 700 million people . . . . Thus we have a unified understanding, a unified will and a unified feeling . . . ."[81]

What reveals itself in post-Cultural Revolutionary China is what George Novack and Joseph Hansen have characterized as a "national bureaucratic tendency with very special features . . ." not unlike the developments under Stalin and, we can add, Mussolini.[82]

The purges that domesticated the revolutionary parties of Mussolini's Italy, Stalin's Russia, and Mao's China have been significantly different among themselves. Nonetheless, they have all served to render the party amenable to the absolute control of the "exceptional" leadership that elitist systems seem to require. Mussolini, once again, provided the most unambiguous illustration of the process employed in the domestication of revolutionary parties. The purge of the party was undertaken to render it submissive. Mussolini insisted that there could be but one "pilot" of the ship of state. Today the children of China sing the political hymn, "Mao is Our Great Helmsman," and perhaps the majority of those men who were Mao's collaborators for a generation, who had served in the party's most strategic offices for more than a decade and a half, have suddenly found themselves turned out as "bourgeois elements," "ghosts," and "monsters."

In Fascist Italy when Mussolini embarked on the program to domesticate the party, Augusto Turati, who was to serve as the principal tool for accomplishing his purpose, stated that the program of Fascism in power "could only be determined by the genius and the thought of the Duce . . . ." Both Stalin and Mao have operated to effect a similar hierarchical system, but they have rarely been as frank. At the time he was domesticating the Bolsheviks with what was perhaps

[81] Kuo Mo-jo, "Commemorating Lu Hsun's Rebellious Spirit," in *Commemorating Lu Hsun* (Peking: Foreign Languages, 1967), p. 40.

[82] G. Novack and J. Hansen, "The Upheaval in China—An Analysis of the Contending Forces," in Peng Shu-tse et al., *Behind China's "Great Cultural Revolution,"* (New York: Merit, 1967), p. 62.

245

the bloodiest political purge in history, Stalin was having the "democratic" constitution of 1936 prepared by a constitutional commission that included Bukharin and Radek among its members—men who were themselves to be destroyed in the purge a short time later. For all the democratic locutions of the "Stalin Constitution," there was precious little democracy in Stalin's Russia; and for all the appeals to the "masses" and to the principles of the "Paris Commune," there appears to be no more in Mao's China.

Lenin, Stalin, and Mao have continued to employ the speech patterns and phraseology of classical Marxism. As a consequence, at the time the Soviet Union was languishing under the iron rule of one man, it advertised the "most democratic constitution in world history." Similarly, Mao insists that the "party" is pursuing the "mass line" precisely at that point in time when his acts, in the name of a purged "party," have become more and more autocratic.

Mussolini, who had relatively early disabused himself of the language of classical Marxism, simply described the domestication of the revolutionary party for what it was—an *inquadramento*, a disciplining of the party to the purposes of the state, with the will of exceptional leadership the ultimate arbiter of state purpose. Mussolini was prepared, with little equivocation to recognize the implications of the elitism he had espoused. The vanguard party, which brought revolutionary consciousness to the masses, was the repository of revolutionary will. An indecisive and unorganized will malfunctions. Ultimately that will must articulate itself in one unified and decisive expression: most auspiciously in the thought of the one-world historical individual. The party handbooks simply and candidly described the form of government Fascism had brought to Italy as "charismatic." What we have learned to call "the cult of personality" becomes a special feature of radical political systems (although its rudiments are clearly present before that) as a consequence of the domestication of the party and the exceptional leader's accession to absolute control.

Nothing in classical Marxism would have suggested these

246

developments; these developments found their origins in non-Marxist sources. The elitism that became so prominent in Lenin's thought can be traced to the influence of Cherny-shevsky; that of Mao can be traced to the influence of Li Ta-chao. Mussolini had picked up the threads of a similar conception in the works of Pareto, Michels, Le Bon, and Sorel—but particularly Alfredo Oriani. These non-Marxist influences on radical thought ultimately produced some of radicalism's most distinctive features. As non-Marxist elements became more and more prominent, more and more of classical Marxism was sacrificed.

The sacrifice has been occasioned, in large part, by one major preoccupation. Throughout the twentieth century, radicalism has been increasingly preoccupied with strategies for mass-mobilization. Where classical Marxism had conceived the process as "spontaneous," contemporary radicals have seen mobilization as a consequence of special effort on the part of a self-selected minority of men. Such mass-mobilizing revolutionary parties have tended to create political environments in which they themselves, as a party, require domestication.

All this, the mobilization of masses and the subsequent domestication of the revolutionary apparatus, seems to require mobilizing issues—special collective concerns around which men can organize themselves, causes for which they will sacrifice and to which they can be disciplined. One of the more unusual features of the new radicalism has been its regular invocation of nationalism as just such a cause, just such a mobilizing collective concern. Where classical Marxism was to conceive nationalism as a bourgeois prejudice, the new radicalism has recognized it to be perhaps the single most effective device for mobilizing masses.

MAOISM AND THE ELEMENTS OF RADICAL STYLE

One of the principal concerns of contemporary radicalism has been mobilization. Elitism has been its response to the absent revolutionary disposition of the "masses," and nationalism has been its most effective mobilizing appeal. But more than that, radical mass-mobilizing movements have found it necessary to mobilize the young. The young have offered special recruitment advantages to mass-mobilizing radical movements. The young are abundant in number; they have high energy levels; they have not as yet assumed clearly defined social roles; they are politically unsophisticated, and are consequently more easily mobilized. Youth provides an important recruitment resource during at least two critical periods in the life of radical movements: (1) during the revolutionary struggle for power; and (2) at the point in the stabilization of the revolutionary regime when the leadership decides on the domestication of the revolutionary party. When Mussolini domesticated the Fascist Party, he restocked its vacancies largely with young people trained in the Fascist system. Stalin similarly restocked the domesticated Communist Party of the Soviet Union with the young after the purge of the thirties. Mao is not only prepared to restock his newly reorganized party the same way, but he employed the young to destroy the bureaucratic infrastructure of the revolutionary party.

Because Mao's struggle with the party was so intense and because the young played an important part in the domestication process, certain elements of style that made their appearance most emphatically during the Great Cultural Revolution are, for our purposes, very instructive.

The Red Guard movement, for example, was self-characterized as a movement of the young against the old. Like the Futurists of pre-Fascist Italy, the Red Guard identified the objects of its disapprobation as those things that were "old," "traditional," and "foreign." At times it appears that the "class war" invoked during the Great Cultural Revolution was, as a matter of fact, not a class but a generational struggle. Those functional and strategic members of the party and bureaucratic apparatus "over forty" seem to have qualified as "capitalists" and the young, who have no power, as "proletarians." The Red Guards were charged with "destroying the 'four olds' (old ideas, culture, customs and habits) . . . and [fostering] 'four news' of the proletariat."[83] The representatives of the "four olds"—the "bourgeois authorities," the "old professors"—the institutions maintained to preserve the elements of the "four olds"—the museums and archives—all came under attack. In some cases the attacks were so threatening that the military had to intercede to protect some of China's cultural treasures as well as the health and well-being of its most accomplished scholars. The purpose of the attacks was, however, served. The attacks on the "four olds," those "in authority over forty," were apparently calculated to disestablish sources of resistance to Mao's "revolutionary romanticism," and in so doing to provide for the total and effective mobilization, behind Mao, of what remained of the party along with the temporarily leaderless masses.[84]

In order to disestablish the functional and strategic bureaucracy, Maoist youth glorified "redness" at the expense of "expertness." Youth, revolutionary ardor, Maoist commitment, were all given precedence over accomplishment governed by some set of objective criteria. Even Kuo Mo-jo, President of the Chinese Academy of Sciences, long considered the most prestigious representative of China's communist intellectuals and the most respected of national scholars, was publicly humiliated by the Red Guards in their program against the "four olds" and the "over forties" in authority. It is interesting to note that the Chinese characterize the entire "revolution" in terms of the "unlearned" having "overthrown" the "learned"—a characterization similar to the injunction issued by Marinetti and Papini that the "fools" take up their positions against the "wise" and the "learned."[85] As early as the "Great Leap Forward" there had been the insistent suggestion that science and technology need not

[83] "Carry the Great Proletarian Cultural Revolution Through to the End," in *The Great Proletarian Cultural Revolution in China*, No. 9 (Peking: Foreign Languages, 1967), p. 5.

[84] Lifton, *Revolutionary Immortality*, p. 53.

[85] Yao Wen-yuan, "Commemorate Lu Hsun and Carry the Revolution Through to the End," in *Commemorating Lu Hsun*, p. 19; cf. p. 5.

be the province of the "learned." Technicians and scientists were harassed by nonexperts emboldened by the assumption that revolutionary ardor and intuition constituted functional substitutes for special skill and learning.[86] Futurists had made the same claims for futurist "science," the product of intuitive insight and youthful ardor.

The similarities do not terminate with the identification with the "new" and the "young" against the "old"—the "unlearned" against the "learned." An entire syndrome of analogous elements relating the style of the Red Guards with that of the Futurists and the Fascists can be catalogued.

The attack on the "old," the "traditional," was expressed by both the Futurists and the Red Guards in terms of "anti-authoritarianism" and "anti-bureaucracy." Both youth movements advocated an anti-gerontocratic, anti-bureaucratic, and decentralized political system. Particularly in the early weeks of the Red Guard movement old men were physically abused, professors and scholars publicly humilated in what could only be described as intergenerational violence. Sustained attacks were directed against the bureaucracy. Joan Robinson, in fact, interprets the Great Cultural Revolution as a "revolt" against "the incipient new class of organization men in the Communist Party."[87] However implausible, the judgment reflects the reality manifest in the sustained attacks that the Red Guards made against "authority" and the "bureaucracy." At about the same time as the attacks on authority and bureaucracy were undertaken, the talk of the "Paris Commune" suggested that the Great Cultural Revolution was calculated to produce the radical democracy that Marx had anticipated as the "dictatorship of the proletariat." China would become a voluntary association of communes in which administration was in the hands of representatives

[86] Kang Chao, "The Great Leap," in F. Schurmann and O. Schell, *The China Reader, Communist China* (New York: Random House, 1967), III, 416; cf. Schram, *Political Thought*, p. 83.

[87] Robinson, *The Cultural Revolution in China*, p. 28; cf. Lifton, *Revolutionary Immortality*, p. 37.

250

selected by universal suffrage and subject to referendum and recall. Lin Piao's speech (of November 3, 1966) to the Red Guard alluded to a new government for China patterned on the "principles of the Paris Commune."[88]

Needless to say, whatever evidence we have indicates that no effort has been undertaken to implement such suggestions. The Red Guards have themselves been domesticated after serving in the domestication of the revolutionary party. We have already suggested that the newly constituted party has directed its criticism against "ultra-democratic" political postures and "ultra-decentralizing" tendencies. What is important for our purposes is to recognize the disposition on the part of the youth movement to employ the locutions we have identified as characteristic of the style of the new radicalism.

More ominous than these elements is the disposition on the part of the "revolutionaries" to conceive violence and war, and military style, as of special significance for the "revolution." We have suggested that mass-mobilizing movements tend to conceive the universe as polarized, the community of men divided into those morally impeccable and those morally impaired. The young are, apparently, particularly disposed to so characterize humanity. For the Futurists, and the Fascist youth groups and *squadristi* that adopted their style, human associations were composed on the one hand of the intuitive, the generous, the spirited, the pure and unsullied and on the other of the depraved, those concerned only with material reward, the selfish, the calculating "experts"—in effect the "bourgeoisie." The distinctions made by the Red Guards are the same. The "nonrevolutionaries" are "bourgeois ghosts" and "reactionary monsters"—they are "bad eggs"—they all "stink," they are "just rotten trash," to be "detested," to "be beaten." The "revolutionaries" will

---

[88] "Comrade Lin Piao's Speech at the Peking Mass Rally to Receive Revolutionary Teachers and Students from all Over China," in *The Great Cultural Revolution in China*, No. 8 (Peking: Foreign Languages, 1967), p. 3.

"smite their dog mouths and . . . bayonets shall taste blood!"[89] One of the most popular of the quotations from Chairman Mao is "Everything reactionary is the same; if you don't hit it, it won't fall."[90] Like the Futurists the Red Guards have committed themselves to "clear out" and "sweep away" all "the old forces, ideas, cultures, customs and habits and trample underfoot all ancient scriptures, precious idols, traditional or secret nostrums . . ." for "destruction come first, and construction in the course of destruction."[91]

The militancy of the Red Guards would appear to be a function of their belief in a radically polarized environment. If the forces of good and evil are to be so clearly distinguished—and if the forces of evil are so transparently malevolent—anything less than a violent struggle against them would be morally repugnant. As a consequence, the disposition of the Maoists to entertain invocations such as "All our work is preparation for war," and "The world can be changed only by using gun barrels," becomes comprehensible. One of the statements chosen for inclusion in Mao's book of quotations, now universally distributed throughout China, reads: "Some people ridicule us as advocates of the 'omnipotence of war.' Yes, we are advocates of the omnipotence of revolutionary war; that is good, not bad, it is Marxist."[92]

"Struggle," both the internal and the international "class struggle," has become a central theme in Maoism. Schurmann has simply identified "struggle" as "the central value of the Chinese Communists' ideology."[93] But it is a specific kind of struggle that constitutes the supreme test of human will: that struggle is "revolutionary" war—and any war that

[89] Lifton, *Revolutionary Immortality*, pp. 39f.

[90] Huang Ping-wen, "Learn from Lu Hsun, Be Faithful to Chairman Mao for Ever," in *Commemorating Lu Hsun*, p. 22.

[91] Editorial in *Hunggi*, No. 14, 1966, in *ibid.*, p. 44.

[92] *Quotations from Chairman Mao*, p. 34. Cf. Lifton, *Revolutionary Immortality*, pp. 51f.

[93] Schurmann, *Ideology*, p. 44.

Mao involved himself in would be, *ipso facto*, "revolutionary." In his more recent interview with Edgar Snow, Mao
made it clear that his misgivings concerning the youth of
China were a consequence of his conviction that they had
not experienced the moral training that only war can provide. Mao's preferences, his style, the product of both temperament and experience, are for *military* solutions. His
language, and the language of the Red Guards he invoked,
was the language of military strategy. His emphasis was,
and is, on the martial virtues. "The language of war, strength,
and courage runs like a red thread through all of Mao's
works. This is not merely one of the *important* strains in
Mao's personality and thought; it is almost the *central*
strain."[94]

War is for Mao and his revolutionaries the supreme test
of human will, endurance, and courage. All the hero-models
provided for the Red Guards were soldiers in the People's
Liberation Army. Their virtues were courage, endurance,
sacrifice, dedication, and obedience—in effect, military virtues. The communiqué of the Eleventh Plenary Session of
the Eighth Central Committee meeting of the party (August
1966) announced its approval of the "brilliant policies of
decisive and fundamental importance put forward by Comrade Mao Tse-tung . . . ," one of which was a call "for the
whole Party to grasp military affairs and for everybody to
be a soldier . . . ." Since that time the army has become
directly involved not only in the reorganization of the control apparatus of government but in the direction and control of education, industry, and agriculture as well.[95]

Invoking military virtues as a guide to conduct carries a
number of consequences. The first, and perhaps most obvi-

[94] Schram, *Political Thought*, p. 125; *Quotations from Chairman
Mao*, p. xi, cf. Lifton, *Revolutionary Immortality*, p. 65; "The Human
Factor Comes First," in *Political Work: The Lifeline of All Work*
(Peking: Foreign Languages, 1966), p. 5; Mehnert, *Maos zweite
Revolution*, p. 21.

[95] "Revolutionary Committees are Fine (March, 1968)," in W. Chai,
ed., *Essential Works of Chinese Communism* (New York: Bantam,
1969), p. 444.

ous, is the explicit rejection of "humanism" and "pacificism" as sustaining human values. "Humanism" and "liberalism" have become terms of disapprobation. Yao Wen-yuan is outraged that Soviet authors could suggest that Lu Hsun could be conceived of as "humanitarian." "They had," Yao complains, "the effrontery to malign Lu Hsun as a 'humanitarian,' . . ." as someone committed to "the slavish philosophy that advertises 'fraternity' and 'forebearance.' " Hsu Kuang-ping, similarly, is incensed by the Soviet suggestion that Lu Hsun could be a "humanitarian" and that his ideas were "marked with a 'pacifist tendency.' "[96]

Fascist parallels are not difficult to discern. The style of Futurism, the style with which it infused Fascism, was one of militant, one might say more appropriately military, rectitude. Struggle, for Futurism and subsequently for Fascism as well, was a moral necessity that provided excision of all that was old and reactionary. Man's most demanding struggle, war, afforded the opportunity of overcoming all that was effete, decadent, reactionary, and corrupt. The Fascist squads, and ultimately the entire movement, were animated by such a style and sustained by such convictions. Pacifism, in any of its many seductive guises, was morally objectionable.

Fascism, like Futurism, conceived life as an interminable struggle between good and evil, reaction and revolution, with "revolutionary" war affording the supreme test of will, endurance, and virtue. For Fascism, therefore, the moral community was circumstanced very much like a military camp with "each citizen a soldier," and the party organized as a "civil militia." All of this has been characterized as "military romanticism," a term that Stuart Schram has recently applied to the organizational and tactical strategy of Maoist leadership.[97] Such "romanticism" became increasingly emphatic during the Great Cultural Revolution. It has created the highly charged atmosphere that facilitates mass mobili-

[96] Yao Wen-yuan "Commemorate Lu Hsun . . . ," p. 11; Hsu Kuang-ping, "Mao Tse-tung's Thought Illuminates Lu Hsun," in *ibid.*, p. 35.
[97] S. Schram, *Mao Tse-tung* (Baltimore: Penguin, 1967), p. 293.

zation in the service of war or protracted nonmilitary sacrifice.

Mussolini had identified three conditions necessary for the realization of the revolutionary program of Fascism: the unitary party, a totalitarian apparatus in which "all the energy, interests and aspirations of a people are transformed and made manifest," and finally "an atmosphere of high ideal tension."[98] That "atmosphere" is the analogue of the "military romanticism" that provides the recruitment advantages for Maoist new cadres. Although the style that animated the Red Guards revealed itself characterized by the utopian democratic dispositions that seem to characterize youth movements, the carrier movement which ultimately assimilated the youth movement employs the "atmosphere of high tension" to mobilize in the service of the party (or its analogue) and the bureaucratized state.

After the excesses of the Red Guards threatened the organizational continuity of Maoist control, the military and the adult Revolutionary Rebels created control agencies to defend production against dislocations created by "revolutionary" activities by the young. In January 1967 the new control agencies the Maoists were creating issued urgent notices to the "revolutionary forces" which asserted that, "We believe that the masses of revolutionary workers have a high sense of political responsibility towards their great socialist motherland; they will certainly be able to put public interest to the fore, and, proceeding from the overall interests of the state . . . and seize a double victory in the cultural revolution and in production."[99]

In effect, the high ideal tension that finds expression in perpetual struggle, in a form of military romanticism, is an effective mobilizing technique. It serves the interests of the Maoist leadership in its efforts to move the population to sustained and exacting sacrifice "proceeding from the overall interests of the state." Youth movements seem condemned

[98] Mussolini, "Discorso per lo stato corporativo," *Opera*, xxvi, 96.
[99] "Urgent Notice," in *The Great Proletarian Cultural Revolution in China*, No. 10, p. 16.

to serve carrier movements in this fashion. They dichotomize the political environment, invoke enthusiasm, mobilize energies, conjure up apocalyptic visions, exploit unproblematic and utopian values, only to succumb to carrier movements which use them as recruitment agencies and their members as expendable foot soldiers. Mass-mobilizing movements have never conceived youth movements as the source of revolutionary ideals. It now seems relatively clear that the Red Guards of the Great Cultural Revolution had given at least partial expression to a number of student and youth grievances that had been bruited as early as the late fifties. There is very little doubt that the Maoist leadership exploited the student and youth sentiment in order to direct their energies against the party apparatus that had proven recalcitrant. With the disestablishment of the party apparatus, the energies invoked by the Red Guards were channeled into the more "responsible" agencies, the Revolutionary Rebel committees and the army.

Conclusions

If the political radicalism of the twentieth century finds expression in mass-mobilizing movements led by self-selected revolutionary elites whose principal recruitment and control strategy involves appeal to nationalist sentiment, then Mussolini's Fascism is its most illustrative exemplification. The political content, the belief system that informs the movement's strategy and tactics, concerns itself with the maintenance, development, competitive position, and defense capabilities of a politically defined national community. The political style that frequently attends that content is borrowed from an auxiliary or antecedent youth movement that is ultimately absorbed by the movement which becomes its carrier.

In circumstances where the recruitment of the young has particular political advantage, the style of the youth movement influences the political expression of the mass-mobilizing movement. Its influence is limited to the confines estab-

256

lished by the political requirements of the carrier movement. If the youth movement has any specific content that is at variance with the political commitments of the carrier movement, that content is dissipated and the youth movement is ultimately domesticated to the needs of its host. Fascism is the clearest instance of this phenomenon, but the youth and student movements exploited by both Lenin and Mao Tse-tung seem to constitute impressive instances in their own right.

Irrespective of the function of the youth movement either as an antecedent, an auxiliary, or a subsequent adjunct movement, the content of mass-mobilizing movements in the twentieth century appears to be remarkably uniform. Since the opportunities for recruitment are particularly propitious in underdeveloped and status-deprived communities, mass-mobilizing movements have largely manifested themselves in partially or singularly underdeveloped environments. The populations of such environments are initially mobilized by war or invasion or left to their own devices by the precipitous withdrawal of colonial governments and as a consequence became available to a mass-mobilizing movement, employing nationalism as its principal recruitment lure.

Such movements have generally arrogated to themselves tasks of such compelling magnitude that only a conviction in their own impeccable insight into the requirements of history, or the inevitabilities of events, sustains them in their effort. Such a conviction renders them intolerant of opposition. What results is a thrust for dominance that is ill disposed to share power with any real or potential competitors. The unique, or unitary, party is the foreseeable consequence.

In a situation in which the unitary party assumes unopposed control of a nation, a number of problems generates tensions between the leadership and the party. First, and perhaps foremost, the party is staffed by men infused with a special constellation of ideals. They are men who have suffered to make a revolution. Any faulting of any of those ideals on the part of the leadership creates centrifugal tendencies in the unitary party, and "right" and "left" wing "oppositions" begin to manifest themselves. The phenomenon has become a commonplace in the history of radical mass-mobilizing parties. It is prominent in the history of the Bolshevik Party of Soviet Russia, the Fascist Party of Mussolini's Italy, the National Socialist Party of Hitler's Germany, and the Chinese Communist Party of Mao Tse-tung. The party demands domestication. What results is the now familiar purge and the elevation of the party leader to the exalted position of ultimate arbiter of ideological truth.

A second source of difficulty that generates tensions between the immediate leadership of the party and the party itself arises apparently from the necessity of developing a bureaucratic infrastructure to carry out the revolutionary purposes of the party. The bureaucracy begins to develop interests of its own; it invests in institutions and operational procedures it is only slow to modify. The response of the bureaucracy to the changed directives of the leadership is at best slow—and sometimes dysfunctional. To resolve this source of tension the leadership will assume an increasing measure of hierarchical responsibility and the party and the bureaucracy take on more and more the character of a military machine with orders emanating from the top and unquestioning and immediate obedience expected from subordinates.

The result of all this is to produce a "charismatic leader," a party leader endowed with almost supernatural qualities, a leader who is a "universal genius," the "greatest mind in the history of the world," someone who is "never wrong"— men who enjoy, like Stalin, "routinized charisma." These men have become all too common in the twentieth century.

In most countries where they have appeared these movements are modernizing and industrializing—for only in such manner could they restore or provide dignity to a status-deprived community. Where the economy is essentially pre-industrial, the recruitment of peasant masses is facilitated by the dislocations and high emotional saliences that attend protracted wars. When these movements manifest themselves in a marginally developed economy, appeal is made to the agricultural and working classes, since they provide the recruitment base for mass mobilization. In more extensively developed economies appeal is made to working class and petit bourgeois elements.

The second half of the twentieth century has seen such mass-mobilizing movements sweep whole populations into the vortex of revolution. The invocation to revolution is made in a special language style. The vocabulary is frequently "Marxist," but the content is more symbolic than cognitive. "Revolutionary consciousness" becomes the possession of a self-selected elite rather than an identifiable social class. Being the vehicle of world historical truth, that self-selected elite, of whatever class provenience, constitutes itself a unitary party that tolerates no dissent or opposition. Within the unitary party, factionalism and sectarianism are suppressed by the exaltation of the "charismatic leader," who becomes the ultimate arbiter of truth, the incarnation of the "will of the masses," and the source of legitimation for the regime itself.

That any of this has anything whatever to do with classical Marxism is, at best, doubtful. The Marxism of Marx and Engels has endured such extensive and intensive "creative development" that it has become the legitimating rationale for mass mobilizing, developmental dictatorships that share far more features with the paradigmatic Fascism of Mussolini than with any of the anticipations of Karl Marx or Friedrich Engels.

CHAPTER SEVEN

The New Radicalism:
The Caribbean Variant

*Look at the Paris Commune. That was the Dictatorship
of the Proletariat. . . . [N]othing could be more foreign
to the spirit of the Commune than to supersede universal suffrage by hierarchic investiture.*[1]

Engels and Marx (1891 and 1871)

OF all the variants of the new radicalism, Castro's revolution in Cuba is perhaps the most fascinating and the
most perplexing. It is obviously too early to deliver a definitive characterization of what has transpired in Cuba, but
there are features of that complex political phenomena
which recommend themselves to our attention. In the first
instance it has been generally accepted that the revolution
led by Castro, which culminated in the flight of Batista on
the first of January 1959, was not a "communist" revolution
or a "crypto-communist" revolution; nor could its ideology
or programmatic intentions between 1953 and 1960 be characterized as even remotely "Marxist" or "Marxist-Leninist."
Fidel Castro (irrespective of what he might have said, or
will say, in retrospect) could not be conceived to have been
a "communist" or a "Marxist" prior to the "socialist phase"
of his revolution, which began only after two years of absolute power. Only in December 1961 did Castro announce
his "Marxist-Leninist" commitment. Throughout the interim
period, his own characterization of his position varied from
an insistence upon its anti-communist character, through an
identification with an indeterminate ideology he identified

[1] F. Engels, "Introduction," to K. Marx, "The Civil War in France,"
in K. Marx and F. Engels, *Selected Works*, I, 485, and 521.

at the time as "humanism," until his espousal of Marxism-Leninism and communism.[2] No one, friend or foe, has made a convincing case that Fidel Castro was a Marxist or a communist of conviction prior to the close of 1961.

The history of the Cuban revolution reveals a radical, mass-mobilizing movement that was emphatically noncommunist, and perhaps anti-communist, during its "insurrectional" revolutionary phase—a movement that transmogrified itself, or was transmogrified, into something self-characterized as Marxist-Leninist, "socialist," and "communist" only after its leadership had enjoyed secure power for almost two years. The Caribbean radicalism exemplified by Castroism is a singular phenomenon. If it is to be classified as "Marxist," or "Marxist-Leninist," it is a Marxism and a Marxism-Leninism of a most peculiar sort. It was a Marxist movement that was led by bourgeois radicals, enjoying the active and passive support of a nonrepresentative minority of peasants, much of the bourgeoisie, but absent of any significant contact or active support from the proletarians that constituted a larger proportion of the working population of Cuba at the time of the revolution than was the case in either Russia or China on the occasion of theirs. In point of fact the Communist Party of Cuba, the *Partido Socialista Popular*, not only did not actively support the "Marxist" revolutionaries, it actively opposed them until the revolutionary victory was all but secured. Only in February 1958 did the Communists of Cuba lend Castro's guerrilla force any active support.

As late as April 23, 1959, after four months of power, Castro continued to identify, and reject, Fascism, Peronism and communism as members of the same genus: totalitarianism. As late as May 1959, Castro spoke of communism as a system "which solves the economic problem, but which suppresses liberties, the liberties which are so dear to man and which I know the Cuban people feel." He in-

[2] Cf. T. Draper, *Castroism: Theory and Practice* (New York: Praeger, 1965), chap. 1.

261

sisted that the communist states "sacrificed" man as "pitilessly" as did the capitalist states.[3]

If Castro made a Marxist revolution, he obviously made it without any consciousness of being a Marxist. Lenin had argued that the "consciousness" requisite to socialist revolution could be brought to the proletariat "from without" through the intercession of declassed bourgeois elements. Mao maintained that that consciousness could be brought to the peasantry—where there were no proletarians—by a class conscious Marxist vanguard. Castroism somehow managed to bring the consciousness requisite to socialist revolution to a nonrepresentative body of peasants, not only where there were abundant proletarians, but through the medium of an "unconscious" vanguard of declassed and non-Marxist bourgeois elements. Not only that, but it was only after the seizure of power, and after two years of secure control, that —in the words of a sympathetic commentator—socialism was "thrust upon [the proletariat] by the intellectuals who were directing the revolutionary government . . . . The initiative came from above, not by insurrection from below."[4]

In 1891 Friedrich Engels referred to a "blanquist revolution" in the following manner:

Brought up in the school of conspiracy, and held together by strict discipline which went with it, [the Blanquists] started out from the viewpoint that a relatively small number of resolute, well-organized men would be able, at a given favorable moment, not only to seize the helm of state, but also by a display of great, ruthless energy, to maintain power until they succeeded in sweeping the mass of the people into the revolution and ranging them round the small band of leaders. This involved above all,

---

[3] Cf. C. Julien, *La Revolution Cubaine* (Paris: Julliard, 1961), p. 265; and Draper, *Castroism*, p. 37.

[4] J. P. Morray, *The Second Revolution in Cuba* (New York: Monthly Review, 1962), p. 165.

the strictest, dictatorial centralization of all power in the hands of the new revolutionary government.[5]

He went on to indicate that not only was such a strategy wrong but that such circumstances could only generate an environment in which simple dictatorship would flourish. The "dictatorship of the proletariat" was, for Marx and Engels, something quite different from any dictatorship in which a small minority of men could win the masses to their cause by dominating the control apparatus of the state. For Engels a true socialist revolution could only be "spontaneous and irrepressible," involving the "mind and the spirit" of masses, *the majority of class conscious workers.* After the revolutionary victory, the "dictatorship of the proletariat," as Marx and Engels anticipated it, would introduce universal suffrage, referendum, and recall, restricted mandates for popularly elected representatives, and the voluntary association of productive communes. These were the features both Marx and Engels identified as essential to their revolution and the "dictatorship of the proletariat" as they understood it. Lenin, himself, in his *State and Revolution,* identified the same institutional constraints on "dictatorial" power during the *first* stage of postrevolutionary government. Lenin was compelled by circumstances to "violate" the principles of proletarian democracy when the revolution was isolated in an underdeveloped environment. But Lenin's Russia had attempted to provide laws that called for referendum and recall and workers' ownership of the means of production. Such laws were passed in the first euphoric days of the revolution—only to be quickly rescinded.

In Castro's Cuba, on the other hand, such laws have, apparently, never even been contemplated. Irrespective of his many promises concerning free elections, freedom of the press, and the defense of constitutional liberties prior to his accession to power—once in power Castro suppressed op-

[5] Engels, "Introduction," to Marx, "The Civil War in France," in Marx and Engels, *Selected Works,* I, 482f.

position political parties and the opposition press and postponed general elections indefinitely. He has, on his own initiative, assigned ministerial tasks, generated legislation, undertaken vast programs of social and economic change with the popular support provided by monopoly control of the means of public persuasion—strategies of mass mobilization that have been employed in political environments as different as that of National Socialist Germany, Fascist Italy, Stalinist Russia, and Maoist China. Trotsky characterized such control strategies as "plebiscitary democracy"—involving ritual performances where one identified himself as being either for or against the "leader," or for or against the "revolution."[6] Whatever one chooses to call such performances—"participatory democracy," "democratic centralism," or, as Mussolini identified it, "organized, centralized and authoritarian democracy"[7]—it has institutional features which categorically distinguish it from the "dictatorship of the proletariat" as that dictatorship was understood by Marx and Engels and as that dictatorship was anticipated by Lenin in his *State and Revolution*.

However one chooses to construe the revolution in Cuba, it certainly displays singular characteristics. It was led by men who reiterated their "anti-ideological" disposition—men who conceived themselves problem-solvers rather than "theorists." The slogans that animated their sacrifice included traditionally nationalist invocations such as "The Fatherland or death" (*¡Patria o muerte!*). Their revolution was to be "as Cuban as [their] music." It was to be a revolution to unite *all* Cubans—of whatever class, category, race, and status—but one that was most emphatically addressed to the "vast unredeemed masses . . . ; people, who yearn for a better, more diginfied, and more just nation; who are moved by ancestral aspirations of justice. . . ." Castro addressed himself, in his now famous *History Will Absolve*

[6] L. Trotsky, *The Revolution Betrayed*, tr. Max Eastman (New York: Doubleday, Doran, 1937), p. 278.

[7] B. Mussolini, *La dottrina del fascismo* (Milan: Hoepli, 1935), p. 29.

Me!, to the Cuban unemployed, the farm laborers, the industrial workers, the small farmers, the teachers, professors, young professionals, and small businessmen. In effect the revolution was to be composed of all, save the "comfortable ones" who were prepared to "welcome any regime of oppression." It was to be a revolution that would "industrialize the country"—an industrialization that required the extensive intercession of the state. Cuba required industrialization and diversification of its economy—a process that would "make the nation great." In order to fulfill these injunctions Cubans must be brought to a conscious awareness of their *duty* to their nation. Castro repeated the declamation of one of the heroes of his first attack against the Batista regime: "To die for your country is to live on." He repeated the prose of José Martí, the "Apostle" of Cuba's independence, "When one dies in the arms of a grateful fatherland death ends, prison walls break—finally, with death, life begins."[8]

While Castro's actions after the seizure of power distinguish his regime from the "dictatorship of the proletariat" conceived by Marx and Engels, the content that Castro initially gave to his revolution did not distinguish it from the content characteristic of any number of developmental and nationalistic movements common to the nineteenth and twentieth centuries. For Fidel Castro, in fact, it was José Martí, the nineteenth-century nationalist, and not Karl Marx or V. I. Lenin, who was the "Apostle" of his revolution. José Martí, the principal founder of Cuban nationalism, was not only a nationalist, he was committed to the development and diversification of Cuba's economy as well as its economic and political independence from "stronger" and more "wealthy" powers—including both the United States and Spain.

The features shared by the revolutionary movement which began with the attack on the Moncada Barracks on July 26, 1953, and the thought of José Martí provide one of the clues for unraveling the complex skein of the Cuban revolution.

[8] F. Castro, *History Will Absolve Me!* (New York: Fair Play for Cuba Committee, 1961), pp. 33f, 38f, 41, 43, 51, 59, 78.

DEVELOPMENTAL DICTATORSHIP

One of the shared features of the Fascist and the Cuban revolutions that detractors characterize as "opportunism," and their advocates admire as "problem-orientated pragmatism" and "anti-doctrinaire dispositions," was their indisposition to codify commitments in specific programs. Mussolini, like Castro, never tired of identifying his revolution as "anti-ideological," as "dynamic," and in "constant flux." "Fascism," Mussolini insisted, "was not the product of some anticipatory doctrine—it was born of the need for action, and was action." It was a "pragmatic movement," responding to "problems" whose complexity necessitated a constant reconsideration of programs.

When Fascists were charged with having violated one or another of their programmatic commitments, they responded that "life is not static," things are "in constant flux." Fascism was a "permanent revolution." Fascists insisted that there were but two constants around which their changing programmatic commitments gravitated: *increased productivity* of the economic system of Italy and the *grandeur and dignity of the fatherland.*[9] At the meeting of San Sepolcro which saw the foundation of the Fascist movement, Mussolini insisted that the "capstone" of Fascist political convictions was "the maximum of production" for the Italian nation through what he called, at that time, "economic democracy." The first programmatic statements of the Fascists insisted upon the "uplift of the working masses—for if the mass of laborers remain miserable and brutalized, there can be no greatness for a people, neither within its national confines nor in its contact with the external world."[10]

Fascism early identified itself as a developmental nationalism that was populist, anti-ideological, and pre-eminently pragmatic. In their earliest programmatic utterances Fascists recognized that if Italy were to begin a program of

[9] Mussolini, "Atto di nascita del fascismo," *Opera*, XII, 325.
[10] *Ibid.*, p. 327; "Discorso da ascoltare," *Opera*, XIII, 97.

accelerated development, she would have to expect the opposition of the favored nations of Europe who, in their own interests, would obstruct any real program of Italian national renaissance. Italy was a "proletarian nation" opposed by privileged "plutocratic powers." As we have seen, as early as 1920, Dino Grandi, who was later to become one of Fascist Italy's foremost ideologues, spoke of the Russian revolution as the first revolution of an economically disadvantaged and status-deprived nation against the world plutocracies.[11] While the Bolsheviks still talked of "world revolution" made by the "international proletarian class," Grandi insisted that the twentieth century would see nationalist revolutions conducted by men mobilized by *national*, rather than *class* appeals. Grandi anticipated revolutions by "poor" nations against "rich" nations—rather than revolutions undertaken by the international proletariat against the international bourgeoisie.

Grandi, two years before the Fascist accession to power, spoke of the political realities of the contemporary world as surface phenomena generated by tensions endemic to capitalism. He maintained that capitalism is, by its very nature, compelled to seek resolution of its two critical problems: its inability to effectively distribute its commodity produce and its continual and insatiable need for raw materials.[12] Grandi insisted, and Fascists continued to insist for over two decades, that the more mature capitalist powers were disposed to resolve their needs for market and resource supplements by systematically exploiting less developed political communities. Those nations that enjoyed industrial maturity would exploit their material advantages in order to extort concessions from the underdeveloped, and largely agrarian, nations. Such treatment could only generate a reactive nationalism whose recruitment base would potentially include all class, strata and functional components of the exploited population. The revolutionary nationalism that resulted would be populist and anti-plutocratic—it would be a na-

[11] D. Grandi, *Giovani* (Bologna: Zanichelli, 1941), p. 225.
[12] *Ibid.*, p. 150.

tional socialism—it would be the product of a struggle between "proletarian" nations and "plutocratic" nations.

These themes remained constant in standard Fascist literature throughout the history of Mussolini's regime. In
1941, for example, Amato Grandi maintained that war was
a consequence of tensions endemic to capitalism—capitalism
was forever driven to resolve its incapacity to distribute effectively its produce by seeking more and more market
supplements and, in order to satisfy its appetite for resources, perpetually to seek a redivision of the world.
Fascism's mission was to liberate Italy not only from the
yoke of Anglo-American imperialism but from capitalism
as well.[13]

In the contemporary world, Fascists argued, the plutocratic powers exploited their bargaining advantages and
forced underdeveloped, that is to say "poor" and essentially
agrarian, nations into subordinate and disadvantaged relationships.[14] For underdeveloped political communities, political independence, true sovereignty, and collective well-
being could only be the consequence of economic strength,
economic independence, and a viability outside the trammels of a world market dominated by the cartels and mo-
nopolies of the plutocratic powers. "Political autonomy,"
Mussolini insisted in 1936, "or the possibility of an independent foreign policy, cannot be conceived of without a
corresponding capacity for economic self-sufficiency . . . .
All nations seek to free themselves as far as possible from
foreign domination."[15] As early as 1918, even before their
incorporation into the Fascist movement, Italian Nationalists
argued that the First World War had been a war of imperialist redivision from which the United States, England,
and France emerged as dominant—powers from whom
Italy, Germany, and Russia could expect no redress. Without

[13] A. Grandi, *La futura civiltà del lavoro nel mondo* (Bologna: Sti-
assi & Tantini, 1941), passim.

[14] Cf. Grandi, *Giovani*, pp. 38f.

[15] Mussolini, "Il piano regolatore della nuova economia Italiana,"
Opera, xxvii, 242.

revolutionary redistribution, the "proletarian nations" could only languish in "a condition of political, economic, and moral inferiority."[16]

Both Nationalists and Fascists contended that Italy's disadvantages could only be resolved by a new national and revolutionary determination to alter the political balance of Europe. Both Nationalists and Fascists insisted that what was required for the redress of that balance was a unified and revolutionary national will. The precondition of that unity of will was an intensive collaboration of all the productive categories of the nation. Fascists (and Nationalists) insisted that Italy's inferiority was a direct or indirect consequence of a lamentable lack of collective national commitment—a commitment due the fatherland irrespective of class provenience.

That Italians failed to manifest the solidarity and revolutionary determination necessary to their historic task was conceived a consequence of the fact that Italy had been largely forged through *diplomacy*, rather than *struggle*. The Fascist mystique of violence was born of a tradition that saw men molded and transformed by violence. Enrico Corradini, one of the founders of Italian Nationalism, and subsequently a principal Fascist ideologue, maintained that what Italy required was the "formation of a national consciousness . . . a spirit of solidarity among its citizens." That such a spirit did not obtain was a product of the circumstances that saw Italy "fashioned through too little war and too little revolution." Italy was too much the artifact of international diplomacy and the by-product of foreign intervention. That Italy was thus "artificially" created left Italians afflicted with unresolved fratricidal antagonisms. To overcome the disabilities of its history as a pawn of foreign powers, as a nation divided by parochial and class interests, Italy was required to attend an arduous "school of discipline and duty . . . an education of national consciousness." "Nations," Corradini insisted, "are not acquired; they are

16 "Il manifesto di 'Politica,'" in F. Gaeta, ed., *La stampa nazionalista* (Rocca San Cassiano: Cappelli, 1965), p. 19, passim.

conquered."[17] As early as 1908, Corradini maintained that *war*, the sanguinary contest between national communities, was the school of collective consciousness. That theme was to find resonance in the hysteria of the Futurist movement and was to become a common theme of Fascism itself.[18]

For the Nationalist, Futurist, and interventionist movements, the First World War provided the occasion for such a "schooling" of national consciousness. It was in the service of the "revolutionary war" that the first Fascist squads were organized. All of Mussolini's writings during the war period reflect the conviction that Italy would emerge from the conflict a nation transformed—fused into an infrangible unity. This theme, the conviction that a selfless and "anti-bourgeois" consciousness could only be the product of the supreme challenge of armed conflict, remained central to Fascism throughout the history of the regime. The First World War was a "revolutionary war" in which a new national consciousness was forged—a consciousness that radiated outward throughout the "masses" of the peninsula through mimetic contagion—a kind of moral mimicry that reflected the image of the warrior-revolutionary. The model for the new consciousness was provided by the men of the trenches, the assault troops—men who had faced the supreme test of will, dedication, and sacrifice. Their right to lead the nation as a vanguard elite was purchased with blood. They were to provide the military models for the new, revolutionary civic consciousness.

When Mussolini maintained that Fascism required that men live in a state of high moral tension and disciplined sacrifice, he was obviously thinking of men under wartime conditions and charged with wartime obligations. The Fascists made no secret of their ideal society—the ideal community was a nation in which the entire population became one "immense militia," infused with the virtues of the war-

[17] E. Corradini, *Discorsi politici* (Florence: Vallecchi, 1923), pp. 113-18.
[18] E. Corradini, *L'ombra della vita* (Naples: Ricciardi, 1908), p. 286.

rior-revolutionary.[19] The warrior-revolutionary was the "new man" which Fascism advertised—a man born in sanguinary struggle for his ideals—a man both warrior and revolutionary, a hero moved by moral rather than material incentives.[20]

In the context of such a political pespective the economic system of the nation served only *instrumental* purposes. If capitalism promised the increments of production requisite to the acquisition of a "place in the sun" for Italy, capitalism would survive. If not, some alternative system would be introduced. Alfredo Rocco maintained that Fascism was indifferent to doctrinal prejudices when it sought to achieve its specific ends,[21] and, in fact, by the mid-thirties Mussolini was calling for an end of capitalism in Italy. Thereafter the Italian economy was increasingly (if ineffectually) controlled by a bureaucratic infrastructure under the direct or indirect control of the Fascist Party.

These doctrinal elements are not peculiarly "fascist"—they are shared by any number of developmental nationalisms. Fascists, in fact, identified them with Mazzini—with some justification. Rocco maintained that "in Mazzini's conception of the citizen as instrument for the attainment of the nation's ends and therefore submissive to a higher mission, to the duty of supreme sacrifice, we see the anticipation of one of the fundamental points of the Fascist doctrine."[22] Giovanni Gentile, in turn, sought to identify Mazzini as a precursor of the Fascist revolution; and Mussolini early argued that the circumstances that attended the reawakening of Italian nationalism with the First World War required a return to Mazzini and a reassessment of Karl Marx. Gentile argued that fifty years after the death of Mazzini some of his teachings were no longer vital. What remained

[19] S. Panunzio, "Gli uomini e le idee," *Gerarchia*, 12, 4 (April 1934), p. 319.

[20] Cf. I. De Begnac, *L'Arcangelo sindacalista: Filippo Corridoni* (Verona: Mondadori, 1943); V. Rastelli, *Filippo Corridoni* (Rome: "Conquiste d'Impero," 1940).

[21] A. Rocco, "The Political Doctrine of Fascism," in *Readings on Fascism and National Socialism* (Denver: Swallow, n.d.), p. 32.

[22] *Ibid.*, p. 46.

vital was his conviction that Italy's problem was that of creating a "unified Italian nation in the concrete form of an independent state." For Mazzini the central issue that faced Italians was to create a nation, a sense of collective unity against foreign influences that all too often dominated the Italian economy, as well as Italian thought and sentiment. Gentile, as a spokesman for Fascist thought, conceived Mazzini's injunction—that man aspire to serve the collective good—as the foundation of Fascist collectivism, the antipode of "bourgeois" egotism, individualism, and anarchy. "The necessity today," Gentile insisted with Mazzini, "is to conceive a higher purpose; no longer that of the individual, but of an association, of humanity . . . ." Nationalism appealed to the active will of a people—committed to the generic purposes of mankind. To serve those purposes Italy must be "before all else and at any cost, united, free and independent."

It was only as a consequence of the First World War, in the supreme challenge of the struggle for national life, Gentile contended, that "the words of Mazzini (the Apostle) were rekindled and perpetuated in Mussolini. And Fascism made its appearance and compelled [Italians] to hear once again the voice of Mazzini in its most profound emphases. [We recognize in Fascism] Mazzini's spiritual conception of the world—the same religious character—the same aversion to individualism—the same conception of the state and the nation, a fundamental and spiritual unity of citizens—the same totalitarian manner of conceiving human life—the same diffidence concerning mechanistic liberalism and abstract classical economy—and therefore the reorganization of social forces into a body in which the atomism of economic laws is subjected to the concrete form of an ethical state, to the very consciousness and conscience of man."[23]

Fascism, as an ideology, displayed all the principal properties of a developmental nationalism. Surprisingly similar ideologies can be found among a variety of political move-

[23] G. Gentile, "Mazzini e la nuova Italia," in *Memorie Italiane* (Florence: Sansoni, 1936), p. 25, 33, 39, 42.

272

ments of the nineteenth and twentieth centuries. Fascists, for example, found subtending similarities between their own movement and that of Kemal Ataturk as well as those that animated the Soviet Union, Portugal, and Falangist Spain.[24]

More recently, Robert Tucker[25] has suggested that within the universe of political systems a distinct class of political regimes, "single-party systems of the nationalist species," can be identified. More specifically, Tucker suggests that "revolutionary mass-movement regimes under single-party auspices" constitute the single most compelling political phenomenon of the twentieth century. These regimes are established in revolutionary struggle against either an external or internal opponent (colonial powers and/or "liberal," "parliamentary," or "oppressive" regimes). They displace the pre-existing establishment in order to undertake a program of national renovation and/or national expansion. Some of these "mass-movement regimes" trace their origins back to predecessors, like Giuseppe Mazzini, who conceived a renovating revolution to be "the product of the active participation of masses of people under the guidance and energetic leadership of an elite organization . . . ." When that "elite organization" arrogates to itself the right of absolute control over the political, social, and economic life of the nation, the result is an authoritarian, hierarchically organized one-party state. Where the apparatus of control extends throughout the social order and constitutes a "transmission belt" for the communication of directives from the central party organs, totalitarianism results.

All such mass-movement regimes tend to be "developmental" in the sense that they have appeared in underdeveloped or partially developed economic environments—or, in singular cases (National Socialist Germany), in environments where, as a consequence of a lost war, a national community finds itself disadvantaged in its competition for

[24] Cf. M. Manoilescu, *Die einzige Partei* (Berlin: Stollberg, 1941).
[25] R. Tucker, "On Revolutionary Mass-Movement Regimes," in *The Soviet Political Mind* (New York: Praeger, 1963), pp. 3-19.

status and security in the modern world. Under such circumstances, revolutionary dynamism is most characteristically directed into the service of economic development or economic expansion. If such a movement loses its *élan*, for whatever reason, it may succumb to a conservative torpor (like Franco Spain) or it may lose its recruitment and mobilization potential and then simply become a repressive and authoritarian personalist or oligarchical regime.

Tucker's suggestions offer one possible analysis of the Castro phenomenon: the Castro revolution, like the Fascist revolution, was a mass-mobilizing developmental nationalism. Like Mussolini, Castro initially articulated broad commitments to political and economic democracy as well as rapid economic expansion. Almost immediately upon the accession to power, however, both mass-movement regimes became authoritarian, mass-based, single-party regimes, to gradually become "personalist" in character and totalitarian in intention. The commitment to political and economic democracy is jettisoned and the emphasis is placed on economic development, political independence, national sovereignty, and collective grandeur. The trajectory, in Castro's case, began with his commitment to José Martí's developmental nationalism.

José Martí and the Intellectual Background of the Cuban Revolution

It seems reasonably clear that when Fidel Castro wrote *History Will Absolve Me!*, he conceived himself a "disciple" of José Martí. He spoke of Martí as the "Master" and the "Apostle." In effect, like Lenin, Mussolini, and Mao, Castro's political convictions were largely fashioned by political thought which originated outside the traditions of classical Marxism—sources outside of the equally broad tradition of Marxism-Leninism as well. The result has been a unique form of "Marxism," a "Latin Marxism" clearly distinct from that of Marx and Engels—and that of Lenin, Stalin, and Mao as well.

The programmatic suggestions found in Castro's revolutionary speeches and writings through and until mid-1961 are compatible with, and find their origins in, the revolutionary nationalism of Martí.

José Martí was born in 1853 and died in battle in the Cuban War of Independence in 1895. He left behind a legacy of social and political thought that was to inspire several generations of Cuban radicals; and after 1930 there were few politically active Cubans, particularly revolutionary students, who had not found succor in his work.[26] Martí was a nationalist, an elitist, an idealist, and irrepressibly committed to the economic, social, and political uplift of Cuba.

There is no necessity to document the nationalism of Martí. There is little that issued from his pen, that was written with political intention, that does not directly or indirectly allude to his disposition to "Serve the Fatherland." From his youth his actions were animated by a commitment to a free and economically developed Cuba.[27] It is equally clear that Martí conceived Cuba's liberation to be the consequence of the *decisiveness* of principled men acting out the duties entailed by a mobilizing *idea*.[28] Ideas must be animated by a "virile will (*la voluntad viril*)," a disposition to sacrifice for the national community—a community that includes members of all races, classes, and categories, the poor and the rich alike.[29] The revolution must be the "soul" of all Cubans of whatever class or origin; it must animate masses (*la gran masa*), masses prepared to struggle with the "book and the rifle" for the realization of their goals.[30]

[26] C.A.J. Hennessy, "The Roots of Cuban Nationalism," in R. F. Smith, *Background to Revolution* (New York: Knopf, 1966), pp. 19-29.

[27] Cf. J. Losada, *Martí: joven revolucionario* (Havana: Comisión de Estudio Históricos, 1969).

[28] J. Martí, "Persona, y patria," in *Obras completas* (Havana: Editorial Nacional, 1963 [hereafter referred to as *OC*]), ii, 278, and "¡Vengo a darte Patria!" *OC*, ii, 254f.

[29] *Ibid.*, pp. 256f.

[30] Martí, "El alzamiento y las emigraciones," *OC*, i, 433f.

While it is true that Martí refused to accede to the interpretation that conceived nationhood to be the consequence of *one* man's efforts, he was clearly committed to an *elitist* conception of revolutionary struggle and national regeneration. He admonished men who imagined themselves creating nations through their own personal will to remember that they were like the tallest trees of the forest, special in that they "tower aloft," but who nonetheless require the forest as the measure of their stature.[31] Martí was an elitist, but a *populist* as well. He spoke of masses of men whose ardor and sacrifice was invoked by the nobility of a select few, those men who "tower aloft," who "rare as mountains . . . can look down from their heights and feel with the bowels of a nation or of mankind."[32] He frequently spoke of "men of a new cast" in whom "nature has placed the need to see justice done." He spoke of "two types of men in constant struggle: those who spring from Nature, vigorous and genuine, active and solitary, recognized and acclaimed only in the moments of grave crisis when they are needed; and those who are molded by conventions, who hide their spirit as though it were a sin, who defend and maintain the established, who live in comfort and happiness . . . ."[33] He spoke of his "New Men" as those "primary and natural characters sprung directly from Nature . . . [each possessed of] an extraordinary will . . ." who provide the direction when peoples "swarm in search of leaders."[34] The qualities of leadership, Martí argued, "seem to appear, through life's mysterious process, in those men privileged to embody the very spirit of the land which gave them birth."[35] Those select spirits are capable of "fusing and transforming" men, to become "instruments of Nature's design . . . ," who by their

[31] Cf. Martí, "Cespedes and Agramonte," in J. De Onis, translator, *The America of José Martí* (New York: Noonday, 1953), pp. 295f.

[32] Martí, "A Federico Henriquez y Carvajal," *OC*, IV, 110; cf. "Emerson," in De Onis, *The America of José Martí*, pp. 219, 224.

[33] Martí, "General Grant," in *ibid.*, pp. 5, 13.

[34] Martí, "General Grant," and "Bolivar," in *ibid.*, pp. 17, 45, 156.

[35] Martí, "José Antonio Paez," *ibid.*, p. 166f.

"vision" bring "free nations into being," but only by keeping in step with the people.[36]

The men who "spring from Nature" united in a revolutionary party that is "the visible soul" of the nation—such men are ill disposed toward books. They are intensely *active* men who employ books only to better pursue their vision of a better social order. Martí entertained the conviction that true wisdom, the recognition that tyranny and oppression obtained, was not the consequence of learning, but a consequence of special intuition possessed by select men. For Martí the "eternal soul divines what science can only suspect. The latter trails like a hound; the former crosses the gorge . . . like a powerful condor."

The leaders of renovating movements not only possess an intuitive wisdom, they also represent a special moral quality. In nations where the many are without dignity, there are those who must of needs represent the dignity of many. "They are the ones who rebel with terrible force against those who rob the people of their liberty, those who rob men of their dignity. Such [select] men contain in themselves thousands, an entire people, the dignity of mankind . . . ." It is their conviction that in speaking they speak for thousands that makes such men revolutionaries, for revolution cannot await legitimation through majority consensus— because the numerical majority may simply fail to appreciate the enormities of the present social order and the requirements of the epoch.[37] Only men with special gifts, capable of mobilizing men to follow them, can resolve revolutionary problems.

Select men, possessed of vision and an intuition of a better social order, mobilize an entire people—without racial, political, social, or class distinction—in the service of a vision. For Martí that vision was the vision of a united and independent Cuba. In order to accomplish that unity and that

---

[36] Martí, "San Martin," *ibid.*, pp. 191f.

[37] Cf. E. Martinez Estrada, *Martí: El Héroe y su acción revolucionaria* (Mexico, D. F.: Siglo XXI, 1966), chap. 2; Martí, "El Partido Revolucionario a Cuba," *OC*, ii, 341.

sovereign liberty, a war of independence from Spain was the first order of revolutionary business. It was the first order of business not only because sovereignty demanded it but because Martí was convinced that true nationhood could only be forged in a revolutionary war. In 1892 Martí wrote that, while everyone was aware of the horrors of war, what was equally obvious was that only the "sublimity" of mortal combat made men conscious of their natural strength, of the advantages of selfless union. Such "spiritual" by-products of war are particularly significant to a young and heterogeneous people. Even if material wealth is destroyed, the spiritual development that attends such contests is of inestimable value.[38] Martí was clearly convinced that war provided the occasion in which those select leaders of mankind, those destined to forge nations, could "fuse" and qualitatively "transform" any collection of men.[39] More than that, he was to argue that nations obtained their mete share of respect from other nations only when they have transformed themselves by such a process.[40] "There can be no fatherland," Martí insisted, "save that which is conquered by a people's own force."[41]

The creation of a suitable national character, the acquisition through struggle of the rights of nationhood, was but the first move in the revolutionary process. To achieve true sovereignty a nation must develop an economic base that permits it a substantial economic autonomy, an industry sufficiently developed to permit it to service its essential internal needs, and an agriculture that is not so dependent upon a single market outlet that a foreign purchaser might unduly influence the internal political system of the producer.[42] Martí argued that advanced countries sought to

[38] Martí, "La guerra," OC, II, 61.

[39] Martí, "San Martin," in De Onis, The America of José Martí, p. 186.

[40] Martí, "Caracter," OC, II, 76f; "¡A Cuba!" OC, III, 47-54; cf. Martinez Estrada, Martí, chap. 3.

[41] Martí, "¡A Cuba!" OC, III, 54.

[42] Cf. E. Roig De Leuchsenring, Martí: Anti-Imperialist (Havana: Book Institute, 1967), pp. 37, passim.

resolve some of their economic problems by exploiting the underdeveloped. He maintained that North American industries offset their problem of market deficiency by "emptying their excessive production into the weakened republics of the American continent . . . ."[43] Only a nation suitably equipped to provide for its own internal needs, and capable of defending itself against imposture, could resist "reciprocal treaties" calculated to exploit.

This was to be accomplished, of course, in a context structured by democratic institutions. Martí spoke of universal suffrage, of the free exchange of information, of a free press, and collective vigilance as the only way of "avoiding the evil of the authoritarian leader (the *caudillo*)" that might arise in the period of a "revolutionary war." He spoke approvingly of "a nation where newspapers are living things, and no sooner does a cause emerge than it has its organ to which all who are interested have equal access, so that there is no injustice or suspicion that lacks a voice, or a newspaper to air it . . . ."[44]

Martí was, in effect, what contemporary radicals would today characterize as a "bourgeois democrat" and nationalist. He was, like Mazzini, broadly humanitarian—and his conception of suitable political institutions, like that of Mazzini, was broadly democratic. His social and political views were nationalist and similar, in many respects, to the views of Mazzini, his European counterpart. The elitism, the populism, the nationalism, the idealism, and the broad democratic sentiments were features common to a whole tradition of nineteenth-century social critics. Mazzini's ideas were to appear selectively in the writings of radical Italians during the first decade of the twentieth century. They found an echo in the work of men such as Oriani, and with increasing selectivity in the thought of Mussolini and Fascist apologists. Martí's thought was to have something of the same destiny.

[43] Martí, "To Cuba," *OC*, III, 56.

[44] Martí, "La guerra," *OC*, II, 63; "General Grant," in De Onis, *The America of José Martí*, p. 47.

THE "IDEOLOGY" OF THE CUBAN REVOLUTON

Until well into 1960 the "ideology" of the Cuban revolution led by Fidel Castro could best be characterized as Martían —and it was so characterized by the spokesmen of the 26th July Movement. They, like most Cubans concerned with political issues, identified themselves as disciples of José Martí in much the same manner as Italians of a multitude of persuasions identified themselves as disciples of Mazzini at the turn of the twentieth century.

As we have indicated, Castro's public pronouncements were self-consciously Martían in character and content. During the entire period from 1955, when the 26th July Movement was officially founded, until after the "insurrection" that led to the seizure of power in 1959, the programmatic goals and the commitments of the movement were, by explicit and formal pronouncement, Martían.

Theodore Draper has made a compelling case for "two revolutions" embodied in the Cuban phenomenon. The first was "bourgeois democratic," pragmatic, nationalist, integralist rather than class oriented, and "indigenously Cuban."[45] As has already been indicated, as early as 1953, one of Castro's explicit political intentions, an intention he did not renounce through 1959, was to restore the Cuban Constitution of 1940, which the Batista regime had violated by the coup of 1952. In the program manifesto of the 26th July Movement, issued from the Sierra Maestra in July 1957, Castro insisted that after his accession to power he would hold "general elections" that would provide an "absolute guarantee" of freedom of association, of information, and of the press as well as all the individual and political rights guaranteed by the Constitution of 1940. The manifesto further maintained that the struggle in the mountains was being conducted to "put an end to the regime of force, the violations of individual rights, the infamous crimes, and to seek the peace we all yearn for through the only possible way,

[45] Cf. T. Draper, *Castro's Revolution* (New York: Praeger, 1962), chap. 1.

which is the democratic and constitutional way of the country." In mid-May 1958, Castro categorically denied that his movement had any intention of experimenting with socialization. He said, on that occasion, "Never has the 26th July Movement talked about socializing or nationalizing the industries. This is simply stupid fear of our revolution. We have proclaimed from the first day that we fight for the full enforcement of the Constitution of 1940, whose norms establish guarantees, rights, and obligations for all the elements that have a part in production. Comprised therein is free enterprise and invested capital . . . ."[46] In the Unity Manifesto of July 1958, Castro had agreed to "guide [the] nation, after the fall of the tyrant [Batista], to normality by instituting a brief provisional government that will lead the country to full constitutional and democratic procedures."

Castro *had* spoken, in his *History Will Absolve Me!*, of nationalizing some utilities companies, but in an interview given to *Coronet* magazine in February 1958 he maintained that he had abandoned those plans. He stated that "I personally have come to feel that nationalization is, at best, a cumbersome instrument. It does not seem to make the state any stronger, yet it enfeebles private enterprise. Even more importantly, any attempt at wholesale nationalization would obviously hamper the principal point of our economic platform—industrialization at the fastest possible rate. For this purpose, foreign investments will always be welcome and secure here." Castro did speak, as early as 1953, of land reform. He advocated a maximum holding for agricultural enterprises and a distribution of excess lands to farming families. He also spoke of encouraging agricultural cooperatives. The Agrarian Reform Law of the Sierra Maestra, dated October 10, 1958, addressed itself to providing land ownership to those who cultivate it. It made no mention of "cooperatives" or "state farms."

In effect, everything Castro advocated between 1953 and 1959 confirmed the self-avowal of the spokesmen of the 26th

[46] Cf. J. Dubois, *Fidel Castro: Rebel, Liberator or Dictator?* (New York: Bobbs-Merrill, 1959), p. 263.

July movement: that the "concepts" and the "fundamental philosophy" of the revolution emanated "without doubt [from] the essence of the political thought of José Martí . . . ."[47] In speaking to the conspirators before the attack on the Moncada Barracks—the attack that marked the commencement of Castro's revolutionary movement—Castro said, "In a short time we shall be either the victors or the vanquished. If we are victors we shall have realized the hopes of José Martí."[48] Among those "hopes" was "the economic and industrial progress of Cuba" in the context of "social justice."

One Martían theme which was not regularly invoked, but which preoccupied some of the leaders of the movement, was "anti-imperialism." In all of his public statements, with but minor exceptions, Castro was careful not to emphasize the "anti-imperialist" aspects of his program for the "independence" and "grandeur" of Cuba. The tactical reasons were obvious. Not only did Castro not wish to alienate the United States at that time, but he did not wish to erode the "national unity" base of his appeal. Many Cubans who were actively supporting his movement were involved in trade and industrial relations with the United States. Any overtly anti-American postures would threaten the "united front" that Castro felt essential to revolutionary seizure of power. Nonetheless, the theme was a constant concern of men such as Raul Castro and still more emphatically a primary concern of Ernesto "Ché" Guevara. As a matter of fact, "anti-Americanism" was endemic to the radical movement in Latin America—Martí had been one of its principal spokesmen.

The revolutionary strategy employed by Castro reflects his convictions that revolutions can be made by dedicated men, invoking the commitment of restive masses. The at-

[47] As quoted, in D. James, *Cuba: The First Soviet Satellite in the Americas* (New York: Avon, 1961), pp. 25f.

[48] As quoted S. Tutino, *L'Ottobre Cubano* (Turin: Einaudi, 1968), p. 203; cf. H. Matthews, *Fidel Castro* (New York: Simon & Schuster. 1969), p. 45.

tack on the Moncada Barracks was calculated to be an "heroic gesture" that would mobilize the masses against the Batista regime. Even the subsequent landing of eighty-two men from the *Granma* in December 1956 constituted a re-affirmation of the Martían strategy of revolution. Eighty-two men were, by their heroic example, to activate the masses. Years later Guevara, in addressing himself to the strategy behind the *Granma* landing, admitted that the strategy was "subjectivistic." Castro, himself, in a letter to Conte Agüero discussing the organization of a revolutionary movement, insisted that there were three conditions "indispensable" to successful revolution: "ideology, discipline and leadership." Then he went on to indicate that while the three were essential it was "leadership" that was basic.[49] Leadership could provide the "catalyst" that would mobilize the popular masses behind the revolution. Again, Castro was making recourse to Martían strategy. Saverio Tutino has characterized the strategy as "Leninist" when, as a matter of fact, it is no less Fascist and was common to nationalist and developmental populist movements as early as the nineteenth century. The Communist Party of Cuba had, in fact, identified Castro's strategy at the time not as Leninist, but as "petty bourgeois" and "*putschist*." Castro's revolutionary strategy was far more Fascist than Marxist.

The "ideology" with which Castro made his revolution was not "Marxist" or "Marxist-Leninist." It was Martían, and as such shared more features with Fascism in terms of strategy and content than it did with Marxism-Leninism. Communist judgments of the time, whether they were made by Cuban communists or foreign Marxist-Leninist sources, were all agreed. The revolutionary movement led by Fidel Castro was not Marxist or Marxist-Leninist, but "petty bourgeois" and "nationalist," a characterization that Marxists of all persuasions had affixed to Fascism throughout the interwar years. Castro had explicitly rejected "socialization" or "nationalization." He had spoken of a "national unity" of all

[49] L. Conte Agüero, *Cartas del Presidio* (Havana: Lex, 1959), pp. 60f.

classes except those irredeemably "reactionary"—commitments made by Mussolini throughout the Fascist period. Castro spoke of mobilizing masses through the agency of a "vanguard leadership," exercising "will" and "determination." He spoke of ideals and of restoring legitimacy—and of "economic and political democracy"—themes common at the founding meeting of the first *Fasci* at San Sepolcro in 1919. Castro in 1959, like Mussolini in 1919, insisted he was against "dictatorship" and "tyranny." When Mussolini came to power in 1922, liberals and laissez-faire economists anticipated a "restoration of normalcy." Similarly, when Castro came to power in 1959, his advent was welcomed by the urban bourgeoisie as the dawning of a new period of "normalcy" and "constitutional democracy."

Castro, furthermore, was irrepressibly *nationalist*, a charge that could hardly be levelled against Marxist-Leninists even in the period of "national liberation movements." One of the traits of Fascism, that Marxists long regarded as species-defining, was its "nationalism." Fascists themselves early argued that "nationalism" distinguished their movement from any Marxist counterpart, and even after Castro's advent to power, the Communist Party of Cuba identified the new government not as Marxist-Leninist, but as being "in the hands of the national and petty bourgeoisie."[50]

More than any of the modern variants of Marxism, insurrectionary Castroism disported Fascist content and Fascist strategy. The developments after 1959 produced changes in the tactics of the revolution, and the tactical shifts, in turn, prompted vast structural and social changes in Cuba that distinguish it from the historic practice of Fascism. While Castro's programmatic commitments were Fascist—the emphasis on increased industrial and economic productivity, the grandeur, independence, and dignity of the nation— Castro did not, ultimately, advocate a program of class collaboration, but rather committed his déclassé revolution to the service of the proletariat and Marxism-Leninism.

[50] Blas Roca, as quoted, A. Suarez, *Cuba: Castroism and Communism, 1959-1966* (Cambridge: MIT, 1967), p. 40.

THE TRANSITION TO MARXISM-LENINISM

All commentators on the Cuban revolution, Marxist and non-Marxist alike, agree that the leadership of the revolution has been "personalist"—inextricably bound up with Castro the man. Herbert Matthews has recently insisted, "One cannot make sense out of the Cuban Revolution without keeping in mind at all times the personal supremacy—at first potential and then real—of Fidel Castro."[51] Like Mussolini, Castro wields personal influence—and like Mussolini, Castro has responded to demands for a "statement of doctrine" with a reply that doctrine "would emerge from the depth of the events, since tying oneself down to inflexible theories in advance would restrict one within excessively dogmatic limits and would obstruct the necessary dynamism of the revolution."[52] Again, like Mussolini, Castro has led a personal following through doctrinal gymnastics of a spectacular sort —but again, like Mussolini, with several central themes providing the logic of his strategy: the *economic advance* and *political independence and grandeur of his nation* as he understands "advance," "independence," and "grandeur." Through all this, and in the pursuit of those ends, Castro has remained the *Jefe Máximo*, the *Duce*, of the Cuban Revolution.

It is clearly too early to offer a definitive account of why Castro decided to identify his revolution as "Marxist-Leninist" and "proletarian," but the outline of a plausible account is available in the literature devoted to the Cuban phenomenon.

First and foremost, Cuba had endured, for decades, what economists are wont to call "high-level stagnation."[53] The *per capita* income of Cubans prior to Castro's revolution was, in fact, relatively high. It compared favorably with the *per*

[51] Matthews, *Fidel Castro*, p. 76.

[52] Suarez, *Cuba*, p. 32.

[53] Most of the material concerning Cuba's "permanent" economic crisis is adapted from J. O'Connor, *The Origins of Socialism in Cuba* (Ithaca: Cornell, 1970).

capita income of Italy, exceeded that of Chile and Brazil, and was incomparably higher than the *per capita* income in China and all of Africa north of the Limpopo. It was the Latin American country which possessed the most railway mileage in proportion to geographic area; it consumed more electrical energy than any other Latin American country save one; there were more automobiles per population ratio than any other country in Latin America; and only Argentina had more radios per population ratio. Nonetheless, wealth was clearly maldistributed, and the economy was, in a significant sense, stagnant. There had been no increase in *per capita* income or in production for extended periods of time. Real *per capita* income had not increased since 1903-1906. Between 1950 and 1958, total production increased at an annual rate of only 1.8 percent, while population growth exceeded 2.0 percent per annum which implied a measurable decline in real *per capita* income during that critical pre-revolutionary period.

The peculiar condition of Cuba's high-level stagnation created a disposition among Cuban political activists that could best be described as "redistributionistic." Since the sum total of welfare benefits disposable within the confines of the Cuban economy was constant, Cuban politicians were largely preoccupied with *redistribution* of that fixed quantum. Political struggles became struggles between "ins" and "outs"—each concerned with a redistribution that would favor his own constituency. Once a contending political group had succeeded in gaining access to the levers of resource and benefit allocation, it would proceed to redistribute them without substantially changing the absolute quantity of available benefits—and the entire process would enter into a new cycle. New "outs," now suffering relative deprivation under the new dispensation, would mobilize for an assault on the levers of power and the sources of patronage. Each contending group was, in fact, composed of a variety of economic classes, population strata and productive categories. The only thing that united them was a desire to redistribute the available benefits that had remained relatively constant since the turn of the century. While all such groups advertised elaborate programs for more rapid industrialization, none of them was capable of breaking the deadlock created by the disposition of forces that operated in the economic system.

Since each new coalition was composed of essentially the same population constituents, there was little disposition to radically alter the system. Any radical change in the system would threaten some constituent components of the coalition. They would be alienated and would make common cause with some other contending "out" group, throw the existing coalition into crisis, and a new cycle in the seemingly constant process would recommence.

Large segments of Cuba's economically active population were, in significant measure, allied to interests in the United States. Cuba's principal agricultural product, sugar, was purchased all but exclusively by the United States. Political decisions in the United States, decisions outside the control of Cubans, largely determined how successful agriculture in Cuba would be at any specific time. As a consequence large land-holding interests in Cuba were bound to the United States by their economic interests. Any transforming political or economic change in Cuba might adversely affect their interests. Thus while many might lament the influence of the United States in Cuba, they were more than circumspect when any moves were made that might antagonize the Congress of the United States. Moreover, many Cuban merchants, importers and exporters of commodities, were intimately tied to the economy of the United States. Any "revolutionary" government that attempted to act out Martí's injunction that Cuba free itself from the trammels of economic intercourse with the "dominant North" could only face massive resistance, both passive and active, from economically significant elements that made up the "revolutionary" coalition.

The peculiar conditions of the Cuban economy made it almost impossible to mobilize large segments of the Cuban population behind a revolutionary program that would seriously alter the economic situation in Cuba. What the various coalitions that animated Cuban politics really desired was a redistribution of benefits. Each "revolutionary" movement in Cuba's history was a coalition movement, and as a consequence was composed of elements that would suffer from any massive economic redirection, even if that redirection were only temporary. At the first threat of radical systemic change, the coalition would fragment, and the proposed "revolutionary" program would be thwarted.

When Castro came to power in 1959 he found himself possessed of a movement, the 26th July Movement, that had all the species traits of a traditional revolutionary "out" that aspired to substitute itself for the discredited "ins." It was evident that Cuba was preparing to enter into another cycle of "revolutionary" governments that could survive only by redistributing the available benefits in differential manner— in order to hold together a coalition of diverse population elements. That the coalition forming the 26th July Movement was unstable was evident in the first defections as soon as the new government began to pass legislation that negatively affected specific interest groups. Under the circumstances Castro had the option of remaining "democratic" and calling for general elections which would have inevitably produced a representative government that would proceed to redistribute the welfare benefits available—in the traditional Cuban manner—or he could seize absolute power and attempt to significantly modify the character of the Cuban economy. It seems as though Castro was caught on the horns of a dilemma; he could either respect his promises for general elections, freedom of expression of opposition opinion, free labor unions, and a free press—*or* he could choose to fulfill his other promises concerning Cuba's rapid and more efficient industrialization, as a necessary condition for achieving "true" sovereign independence from North American influence. Either program would have violated some aspect of the program of the 26th July Movement. It was obvious that should he choose to satisfy the programmatic commitment to general elections, his personal power would be subject to suffrage constraints, renewable at fixed intervals. The past history of Cuba suggested that such coalition "leaders" could only expect to enjoy a precarious hold on power, no matter what their initial popular support. Even Castro's most ardent supporters recognized in him a man that was ill-disposed to surrender the firm grasp on political power. On the other hand, if Castro chose to respect his commitment to economic and political revolution it was obvious that the 26th July Movement could only serve as an inconvenience. He would require a different political apparatus to drive Cuba off dead center. Years later Ernesto Guevara admitted as much. To move the revolution from the "national liberation phase" to the "socialist phase" Cuba required "new sympathizers, cadres, and organizations" that could supplement "the weak organic structure of the initial movement . . . ."[54]

Castro opted to fulfill his program of national development at the expense of his "bourgeois democratic" commitments. In doing so he opted to reject those parts of his program that called for the maintenance of "bourgeois institutions." What he needed was

> a reconstitution of the Party into an effective directive organism, equal to the historic task, [requiring that] an end be put to the plethora of commissions, secretariats, congresses, conferences, plenary sessions, meetings, and assemblies at all levels—national, provincial, regional, and local. . . . [Such things] are the cause of the vice of excessive deliberation which Fidel has spoken of and which hampers executive, centralized and vertical methods . . . .[55]

Castro very rapidly came to appreciate that what he required was not "bourgeois" institutions with all their attendant deliberations and periodic elections, but a hierarchically

[54] E. Guevara, "The Cadre, Backbone of the Revolution," in J. Gerassi, ed., *Venceremos!* (New York: Macmillan, 1968), p. 204.

[55] R. Debray, *Revolution in the Revolution?* (New York: Monthly Review, 1967), p. 102.

constituted infrastructure that would serve as a conveyance belt for his instructions. It seems apparent that Castro did not anticipate precisely how much a protracted strain this would generate. In February 1959, when he first began to realize that he would have to opt for some rather than some other of his programmatic commitments, it seems that he imagined that the rapid expansion of Cuba's economy would involve only a brief dislocation, immediately followed by rapid expansion. At that time he insisted that "in the course of a few short years," given the opportunity, he could raise "the standard of living of Cubans to a level higher than that of the United States and Russia." He still apparently believed that the transition could be made without "totalitarianism."

In retrospect it is obvious that his judgments were totally unrealistic. The effort to create an industrial base in Cuba that would make it "independent" and "grand" would require far more than Castro had anticipated. What he required was a secure power base from which he could manipulate the economy. This drove him to seek popular support from those population elements that would not be threatened by massive changes in the economy, and this implied an erosion of the power base of any opposition. His opposition would obviously come from those segments of the economy that had most to lose—the Cuban middle classes, the large landholders, the comprador capitalists. He could expect to win support from those who had nothing to lose from "nationalization" and "resistance to imperialism"—that is to say, from any policy that sought to amputate Cuba from its economic ties with the United States.

If Castro was to create an independent power base for his policy of economic change and economic independence from the United States, he would have to appeal to the peasantry of Cuba that could only see benefit from massive land redistribution. Appeal to the working class could be made if Castro's government could mobilize sufficient patronage to redistribute. This might be done by massive confiscation of "bourgeois" holdings. At the same time this action would destroy the economic and political strength of those population elements that would, predictably, oppose his "revolutionary" program.

These decisions were apparently made under the pressure of events. In February 1959, Castro had insisted that he had no intention of lowering rents. A few months later he undertook just such a policy and thereby won the immediate support of large sections of the urban working class. In the interim, apparently, Castro had made his decision to erode the power base of the bourgeoisie. Confiscation of property as a penalty for crimes against the revolution, and the initial land reforms, gave the revolutionary state patronage resources on a scale unprecedented in Cuban history. As confiscations and nationalization proceeded, the state could allocate welfare benefits on such a scale that large sections of the population, hitherto passive or indifferent, could be won to the regime. Members of Batista's army, for example, received pay and benefits from the revolutionary government and were incorporated into the new armed forces. Castro succeeded, thereby, in eliminating the possible influence of the "Rebel Army" which had brought him to power but which was composed, to a significant degree, of men committed to "bourgeois" and "democratic" goals. Peasants, in turn, were immediate beneficiaries of land reform programs—and another source of opposition, the latifundists, was canceled out.

Castro realized that he had to seek a population base as support for his developmental program. He could not expect support from the bourgeoisie, which aspired to nothing more than a redistribution of available welfare benefits. They demanded a fulfillment of the democratic goals of the revolution. Castro opted to pursue the developmental program. That program offered him the opportunity of long tenure in office, an independent power base for his tenure, and the hope of sovereign independence, both political and economic, for the "Fatherland."

The first stage of the "socialist phase" of the revolution was characterized by a redistribution of patronage unparalleled in Cuban history. The redistribution was undertaken in the hope that it would provide the energy for a short transition to abundance. Castro seemed convinced that a "few short years" would see such a spectacular growth of benefits that the system would not suffer dysfunctional tensions. The singular redistribution effected by Castro provoked large numbers of the middle class to defect—and the 26th July Movement disintegrated.

Castro immediately found himself faced with a crisis of serious proportions. Cuba, if it were successfully to negotiate the "interim" period to a new abundance, having alienated the United States and its own strategic and functional elites, had to seek alternate sources of support. Soviet Russia early made gestures of assistance—which Castro eagerly accepted.

By this time Castro realized that he needed several things to make his revolution as he now conceived it. One was a disciplined party to carry out his directives. The second was to erode the support base of any opposition that might mount in Cuba. The third prerequisite was financial and technical support outside the Western Hemisphere.

In the first place he could take over the party structure of the Partido Socialista Popular, the Communist Party of Cuba, which, irrespective of how ineffectual it had been, did have an apparatus he could effectively employ. The Cuban Communist Party did have "cadres" that satisfied all the demands the Castroites could make of them. In 1962, Guevara described a "cadre" as "an individual who has reached a sufficient level of political development to be able to interpret the general directives issued by the central power, to assimilate them, and to transmit them as ideas to the masses."[56] "The initiative," Guevara insisted, "generally comes from Fidel or the high command of the revolution: It is explained to the people, who make it their own."[57]

The 26th July Movement simply did not have a party structure suitable for such "cadres" or the purposes to which

[56] Guevara, "The Cadre . . . ," in Gerassi, *Venceremos!*, p. 205.
[57] Guevara, "On Man and Socialism in Cuba," in *ibid.*, p. 389.

they were to be put. The 26th July Movement was an essentially "bourgeois" movement. Castro, given his new emphasis on the economic and developmental goals of the revolution, could expect to have middle class opposition. Castro found both the 26th July Movement, and the bourgeoisie it housed, a disability. By eliminating the movement and assimilating the Communist Party of Cuba to his purpose, Castro could resolve two of his major problems.

More than the erosion of opposition and the provision of effective party control over Cuban society, Castro needed material resources, entrepreneurial, and economic expertise, and political and military support. Given his program, he could anticipate that no accommodation would be possible with the United States. The Soviet Union offered the supports necessary for Castro's regime.

Castro could solve the problem of providing himself with a "disciplined" party that acted as a conveyance medium for his directives by absorbing the apparatus of the Communist Party of Cuba, which had an elaborate control infrastructure and suitably trained political cadre. He could provide himself with critically necessary skilled personnel and resources by allying himself with the socialist bloc. In order to accomplish both most effectively, Castro needed only to identify himself as a "Marxist-Leninist." He could then commandeer the Communist Party apparatus and appeal to the socialist bloc as a "comrade." In December 1961, Castro announced that he was a "Marxist-Leninist."

In creating a party that would be responsive to the directives emanating from the *Lider Maximo*, Castro proceeded to "domesticate" the revolutionary party that brought him to power. Just as Mussolini, Stalin, and Mao found it necessary to domesticate a recalcitrant party in order to make their revolutions, Castro has found it necessary to dismantle his revolutionary party, absorb the organizational apparatus of the Partido Socialista Popular, and restock it with members of his own choice. The Communist Party of Cuba that Castro created is now apparently stocked largely with "reliable" members of the 26th July Movement and those members of the "old" communist apparatus that have survived Castro's critical scrutiny.

The result has been a personalist and hierarchically structured party. Castro is the *"Jefe,"* the *Duce*—and Cuba abounds with the slogan, *"Comandante en Jefe—¡Ordenes!"* ("Commander in Chief—we await your orders!"). The slogan is, of course, more than reminiscent of the popular Fascist slogan: *"Credere, Obedire, Combattere!"* ("Believe, Obey, Fight!"). It not only characterizes the hierarchical structure of power but captures the prevailing attitude toward dissent. More than that it characterizes the disposition to "instill" in the "masses" an appropriate "revolutionary consciousness,"[58] a task which Mussolini conceived as the fundamental obligation of the party. The class consciousness, the revolutionary or socialist consciousness that Marx and Engels conceived to be the product of the life circumstances of the proletariat, is now conceived by the leaders of single party mass mobilizing regimes to be the artifact of monopoly control of education. The party assumes pedagogical responsibilities unanticipated by classical Marxism —and first fully articulated by Mussolini.

"The men of the party," Guevara insisted before his death, "must take this task upon themselves and seek the achievement of the principal aim: to educate the people." Most important to the task is party control over the education of the young, for the young are the "malleable clay with which the new man, without any of the previous defects, can be formed."[59] Conjoined with the enterprisory responsibilities the single party has assumed is the pedagogical responsibility which is its natural corollary. That responsibility is expressed metaphorically by referring to the "people" or the "masses" as "artist's material" for the creation of the "new man" (Mussolini's characterization of the process)—or to the "people" as being "blank" and therefore suitable subjects

[58] Castro, as quoted, in L. Lockwood, *Castro's Cuba, Cuba's Fidel* (New York: Random House, 1969), p. 24.

[59] Guevara, "On Man and Socialism in Cuba," in Gerassi, *Venceremos!*, pp. 396, 397.

for the "painting of beautiful pictures" (Mao's characterization).

What the process requires, of course, is a consummate artist—someone who intuits the real interests of the masses —who is capable of creating the most complex things literally out of nothing—who can, in effect, create the "objective" out of the "subjective." Guevara, in his discussion of the role of Castro in the Cuban revolution, insisted that "Fidel Castro did more than anyone else in Cuba to create out of nothingness the formidable apparatus which today is the Cuban Revolution."[60] Saverio Tutino echoed these judgments in referring to Castro as one of the "unique features" of the Cuban phenomenon, and then indicating that Castro employed voluntaristic elements to catalyze objective conditions which had, until that time, remained inert.[61] Herbert Matthews, in turn, has simply characterized Castro as "a perfect example of Max Weber's charismatic leader," something that Roberto Michels said of Mussolini in 1927— a characterization of leadership common to Fascism and embodied in its party manuals. Until the advent of Castro, Marxist-Leninist radicals have never been disposed to identify their leaders as "charismatic." Marx and Engels, and Lenin as well, knew nothing of charismatic leaders, much less conceived them as intrinsic to the creation of a Marxist society or the creation of "new men." But then they didn't conceive of men as "clay" to be "molded."

With the domestication of the revolutionary party and the creation of a party that serves as a control mechanism for the single-party state, the appearance of a "charismatic leader" is an almost predictable consequence. In Castro's case (as was the case with Mussolini), he always had a personalist entourage prepared to follow him wherever he chose to go. Like Mussolini, Castro created an institution suitable to hierarchical and charismatic control *after* the seizure of power. Mussolini waited three years. Castro waited less than two.

[60] Guevara, "Cuba—Exception or Vanguard?" in *ibid.*, p. 132.
[61] Tutino, *L'Ottobre Cubano*, p. 191.

Guevara spoke of Castro as having all the qualities of a great leader: "audacity, strength, courage, and untiring perseverance in discovering the will of the people. . . . a capacity to assimiliate knowledge and experiences quickly, to understand the totality of a given situation without losing sight of details, an unbounded faith in the future, and a breadth of vision which allows him to see further and more accurately into the future than his comrades. With these qualities, with his capacity to unite, to oppose debilitating divisions, to lead all the actions of the people [is conjoined his] love of the people, his faith in the future, and his capacity to predict it . . . ."[62] The revolution in Cuba is identified with a body of thought—the thought of Fidel Castro. Only he can legitimize the correct interpretation of Marxism-Leninism.

In his protracted struggle with the "old" Communist Parties of Latin America, Castro has been charged with monopolizing for himself the right to determine what is and what is not contemporary Marxism-Leninism. In 1967 the Venezuelan Communist Party charged Castro with a disposition to "arrogate to himself the role of revolutionary 'Pope.' "[63] It has become increasingly clear that Marxism-Leninism in Cuba is, in the last analysis, what Castro says it is. Castro has denounced the communists of Mao as "blackmailers" and "pirates"—and they, in turn, have condemned him as "revisionist." Castro himself has insisted that "no formula is always applicable to the letter, and that, in general, in political and social matters formulas are always bad. . . . We are developing our ideas. We understand that Marxist-Leninist thought requires unceasing development; we understand that some stagnation has taken place in this field, and we even see that formulas that can, in our opinion, lead to devi-

[62] Guevara, "Cuba—Exception or Vanguard?" in Gerassi, *Venceremos!*, p. 132.

[63] "The Venezuelan Communist Party Replies to Fidel Castro," in L. E. Aguilar, ed., *Marxism in Latin America* (New York: Knopf, 1968), p. 260.

ation from the essence of Marxism-Leninism are widely accepted."[64]

In effect, it appears quite clear that Castro has "creatively developed" Marxism-Leninism to a new stage. Like Mao, Castro is the final arbiter of what Marxism-Leninism is. Moreover, since Castro is the ultimate arbiter of what are and what are not revolutionary thought, attitudes, and behavior, he defines, by implication, what is to count as "counterrevolutionary." Beginning with men like Hubert Matos and Pedro Diaz Lanz, men of his original revolutionary party, through men like Anibal Escalante, leaders of the "old" Communist Party, Castro has identified "counterrevolutionary" in accordance with his own lights. The criteria for making such a determination are personal and political. "Proletarian" is what Castro says it is; "bourgeois" is equally what Castro says it is. The ultimate determinant is "the thought of Fidel Castro." And all the time Castro proceeds "intuitively."

Castro has not concealed the fact that he is unlettered in Marxism-Leninism. He has never tired in reiterating that he is not an intellectual, but a revolutionary. In the now famous speech in which he made a self-avowal of his Marxism-Leninism, he admitted that he could bring himself to read no more than the first 270 pages of the first volume of Marx's *Kapital*. Raul Castro indicated to Herbert Matthews that Fidel had read literally nothing in the corpus of Marxist literature. "We read about three chapters of [*Das Kapital*]," Raul confided, "and then threw it aside, and I am certain that Fidel never looked at it again."[65] At best Castro has read *The Communist Manifesto* and some fragments of Lenin. Castro is the last of a long line of radicals that have become Marxists without having, or before having, read very much of Marx. Mao was a Marxist before he could read anything more than *The Communist Manifesto*. He had

[64] F. Castro, "May Day Speech, May 1, 1966," in *Fidel Castro: Major Speeches* (London: Stage 1, 1968), p. 41.

[65] Quoted, Matthews, *Fidel Castro*, p. 187.

297

become a Marxist through the work of Li Ta-chao—and the remainder of his life remained faithful to the elitist, nationalist, and developmental convictions that infused Li's thought. Castro is a similar Marxist, having found his Marxism in the elitist, nationalist, and developmental anti-imperialism of José Martí. Mao and Castro became Marxists for the same reason that Mussolini abandoned it—in order to become mass-mobilizing revolutionary nationalists, anti-imperialists, and developmental strategists.

THE MARXIST-LENINIST INTERPRETATION OF THE CUBAN REVOLUTION

Almost immediately after the appearance of Cuban socialism, attempts were undertaken to provide a suitable Marxist-Leninist interpretation of the entire phenomenon. The interpretation was to cover not only the socialist phase but, more significantly, the "insurrectionary," or "national liberation" phase as well. The result has been a singular development of Marxist theory. The principal spokesmen of this interpretation have been men close to Castro and understood to "represent" his thought. Ernesto "Ché" Guevara has been the theoretician who has attracted perhaps the largest following, but it has been the work of Regis Debray that has generated the most sustained and perhaps most significant discussion.

The "interpretation" of the Cuban Revolution began almost immediately after Castro's accession to power. It focused on, at that time, and still continues to emphasize, the role of the guerrilla in the revolutionary struggle. In February 1959, less than two months after the flight of Batista, Guevara published a brief essay, "What is a Guerrilla?" in *Revolución*. From that point on the "theory" of the Revolution has matured into several books, one by Guevara, *Guerrilla Warfare*, and another by Regis Debray, *Revolution in the Revolution?* Several articles were devoted to a Marxist interpretation of the Revolution, among which Debray's

"Castroism: the Long March in Latin America," is perhaps the most significant.

Guevara's first contributions to the on-going discussion were not particularly illuminating. In his first public statements he did little more than inform his readers that "liberation" could come to oppressed nations through the agency of "guerrillas"—and "guerrillas were, essentially, fighters for liberty; the elect of the people, a fighting vanguard of a people in their struggle for liberation." Guerrillas were the "armed vanguard" of the "people" who embodied in themselves the "best qualities of the best soldiers in the world." They were men dominated by a rigorous and interior discipline. They were social reformers, and because they chose to confront their opponents in the countryside, and required the active and passive support of the peasantry, they were "first of all rural revolutionaries."[66] All of which was not particularly illuminating, nor much of an interpretation.

Theodore Draper has characterized Guevara's article of 1959 as containing the "rudiments of a theory." More than that, perhaps, is the fact that Guevara devoted his energy to glorifying the aims, the methods, the attitudes and dispositions of the *warriors* of social revolution. He identified them as the elect, as some sort of "guiding angels." The guerrilla warrior was being groomed as a model—and military discipline advanced as a social ideal. The article on the characteristics of the guerrilla was immediately followed by two short pieces devoted to the solidarity and camaraderie generated by *armed struggle*, in which masses of men devote themselves to the realization of specific goals. In his "Morale and Discipline of Revolutionary Fighters," Guevara exalted "morale" as both an ethical and heroic quality that guerrillas must possess. They are possessed, for example, of the heroic conviction that "To Die for the Fatherland is to Live!" More important than both moral elements is the *dis-*

[66] E. Guevara, "Che cos'é un guerrigliero?" in *Opere* (Milan: Feltrinelli, 1968), I, 229-32.

cipline that unites them. That discipline is an interior conviction—an indisposition to deviate "a centimeter" from the revolutionary line. The guerrillas, Guevara insisted, are to act as models for the civil population. In a speech delivered on the 27th of January, 1959, less than a month after the seizure of power, Guevara announced that "the entire people of Cuba" must become a guerrilla vanguard in order to fulfill the vision of José Martí: to bring "social justice" to Cuba, to introduce extensive land reform, to accelerate industrial production and to achieve true independence from "foreign monopolists."[67]

Before the publication of *Guerrilla Warfare*, therefore, Guevara outlined the substance of his "theory" of the Cuban Revolution. At the time he first articulated it, he did not relate it to Marxism, but clearly and accurately identified it as a restatement of the vision of José Martí. The revolution was animated by an idea, made real by the willed and determined acts of disciplined men in sanguinary struggle— in war. It was a revolution dedicated to a "national renaissance"—to the rapid expansion of industry, the diversification of agriculture, and the consequent creation of true independence and sovereignty for Cuba. Neither the program nor the strategy designed to achieve it was identified as Marxist. They were identified as Martían in content and in strategy—as indeed they were.

The conviction that warriors would constitute the elect of a people—that by their example a people might be revitalized and mobilized to the service of a greater fatherland —is a Martían conviction. Martí insisted, both by implication and explicitly, that "subjective conditions" could create the "objective conditions" necessary to a saving revolution. When Guevara wrote his *Guerrilla Warfare* in 1960, he simply reasserted a Martían conviction: "It is not necessary to

[67] Cf. Guevara, "La solidarietà nel combattimento," "Morale e disciplina dei combattenti rivoluzionari," and "Responsibilità sociali dell'Esercito Ribelle," in *Opere*, i, 243-61.

wait until all conditions for making revolution exist; the insurrection can create them."[68]

Guevara, no more than Martí, ever provided a rigorous account of how the revolutionary *foco* could create the conditions for revolution. At one point, for example, he came precious close to maintaining that the charismatic leader, Fidel Castro, provided the sufficient conditions for the revolution. In his *Guerrilla Warfare*, on the other hand, he maintained that guerrilla revolution would be impossible if "the possibilities of peaceful struggle have not yet been exhausted." He provided no indication of what the index might be that identified the circumstances when peaceful struggle was no longer possible.

It seems fairly obvious that Guevara possessed no confirmable convictions about the conditions necessary or sufficient for revolution. The abysmal failure of his Bolivian adventure seems to provide sufficient evidence of that. It is difficult to know what moved Guevara to attempt to establish a *"foco insurreccional"* in Bolivia in 1966—but, unless one were to hypothesize that he was seeking self-destruction, one can only conclude that he conceived the conditions for making a guerrilla-led revolution in Bolivia as obtaining. Marvin Resnick, in an intuitive judgment, argues that Guevara had "absolute faith in the ability of the guerrilla to change the world" and that he imagined that he, himself, could supply "the final ingredient"—a "charismatic leader" —that would make revolution in Bolivia.[69] If such were the case, then Guevara seems to have committed himself to the proposition that the guerrilla *foco* had the Martían faculty of fusing and transforming men by its example—and essential to that example was a man of special caliber—the guerrilla leader.

In these circumstances, then, the "radical" revolutionary

[68] E. Guevara, *Guerrilla Warfare* (New York: Monthly Review, 1961), p. 15.

[69] Marvin D. Resnick, *The Black Beret: The Life and Meaning of Ché Guevara* (New York: Ballantine, 1969), pp. 208, 289.

as Cubans conceive him is more the counterpart of the Fascist *Arditi* or *squadristi* than he is of the Leninist revolutionary. The Fascist *squadrista* emphasized action, rather than thought. Conceiving himself always in military contexts the *squadrista* emphasized loyalty, obedience, and discipline before he concerned himself with "theoretical consciousness." When Lee Lockwood asked a survivor of the guerrilla band that Castro led in the Sierra Maestra whether he had ever concerned himself with political ideology he could only respond with a guffaw. He replied that under the circumstances there was no time for that, and concluded, "We let Fidel do our thinking for us."[70]

This was precisely the style of the Fascist *squadristi*, the street fighters of Mussolini. They were the vanguard of the Italian people, a "new and heroic generation," "unconditionally dedicated to the Cause," and "devoted to its supreme leader," falling in battle for the "salvation of their nation and of universal civilization."[71] For *squadristi* it was dedication, sacrifice, and obedience, generated in sanguinary conflict, that would change the shape and character of the world. For *squadristi*, violence was the school of revolution. They had developed a Sorelian theme, couched it in Futurist locutions, and produced the *ethos* of the *squadristi*. For them sterile intellectuality played, at best, a secondary role in the revolutionary process. They were unconcerned with formulae. They were committed to the "moral regeneration" born of violence that would dissipate bourgeois apathy and egotism.

Both Castro and Guevara have candidly reiterated that the guerrilla *foco* that made the revolution had no clear ideological commitments. They had "neglected" theory. Guevara, in 1960, admitted that "the principal actors of this revolution had no coherent theoretical criteria . . . ." What they did have was a recognition of "the value of armed insurrection"—the circumstances that produce the "strength

[70] Lockwood, *Castro's Cuba*, p. 23.

[71] G. Fracastoro di Fornello, *Noi squadristi* (Verona: Albarelli-Marchesetti, 1939), pp. 53ff.

that any man has when, with a weapon in his hand and the will to win in his heart, he confronts other men who are out to destroy him."[72]

Mussolini characterized these features by saying that "Fascism was not the nursling of a doctrine previously worked out at a desk; it was born of a need for action and was action. . . . The years which preceded the March on Rome were years in which the necessity of action did not permit complete doctrinal investigations or elaboration. . . . There were discussions, but what was more important and sacred—there was death. Men knew how to die. The doctrine—all complete and formed, with divisions into chapters, paragraphs, and accompanying elucubrations—might be missing; but there was something more decided to replace it, there was faith."[73]

It is reasonably clear, to both Marxist and non-Marxist observers, that the loyalty of Cubans to Castro is a personal loyalty, and that loyalty is exemplified in the attachment to him of his guerrillas. Cubans have followed Castro through kaleidoscopic changes of political persuasion—from the "bourgeois liberalism" of the 26th July Movement, through the "humanism" of the first phase of the post revolutionary, through to the "communism" of the contemporary period. The Cubans have faith in their leadership. And it is equally clear that the leadership had only an obscure idea of where it was headed. When Lee Lockwood confided to Castro that he did not know that the revolution that was being made in the Sierra Maestra would turn out to be "communist," Castro candidly replied, "Neither did I."[74]

Even today there is no evidence that Castro has anything more than the most superficial acquaintance with the basic works of Marx, Engels, or Lenin. Although Ricardo Rojo has has suggested that Guevara had read the Marxist classics

[72] Guevara, "We are Practical Revolutionaries," in Gerassi, *Venceremos!*, pp. 120, 126.

[73] Mussolini, "Dottrina del fascismo," "Dottrina sociale e politica," Sections 1 and 2, *Opera*, xxxiv, 122-24.

[74] Lockwood, *Castro's Cuba*, p. 294.

and the collected works of Lenin as early as 1955, Herbert Matthews has insisted that Guevara, until the day of his death, never acquired more than a "superficial knowledge of scientific Marxism"—and that "the Castroites played their Communist music by ear."[75] In effect, the guerrilla makes a revolution by dedicating himself to armed struggle for an idea which will only be progressively revealed by leaders who only progressively discover it. What counts are the military virtues of the guerrilla: a heroic will to collective and individual sacrifice. The revolutionary struggle, itself, will somehow insure the prevalence of the "revolutionary" ideology.

Even before Guevara's death in Bolivia there was some concerted attempt to provide a more substantial theoretical account of this somewhat curious process. Regis Debray charged himself with providing a rationale for the process that brought Castro's revolutionary government to power. In a series of essays culminating with *Revolution in the Revolution?* Debray attempted to outline the elements of a new Marxism. The results are no less curious than the phenomenon the writings were calculated to illuminate.

Debray has insisted that Castro's successful revolution has "rehabilitated Marxism" by adapting it to a social reality that is atypical by European standards. What is necessary is a return to the inspiration of Marxism-Leninism rather than the importation of "prefabricated strategies."[76]

Guevara had intimated as much in his *Guerrilla Warfare*. He had challenged "old dogmas." Debray was more explicit. He renounced the "old Marxism." How much of the old Marxism was to be jettisoned and how much of Marxism was to be transmogrified only became apparent after Debray had completed several major essays.

It seems evident that Debray has attempted to elaborate

[75] Matthews, *Fidel Castro*, p. 191; cf. R. Rojo, *My Friend Ché* (New York: Grove, 1968), p. 69.

[76] R. Debray, "Problems of Revolutionary Strategy in Latin America," in *Strategy for Revolution* (New York: Monthly Review, 1970), pp. 126, 128.

a theoretical infrastructure for the loosely argued theses of Guevara and the stream-of-consciousness ideology of Castro. Castro and Guevara, when they made their revolution, were both young and recently students. Debray has elevated this factual circumstance into a theoretical proposition. What the revolution represents, Debray informs us, is a *"dramatic divorce between generations."* The most active aggregate of political actors in the Latin American situation is the "poor peasantry," innocent of theoretical sophistication, conjoined and led by a conscious leadership which originates in student circles. The students are the "head of the anti-imperialist struggle in Latin America."[77] The "Fidelista Movement" is the "point of divorce between two generations."

Marxism, for Debray, has taken on the features of generational conflict—with students and the young becoming the intellectual vanguard of the "poor peasants"—in order to make the "proletarian revolution"! More than that, the proletariat of Latin America does not, in Debray's judgment, feel particularly disposed to make Marxist revolution (any more than Cuba's proletariat was so disposed). In fact, the proletariat constitutes, for Debray, the "privileged" element of Latin American society. Debray goes even further to suggest that the "city can bourgeoisify the proletarians." He refers to the cities as "lukewarm incubators" that "make one infantile and bourgeois."[78] The "proletarian" revolution must be made for the urban proletarians by poor peasantry which constitute the force of the revolution, but not its consciousness. This is provided by the young student warriors. The poor peasants can only become a vanguard force "if it is accompanied by a leadership of an intellectual type." Again we have a notion of elemental forces being fused and transformed by heroic warriors—a tradition common to Martí, the Futurists and Mussolini, but hardly Marxian in any identifiable sense.

Whenever it was suggested to either Marx or Engels that

---

[77] Debray, "Problems . . . ," "Interview with Havana Students," in *Strategy for Revolution*, pp. 132, 170, 171.

[78] Debray, *Revolution in the Revolution?* pp. 71, 76f.

students or intellectuals would lead the proletarian revolution, they both insisted that "the emancipation of the working classes must be conquered by the working classes themselves. We cannot therefore cooperate with people who openly state that the workers are too uneducated to emancipate themselves and must be freed from above . . . ." They systematically and emphatically rejected the notion that "the working class is incapable of its own emancipation."[79] Moreover, their judgments about student revolutionaries were not calculated to move them to identify students as the "ideological vanguard"—should they have chosen an "ideological vanguard." Engels, for instance, frequently referred to student revolutionaries in his analyses. While he does speak of them, in one phase of the revolution of 1848, as forming the "nucleus . . . of the revolutionary force," he characterized them as "those 'representatives of intellect,' as they liked to call themselves, [being] the first to quit their standards, unless they were retained by the bestowal of officer's rank, for which they, of course, had very seldom any qualification."[80] In 1890, in discussing the role of students in the German Social Democratic Party, Engels again characterized them as "young declassed bourgeois" who "rush into the Party" to "occupy most of the editorial positions on the new journals which pullulate and, as usual, they regard the bourgeois universities as a Socialist Staff College which gives them the right to enter the ranks of the Party with an officer's, if not a general's, brevet. All these gentlemen go in for Marxism, but of the kind you were familiar with in France ten years ago and of which Marx said: 'All I know is that I'm no Marxist!' And of these gentlemen he would probably have said what Heine said of his imitators: 'I sowed dragons and reaped fleas.' "[81]

[79] Marx and Engels, "Circular Letter," September 17-18, 1879, in K. Marx and F. Engels, *Selected Correspondence* (Moscow: Foreign Languages, 1953), pp. 388-95.

[80] F. Engels, *Germany: Revolution and Counter-Revolution* (New York: International, 1933), pp. 41, 103.

[81] Engels to Lafargue, letter dated August 27, 1890, in F. Engels and P. and L. Lafargue, *Correspondence*, tr. Y. Kapp (Moscow: Foreign Languages, 1960), II, 386.

Both Marx and Engels saw the proletariat maturing to its social, economic, and political responsibilities as a consequence of its long struggle against capitalism. While they recognized that the workers might be temporarily "bourgeoisified" by circumstances, Engels made it quite clear that the mission of the proletariat could only be carried out by the proletariat.[82] In the 1890 introduction to *The Communist Manifesto* Engels insisted that "For the ultimate triumph of the ideas set forth in the *Manifesto* Marx relied solely and exclusively upon the intellectual development of the working class, as it necessarily had to ensue from united action and discussion."[83]

Debray has not only accepted the Leninist conviction that the proletariat is intrinsically incapable of attaining the consciousness requisite to socialism, he has insisted that the proletariat must necessarily be "bourgeois" because of the very character of urban life. The distinction between "proletariat" and "bourgeois" is not an economic one. It is totally unrelated to relations of production, functions in the economic system, income or ownership. To become a "proletarian" all one need do is fight in a guerrilla band! Surely a curious "Marxist" notion. In order to become a proletarian one must clear a "corner of the forest so as to be able to grow crops"— one must undertake "collective working of the soil, by hunting, etc. These material conditions force the guerrilla *to proletarize itself* morally and to proletarize its ideology. Whether its members are peasants or petit-bourgeois, the *foco* can only become an army of proletarians."[84]

Debray is grappling once again with the problem of the nonrevolutionary proletariat. The same problem that has bedeviled Marxism since the turn of the century has resurfaced. Debray's response—while novel—shares features with

[82] Cf. Engels, 1892 introduction to F. Engels, *The Condition of the Working Class in England in 1844* (London: George Allen & Unwin, 1950).

[83] Engels, "Introduction of 1890," "Communist Manifesto," in Marx and Engels, *Selected Works*, I, 31.

[84] Debray, "Castroism . . . " in Debray, *Strategy for Revolution*, p. 68.

that of Lenin, Mussolini, and Mao. What is required to make a revolution is a vanguard elite, mobilizing *any* population element that affords it access. Everyone becomes a "proletarian" by being committed, with discipline and sacrifice, to a "revolutionary line." The sorting criteria are clearly political, in fact military, and not economic.

At one time to be "proletarian" for Marxists meant to be a "class of modern wage-laborers who, having no means of production of their own, are reduced to selling their labor power in order to live." For Leninists a "proletarian" was someone who followed the political line of the Bolsheviks. For Debray a "proletarian" is anyone who fights in a guerrilla band that Debray approves of. Debray has stigmatized various, if not all, communist parties in Latin America as irredeemably bourgeois. The true proletarians are those who fight in guerrilla bands, even if their ideology (as was the ideology of the Castroites) appears, for all the world, to be "petit bourgeois nationalist." Neither Castro nor Guevara knew that they were Marxist-Leninists when they fought in the Sierra Maestra. They had, as Cuban radicals have ever after insisted, become, somehow, "proletarians" unbeknownst to themselves.

Mussolini never tired of reiterating that the Fascists were true "proletarians," serving a "proletarian fatherland." Fascists insisted that the effort to characterize men as "proletarians" and as "bourgeois" because of their economic and social circumstances was perverse. A worker might have a "bourgeois" disposition—and a member of the bourgeoisie might have a "proletarian" outlook. The distinction was a moral, that is to say, a political one. More emphatically, it ultimately came to be a military distinction. Those prepared to fight for the Fascist revolution were true "revolutionaries" and "proletarians"—whatever their objective class characteristics—and those who refused were "bourgeois."

Maoism has run something like the same course. In China a "proletarian" is one who does not deviate "a centimeter" from Mao's thought. The true proletarian is prepared to fight for the revolution. Even if one's class credentials are in perfect order, and one chooses to oppose Mao for whatever reason, he condemns himself as "bourgeois."

In the case of Castroism, the emphasis on youth, generational conflict, action as antecedent to thought, on the transforming function of military conflict, on the invocation of nationalist sentiment, are all instances of Fascist *style*.

The constituents of Fascist *content* regularly surface in Castroism as well. The Fidelistas emphasize the sovereign independence, economic development, and grandeur of the nation. They insist upon the necessity of breaking out of the confines of foreign domination; their enemy is imperialism. They have committed themselves to the effort to create a substantial degree of economic autarchy—economic self-sufficiency—and to create an intercontinental unity of "anti-imperialist" nations.[85] To achieve these ends they must mobilize all human and material resources. The population is conceived as "elemental," as material to be molded, into which a "new consciousness" is "instilled" through monopoly control of the means of communication. All of which is essentially Fascist and non-Marxist in content.

What is particularly interesting in Debray's account of Castroite Marxism is his explicit recognition that Castroism necessarily involves a fusion of *nationalism* and communism. Mussolini early characterized Fascism as a fusion of socialism and nationalism—and for years Marxism conceived this fusion a betrayal of the internationalist thought of Marx. Debray, on the other hand, conceives of the fusion as the fulfillment of Marxism. "Fidelism," we are told, is a "synthesis of two currents, national and international, nationalist and Communist." Debray went on to characterize some of the features of "Fidelism": ". . . the domination of an

[85] The Programme Manifesto of the Fascist Republican Party of Verona, published in 1943, included the plank which insisted on an inter-European consortium of nations to "abolish the capitalist system and to struggle against the world plutocracies. . . ." Cf. A. J. Gregor, *The Ideology of Fascism*, p. 388 and pp. 356f.

irreplaceable chief in charismatic contact with the masses, his undisciplined, stormy nationalism, his inability to 'depersonalize,' to provide a political programme and a party structure or to come to understandings with other political organizations . . . ." "Fidelism" requires a leader with "passion, [a] large popular following . . . , courage, . . . realism, [a] profound and reasoned hatred of imperialism, [and] honesty." This would constitute a "variety of Fidelism." In countries such as Argentina, "Fidelism" would have a very special "physiognomy"—"that of an essentially urban working-class movement in which the images of Lenin, of Evita Peron and of Fidel mingle in [an] unstable synthesis." Debray insists that there "is a far closer relationship [than 'old' sectarian Marxists appreciated] between Fidelism and the two most historically important forms of South American nationalism, which can today be called Bonapartist nationalism: Peronism in Argentina and the populism of Vargas in Brazil."

Peronism and the political persuasion of Vargas have for some considerable time been characterized as "fascistic." Debray is unembarrassed by the association and decries the sectarianism of the "old Marxism" which led Marxists of Latin America to "ally with reactionary forces against Peronism . . . ."[86]

The relationship between what Debray calls "revolutionary nationalism or Fidelism" and Fascism is far more intimate than contemporary radicals are prepared to admit. The political commitments with which Castro came to power were all but indistinguishable in style and content from the original programmatic commitments of Mussolini in 1922. The circumstances that generated the distinguishing features of Castroism after 1960 and those that produced the characteristics of the Fascist regime from 1925 through 1943 were the consequences of factors having little bearing on the initial ideological commitments of either.

[86] Debray, "Castroism . . . ," in Debray, *Strategy for Revolution*, pp. 54, 77-81.

FASCISM, CASTROISM, AND THE SOCIALIST REVOLUTION

After the palace *coup* that deposed Mussolini in 1943, Mussolini provided a frank characterization of the history of Fascism. He admitted that the revolutionary program of the Fascist movement had been confined by the constraints imposed by non-Fascist allies: the propertied and industrial classes who, allied with the Church, the monarchy, and elements of the army, obstructed Fascism's free passage. Mussolini insisted that Fascism had been systematically betrayed by those bourgeois elements it had been incapable of isolating and excising. He recognized that the Fascist revolution had been faulted because the capitalist class had maintained, throughout the Fascist period, an independent power base which permitted it to deflect the purposes of the revolution, and from which the forces at the disposal of Fascism were incapable of dislodging it. Mussolini recognized that only by eroding that base, by socializing large-scale industrial enterprises, would it be possible to even attempt an implementation of Fascism's "maximal" program.[87]

Mussolini recognized, belatedly, that the configuration of forces that obtained at the time of the March on Rome had succeeded in largely containing the Fascist revolution. Confined by the industrial bourgeoisie and traditional institutions like the monarchy and the army, Fascism had lapsed into a "dyarchy," an uneasy combination of revolutionary and conservative elements behind a facade of monolithic totalitarianism.[88]

Mussolini insisted that Fascism was not opposed to socialism in and of itself. Fascism had found itself opposed by the "old" socialist parties because of the peculiar confluence of circumstances that attended Italy's entry into the First World War and the period which followed. The "old" so-

[87] Mussolini, "Soliloquio in 'Libertà' all'Isola Trimellone," *Opera*, XXXII, 171, 177-79; "Rivoluzione sociale. Primi sintomi," *ibid.*, p. 267; "Le basi della nuova economia," *ibid.*, p. 294.

[88] Mussolini, *Storia di un anno*, in *bid.*, XXXIV, 406-16.

cialists had refused to recognize the revolutionary nature of the war. They refused to commit themselves to the productionistic and nationalistic program of "national syndicalism." The ensconced bourgeoisie, who resisted socialism for their own reasons, were driven to support Fascism (not without misgivings). Mussolini found himself in unhappy alliance with non-Fascist allies. The alliance remained relatively stable because Mussolini was prepared to admit, in 1922, the possibility that capitalism might possess sufficient vitality to support the productionistic program of Fascism. It was only in 1934 that Mussolini was prepared to argue that capitalism did not have the qualities necessary to fulfill the goals of the revolution. From that point on Fascism attempted to extend increasing controls over the entrepreneurial bourgeoisie. The effort met with systematic resistance at almost every juncture. The struggle continued until the very outbreak of the Second World War, when the Fascist system was thrown into the crisis from which it did not emerge.[89]

The phoenix Fascism that arose in the north of Italy from 1943 through 1945 was supported by German arms and won little support among the Italian working class. Nonetheless, Mussolini attempted to do something he had not been able to accomplish for twenty years: the socialization of Italian industry. His intention was clear. He wished to destroy the independent power base from which the capitalist class had resisted the totalitarian aspirations of Fascism. Mussolini attempted to impose socialism on Italy from the top. The only lever of power that remained to him was the passive support of the Germans who were concerned, by and large, only with the maintenance of the productive levels of Italian industry. Their concern was to support the German war machine. They were ill-disposed toward Mussolini's "socialist experiments." The capitalists of North Italy sought Ger-

---

[89] For a competent discussion of the relationship between Fascism and the industrial capitalists, cf. R. Sarti, *Fascism and the Industrial Leadership in Italy, 1919-1940* (Berkeley: University of California, 1971).

man protection to insulate themselves from Fascist socialism.

It was at this time, in support of Fascism's program of socialization, that a number of socialists and communists joined the Fascist ranks. Nicola Bombacci, a former Communist Deputy, for example, was Mussolini's intimate adviser during this final period. Mussolini took the initiative and released a number of socialists from custody in order to bridge the distance that separated the socialists from Fascism. Piero Pisenti, the Fascist Minister of Justice, made concerted efforts, at Mussolini's urgings, to enlist the aid of organized socialists in the Fascist program of socializing the Italian economy. Eight days before his death, in an interview with Gian Gaetano Cabella, Mussolini insisted that Fascism must ultimately accomplish the unrestricted socialization of the economy. Friends and enemies alike recognized Mussolini's preoccupation with socialization. Mussolini's belated efforts failed. But that the effort was made —that Mussolini was serious in his program—is instructive. It suggests that under suitable conditions Fascism and Fascists can, perhaps must, adopt a socialist program.[90]

Debray and a number of Castroites have suggested as much. Nationalist revolutionaries, such as Peron, must either fault their programs, Debray has suggested, or divest themselves of their conservative allies. Peronism, had it been able effectively to defend itself against the alliance of the latifundists, the comprador and entrepreneurial capitalists, and the army, would have realized a "Fidelista" program. Ricardo Rojo, one of the early associates of Guevara, has indicated that only the "myopia" of the "old left" militated against their recognition of the revolutionary character of Peronism. Even Guevara's father has provided evidence that radicals are prepared to make a distinction significant for our analysis. He was opposed to—and taught his son, Ernesto, to oppose—Peron. But one should make a distinction

---

[90] I have developed the discussion of Fascist socialism in more detail in my book, *The Ideology of Fascism*, chapter seven.

between Peron and Peronism. Not to have done so was an "error."[91]

The relationship between Fascism and the "Marxism" of contemporary radicals is, as has become increasingly evident, complex and ambivalent. In Castroism the complexity and ambivalence are revealed in perhaps their most transparent form. The criticisms leveled against Debray's theoretical account provide illustrative evidence of the thesis here suggested. Nelson Amaro Victoria, for example, has indicated that the institutionalization of *"charismatic leadership"*—a phenomenon first observed in Fascist Italy—has given the "Marxist revolution traits that [are] very similar to those of Nazi and Fascist regimes, in which one individual was the supreme authority."[92] Clea Silva's criticism, in turn, focuses on the "military romanticism" of Debray's account in which, of the necessary and decisive factors in revolution, military struggle, the sanguinary conflict, becomes decisive —and "revolutionary theory" emerges from the contest. It does not obtain *prior* to the armed conflict. Silva suggests that this is to invert "Marxist" tactics and strategy.[93] The military romanticism to which Silva refers is a feature common to revolutionary nationalisms, like that of Mussolini, the Futurists, the Italian nationalists, and the nationalism of José Martí—but it is hardly Marxist in any identifiable sense. James Petras' criticism concerns the *elitist* character of Debray's account. Debray's characterization of the guerrilla *foco* as the "little motor" that activates the "large motor" is more than reminiscent of the Mussolinian conviction that an aggressive, dedicated paramilitary elite can activate

[91] Rojo, *My Friend Ché*, p. 19; F. Pierini, *"Ché" Guevara* (Milan: Longanessi, 1968), p. 78. Guevara entered into formal alliance with the Peronistas, cf. D. James, *Ché Guevara* (New York: Stein and Day, 1970), pp. 182-87.

[92] N. A. Victoria, "Mass and Class in the Cuban Revolution," in I. L. Horowitz, ed., *Masses in Latin America* (New York: Oxford University, 1970), p. 559.

[93] C. Silva, "The Errors of the *Foco* Theory," in P. Sweezy and L. Huberman, *Regis Debray and the Latin American Revolution* (New York: Monthly Review, 1968), p. 23.

the masses. Debray, like Mussolini, has little confidence in the working class (they tend to be "reformist"), the trade unions (they are "economist"), urban populations (they are "bourgeois"), or the peasants (they are ignorant of their ultimate interests). They can be "mobilized," "detonated," and provided "consciousness" by declassed bourgeois intellectuals and specifically a group of self-selected students and paramilitary activists and guerrillas.[94]

Peter Worsley's criticism expands on Petras' objections. "There remains [in Debray's account]," he maintains, "the band of hunted men, acting and creating the revolution, increasingly focused upon themselves and preoccupied with the military act. It may be that the Sorel whose name appears in his book (true, to be rejected) is not too far below the surface. . . ." "The *foco*, the act, become primary. . . . [The] absence of theoretical programmatics is authentically Cuban, the emphasis upon *creating* the revolution authentically Castroist." The Cuban radicals were, in fact, "revolutionists and voluntarists."[95]

All of this "mistrust of masses and ultra-voluntarism," conjoined with a romantic elitism, generates a "demand for an authoritarian dictatorial organization that makes the bureaucratic Communist parties look like paragons of democratic virtue." What Debray's account produces, according to Petras, is an "ultra-centralized personality cult"—whose historical analogues are far too obvious to merit comment.

That Castro's fascism escaped the *containment* suffered by Mussolini's Fascism, and the *extinction* suffered by the fascism of Spain's José Antonio, was a consequence of a number of factors that can only be schematically outlined here.

Castro came to power with a party that was composed of a multiplicity of interest groups representing various segments of Cuba's population. They were bound together by

[94] J. Petras, "Debray: Revolutionary or Elitist?" in Sweezy and Huberman, *ibid.*, p. 110, 114.

[95] P. Worsley, "Revolutionary Theory: Guevara and Debray," *ibid.*, pp. 132, 136, 137.

a vague ideology that was largely fascist in content and character. Implicit in that program were two mutually incompatible elements: commitment to parliamentary democracy and economic laissez faire—and an aspiration to rapidly diversify and industrialize the economy of Cuba—while detaching the nation from integration in an "imperialist" system. The original Fascist program of San Sepolcro had the same features. Mussolini spoke of "broad political and economic democracy" and a restoration of the "manchestrian state" throughout the first years of the Fascist Party's activities. At the same time, at the founding meeting of the movement, he spoke of increasing the productivity of Italian industry and the struggle against the "world's plutocracies."

Castro found, as Mussolini would discover, that one could not accomplish all these "historic mandates." The critical question that faced both men turned on creating a power base from which the revolutionary party could draw sustained support during the dislocation that would inevitably follow efforts to realize their programs. Castro had the general support of the working class movement in Cuba in the euphoric period that immediately followed his accession to power. Mussolini, on the other hand, had insufficient leverage with organized working class parties, long involved with orthodox socialist parties who maintained a sectarian resistance to Fascism. Mussolini found himself opposed by large segments of the organized working class because the socialist and communist parties in Italy had a long tradition of effective working class mobilization. The "sectarians" had identified Mussolini as a "renegade."

Castro could count on effectively dominating the working class movement. Mussolini could not. Castro could move against the bourgeoisie, given the circumstances which permitted him to win the working class to his support. Mussolini could not. Mussolini was driven to accommodate bourgeois factions. He had made serious and persistent efforts to win orthodox socialists and organized working class groups to his "revolution." He was unsuccessful. Castro, although his movement was initially no less bourgeois in composition, could rapidly divest himself of bourgeois support when it became obvious to him that what they aspired to was a redistribution of the constant sum of welfare benefits that obtain in Cuba's stagnant economy.

Under the circumstances that prevailed in Italy following the March on Rome, Mussolini permitted himself to be convinced that capitalism still had sufficient expansive capacity to realize the Fascist developmental program. Mussolini argued that a "surgical" treatment of the economy would create massive dislocation and would alienate bourgeois support, would mobilize still further the working class resistance, and threaten his regime. The disenchanted could then invoke in their support the established and still viable institutions of the monarchy and the army against the Fascists. Moreover, a Fascist Italy suffering massive dislocation during the transitional period could expect no outside assistance that might offset the loss of the functionally strategic bourgeoisie should the decision be made to seek exclusively worker and peasant support.

Castro, on the other hand, had effectively destroyed the credibility of almost all preexistent institutions, including the army. He had absolute control over the deployment of force on the island. Moreover, he very soon learned that the Soviet Union was prepared to underwrite any experiments he chose to conduct if those experiments were calculated to embarrass the United States. Castro's revolution very rapidly went into a phased "radicalization." As he announced the postponement of elections he made overtures to the "underprivileged masses" by passing reductions in rent, in increasing distribution of land to peasant farmers. The distribution of such patronage provided him a base from which to operate while he lost the support of those elements of the population who still conceived that the revolution had been fought to restore the "responsible guarantees" of the 1940 Constitution. Castro then began to emphasize the productionistic plank of his program. The talk became more and more of "industrialization" and "development" and less and less of "elections." In early 1960 the Soviet Union committed itself

317

to a trade agreement with Havana that assured Cuba that the Soviets would purchase significant quantities of Cuban sugar and would afford Cuba Soviet credit of one hundred million dollars, at minimal interest, with which to expand the base of Cuban industry. This was followed by agreements with East Germany. As assistance from the socialist bloc materialized, the latent anti-Americanism that had always animated the Martían convictions of the Cuban radicals matured. The postures assumed by the United States abetted the tendency and also increased Castro's nationalistic support base in Cuba. The anti-imperialist plank of Castro's platform became more prominent. The comprador bourgeoisie, those whose interests allied them with the United States, were further and further alienated. Castro could then "nationalize" the holdings of Cubans and increase the patronage he could allocate, to increase the support afforded him by the more marginal sectors of Cuba's population.

As Castro's rapprochement with the Soviet Union became more intimate, more and more of the members of the 26th July Movement fell away, and the movement was restocked with marginal elements. The move was made to organize all the "revolutionary" forces in the reconstituted Partido Socialista Popular.

The nationalization of foreign interests and subsequently of Cuban firms was not preceded or followed by meetings, demonstrations, or any public expressions of the "popular will." They were simply dictated by executive order. Castro distributed official positions throughout what was now "national industry" to those who followed his program and thereby created a committed support base for his totalitarian system. Even the PSP, as late as the Party Congress in August 1960 counseled against the nationalization of Cuban enterprises. Castro proceeded very rapidly to out-distance the "Marxists."

The subsequent flight of the bourgeoisie from Cuba liquidated the possibility of any internal opposition to Castro's regime. Castro created Committees for the Defense of the Revolution, one committee on each block throughout the urban areas of the republic. Anyone who was against Castro was against the revolution. Any resistance that mounted anywhere was swiftly dissipated by Castro's newly organized militia. When the housewives of Cardenas organized a protest to deplore food shortages, the regime responded with a show of force that included tanks and machine guns.

The regime very rapidly developed all the totalitarian features that now characterize it. While the per capita income of Cuba has significantly declined, agricultural production fallen, and the cumulative deficit of payment in international transactions amounts to considerably more than one and a half billion pesos, the patronage that large-scale nationalization has provided, accompanied by the massive support of the Soviet Union, as well as the dissipation of any organized resistance to the regime through emigration and systematic surveillance, has provided Castro's revolutionary regime a viability that has carried it through a series of crises that would have destroyed any number of other less well-integrated political systems.[96]

The circumstances for Cuban socialization were so auspicious that Cuba has succeeded in socializing more of its economy in less than a decade than has been the case in Russia in over five, and China in more than two, decades. For Mus-

[96] An account of Cuban economic circumstances can be found in C. Mesa-Lago, "The Revolutionary Offensive," in *Transaction, 6,* 6 (April 1969), 22-29, 62. For an instructive summary of the phases of mobilization in support for the regime, see Victoria, in Horowitz, ed., *Masses in Latin America*, pp. 547-76. An account of Cuba's developing relationships with the socialist nations is given in Suarez, *Cuba.* A summary account of the Cuban phenomenon can be found in R. E. Ruiz, *Cuba: The Making of a Revolution* (New York: Norton, 1968). A sanguine account of Cuba's economic development can be found in L. Huberman and P. Sweezy, *Socialism in Cuba* (New York: Monthly Review, 1969), and E. Boorstein, *The Economic Transformation of Cuba* (New York: Monthly Review, 1968). A discussion of the transformation of Cuba's political life is available in R. R. Fagen, *The Transformation of Political Culture in Cuba* (Stanford: Stanford University, 1959). An extended discussion of the tensions between Castroism and Marxism-Leninism can be found in A. G. Petit, *Castro, Debray contre le Marxisme-Leninisme* (Paris: Laffont, 1968).

solini's Italy few, if any, of the conditions that would have fostered socialization obtained. Only external support from Germany, after the bourgeoisie and "bourgeois institutions" had abandoned Fascism, permitted Mussolini the occasion to make a last, desperate attempt to introduce a fascist socialism to Italy.

The Cuban revolution was made by a revolutionary cadre committed to an essentially nationalist and fascist program. It became socialist as an afterthought when it became fairly obvious that it could not achieve its goal without excising those elements from the economy that obstructed its course. This excision was made possible by the confluence of special local and international circumstances.

Whether Cuba succeeds or not in its program for national development, intercontinental anti-imperialism, and Cuban grandeur is a matter of little significance for the purposes of our account. The lesson it seems to teach is that it takes resolute fascists, and a collection of very special circumstances, to make a socialist revolution in the twentieth century. Cuban radicals have resolved the dilemma of the non-revolutionary proletariat and the historic role of nationalism by transforming classical Marxism into a Caribbean variant of fascism.[97]

[97] "It is tempting to compare the distinctive colouring which Castro has given to Cuban communism with fascism; there is Castro's evident belief, with Chibás but also with Mosley or Hitler, that political power lies in 'the response of a large audience to a stirring speech.' There is the willingness of large sections of the population, including intelligent and humane people, to surrender their individuality to Castro as men did to Fascist leaders. There is the persistent elevation of the principle of violence and the appeals to martial reactions in the regime's propaganda; and there is the cult of leadership, the emphasis on physical fitness in the education system, and the continual denigration of bourgeois democracies. The very statement of Guevara's in *Socialism and Man* which defines the drives of Cuban socialism shares with fascism, as with expressionism, 'the urge to recapture the "whole" man who seems atomized and alienated by society,' a man who could not find himself among the 'commonplaces of bourgeois democracy,' as Guevara put it. The 'New Man,' held to be typified by Guevara, a hero, and man of action, will and character, would have been admired by

French fascists such as Brasillach or Drieu or by D'Annunzio, of the wild demagogic epoch of the Republic of Fiume, who himself has seemed to at least one commentator to have been Castro's intellectual precursor. Castro's moralizing and his desire to break with material aims reflects fascist regenerationism; and his presentation of himself as the thoughtful and benevolent father resembles Mussolini. In fact, of course, the fascist revolutions of the 1930's cannot be understood (anymore than Castro's can) if observed wholly negatively, or if it is forgotten that even the Nazi revolution 'satisfied a deeply felt need for activism combined with identification [with] . . . a classless society.' Fascism was a heresy of the international socialist movement and several fascist leaders had once been men of the Left: it is possible to imagine Castro moving in time (or, more probably, at a certain time) from extreme Left to what passes for extreme Right. The charismatic leader, both left and right, after all, lives against an artificial background. As George Kennan put it, 'He creates [the background] for himself; but he believes in it implicitly and in part he generally succeeds in making it seem real to others as well. And his role, as he plays it, may be none the less heroic and impressive for this artificiality of the scenery.' Of no one is this percipient comment more true than of Castro who is also, of course, the heir of the Latin American continent's tradition of caudillismo." Hugh Thomas, *Cuba: The Pursuit of Freedom* (New York: Harper and Row, 1971), pp. 1490f.

CHAPTER EIGHT

Nonregime Radicalism:
The Student and Black Variants

ONE of the most interesting features of the nonregime radicalism in the industrially developed nations is that, as a political phenomenon, it is all but exclusively identified with the young. When one speaks of the "New Left" in the United States, for example, one is speaking, by and large, about the youth of the nation, more specifically the youth of college age—the post-adolescents entering college, as well as the graduate students in our institutions of higher learning. Whatever "youth masters" there are succeed, at best, in half-articulating the political sentiments of the young. Someone, somewhere, has suggested that Dr. Spock and Eugene McCarthy were created by the youth of the United States. As much might be said of Herbert Marcuse and his confreres. The non-young have a "radical" viability as long as they echo the sentiments, the convictions, and the postures of a vocal minority of our young. These are circumstances common to the radical youth and their adult spokesmen in most of the industrially advanced countries.

In their more exacerbated moments, the most radical of our radical youth will not hesitate to repudiate their adult spokesmen. In 1967, for example, Marcuse was given a thunderous ovation by the students of Berlin; in 1968 he was hooted and jeered. His reception at Columbia, during its troubled days in 1968, was equally unfortunate. Recently in Frankfurt, at the Institute for Social Studies—the one-time home of Marcuse and the intellectual base for the progenitors of West Germany's S.D.S. (*Sozialistischer Deutsche Studentenbund*)—Professors T. W. Adorno, Max Horkheimer, and Jürgen Habermas were forced to call upon the local constabulary to dispossess radical students who had forcibly occupied the Institute and were employing its facilities to organize a demonstration against the Chancellor of Germany. The young and the non-young of the radical left are in uneasy alliance. And the initiative rests with the young.

"Radicalism," in our own time, and in the industrially advanced, nonsocialist nations, is largely if not exclusively, a generational phenomenon. The "radicals" have shown little disposition to be true to any one specific theoretician or collection of theoreticians. In radical tracts one can find references to Nietzsche as readily as Nkrumah, to Bakunin as readily as Sorel, to Hegel as readily as Sartre. While much of radical rhetoric is alive with the language of Karl Marx, the Marxism of contemporary student radicalism is more shadow than substance, more intestinal than cerebral. The prescription, "Don't trust anyone over thirty!" does seem to capture a genuine radical sentiment—and Marx was, after all, over thirty.

As a generational, nonregime political phenomenon, student radicalism is agonizingly diffuse. What passes as the "radical student movement" is a complex phenomenon composed of variegated constituents of varying degrees of political significance. Most of the component groups and individual leaders of the movement celebrate the fact that they are not confined by "theoretical abstractions"; they insist that they are moved by events and adapt theory to practice. While there has been a more recent emphasis on analysis and theory, the more general disposition on the part of student radicals has been to preoccupy themselves and their energies in action. Student radicals talk glibly of action being "the only reality; not only reality but morality as well . . . ." One is admonished by radicals to "Trust your impulses," and advised, "There is no program. Program would make our movement sterile." This is conjoined with the conviction that it is the "insistence on ideological exactness rather than action, that has held the revolution back in this country as much as the actions of the people in power."

Other student radicals speak with equal equanimity of a "lust for violence . . . ."[1]

These sorts of assertions have had calculable effect. Commentators speak painfully of the "new barbarians."[2] More interesting than that, an increasing number of analysts have identified student radicals as contemporary fascists. Juergen Habermas, one of the intellectual progenitors of the German New Left, coined the expression "fascism of the Left" (*Links-faschismus*) to characterize the political postures of his radical students. Since that time the characterization has been reinvoked by a number of observers from all stations along the political continuum. Guenther Albrecht Zehm developed the theme with an analysis of the ideology of radical students. In response, Max Beloff insisted that "the student movement is not 'left-wing fascism,' it is 'fascism'; there is no other term that so aptly places it in its historic context." Lewis Feuer, in turn, maintains that "the student movements partake of a fascism of the left." Edmund Glenn speaks simply of "the fascism . . . of the student rebels . . . ," while Bruno Bettelheim refers to a student "fascism of the Left."[3]

That the characterization of student radicals as "fascists" is shared by commentators on both the "Left" and the "Right" is in itself instructive and interesting. Even a Marxist historian with the credentials of Eugene Genovese has warned us of the "pseudo-revolutionary middle-class totali-

[1] Free (A. Hoffman), *Revolution for the Hell of It* (New York: Dial, 1968), pp. 9, 12, 80, 89; D. Rader, *I Ain't Marchin' Anymore* (New York: Paperback, 1969), pp. 116; cf. pp. 77, 87, 96.

[2] D. J. Boorstin, *The Decline of Radicalism: Reflections on America Today* (New York: Random House, 1969), pp. 121-34.

[3] G. A. Zehm, "Gibt es einen linken Faschismus?" in H. J. Schöps and C. Dannenmann, *Die rebellischen Studenten* (Munich: Bechtle, 1968), pp. 116-23; M. Beloff, "Universities and Violence," L. S. Feuer, "Patterns of Irrationality," in *Survey, 69* (October 1968), pp. 39, 51; E. S. Glenn, "The University and The Revolution: New Left or New Right?" in G. R. Weaver and J. H. Weaver, *The University and Revolution* (Englewood Cliffs, N.J.: Prentice Hall, 1969), p. 118; B. Bettelheim, *Obsolete Youth: Towards a Psychograph of Adolescent Rebellion* (San Francisco: San Francisco Press, 1970), p. 6.

tarians . . . of the left wing student movement."[4] Habermas' "left-wing" credentials are, of course, no less impeccable— and his judgment equally explicit. There is an identifiable syndrome of "fascistic" traits that has come to characterize student radicals. Russell Kirk, on the "Right," alludes to just such a collection of syndromatic traits.[5] Such judgments, coupled with the sober assessments of political analysts of the stature of Walter Laqueur, commend themselves to our attention. In what sense does the nonregime student radicalism of the nonsocialist industrialized nations represent a variant of fascism?[6]

The Student Movement in Industrially Advanced, Nonsocialist Nations

Any number of conceptual and empirical problems make it difficult to address oneself to an adequate analysis of what is now spoken of as the "student movement" in the industrially advanced, nonsocialist countries. The question which immediately presents itself is one of definition: what is to count as *the* student movement? In the United States there are approximately seven million students in institutions of higher learning. In Japan there are about one and a half million students currently enrolled in universities; in Italy and France there are approximately 600,000 in each country. In Germany there are about half as many, and in England there are about 200,000 currently attending universities. Of these numbers, informed estimates identify about two or three percent as "hard core radical students." Most students could not, under any classificational schema, be counted as "politically active." The bulk of students, American, Japa-

---

[4] Cf. D. P. Moynihan, "Politics as the Art of the Impossible," *The American Scholar, 38*, 4 (Autumn 1969), p. 575.

[5] R. Kirk, "The University and Revolution: An Insane Conjunction," in Weaver and Weaver, *The University and Revolution*, pp. 75f.

[6] Oskar Negt has written a reply to Habermas' suggestion that the German New Left represents a form of "Left fascism"; O. Negt, "Studentischer Protest, Liberalismus, 'Linksfaschismus,'" *Kursbuch, 13* (1968).

nese, or European can be identified as "vocationalists" or "professionalists," "collegiates," or "ritualists"—that is to say they attend institutions of higher learning in order to equip themselves to take up a vocation or profession, or they attend because they find college life attractive or because attendance is expected of them. They are, like most of their parents, apolitical. They may, on occasion, be mobilized for one or another political (or nonpolitical) cause, but they remain in general uninvolved. Students who do join "new left" campus organizations, who attend meetings and pay dues, are very few in number. At its peak, the Students for a Democratic Society, one of the more active radical student organizations on American campuses, had approximately seven thousand members who paid dues to the national headquarters. Approximately ten times as many students were members of local chapters. The S.D.S., at the most generous estimates, included about one percent of the students on American college and university campuses. The entire organized student left included no more than three percent of the student population of the United States of America. Much the same can be said of the organized student radicals in Britain, Germany, Italy, France, and Japan.

It is difficult to estimate the amount of sympathy the organized radical students enjoy or enjoyed. There is some evidence that a large minority of students at least passively sympathize with the *goals* expressed by organized radical groups (while generally objecting to their *methods*), and on some campuses, under crisis conditions, student radicals have been able to mobilize a simple majority to support their specific issue-orientated demands. In general, however, the majority of politically active students remains within the limits of political "orthodoxy," however that "orthodoxy" is defined. The largest number of students active in politics remain members of "orthodox" political organizations even if they are occasionally mobilized to "radical" causes. In the United States the Young Republicans and the Young Democrats have a total combined membership of approximately

250,000 members on American campuses, and a 1967 survey of American college students indicates that a plurality favored Richard Nixon in the 1968 presidential election. As late as 1966, four national surveys indicated that 75 percent of all American college and university students supported the American policy in Vietnam.

Student radicalism (whatever "radicalism" is taken to mean in such a context) is, in effect, a minority phenomenon involving relatively few students. This is not to suggest that the "movement" is not of political significance. Radical students, for example, played a significant role in precipitating the political crisis in France in May 1968. Japanese students mobilized massive riots against the Japan-U.S. Security Treaty in 1960 and were thus instrumental in forcing the resignaton of the Kishi government. Nonetheless, we *are* dealing with a very small minority of students—and it is essential that we remain cognizant of that fact.

Not only is the student movement a minority phenomenon, it is composed, as has already been suggested, of a multiplicity of elements which, in times of stress can mobilize around an issue, but which often find themselves involved in intramovement factional struggle. The recent disintegration of the American S.D.S. is a case in point. The S.D.S. is now divided up into an "orthodox" faction, a "Maoist" faction, and an "extremist" faction (the Weathermen), whose interrelationships are often more strained than the relationship between the radicals and the "Establishment." In France there has been protracted in-fighting among the various radical groups, some identifying themselves as anarchists, some as Trotskyites, others as Maoists, and still others as Castroites. The distinctions between the factions seem to be of sufficient significance to generate considerable mutual ill-will.

Because we are concerned with a nonregime movement involving a relatively small number of students entertaining a complex variety of volatile ideological opinions, any discussion about "student radicalism" can only be very general

327

and, by and large, impressionistic.[7] Student radicals have been very eclectic in gathering together a political belief system. Few could be responsibly characterized as "orthodox" anything. As will become quite evident, literally none could be characterized as classical Marxist. Few could pass as orthodox Leninists or orthodox Maoists (whatever that might be taken to mean). Finally, in view of the fact that Castroist ideology has not been standardized in any serious sense, student preoccupation with Castroism is more *affective* than *intellectual*. Paul Jacobs and Saul Landau characterize this disposition by indicating that American student radicals "found a new hero in Castro, the *man of action, the man without an ideology . . . .*"[8]

The fact is that the radical student movement in the advanced industrial nations outside the socialist sphere has, since its inception, exhibited a marked inclination "for activism and a spirit of anti-intellectualism . . . ."[9] This disposition has been regularly identified by both enthusiasts for and detractors of the "movement." Michael Harrington has spoken of the new radicals as "the privileged children of the affluent middle class. . . . numbered in the thousands, a mere fraction of their generation, only a small percentage even among college students. They are courageous, dedicated, and existential in a way that sometimes borders on the anti-intellectual. So they are rather weak on social and

[7] Student radicalism has generated a very large body of literature. The descriptive literature that I have found most helpful includes L. S. Feuer, *The Conflict of Generations: The Character and Significance of Student Movements* (New York: Basic Books, 1969); K. Keniston, *Young Radicals: Notes on Committed Youth* (New York: Harcourt, Brace & World, 1968); S. M. Lipset, ed., *Student Politics* (New York: Basic Books, 1967); "Students and Politics," *Daedalus*, 97, 1 (Winter 1968). A very general discussion can be found in J. A. Califano, Jr., *The Student Revolution: A Global Confrontation* (New York: Norton, 1970).

[8] P. Jacobs and S. Landau, *The New Radicals* (Harmondsworth: Penguin, 1966), p. 21.

[9] *Ibid.*, p. 20.

328

political theory . . . ."[10] Jack Newfield has spoken of the student New Left as evincing an "indifference to ideology, discipline, economics, and conventional political forms. . . . Occasionally they have been negative to the edge of nihilism. . . . [Some] segments of the New Left are anti-intellectual, sometimes even anti-rational." With respect to the members of the American S.D.S. Newfield has gone on to lament:

There is an appalling anti-intellectualism among the newer S.D.S. members. Not only do they read few novels and almost no scientific or philosophical literature, they have read little within the radical tradition. Of twenty-five activists interviewed, none had ever read Rosa Luxemburg, Max Weber, Eduard Bernstein, John Dewey, Peter Kropotkin, or John Stuart Mill. Less than five had actually read Lenin or Trotsky, and only a few more had ever read Marx. . . . Even the few who regretted never having read Mill and Weber insisted they could learn more from events that touched their own lives than from any book.[11]

Critics such as Daniel Moynihan characterize radicals as "anti-ideological, even anti-intellectual."[12] Leslie Fiedler simply identifies them as the "new irrationalists." "Disinterested scholarship," he went on, "reflection, the life of reason, a respect for tradition stir (however dimly and confusedly) chiefly their contempt."[13]

The identification of such dispositions on the part of radical students is surprisingly general. The "anti-intellectual" and "irrationalist" disposition seems to be one of the most general criterial attributes shared by the class of political

[10] M. Harrington, "Introduction" to J. Newfield, *The Prophetic Minority: The American New Left* (London: Blond, 1967), p. 13.

[11] *Ibid.*, pp. 23, 120, 121.

[12] D. P. Moynihan, "Nirvana Now," in A. Klein, ed., *Natural Enemies: Youth and the Clash of Generations* (New York: Lippincott, 1969), p. 43.

[13] L. A. Fiedler, "The New Mutants," in *ibid.*, pp. 206, 208.

actors identified as "radical." Obviously not all share the trait, but its presence is sufficiently general to mark it as a significant element in the political style of radical students. Many commentators, again both enthusiasts as well as detractors, have referred to the irrational quality that attends the political style of student radicalism. Kenneth Keniston, in speaking of "alienated" students who provide the recruitment base for radical student groups, refers to their "positive values" as "expressive or aesthetic" rather than intellectual. Paul Jacobs and Saul Landau refer to youths who make "a virtue of their inability to articulate and analyze coherently. They [speak] 'from the gut,' stumblingly, haltingly, using the language of the new folksingers, deliberately adopting a style that was the antithesis of what they had heard from their professors. . . . They respond instead to the sense and sound of friendship and community, to the exultation they feel when thousands of people link hands and sing. . . ." What they search for is a "feeling of community."[14]

Keniston, referring to these dispositions, has spoken of a "post-modern style." While such a characterization is based upon restricted data, and the class of radicals is ill-defined and includes, at best, an exiguous minority of American students, the notion of a radical *style* is suggestive in the context of our survey. Keniston urges that

> emphazing "style" rather than ideology, objectives, positions, or traits . . . [suggests] that the similarities in post modern youth are to be found in the *way* they approach the world, rather than in actual behavior, formal beliefs, or goals. . . . In . . . a revolutionary world, where ideologies come and go and radical change is the rule, a style, a way of doing things, becomes more tenable and more important than any fixed goals, ideologies, programs, institutions, or psychological traits.[15]

[14] K. Keniston, "The Alienated," in *ibid.*, p. 259; Jacobs and Landau *The New Radicals*, pp. 22, 15.
[15] Keniston, *Young Radicals*, p. 275.

Theodore Roszak has celebrated the advent of this style among student radicals in his *The Making of a Counter Culture*. The new style requires no less than "the subversion of the scientific world view . . . . In its place, there must be a new culture in which the non-intellective capacities of the personality—those capacities that take fire from visionary splendor and the experience of human communion—become the arbiters of the good, the true, and the beautiful." The emphasis is not only on the exploration of "non-intellective consciousness," but, more than that, a disposition to identify "truth" with *feelings* rather than any intersubjective criteria of admissibility. The ultimate warrant for truth claims is provided not by publicly accessible evidence but rather via "visionary powers" that "move souls." Roszak speaks of "the beauty of the fully illuminated personality as our standard of truth . . . ." The radical students are admonished to "reject the small souls who know only how to be correct, and cleave to the great who know how to be wise."[16]

If *reason* is understood to refer to that process of truth certification that has historically established itself as generating the most reliable truth claims—the standard process of characterizing as corrigibly true only those claims that can specify the public and neutral evidence that supports them—then the radical style is more than anti-intellectual. It is irrational. Radicals do not produce defensible truth claims for public scrutiny. Their truths tend to be certified largely by strong *feelings*. In referring to participants in the Vietnam Day Committee activities, Jacobs and Landau maintain that "the absence of ideological discussion is not because the membership does not have political views or leanings; they do, but they are based on impulsive right-wrong feelings as much as on reasoned analyses."[17]

The disposition to support truth claims through reports of subjective feelings is pervasive among student radicals. It

[16] T. Roszak, *The Making of a Counter Culture* (Garden City, N.Y.: Doubleday, 1969), pp. 50f., 237f.

[17] Jacobs and Landau, *The New Radicals*, p. 74.

finds its most transparent expression in the irrationalism of Jerry Rubin and Abbie Hoffman.

THE YIPPIES AND THE RADICAL STYLE

Jerry Rubin, one of the "founders" of the Youth International Party, the "Yippies," has provided stream-of-consciousness accounts of the radical style (what he himself calls a "life-style"). One of Rubin's central theses is that learning can only be the consequence of *action*—what he calls "Apocalyptic Action." Action, in turn, is motivated by "myths." History, he insists, finds its motive force in myths. Myths provide "a model to identify with . . . . The reality [is] there. A myth [is] needed to coalesce the energy." The myth is a piece of theater. It is an acting out. It is general, vague, and ambiguous. "Let's not let details get in the way of the myth," Rubin has insisted, "we gotta choose a symbol so evil that we can do anything we want and get away with it." Such a myth may be, and frequently is, a mass of contradictions. Its sole requirement is that it "touch" a "common but nameless emotion." It need not be consistent nor comprehensible. One cannot communicate with words— "words have lost their emotional impact, intimacy, ability to shock and make love. Language *prevents* communication." As a consequence Rubin has admonished student radicals to "Act first. Analyze later. Impulse—not theory—makes the great leaps forward." What radicals are required to produce is "a spectacular myth of revolution." The necessary corollary is that "goals are irrelevant. The tactics, the actions are critical."

The role of the revolutionary is to create a myth, understood in terms of theater. In the service of this strategy symbols, condensed imagery, hyperbolic speech, and uniforms create models for revolutionary behavior. " 'Critical' or 'abstract thinking' is a trap. . . . Look at both sides of the argument, take no action, take no stands, commit yourself to nothing, because you're always looking for more argu-

332

ments, more information, always examining, criticizing. . . .
Our generation is in rebellion against abstract intellectual-
ism and critical thinking. . . . The goal of the revolution is
to eliminate all intellectuals . . . ." What the revolutionary
must understand is that "language does not radicalize people—what changes people is the emotional involvement of
action." The politicians can only be reached through "the
language of power and violence."[18]

The noncognitive style that finds expression in Rubin's
nonprose, finds its echo in the nonprose of Abbie Hoffman.
Hoffman insists that "clarity, alas, is not one of our goals.
Confusion is mightier than the sword! . . . Don't rely on
words. . . . Rely on doing—go all the way every time. . . .
Accept contradictions, that's what life is all about. . . . The
truth lies through insanity. . . . Fantasy is freedom. Anybody
can do anything. . . . We are living contradictions . . . ."
What is required for the production of revolution is a "vast
myth."

The "myth" occupies a central role in the noncognitive
style of the self-proclaimed most radical of radicals. The
myth has a mobilizing function. It is never precise, for that
"would allow it to be trapped and molded. It must have the
action of participation and the magic of mystique. It must
have a high element of risk, drama, excitement and bullshit."
With evident approval Hoffman cites Sorel: "As long as
there are no myths accepted by the masses, one may go on
talking of revolts indefinitely, without ever provoking any
revolutionary movement."[19]

All of this is celebrated as the "End of Reason," a generational conflict that pits the old against the young. It is a
revolution of "total feeling." It is a movement of young
"warrior-poets" ready to employ "whatever means necessary" to "totally destroy the enemy." The means necessary

[18] J. Rubin, Do It! (New York: Simon and Schuster, 1970), pp. 68,
82, 104, 109, 116, 125, 142, 213, 249, 252.
[19] Hoffman, Revolution for the Hell of It, pp. 26, 31, 39, 43, 80,
102, 103, 177.

may include the burning of books, attacks on individuals and institutions guilty of any complicity in the crimes of "Pig Nation," the United States of America.[20]

The principal function of such "Apocalyptic Acts" is not to overthrow the system; it is rather a calculated strategy undertaken to "force people to change their lives overnight." The fact is that radicals such as Rubin and Hoffman conceive the "masses" as infinitely manipulable and subject to instant conversion. Rubin insists that "if the Yippies controlled national TV, [they] could make the Viet Kong and the Black Panthers the heroes of swooning Amerikan [sic] middle-aged housewives everywhere within a week." Largely for this reason such radicals advocate "mass politics." "To our parents," Rubin indicated, "crowds bring back memories of Hitler and mass hysteria. To us crowds mean freedom."[21]

Radicals of the caliber of Rubin and Hoffman are not only irrationalists—conceiving "truth" to be a function of "action" and personal "feeling" rather than "thought" and intersubjective certification—they are anti-rationalists in the sense that they are committed to a mobilizing strategy predicated on the invocation of emotion through inflated speech, condensed imagery, and the exploitation of sentiment.

There is little difficulty in unearthing the historic analogue of Yippie style. Marinetti's Futurists were committed to the same noncognitive style. Their movement was no less irrational, anti-gerontocratic, anarchistic, violent, histrionic,

---

[20] Cf. A. Hoffman, *Woodstock Nation* (New York: Random House, 1969), pp. 133, 10; Rubin, *Do It!*, p. 127, 122f. "When in doubt," Rubin prescribes, "burn. Fire is the revolutionary's god. Fire is instant theater. No words can match fire. . . . To take what you need is an act of self-love, self-liberation. While looting, a man to his own self is true. (Shoplifting gets you high. Don't buy. Steal. . . . Kids should steal money from their parents, because that is true liberation from the money ethic: true family.)" *Ibid.*, pp. 127, 122f. "I think people should do whatever the fuck they want, and not because I am trying to organize the working class, but because I think kids should kill their parents." Hoffman, *Woodstock Nation*, p. 8.

[21] Hoffman, *Revolution for the Hell of It*, p. 36.

334

anti-traditional, and romantic. Their advocacy of an anti-science—a strategy for truth determination that involved impulse, instinct and "illuminations" and "fellow feeling, love and humanism"—was no less insistent. Their celebration of "contradiction" and "action rather than 'abstract' thought" was no less unrestrained. Their lust for "life" and "free love" was equally consuming. Their disposition to generate confrontation and political polarization is indistinguishable from that of the contemporary Yippies.

The Futurists not only anticipated the noncognitive style of America's Yippies but their political content as well. The Futurists had demanded an abolition of "elephantine bureaucracies," conscript armies, police and courts. They advocated an "absolute freedom" unrestricted by the constraints of codified law or rule-governed behavior. They advocated the abolition of schools and the advent of "learning through living." They rejected capitalism and imperialism. Their objection to the socialism of their time was predicated not only on their objection to its "cerebral" and "abstract intellectual" character but on the anticipation that socialism would breed a bureaucratism and authoritarianism that would make "participatory democracy" impossible. Whatever coherent political convictions the Futurists entertained could only be characterized as "radical left" if "left" means anything at all.

The Futurists did not consider themselves Marxist because Marxism, as they understood it, was committed to a form of historical determinism that precluded the political influence of "moral factors," which they conceived to be "particularly explosive and determinant."[22] Marxism, for the Futurists, was largely irrelevant. It had become the hobbyhorse of intellectuals.

The Yippies have been no less critical of Marxism no matter how liberally it is interpreted. Hoffman has insisted that "Marxism is irrelevant to the U.S.A., as irrelevant as Capitalism."[23] Rubin has simply rejected anything that might

[22] Marinetti, *Teoria*, p. 363.
[23] Hoffman, *Revolution for the Hell of It*, p. 36.

pass as Marxist analysis. His explicit objection is to what he identifies as "The Laws of Marxism"—Rubin maintains that "white middle class youth" constitute a revolutionary class that is "exploited and oppressed" and that the "revolution" is, in fact, not Marxist but generational. Rubin rejects the revolutionary theories and strategies of the "Communist Party, Trotskyites, Progressive Labor, Independent Socialists," and so on. In fact, Rubin and Hoffman both reject what they identify as "the left." Rubin maintains that "the left" has turned communism into "a church."[24] Hoffman, in turn, insists that the most elementary social facts of the twentieth century have not succeeded in penetrating the "plastic domes" of "Marxist theoreticians." In his inimitable style Hoffman informs his readers that "the left sucks," and "masturbates continuously"—characterizations hardly advanced as evidence of his approval.[25]

There is clearly no Marxism to be found among the radicals that collect around the Yippies. Nor are they committed to either identifiable goals or specific programs. They are committed only to irrationalism as a life style, to action for action's sake, to myth and contradiction. People are mobilized; political actors act out a myth that serves both as a source of "truth" and a "model" for participants; and the result is "Yippie politics." All of which is painfully familiar. It is a caricature of "Futurist politics."

The irrationalism of the Yippies, their appeal to the act as a repository of truth, their commitment to myth as an infallible source of wisdom, their anti-programmatic and anti-gerontocratic postures, their irrepressible anarchism and personalism, their invocation of "masses" and "crowds," their anti-Marxism, their quaint sexuality and adolescent hunger for "community," are indistinguishable from the postures and dispositions of Italy's Futurists, the progenitors of Fascist style.

[24] Rubin, *Do It!*, pp. 115, 113.
[25] Hoffman, *Woodstock Nation*, pp. 106, 29, *Revolution for the Hell of It*, p. 89.

The Non-Marxism of the Student Left

The relationship which the Yippies enjoy with the more orthodox New Left is evidence of a measure of tolerance that suggests several things: (1) the New Left is prepared to act as a carrier movement for elements such as the Yippies; and (2) such an accommodation is only possible because classical Marxism has been so eroded by time and circumstance that it no longer provides selective criteria for radical students. One of the circumstances that has produced the erosion of Marxism in the United States has been the historic absence of a revolutionary proletariat. The New Left may aspire to "radicalize" the American working class—they may talk of an eventual rapprochement between students and working men—but the historic fact remains that the proletariat of the advanced industrial nations is nonrevolutionary.

John Kautsky and Roger Benjamin have plotted the relationship between the common indices of industrial maturity and the disposition of workers to join the Communist Party, and have found a *negative* correlation between economic maturity and Communist Party membership. A nation characterized by a high level of urbanization, a reduced proportion of its working population involved in agricultural production, with a relatively high level of per capita production and high international financial status evidences a low incidence of Communist Party membership. Where proletarians constitute decisive elements in the working population, where capitalism is most highly developed, one finds the least disposition on the part of wage laborers to undertake systemic revolution.[26]

C. Wright Mills, in a statement now identified as one of the founding documents of the student New Left, insisted that he could not understand why the left conceived "the working class of the advanced capitalist societies as *the*

[26] J. Kautsky, *Communism and the Politics of Development* (New York: Wiley, 1968), chap. 10.

historic agency, or even as the most important agency, in the face of the really impressive historical evidence that now stands against this expectation. Such a labor metaphysic . . . is a legacy from Victorian Marxism that is now quite unrealistic." Mills went on to suggest, on the other hand, that the "intellectuals" constituted "a possible, immediate, radical agency of change."[27]

The theme is reiterated by Herbert Marcuse, one of the intellectual luminaries of the New Left. "[The] New Left is, again with exceptions, not bound to the old working class as the sole revolutionary agent. . . . If you reflect on this . . . you will admit that this . . . is a real nightmare for 'old Marxists.'" And further, "In the capitalist world, [the bourgeoisie and the proletariat] are still the basic classes. However, the capitalist development has altered the structure and function of these two classes in such a way that they no longer appear to be agents of historical transformation. An overriding interest in the preservation and improvement of the institutional *status quo* united the former antagonists in the most advanced areas of contemporary society." One of the principal agents of social change is the strata of intellectuals "whose consciousness and instinct break through or escape social control."[28]

The rejection of the proletariat as the principal agent of historic change and the invocation of "intellectuals" whose "instincts" motivate revolution do constitute nightmare elements for any self-conscious Marxist. Marcuse is painfully specific. He recognizes that his notions constitute a deviation from Marxist theory specifically in terms of conceiving revolutionary change to be the product of the initiative of intellectuals motivated by "biological and aesthetic needs." He recognizes that this reinterpretation and deviation moves him beyond Marxism to increasingly emphasize "subjective" rather than "objective" factors. His analysis leads him "into

[27] C. Wright Mills, "Letter to the New Left," in P. Long, ed., *The New Left* (Boston: Sargeant, 1969), p. 22f.

[28] H. Marcuse, *Five Lectures* (Boston: Beacon, 1970), pp. 83f.; *One Dimensional Man* (Boston: Beacon, 1964), pp. xiif.

a dimension of the human existence hardly considered in Marxian theory—the 'biological' dimension in which the vital, imperative needs and satisfactions of man assert themselves." Since only a minority of men are driven by Marcuse's liberating "instincts," it is obvious that his revolution would be minoritarian. "We would have to conclude," he informs us, "that liberation would mean subversion against the will and against the prevailing interests of the great majority of people." There is an explicit rejection of parliamentary procedures and an equally explicit invocation of elite rule.

> Who has the right to set himself up as a judge of an established society, who other than the legally constituted agencies or agents, and the majority of the people? Other than these, it could only be a self-appointed elite, or leaders who would arrogate to themselves such judgment. Indeed, if the alternative were between democracy and dictatorship (no matter how "benevolent"), the answer would be noncontroversial: democracy is preferable. However, this democracy does not exist, and the government is factually exercised by a network of pressure groups and "machines," vested interests. . . . These are not derived from the sovereign people. The representation is representative of the will shaped by the ruling minorities. Consequently, if the alternative is rule by an elite, it would only mean replacement of the present ruling elite by another.[29]

One doesn't have to be possessed of total recall to remember that such was the rationale for minoritarian revolution that Mussolini advanced as early as 1913. Marcuse's political postures are not only irrepressibly elitist[30] but clearly fascist rather than Leninist much less Marxist. Marcuse's appeal to "biological" "instincts," to the repression of opposition, to

[29] Marcuse, *An Essay on Liberation* (Boston: Beacon, 1969), pp. 52f., 16, 70.

[30] R. Marks, *The Meaning of Marcuse* (New York: Ballentine, 1970), p. 99, cf. pp. 114-19.

violence as a legitimate form of political action are all manifestly fascist.

The task which Marcuse assigns to his new, minoritarian,
and self-selected elite is to generate a new " 'biological' solidarity in work and purpose, expressive of a true harmony
between social and individual needs and goals. . . . It is the
image of this solidarity as elemental, instinctual, creative
force which the young radicals see . . . ." The rebellion
then—initiated by the self-selected elite possessed of some
saving vision of "instinctive solidarity"—would be charged
with transforming the "instinctual basis of society." The
revolution must reach into the "infrastructure of man,"
". . . and unless the revolt reaches into this 'second' nature,
into [the majority's] ingrown patterns, social change will
remain 'incomplete,' even self-defeating." It is obvious to
Marcuse that under present circumstances the individual
cannot be "the judge of his own happiness." The "majority
of organized labor shares the stabilizing, counterrevolutionary needs of the middle classes"—a condition that is "fostered in the instinctual structure of the exploited."[31]

The resistance to the oppression of the majority arises
only among the young and the intellectual. The social and
political changes necessary for Marcuse's true liberation require a "qualitative" change in men's "physiology and psychology," in the generation of an "aesthetic morality" that
would require the suppression of what Marcuse's elite clearly conceives to be "false words and wrong deeds which . . .
contradict and counteract the possibilities of liberation."
The only truth that can be responsibly tolerated by Marcuse's intellectuals—the young and the hippies whose "bodies are unsoiled by plastic cleanliness," and who are possessed of the "sensuous power of the imagination"—is *their*
personal truth.[32] What is required is an "educational dictatorship," which is, according to Marcuse, less of a risk than

---

[31] Marcuse, *Essay on Liberation*, pp. 88, 4f., 14ff.

[32] Marcuse, "Repressive Tolerance," in R. P. Wolff, B. Moore, and
H. Marcuse, *A Critique of Pure Tolerance* (Boston: Beacon, 1965),
p. 88; *Essay on Liberation*, p. 30.

the system which characterizes "liberal" society at the present time.[33]

It is evident that the principal source of Marcuse's difficulties as a "non-Marxist Marxist" is the absence of a revolutionary working class—a class that classical Marxism conceived to be the vehicle of a liberating world revolution. Marx conceived the proletariat as revolutionary as a consequence of pervasive and increasing deprivation that not only provided the occasion for systemic revolution but also schooled that majoritarian class to appreciate its real and *rational* interests. Both Marx and Engels conceived revolutionary consciousness to be the product of a rational appreciation of the transparent disabilities of advanced capitalism. Marcuse and all the spokesmen of the New Left have been compelled to abandon that vision of the saving revolution. Howard Zinn has insisted that "the traditional Marxian idea of a revolution taking place because of a breakdown in the capitalist mechanism and an organized class-conscious proletariat taking over, is hardly tenable today." The New Left must commit itself to "revolutionary action" which is "not . . . preoccupied with prediction or with measuring immediate success . . . ." This is what Zinn calls an "existentialist emphasis on the necessity for action—based on conscience, avoiding that cool and careful weighing of 'the realities' . . . ." "We are unabashed," Zinn goes on, "in declaring our subjective wants and desires—without needing a 'scientific' basis for such wants." As a consequence classical Marxism becomes totally irrelevant to the revolutionaries of the New Left. "I confess," Zinn continues, "that I cannot see how [Marx's] dense Volume II of *Das Kapital* . . .[is] essential to revolutionary theory. . . . Even so brilliant a theory as that of surplus-value—how relevant is it to social action?" Marxism, in fact, gives least guidance to "the most urgent theoretical problem of the New Left . . . : how do we change society."[34]

[33] Marcuse, *One Dimensional Man*, pp. 40f.

[34] H. Zinn, "Marxism and the New Left," in Long, *The New Left*, pp. 66, 68, 64.

Marcuse has been equally explicit. Modern industrial reality "seems to cancel the Marxian notion of the 'organic composition of capital' and with it the theory of the creation of surplus value."[35] Thus Marcuse rejects most of the partially formalized theory to which Marx devoted his life and on which all the less general entailments rest for their ultimate warrant. The consequences are that Marcuse rejects not only Marx's conception of the role of the proletariat in historic transformation but most of the substance of Marxism as well. Rather than Marxian theory, he invokes quaint and curious instincts such as the "death instinct" and "eros" to explain contemporary events. Precious little of classical Marxism has survived the "creative development" at the hands of some of the principal spokesmen of the New Left.

What results is no less than a variant of Fascism. When Mussolini began his searching review of classical Marxism he opted for a revolutionary theory predicated on the supposition that men in the aggregate were moved by psychological and emotional impulses by and large determined by what Pareto called "residues," "prepotent dispositions." "Residues" were, for Pareto, prepotent dispositions to behave, which gave rise, in turn, to "derivations," the variable, "mythic" form in which those dispositions found expression. Mussolini argued that men were disposed to organize themselves in collective solidarities predicated on what Mosca and Michels called "political formulae" or "myths." The political myths or derivations of which they spoke were the products of a directive elite, intellectuals in our own time, who advanced the formulae as pedagogical guides to collective orientation. Mussolini insisted that Marx had not delivered an adequate assessment of human motivation. Marx must be supplemented and transcended through an appreciation of the "realities" of the twentieth century. The proletariat could make no revolution without the intercession of a self-selected minority of revolutionary intellectuals who would organize the energies of men via political myths, imaginative non-intellectualistic formulations.

[35] Marcuse, *One Dimensional Man*, p. 28.

Not only had Marx failed adequately to assess the role of political myths in mass mobilization, Mussolini contended, but his economic analyses had themselves been revealed as wanting. Marxism, therefore, became more and more irrelevant to Fascist strategy and tactics. Fascism simply abandoned "the economic laws of Marxism" as constraints on the revolution. The revolution must define itself in *act*. Action, rather than empty formulations, inspired revolutionary ardor among the mobilizable population elements available to the directive revolutionary elite.

After the revolution the Fascists would create the "new man"—the product of a controlled educational environment —the pedagogical task which elite rule imposes on revolutionary leadership.

Since every society is dominated by a ruling minoritarian elite which inures the majority of men to control through the functional myths of the system, Fascists argued, the substitution of elites can only be the consequence of violent confrontation between established and contending elites. The commitment of each elite is embodied in a political formula which defines the obligations of the revolutionary masses. A contending minoritarian elite can only reject the functional formulae of the ensconced conservative minority. In so doing they invoke repression. The response to repression by one world view is, within the context of the established order, violence. Revolutionary violence is opposed to institutional force (a conceptual distinction Mussolini adopted from Georges Sorel).[36] Such an account provides, in schematic outline, the character of Fascist "confrontation politics"—the rationale for political violence.

Mussolini's rationale for political violence is all but indistinguishable from that of Marcuse and his New Left adherents. Marcuse insists that in order to reopen the closed confines of the "one dimensional society," in which the vast majority of men are inured to prevailing "false consciousness," one requires the employment of "apparently undemo-

[36] Cf. A. J. Gregor, *The Ideology of Fascism* (New York: Free Press, 1969), chaps. 2 and 3.

cratic means." One "withdraws tolerance" from those groups which violate what the New Left, given its revolutionary world view, sees as "repressive, chauvinistic and antisocial." The "liberating violence" of the New Left must necessarily violate "ethical standards"—for, Marcuse reminds us, "since when is history made in accordance with ethical standards?" Only their own conscience can be the ultimate judge of the necessity of violence on the part of revolutionaries—and in the last analysis, "the end justifies the means."[37]

The fascination with political violence has become a central theme in the literature of the New Left. Often even Marcuse has been forced to deplore its indiscriminate use. But its "liberating" function is more and more conceived as central to revolutionary tactics by some of the most prominent spokesmen of the New Left. Marshall McLuhan, for example, has argued that not only is violence necessary for making a revolution—but it serves intrapsychic and mobilizing purposes as well. "Violence and struggle," McLuhan maintains, "are themselves the means of creating new identity."[38] This thesis is elaborated upon by Frantz Fanon, now so popular among student radicals. His contention is more elaborate and more revealing. "At the level of individuals," Fanon contends, "violence is a cleansing force." It frees man from "his inferiority complex and from his despair and inaction; it makes him fearless and restores his self-respect." More than that, violence is an effective mobilizing tactic. It is "violence that unites the people." "Violence alone, violence committed by the people, violence organized and educated by its leaders, makes it possible for the masses to understand social truths and gives the key to them."[39] "Violence," Jean-Paul Sartre, another favorite of the New Left, informs us,

[37] Marcuse, "Repressive Tolerance," pp. 102f., 117; *Essay on Liberation*, p. 73; "Ethics and Revolution," in R. T. De George, *Ethics and Society* (Garden City, N.Y.: Doubleday, 1966), p. 147.

[38] M. McLuhan, "Retribalized Makers," in Klein, *Natural Enemies*, p. 343.

[39] F. Fanon, *The Wretched of the Earth* (New York: Grove, 1963), pp. 73, 117.

". . . is man re-creating himself."[40] Fascists, half a century ago, argued the same theses.

Both Marx and Engels, on the other hand, conceived violence as a sometimes *necessary evil* that attends revolution. Marx argued that revolution could come to the most advanced industrial nations *without* violence—simply because advanced industrialization would create a rational awareness of an alternate society *among the vast majority* of the population. Engels insisted that the proletariat might be driven to violence, but only *when the bourgeoisie found itself compelled to violate the constitutional norms that protected the will of a sovereign people.* Neither Marx nor Engels conceived violence as a mobilizing tactic, a long-range strategy, a resolution for feelings of unworthiness, a source of truth, or the occasion for the "recreation" of man. Mussolini, and Fascists in general, on the other hand, conceived violence as a mobilizing tactic, a means by which conservative political formulae might lose their capacity to mesmerize the masses. Fascists also insisted that violence was an irrepressible moral necessity if men were to shake off the trammels of bourgeois sentimentality and egotism. Only when one faced life's greatest challenge in preparing to sacrifice for one's beliefs would one transcend the limitations of the bourgeois world view with its selfishness, its materialism, and its lack of moral commitment.

Mussolini conceived that the fulfillment of man could only be purchased at the price of committing oneself to a "collective life"—a life within a moral community for which one is prepared to make ultimate sacrifice. War and violence served these moral ends for Fascism.

The rationale advanced by the intellectual spokesmen of the New Left provides justificatory arguments for the activism, the violence, and the irrationality of the most radical elements of the New Left. All these spokesmen conceive "truth" to be the product of some arcane enterprise distinct from what is characterized as the "operationalism" and the

[40] Introduction to Fanon, *ibid.*, p. 18.

"logical-empiricism" that has become central to the rationality of the mature industrial societies outside the socialist sphere. Marcuse maintains that revolutionaries must embrace a strategy he calls "dialectical," one untrammeled by precision and rigor, and which finds "contradiction" compatible with truth.

He offers a number of formulations which characterize his "dialectic." They include formulae such as "Reason = Truth = Reality" conjoined with a claim that "epistemology is in itself ethics and ethics is epistemology," which seems to mean that the search for truth delivers moral principles and moral principles are "reality" and "reality" is "reason" —all of which is predicated on "intuition," which is a form of cognition "in which the object of thought appears clearly as that which it really is . . . ." Since "intuition" can deliver such truths about reality, and truths about reality are identical with ethical truths, what we seem to have is a restatement of moral intuitionism, an appeal to personal conscience for the justification of whatever acts the individual chooses to undertake.[41]

This quaint rationale (which less tolerant critics have called simple nonsense) is couched in terms of "definitions as meaningless as the terms defined," in sentences loosely formulated and dense. Even New Left commentators have recognized a disposition on Marcuse's part to "aphorize" rather than undertake "disciplined thinking"—the literary counterpart of the New Left's disposition to talk in slogans and communicate through graffiti.[42]

In this sense the rationale for New Left style is a caricature of Fascist justificatory argument. Only few Fascist theoreticians succeeded in justifying irrationality and intuitionism to the same measure as Marcuse, Theodore Roszak, and R. D. Laing. Roszak's notion of "myth" as "crystallizing the

[41] Marcuse, *One Dimensional Man*, pp. 12f., 124f.

[42] Marks, *The Meaning of Marcuse*, p. 56; J. Cohen, "Critical Theory: The Philosophy of Marcuse," *New Left Review*, 57 (September-October 1969), 35-51.

great, central values of a culture," his appeal to "imaginative exuberance, for moral purity, for passion," and to a "new shamanism" in which men will "lose themselves in nature," a harkening to a "cultural stage buried in the primitive past of our society," are all themes that were recurrent in a special *genre* of Fascist literature. R. D. Laing's insistence that "we can put no trust in princes, popes, politicians, scholars or scientists, . . . [but] with the greatest precautions, we may put trust in a source that is much deeper than our egos . . ." was long ago anticipated by Julius Evola in his attempt to provide a noncognitive rationale for Fascist style and strategy.

Evola maintained, for instance, that "Wisdom" (*Sapienza*) could only be the product of a most "intimate silence" accompanied by "acts"—a consequence of "living life" rather than the conclusion of "arguments and books." True knowledge is found in "transcendental thought," in the "Wisdom" of the past—not in "shamanism" perhaps, but in the Hermetic and Pythagorean mysteries or the Vedic texts. What one must resist, Evola insisted, is "positive science," since its requirement of public and intersubjective truth conditions are irretrievably "democratic." "Wisdom," for Evola must be "personal," rooted in the deepest recesses of the "absolute individual," acquired "neither in books or universities nor transmitted by words . . . ."[43]

The contemporary vogue among radical students for phenomenology, numerology, astrology, ancient wisdom, sacred texts, intuition, and mysticism was long ago anticipated by a collection of minor Fascist ideologues. While Mussolini had little patience with such attempts to justify Fascist style and strategy, he was content to permit their distribution. Mussolini insisted that, while the masses are mobilized by myths and mysticism, the directive elect were required to

[43] J. Evola, *Imperialismo pagano* (Rome, Atanor, 1928), pp. 12, 72, 76; cf. also Evola, *Rivolta contro il mondo moderno* (Milan: Hoepli, 1934) and *Fenomenologia dell'individuo assoluto* (Turin: Bocca, 1930).

formulate policy on the basis of the best available evidence. He refused to grant that truth was the product of "intuition," the "dialectic," or rummaging about in the inner recesses of the self.[44] Nonetheless, Fascist literary hacks did turn out an inordinate amount of mystic and intuitionistic irrationalist literature, which in many respects is indistinguishable from their New Left counterparts. The "higher rationality" to which Evola appealed fifty years ago has the species characteristics of the "new rationality" of Marcuse, Roszak, and Laing.

Irrationalism, the conviction that public reason cannot mediate the differences between men, that truth is the product of some special noncognitive mode—whether it be the "dialectic" or the new "shamanism"—can lead only to violence or manipulation as the ultimate arbiter between contesting groups. The insistence on the part of some New Left theoreticians that "positive science," "empiricism," and reasoned discourse are, in principle, incapable of reducing the distance between opponents, can only serve as a justification for violence or the manipulation of "myth," "instinct," or "emotion."

Activism, voluntarism, intransigence, the disposition to invoke violence and exploit the gullibility of the masses share a common logic with anti-intellectualism and irrationalism. Such a logic was implicit and explicit in Futurism. It is equally implicit and explicit among our student and non-student Yippies. The intellectual youth masters of the New Left have attempted its justification. In doing so they have invoked a caricature of Fascist argument and abandoned not only the substance but the spirit of classical Marxism. Lenin would have been equally embarrassed by their postures. Whatever else he was, Lenin was a rationalist in the strict sense of the rationalism of the Enlightenment. He was convinced that Marxism was positive science—and that truth was a product of scientific inquiry. Lenin, in effect, while he may have adopted Fascist content, resisted Fascist style. The New Left has embraced it.

[44] Cf. Gregor, *Ideology of Fascism*, 113-27.

THE NEW LEFT AND FASCIST CONTENT:
RADICAL ANTI-NATIONALISM

If a case can be made for the adoption of Fascist *style* by significant elements among the student New Left, it is frequently argued that the *content* of the New Left clearly distinguishes it from Fascism. The student New Left in the advanced capitalist countries is invariably anti-nationalist as well as consistently anti-authoritarian and anarchistic.

Joseph Califano, in his survey of student movements in the nonsocialist industrial countries, concludes that radical students "have little respect for and virtually no sense of nationalism."[45] Futurists and Fascists, on the other hand, gave expression to an irrepressible nationalism.

The vast majority of commentators, both detractors and enthusiasts, further describes the radical student movement as anti-authoritarian and anarchistic. Bernd Rabehl simply describes radical students as members of an "anti-authoritarian movement," and Daniel Cohn-Bendit sets most of the tone for student radicalism with his rejection of all forms of authoritarianism.[46] Fascism, on the other hand, was nothing if it was not authoritarian and hierarchical.

Anti-nationalism, of course, is something of an anomaly among radical movements in the twentieth century. Not a single successful political revolution in our century has failed to enjoy the support of a pervasive nationalist sentiment. Bolshevism very rapidly fell back to nationalism. Maoism would never have been successul had it failed to invoke peasant nationalism; and Castroism was animated by, and remains infused with, a consuming nationalism.

Radical students in the industrialized, nonsocialist nations, on the other hand, have developed a strange disposition that manifests itself in deprecating everything about

[45] Califano, *The Student Revolution*, pp. 64, 38.

[46] B. Rabehl, "Von der antiautoritären Bewegung zur sozialistischen Opposition," in *Rebellion der Studenten oder die neue Opposition* (Reinbek bei Hamburg: Rowohlt, 1968), 151-78; D. Cohn-Bendit, *Obsolete Communism: The Left-Wing Alternative* (New York: McGraw-Hill, 1968).

349

their individual nations, its traditions, its character, and its culture. Unlike the successful revolutionaries of the twentieth century, the student radicals rarely if ever talk about restoring the "grandeur" of the nation, reestablishing its traditions, or mobilizing people in its service. They speak of their nations as totally bankrupt and corrupt, incorrigibly evil and irretrievably debased. The United States of America, as a case in point, is, for radicals, "old, weary and consumptive." America is a "sick society"; it is the "Pig Nation." Jerry Rubin insists that the only cause that can mobilize radical students is "anti-Americanism."[47] The trajectory followed by many student radicals is graphically traced by Dotson Rader in his *I Ain't Marchin' Anymore*. Beginning with a belief in America and its institutions, the dissenting students gradually convinced themselves, or became convinced, that America was "violent and corrupt," that they could "no longer [believe] in the essential decency of the American people, that given the truth the majority had the honesty and the compassion and the guts to do what was right and necessary."[48]

Ranging from a total disinterest in patriotism and nationalism to a violent rejection of the nation and its history and traditions, many if not most student radicals are manifestly anti-nationalist.

While all this is true, the anti-nationalism of student radicals displays a curious ambivalence. Student radicalism will all but invariably *support the nationalism so rife in underdeveloped nations*. They are unembarrassed by the overt nationalism of Castro's Cuba or Mao's China. They have at various times supported Arab nationalism and the nationalism that inflames the African states. No matter how repressive such regimes might be, no matter how violent their postures, how sanguinary their actions, student radicals will support "Third World" nationalism. No matter how conclusive the evidence available that establishes the arbitrari-

[47] J. Rubin, "Don't Trust Anyone over Thirty-Four," *Berkeley Barb*, 6, 5 (February 2-8, 1968).
[48] Rader, *I Ain't Marchin' Anymore*, pp. 82f.

ness of Nkrumah's regime, for example, student radicals still reinvoke its memory with nostalgia. No matter how repressive Mao's regime is with respect to ethnic minorities in China, student radicals mount no protest. When housewives in Cuba protested food rationing and their protests were silenced with a display of armed might that included tanks and machine guns, students in the advanced industrial countries raised no outcry.

The logic of student engagement in these instances is perhaps best revealed in a simple dichotomy. Student radicals have bifurcated the world into two camps, the "proletarian nations" as opposed to the "have nations." And they have pledged their uncritical loyalty to the nationalism of "proletarian states." Marcuse has called attention to this aspect of New Left thought. He suggests that the advanced industrial nations, both those identified as "capitalist" and those spoken of as "socialist," have made common cause against the "have-nots"[49]—what the Fascists had, early in this century, called the "proletarian nations." In the "proletarian nations" many of the theoreticians of the New Left have found not only a *surrogate proletariat* but a *surrogate nationality*. Rudi Dutschke, one of the most prominent of West Germany's radical students, has declaimed that "the underprivileged of the world provide the actual mass base for the historic liberation movement . . . ." Bernd Rabelh has spoken of the radical students' "voluntary identification with the revolutionaries of the Third World. . . . These radical students conceive themselves the agents of the Third World in their war of liberation against the metropolitan powers. . . ."[50]

Radical students have, in effect, resolved the problem of nationalism that revolutionaries inherited from Marxism by *adopting* a nationalism: Cuban nationalism, or Chinese na-

[49] Marcuse, *Essay on Liberation*, p. 85.

[50] R. Dutschke, "Die Widersprüeche des Spätkapitalismus, die antiautoritären Studenten und im Verhältnis zur Dritten Welt," p. 85, and B. Rabehl, "Von der antiautoritären Bewegung . . . ," pp. 164, 165, in *Rebellion der Studenten oder Die neue Opposition*.

tionalism, or North Vietnamese nationalism or all these nationalisms together. They will deck themselves with the symbols and tokens of foreign nationalisms. More and more frequently radical students will not rest content with objections to American foreign policy—they will adopt the flags, uniforms, and slogans of foreign nationalisms. They become participants in a "national war of liberation"—only the nation they support is North Vietnam or Cuba, or China, or perhaps any or all of the African states.

In their commitment to the nationalisms of the Third World, radical students very rarely undertake any systematic study of one or another developing society to assess its potential for "democratic" development, for the "soulful socialism" they advocate. They lend themselves uncritically to a carrier movement that represents a virulent nationalism—Cuban nationalism, North Vietnamese nationalism, Chinese nationalism, or any number of other nationalisms—as long as they are the nationalisms of "proletarian nations."

The entire discussion of proletarian nations, while frequently couched in Leninist terms of "imperialism," shares far more kinship to Fascist notions. Lenin continued to remain convinced that the revolutions in the backward areas of the world would ultimately invoke the proletariat of the advanced West—without whom socialism could not be achieved.[51] Fascists, on the other hand, insisted that the proletarian nations would have to forge their nationhood, achieve dignity and a place in the sun, employing their own energy—in sanguinary struggle against the "plutocratic powers."

In the conditions that prevail in the modern world there is no suggestion that the nationalisms of Cuba, China, and North Vietnam will ultimately give way to an "internationalism" devoid of nationalism. Castro's Cuba has all too frequently given evidence of its indisposition to surrender its national sovereignty to any "socialist" international. China

[51] A. J. Gregor, *A Survey of Marxism* (New York: Random House, 1965), pp. 227-37; M. Lewin, *Lenin's Last Struggle* (New York: Random House, 1968), chap. 1.

is equally independent. North Vietnam no less so. In point of fact the "proletarian internationalism" to which Lenin aspired has dissolved in the revolutionary nationalism of the twentieth century. The New Left is disposed to "identify" with that nationalism—only it is an uncritically adopted nationalism; it is Cuban, Chinese, or a vague Third World nationalism that gives radical students the sense of community and purpose that nationalism provides. Radical students have shown themselves more than prepared to identify with the nationalistic charismatic heroes of the Third World: with Castro or Guevara, with Ho Chi Minh or Mao Tse-tung.

If the radical New Left has succeded in caricaturing Fascist style, elements of the New Left have succeeded in re-creating Fascist content by adopting as their own an unselected set of foreign nationalisms. The conviction that "the proletariat of American capitalism is the international proletariat of the third world"[52] has committed many radical students to nationalisms no less emotional, no less chauvinistic, no less militant than any nationalist commitment made by any Fascist.

Radical students, and their adult spokesmen, seem vaguely aware of the curiosity of their political postures. Marcuse, himself, has recognized that many, if not all, the nationalisms supported by radicals may very well generate societies of "total administration more violent and more rigid than that traversed by the advanced societies which can build on the achievements of the liberalistic era." He goes on to lament: "To sum up: the backward areas are likely to succumb either to one of the various forms of neo-colonialism, or to a more or less terroristic system of primary accumulation."[53]

The anti-nationalism of radical students in the advanced industrial countries is thus a curious and ambivalent anti-nationalism. Its obverse is an adopted nationalism which commits radical students to the support of political systems which give every evidence of developing into bureaucratic,

[52] J. S. Kunen, *The Strawberry Statement: Notes of a College Revolutionary* (New York: Avon, 1970), p. 155.
[53] Marcuse, *One Dimensional Man*, p. 47.

"administered societies" in which terror becomes an instrument of policy. More than that, the nationalisms with which they have identified are characterized by one-party regimes, controlled information, charismatic and hierarchical leadership, and a military-heroic and histrionic style that can only be identified as fascistic. That radical students frequently conceive the proletarian nations of the Third World as the vehicle of the saving revolution indicates their Fascist, rather than their Leninist, much less Marxist persuasion. Lenin never conceived of the underdeveloped regions of the globe ushering in the Marxist millennium. Until the end of his life he remained convinced that the historic agent of revolution was the proletariat of the advanced countries of the West. Only they, according to Marxist theory, could have achieved the degree of intellectual and technical maturity adequate to the governance of an advanced industrial economy, and only they would inherit the very material base which would make a classless society a reality.

The non-Marxist character of student radicalism becomes increasingly apparent precisely at this juncture. Student radicals recognize the nonrevolutionary character of the proletariat of the advanced industrial nations. Much of Marcuse's prose, for example, is devoted to an analysis of this painful reality. Marcuse talks of the "radical and total rebellion" on the part of student radicals standing in stark contrast to "the absence of a class basis for this radicalism on the other." Elsewhere he laments that the forces of "liberation" find themselves "without a mass basis." He goes on to indicate that "today we cannot identify any specific class or any specific group as a revolutionary force . . . ."[54]

The Fascists had early advanced such arguments. The class analysis of Marxism was inadequate to the facts of the twentieth century. Revolution was not a specifically class phenomenon. "Bourgeois mentality" was not the exclusive possession of the bourgeoisie. Groups that could *not* be iden-

[54] Marcuse, *Essay on Liberation*, p. 79; "Liberation from the Affluent Society," in G. Bateson et al., *To Free A Generation* (New York: Collier, 1969), pp. 176, 187.

tified solely or essentially by class characteristics provided the revolutionary will, energy, and demographic base for revolution—and, within the larger context, revolution was the consequence of "proletarian nations" undertaking wars of liberation to free men from the dominance of the "plutocratic powers." One of the principal propaganda theses of Fascism during the Second World War was "the struggle between two worlds": the "proletarian" against the "plutocratic" and "imperialist" nations. The Axis powers exploited the theme sufficiently to win the collaboration of many nationalists in the Third World. Both Sukarno and Chandra Bose expressed sympathy with the "anti-imperialism" of the Axis. The nationalist Neo-Destour of Tunisia received active support from Fascist Italy, and Nasser of Egypt entertained contact with the Fascists and National Socialists. All the elements were to resurface after the war as national movements of liberation—to become the surrogate proletariat of the New Left.[55]

The student New Left has not succeeded in resolving the problems of the nonrevolutionary proletariat and nationalism. Finding themselves denizens of an environment which offers no mass base for their radicalism, much of their radicalism degenerates into a frustrated caricature of Fascist style. Incapable or unwilling to mobilize by using native nationalism, they have adopted foreign nationalisms. The rationale advanced to support that adoption has little, if anything, to do with Marxism or Leninism. They have simply opted for an inverse Fascist content. They support "proletarian nations" against the "imperialist nations."

The New Left and Fascist Content: Anti-Authoritarianism

That the student radicals advertise themselves as anti-authoritarian, in fact, anarchistic, is so generally accepted that documentation is hardly necessary. Student radicals have

---

[55] Cf. L. Garruccio, *L'industrializzazione tra nazionalismo e rivoluzione* (Bologna: Mulino, 1969), p. 17.

regularly denounced not only the United States but the Soviet Union and the "orthodox" Communist Parties as authoritarian and bureaucratic. It is not uncommon, today, to hear radical students or their senior spokesmen express sentiments concerning the Soviet Union of the following sort:

> The proletarian dictatorship, which naive souls believe is an inevitable transition stage to real Socialism, has today grown into a frightful despotism and a new imperialism, which lags behind the tyranny of Fascist states in nothing. . . . The development of the Bolshevist bureaucracy in Russia under the alleged dictatorship of the proletariat has never been anything but the dictatorship of a small clique over the proletariat and the whole Russian people . . . .[56]

Rudi Dutschke speaks of an "authoritarian hegemony that extends from Washington to Vladivostok." Danny Cohn-Bendit has asserted that "the Bolsheviks were responsible for holding back the struggle of the masses . . . and later for turning the revolution into a bureaucratic counterrevolution . . . ."[57]

Radical students seem genuinely animated by anti-authoritarian sentiments. At this point in history, however, it is necessary to remind ourselves that the Futurists of Marinetti were more anarchistic than the anarchists, and it was Mussolini, in 1920, who called for a return to Max Stirner—one of the fathers of modern anarchism. No revolutionaries could be more anarchistic, anti-structuralist, and anti-hierarchical than were the Futurists—and yet the Futurists passed, without remainder, into the Fascist ranks. The Russian Futurists served the purposes of the Bolsheviks.

The fact is that a movement committed to anti-ideological and anti-intellectual postures, embroiled in activism and in-

[56] R. Rocker, "Anarcho-syndicalism," in Long, *The New Left*, p. 48.
[57] Dutschke, "Die Widersprüche . . . ," p. 92; Cohn-Bendit, *Obsolete Communism*, p. 201.

tuitionism, unconfined by programmatic goals or principled strategies, can lend itself to anything. When an anti-authoritarian and anti-hierarchical movement can applaud the authoritarianism of Mao Tse-tung and the hierarchical dispositions of Fidel Castro, almost anything is possible.

Mussolini's Fascism was, by his own definition, "unprejudiced" (*anti-pregiudiziaiole*). Fascists were prepared to accept into their ranks radical syndicalists (in large numbers), activistic Sorellians, anarchistic Futurists (as critically important cadre of the first *Fasci*), and simple anarchists (the anarchists made common cause, for a time, with Gabriele d'Annunzio and the Arditi). Mussolini, in fact, bruited some anarchistic sentiments and defended the anarchist leader Errico Malatesta in 1920. As we have already indicated, the Futurists, who identified their political position as more anarchist than that of the anarchists, found no difficulty in making common cause with Fascism.

Any political movement that insists that life and politics are contradictory, and that one must assume "dialectical" postures vis-à-vis contemporary reality, can be expected to manifest the most unpredictable patterns of behavior. One need but consider Castro's exaltation of freedom, liberty and constitutionality—his rejection of military conscription as a violation of basic human rights—his objection to "bureaucracy"—and compare it with the new institutionalized features of his regime, to recognize how very rapidly "anti-structuralist" and "anti-authoritarian" convictions can be transmogrified by a revolutionary movement having no specific strategies and no specific goals. Similarly, one need but recall the anti-authoritarian sentiments voiced by Mao's Red Guards and compare the intention with the reality of China's hierarchical system, to find oneself beset with more than some misgivings.

One can entertain only a faint sense of security in the reiteration of anti-authoritarian commitment on the part of radical students. The institutional features of Fascism did not become fully manifest until some considerable time after the stabilization of power. By that time Fascism had fully absorbed the radical student movement—and fully contained all its "anti-authoritarian" pretensions.

An anti-authoritarian movement that manifests only admiration for authoritarian and hierarchical systems like that of China and Cuba, composed of activists animated by an irrepressible conviction in the impeccability of their own moral insights, impatient with the "vast majority" of men afflicted with "false consciousness," prepared to employ any means to achieve obscure ends, is one that can hardly allay our misgivings by voicing anti-bureaucratic sentiments.

Given the pressures of insurrectional activities, the necessities of continuity and experienced leadership, the recruitment and mobilization advantages of having "charismatic" leadership—one would expect student movements to display more and more of the features of Fascist populism. Just as Fascist content seems to require Fascist style, *Fascist style tends to generate Fascist content*. Should an anti-authoritarian movement enjoy any significant increments in the prospects of success, one can expect it to take on Fascist leadership, organizational and strategic characteristics. This has been the case with so many of the mass-mobilizing revolutionary movements of the twentieth century, no matter how firmly they articulated their initial "anti-authoritarian" intentions, that one has little reason to believe that the radical student movement could avoid such an involution. One need but recall the anarco-syndicalist aspirations of Lenin's *The State and Revolution*, and compare them to the state apparatus and leadership characteristics that almost immediately became institutionalized in the Bolshevik regime, to realize that the most heartfelt intentions of revolutionaries are readily sacrificed on the altar of political success and secure political tenure.

Leopold Labedz has maintained that "the only common feature of the students' revolt is their rebellious mood, and its historical originality is that it appeared in the highly industrialized countries. Neither its practice nor its 'theory' are coherent enough to be seen as an attempt to seek ratonal goals by rational means. . . . It is a mixture in which ironically, elitist philosophy and dictatorial practice are supposed to serve as a guide to a participatory democracy in a permissive society. . . . Many of the postures and fads displayed in them look like a parody of similar manifestations in the past, in a situation very different, and the young actors seem insufficiently aware of this. . . . The followers of a movement which exalts romanticism, anti-rationalism, *Gemeinschaft* (the community feeling), makes action a self-justificatory criterion, and who are fascinated by violence, can—and do—evoke memories of a movement which extolled all these elements not so long ago . . . ."[58]

It goes without saying that when one isolates the fascist elements in student radicalism one has not *identified* the latter with its prototype. The radical student movement is not fascist. Its nationalism, characteristically, is a *fictive* nationalism—either the adopted nationalism of the Third World or the fantasy nationalism of "Woodstock Nation." Student radicals, responding to the felt need of a community, have chosen to make foreign nationalisms their own or have created a drug-induced "nation" out of their hard-rock music festivals. Abbie Hoffman's nationalism, his appeal to the radical youth of the United States to create "a nation within the nation," is a pathetic *caricature* of Fascist nationalism. The cultural chauvinism, the intolerance, the aggressiveness, and the aspirations of "Woodstock Nation" constitute the nonviable surrogate nationalism of an adolescent and/or psychopathic fascism, the analogue of Lenin's "left wing communism, an infantile disorder." Student radicals have attempted to resolve the two basic problems of classical Marxism—the absence of a revolutionary proletariat and the reality of nationalist sentiment—by creating a *surrogate* proletariat and adopting a *fictive* nationalism for themselves. In that sense the student radical movement contains elements that represent a caricature of Fascism—a "left wing fascism—an adolescent disorder."

[58] L. Labedz, "Students and Revolution," *Survey*, 68 (July 1968), 5, 20.

The Black Variant of Fascism

If the most extreme elements of student radicalism have an insubstantial and adolescent quality—and their fascism is a caricature of the prototype—the fascism of black radicals is far more substantial, more interesting, more serious, and, ultimately, more dangerous. The fascism of "black nationalism" is grounded in the reality of black experience in the United States. It is the product of an historical and intellectual tradition that has always been vital among blacks; and as a political style and strategy it succeeds in invoking response among an appreciable number of black men. In that sense, the fascism of black nationalism is more substantial, interesting and serious. That as a political strategy and a style of political rhetoric it has found appreciable response in the black community makes it dangerous—not only to the white community but to the black as well.

The characterization of black nationalism as "black fascism" has become fairly commonplace. Gene Marine alludes to the disposition of commentators to so characterize the Black Panthers—the most contemporary variant of black nationalism.[59] But the association with Fascism goes much further back than the Black Panthers and has far more substance than tangential references to military trappings, violent postures, and paramilitary discipline. Mass-mobilizing black nationalism arose in this century under the leadership of Marcus Garvey, the founder and leader of the Universal Negro Improvement Association. The UNIA was founded by Garvey, a West Indian, in 1914—and in 1917 the first American branch was established in Harlem. From that point until the mid-twenties the membership of the association expanded, and Garvey claimed that six million Negroes

---

[59] G. Marine, *The Black Panthers* (New York: Signet, 1969), p. 37; cf. N. Hill, *The Black Panther Menace: America's Neo-Nazis* (New York: Popular, 1971); M. Curtis, "Retreat from Totalitarianism," in C. J. Friedrich, M. Curtis, and B. R. Barber, *Totalitarianism in Perspective* (New York: Praeger, 1969), p. 112.

had enrolled.[60] In 1928 he insisted that the UNIA had eleven million members scattered over the globe. While the most responsible estimates of the actual membership of the UNIA give figures far less substantial,[61] there is no doubt that the Garvey movement was the first Negro mass-mobilizing movement of the twentieth century; and it was Garvey himself who, in 1937, characterized his movement as "fascist." Garvey, after the Fascist invasion of Ethiopia, had denounced Mussolini and his "violent, Roman hogs," but went on, nonetheless, to say that "We were the first Fascists. . . . Mussolini copied Fascism from me . . . ."[62]

E. David Cronon has suggested that the UNIA, "with its fierce chauvinistic nationalism and strongly centralized leadership, had fascist characteristics," but that Garvey was not "aware of all the connotations of . . . fascism . . . ."[63] All of which may well be true. Garvey surely was unaware of many of the "connotations" that would collect around fascism as a consequence of a lost war. The term in our own time serves as little more than an epithet. It has become a simple term of derogation—having little, if any, cognitive meaning. Garvey, however, understood the term as it was employed in his time—to refer to a mass-mobilizing political movement, characterized by its proper style, strategy, and content. He understood Fascism as a revolutionary and developmental nationalism—and attributed the failure of his fascism, equally revolutionary, developmental, and nation-

[60] Cf. R. Ottley, *New World A-Coming* (New York: Farrar, Straus & Giroux, 1943), pp. 68-81; A. Edwards, *Marcus Garvey* (London: New Beacon, 1967), p. 39.

[61] M. Garvey, *Philosophy and Opinions of Marcus Garvey* (New York: Atheneum, 1969), II, 131, 183, 212. Cf. E. D. Cronon, *Black Moses: The Story of Marcus Garvey and the Universal Negro Improvement Association* (Madison: University of Wisconsin, 1955), pp. 204-207.

[62] J. A. Rogers, *The World's Great Men of Color* (New York: Rogers, 1946), II, 602.

[63] Cronon, *Black Moses*, p. 199.

alist, to the influence of "Negro reactionaries" who "sabo-taged" it.

Garvey's characterization of his movement as "fascist" is more than reasonable. Even his claim of priority has some substance. The first tentative outlines of his political move-ment were formulated in 1914, when Mussolini was first reordering his specifically socialist commitments. Garvey anticipated much of the Fascist political style, Fascist or-ganizational structure, and Fascist programmatic goals sev-eral years before the official meetings at San Sepolcro that founded the "first Fascism." Both characterized themselves as mass-mobilizing developmental nationalisms.

A mass-mobilizing movement appeals, characteristically, to a volatile constituency animated by a pervasive sense of general deprivation, of political alienation, status insecurity, and role ambivalence. Mobilizable individuals are generally characterized by an insistent disposition to redefine them-selves by entertaining a belief system that offers them the promise of status and place, specific role functions, and prestige enhancements. A leader who appeals to such a constituency is generally gifted with qualities we now iden-tify with "personal charisma"—oratorical skills and personal magnetism that inspire confidence. In circumstances of pro-tracted crisis, such a leader enjoys "situational charisma" and a "mass" collects around him. Protracted crisis erodes traditional loyalties. If a population is dislocated, recently inmigrant, particularly from rural to urban areas, for exam-ple, it is destabilized, and its members provide the material for mass mobilization. Such a mass is susceptible to appeals that tap free-floating discontent. Individuals that constitute the "mass" do not identify themselves with specific class or occupational functions in the established society, for such individuals have no socially defined roles in their new envi-ronment. Such traits, conjoined with a pervasive sense of the desirability of change, render such a mass eminently mobi-lizable.

In an environment where such a mass is available, a leader can collect a following by articulating a program that holds real or fictive promise of restoring a lost sense of community, security, upward mobility, and/or purpose. In order to restore a lost sense of community—a sense of collective identification—a leader may, for example, exploit collective traits of high visibility or alternatively provide high visibility by introducing uniforms or identifying symbols. The new community so invoked is identified with collective travail, past glories, anticipated future victories, and/or a cosmic destiny that will reorder contemporary priorities and restore lost values or fashion new ones.

In the twentieth century such movements have regularly employed the expressive language and the symbolism of nationalism to create the reactive sense of community necessary to the organization of a mass movement. Restive masses in the twentieth century have not collected themselves behind the standards of class, as Marx anticipated, but rather around the affective imagery of nationality. The new radicalism of our time has been unable to move masses with the rationale inherited from Marx—with his conception of "a class in-and-for-itself," possessed of the rational appreciation of its collective interests. The new radicalism has moved masses through the employment of nationalist exhortation. The masses they have moved have not been long-established urban working classes, but dispossessed masses, masses destabilized by protracted war, economic dislocation, or urban inmigration. The *established* working classes have regularly proved "conservative" and "reformist" in disposition. Having well-defined social roles, long-established urban working classes have been unmoved by revolutionary Marxist appeals. Mass movements have been composed of the young, the downwardly mobile, the status-threatened, the rural inmigrants or peasantry dislocated by war or foreign invasion, that is to say, groups without stable social roles.

Paradigmatic Fascism appealed specifically to such elements. It was a commonplace in Fascist Italy to characterize the most aggressive Fascist elements as composed of *spostati*, the "displaced." The *spostati* of Italy—the young, the war veterans, the inmigrants to the urban industrial areas—

provided the population resources for the Fascist movement. The appeal to such groups could not be made in terms of the traditional economic classes. The appeal was made in terms of the expressive language of nationalism. By 1914 Mussolini recognized that national sentiment provided the psychological stuff of which a mass-mobilizing revolutionary movement could be fashioned. In 1917 Marcus Garvey made the same discovery.

Garvey appealed to the general sense of reactive group identity that characterized the new urban Negro inmigrants. He made no appeal to class identity defined in terms of economic categories. He appealed to what he identified as "national solidarity." For Garvey, "nationhood" rather than class identity offered the hope of black salvation. "Nationhood," Garvey insisted, "is the only means by which modern civilization can completely protect itself. . . . Nationhood is the highest ideal of all peoples." Nationhood, he went on, exists only on a "solid industrial foundation," a foundation which provides the power not only to protect its vital interests but to proceed to the creation of "empire." Only such national power can protect the individual and the community.

While Garvey was forever prepared to invoke moral suasion in his nationalist and developmental exhortations, he admitted that "man is becoming so vile that today we cannot afford to convert him with moral, ethical, physical truths alone, but with that which is more effective—implements of destruction." Any nation that aspires to justice must "think in terms of blood"—redemption can only come when men are prepared to kill and be killed. "Force," Garvey insisted, "is the only element [the opponents of the Negro nation] recognize." "Power," he continued, "is the only argument that satisfies man."[64]

Garvey saw the twentieth century as a period of increasingly sanguinary struggles between oppressed and oppressing nations, between dependent and dominant political

[64] Garvey, *Philosophy and Opinions*, i, 6, 8, 9, 11, 16, 18, 21; cf. ii, 34, 36, 103, 110, 115, 133, 222.

communities. The demand for national independence would be the revolutionary rallying cry of this century. As a consequence he conceived of a black nation arising out of the political activities of a hierarchically structured mass organization of Negroes. For Garvey there was "nothing in the world as serious as leadership" in the international struggle for place. He was convinced that the masses of men "drift along recklessly," making "no effort to regulate or arrange their own lives and outlook"—they "give no thought toward the future. . . ." It remains, Garvey argued, for a "small number of active minds" to "lay out the course of salvation; and it is to these we look for direction in all those things that affect the human race." As a consequence Garvey's conception of the "ideal state" to which his nationalism aspired was one in which, once elected, the leader of a nation "should be endowed with absolute authority to appoint all his lieutenants from cabinet ministers, governors of States and Territories, administrators and judges to minor officers."[65]

Garveyism was a form of mass-mobilizing, developmental, and authoritarian nationalism. It emphasized personal and charismatic leadership directing a hierarchical and paramilitary organization. Its appeal was consciously directed toward the dispossessed, the impoverished, and alienated, the young and underprivileged. It was anticapitalist, advocating strict state control over capital in excess of five million dollars. Its style was expressive, histrionic. It marshaled its membership into paramilitary groups such as the African Legion and the African Motor Corps and the African Air Corps. Its tactics included the suppression of opposition by violence and vituperation. Its political mythology appealed to the past grandeur of black peoples, the empires of Egypt, Ethiopia, and Timbuctoo. Blacks were admonished to teach their children that they were the "direct descendants of the greatest and proudest race who ever peopled the earth." Garveyites were inspired by visions of future supremacy: "Give the Negro," Garvey

[65] *Ibid.* I, pp. 94, II, 12, 24, 52, 74, 84.

prophesied, "fifty years of unhampered or unmolested freedom of action and in less than that time he will prove to the world that he is the greatest genius Nature ever fashioned and the most liberal and charitable of God's creatures."[66]

Animated by this vision, Garvey sought to create what he called the "New Negro," the appropriate denizen of the future "Empire for Negroes." Garvey's purpose was to "arouse the consciousness of four hundred million Negroes to the hope of Empire." To accomplish those ends Garvey insisted that the black nation "must be strong," in order to survive as the "fittest race" in the inevitable "death struggle" that he anticipated. Blacks, Garvey maintained, must hold themselves "in readiness for that great catastrophe that is bound to come—that of racial extermination, at the hands of the stronger race—the race that will be fit to survive."[67]

Garvey appealed to what Enrico Corradini called the "sacred egotism" of the race, the disposition of the individual to sacrifice his private interests in the service of a community of "his own"—a community that Corradini identified with an "association of similars," those who share one history, one blood, and one destiny. Corradini, like all the nationalists that passed into the Fascist ranks, insisted that the fundamental unity of the "race" was more substantial than any class differences that divided it. Garvey voiced the same conviction. Corradini and the Fascists excoriated the socialists and Marxists for failing to appreciate that fact. Garvey was equally opposed to class divisions among blacks —and was as vehement in his rejection of classical socialism as were the Fascists.[68]

At almost the same time that Garvey was lamenting the

[66] *Ibid.*, II, 72, 82, 337.

[67] *Ibid.*, II, 133, 319, 222; I, 12, 63; cf. I, 20, 66.

[68] "I am against the brand of communism that is taught in America, because it is even more vicious than all the other ism's put together. . . . I would rather be dead than live under Government administered by such characters." *Ibid.*, II, 333f.

threats to black survival in the twentieth century, Mussolini was voicing the same lamentations concerning the survival of the Italians and Europeans in general. Garvey spoke of "race suicide" through a declining birth rate—Mussolini addressed himself to the same issue. Garvey advocated the development of a "national power" as a defense against prevailing threats; Mussolini proposed the same solution.[69] The twentieth century demanded of revolutionaries a program of "new national solidarity," a collective disposition to sacrifice for the collectivity, a collectivity innocent of class divisiveness, united by a glorious past, and aspiring toward a special destiny. The immediate requirements were discipline and sacrifice in the service of industrial expansion for the nation, an enhancement of collective self-confidence in order to animate the drive for a "place in the sun" and a resolute demand for an "equitable" redistribution of global resources. Both Garveyites and Fascists saw their constituency composed of the underprivileged and dispossessed, "proletarians" opposed to "capitalists." Their charismatic object of loyalty was the nation or the race (Fascists, as we shall see, used both terms interchangeably, as did Garvey). Their opponents were the "selfish" and the privileged. Only a movement of "revitalization," a determined effort to create a new consciousness among the masses, could redress longstanding deprivations. Neither the Fascists nor the Garveyites conceived disarmament as a serious possibility until there was a global redistribution of resources. Both objected to the international League of Nations as a conservative force in the maintenance of the prevailing and inequitable *status quo*. Garveyites, like the Fascists, insisted that war would be inevitable as long as gross international disparity in industrial development and access to available resources persisted.

Garvey, like the Fascists, insisted that the sentiment of solidarity upon which viable organizations in the twentieth century might be built was associated with biological and

[69] Cf. Mussolini's introduction to R. Korherr, *Regresso delle nascite: morte dei popoli* (Rome: Littorio, 1928), pp. 7-23.

cultural affinities rather than class roles. Garvey spoke of a confraternity of "nationality" or "race" in precisely the same fashion as Fascists. When Garvey spoke of the "race" he equated its reference with that of "Negro nation." A similar systematic ambiguity between racial and national identity was characteristic of Fascist doctrine. When Mussolini spoke of the "Italian race" it was transparently a reference to the Italian nation. Garvey's references were, of necessity, much more vague. Mussolini spoke of a politically defined collection of individuals related by history, language, and general culture, living in a relatively well-defined geographic space and related by extensive intermarriage for a millennium. Garvey, like the black nationalists that were to follow him, addressed himself to a community of men possessed of a reactive identity, a community whose consciousness of kind was at least in part the product of a rejection by the larger community with which they shared territory, government, history, and culture. Garvey spoke of a black nation that was to exist, that in his time had no foundation in land, that had no history as a separate political entity. He addressed himself to a collection of men scattered throughout the world, denizens of a variety of nations, colonies, and dependencies. While Mussolini's invocations concretized themselves by referring to Italians, Garvey's became increasingly diaphanous by referring to the "race." The Fascist invocation to rapid industrialization and national discipline mobilized masses in the service of a real political community. Garvey's appeal was directed to a dispossessed caste involved in, and yet not a part of, a multiplicity of nations at various stages of industrial and political development.[70] There was no specific nation to which Garvey could appeal. There was only a race defined largely by the rejection it suffered at the hands of white men. Garvey's fascism, as a consequence, was a nonviable and fantastic fascism, confused in its appeals to nationalism in

[70] Cf. Garvey, *Philosophy and Opinions*, i, 23, 31f., 33f., 40f., 43f.; ii, 110.

circumstances where nationalism was inappropriate or ineffectual, unrealistic in its program of black repatriation to Africa, unconvincing in its proposed solution to the problems that beset black Americans.

Garvey advocated the repatriation to Africa of a significant portion of black Americans—a repatriation that few were seriously disposed to entertain. At the same time he insisted that the blacks who remained in the United States remain loyal to a government which he maintained was dominated by the "white race," a race possessed of an irrepressible disposition "to subjugate, to exploit, and if necessary exterminate the weaker peoples with whom they come in contact." Those blacks who were to remain in the United States were counseled to recognize that the white race would *never* grant social equality. Garvey insisted that history had demonstrated "proof positive" that the constitution and the laws of the United States were "never intended for [blacks] as a people." He understood that the "Anglo-Saxon" was "full of greed, avarice, no mercy, no love, no charity." The "vast masses of the white race" could never countenance the social equality of blacks; "the humanity of white America," Garvey insisted, "will seek self-protection and self-preservation, and that is why the thoughtful and reasonable Negro sees no hope in America for satisfying the aggressive program of the National Association for the Advancement of Colored People" which advocated social equality and integration of the races. Garvey maintained that wherever there was a reasonably large incidence of blacks there would forever be "the same problem of hostility, riots, lynchings and burnings." "The appeal to Christian love," he went on, "is a farce, and the white man . . . preaches it only to suit his own conveniences. . . . Political, social and industrial America will never become so converted as to be willing to share up equitably between black and white."[71]

Thus, while Garvey advocated the repatriation to Africa of "eight or ten million" blacks, he insisted that those blacks

[71] *Ibid.*, I, 13, 47, 81; II, 40, 44, 46, 49.

remaining respect the United States government as the "greatest democracy in the world . . . . the greatest government in the world. . . ." He insisted that, irrespective of the cupidity he recognized in whites, in their disposition to exploit, oppress, and ultimately to exterminate, he loved "America for her laws, constitution and her higher sense of fairplay and justice. One can always find," he concluded, "justice in America." On the other hand the UNIA insisted that "in certain parts of the United States of America our race is denied the right of public trial . . . [and is] lynched and burned by mobs, and such brutal and inhuman treatment is even practiced upon our women." Garvey and the UNIA went on to indicate that blacks are unfairly taxed and are segregated by law and discriminated against in terms of employment. Garvey demanded that "wheresoever they form a community among themselves, [blacks] should be given the right to elect their own representatives to represent them in legislatures, courts of law, or such institutions as may exercise control over that particular community." He insisted that blacks should refuse to obey the tax laws of a state where a black is "denied representation on account of his race and color." He advocated the disobedience to those laws which single out the Negro to his disadvantage, and insisted that "the Negro should adopt every means to protect himself against barbarous practices inflicted upon him because of color." Furthermore, any tactic is "justifiable" to protect the race against oppression. He went on to insist upon "complete control of our social institutions without interference by any alien race or races," and further that "no Negro shall engage himself in battle for an alien race without first obtaining the consent of the leader of the Negro people of the world. . . ." He argued that, wherever blacks constituted a "majority" in a community, they should "run those communities." On the other hand he emphatically denied that the UNIA was "seeking to build up another government within the bounds or borders of the United States of America. . . ." He maintained that "If we want Africa, as we surely do, we must reasonably make up our minds to yield some things and make concessions in America. . . ."[72]

Garvey's fascism was a confused and confusing melange of back-to-Africa aspirations, a redress of grievance formula which committed blacks to what Garvey himself, given his judgments about the "white race," could only characterize as an unrealistic struggle with the irredeemably prejudiced and rapacious white majority. Garvey advocated a program of black repatriation to Africa—a program that won the support of the Ku Klux Klan and the notorious Senator Bilbo—but which few blacks were prepared to consider seriously. Alternately, he articulated what could only be assessed, given his initial premises, as a hopeless strategy of creating isolated black enclaves throughout the continental United States. Those enclaves would be self-governing, among other things having the right to pay or not pay federal taxes, having the right to decide whether their young men were or were not to be conscripted in the national defense, and having "complete control" over institutions in the enclaves. All these autonomous communities would be surrounded by a malevolent white majority which at best was disposed to oppress blacks, and *in extremis* to exterminate them. Yet such irredeemably malevolent whites would presumably permit blacks to so comport themselves in their enclaves that the federal union would, in effect, be dissolved.

Garvey was compelled to insist upon the malevolence of whites if his program of repatriation to Africa was to win converts in the black communities. Since there was very little prospect of repatriation of all, or a significant portion of, blacks within the foreseeable future, Garvey had to articulate an alternative immediate strategy. But if the alternative strategy worked at all, its success would provide counterevidence to the thesis of unalterable white malevolence. It would suggest that blacks and whites *could* accommodate, in some fashion or other, within the territorial limits of the United States. The short-range strategy would make

[72] *Ibid.*, II, 50, 107, 182, 229, 137f., 140, 141, 122f., 95f., 236.

the long-range strategy unnecessary, or at least less appealing. All this notwithstanding, Garvey attempted to pursue *both* strategies at the same time. What resulted was a volatile fascism, capable of generating episodic enthusiasm, but doomed to long-range failure. All that was necessary to destroy the UNIA was the absence of its charismatic leader. With the deportation of Marcus Garvey from the United States, the Universal Negro Improvement Association all but vanished from the political stage.

The Garvey movement tapped an impressive reservoir of restiveness among the black masses of North America. Garvey succeeded in mobilizing more blacks than any other black political leader in the twentieth century. His variant of fascism was, however, nonviable. There were no immediate goals that could occupy the energies of the mobilized. The business ventures the UNIA supported were hopelessly inadequate to cope with the dimensions of black needs in America. Some of those ventures ended disastrously—and in the case of the Black Star Shipping Line the disaster carried Garvey, himself, down with the enterprise. Garvey's conviction for fraud in conjunction with the sale of stocks in the shipping line fostered by the UNIA marked the beginning of his decline—a decline that was almost as rapid as his rise.

Garvey's movement had exhausted its recruitment potential by mobilizing a small minority of particularly disadvantaged urban blacks. They were relatively easy to mobilize behind a leadership that promised redemption and collective uplift. Recruitment could proceed no further because the programmatic goals of the movement were hopelessly confused and offered no prospects of success. The talk of repatriation remained simply talk. The attempt to develop "black industries" in the confines of the United States simply emphasized the competitive disadvantage in which the American black finds himself. The attempt to attract white allies foundered on Garvey's conviction that whites could not be trusted—particularly "liberal" whites. His attempts to establish a working alliance with the Ku Klux Klan and the

Anglo-Saxon Clubs of America only brought the UNIA into further disrepute. Garvey's vague and petulant anti-Semitism only succeeded in further reducing his credibility.[73]

Fascisms have, in general, been afflicted with an endemic disposition to allow their emphatic nationalism to degenerate into simple racism. Some fascisms, however, have successfully suppressed the disposition. Others, Mussolini's Fascism among them, came very close to aping National Socialist racism.

Black nationalism, as a variant of fascism, has always harbored this disposition, and, while Garvey seems to have sincerely made an effort to resist lapsing into simple racism, and even anti-Semitism, much of what he said could easily be construed as racist. Both Garvey and Mussolini denied that there were superior and inferior races, but both committed themselves to a doctrine of racial purity that proscribed interracial and interethnic marriage. In that regard Garvey was by far the more emphatic of the two. He insisted that miscegenation violated the "laws of nature" and was a moral affront and an historic abomination. Garvey's "distinct racial group idealism" was predicated on the conviction that the "races can be friendly and helpful to each other, but the laws of nature separate us to the extent of each and every one developing by itself." "We believe," Garvey explained, "in the purity of both races. . . . We believe that the white race should protect itself against racial contamination, and the Negro should do the same. Nature intended us morally (and may I not say socially?) apart, otherwise there never would have been this distance."

A similar kind of "racial idealism" was embodied in the *Racial Manifesto* of Italian Fascism. Mussolini insisted that racial separation protected the integrity of "natio-races," breeding populations. He insisted that such separation was not predicated on racial inferiority and racial superiority. Nonetheless, he, like Garvey, lapsed into statements about the grandeur and purity of the "Italian race" that were but

[73] *Ibid.*, II, 71, 338-49, 217f., 260.

373

little removed from racial chauvinism. Garvey's anti-Semitism was no less muted than that entertained by Mussolini until 1938, when the increasing rapprochement with National Socialist Germany produced a hardening of Fascist anti-Semitism.[74]

It was not the muted racism of Garvey's fascism that rendered his movement ultimately ineffectual. His movement very quickly exhausted both its recruitment potential and its credibility. A revolutionary nationalism predicated on reactive identity—that is to say an identity that was the consequence of systematic rejection by the white majority in America—might have been vital if black America could, in fact, constitute itself a nation, possessed of its own geographic space. Garvey's orphaned nationalism might have succeeded by adopting Africa as the Homeland—as the Zionists adopted Palestine—if his movement offered a real hope that blacks would simply become citizens of the United States of America as Jews were citizens. That would have required that the Garveyites commit themselves to a struggle for equal citizenship rights as Americans. But Garvey continued to insist that social, political, and economic equality was simply impossible in the United States and thus committed himself to two conflicting political strategies: (1) he resisted those allies that might have assisted the UNIA in obtaining equal citizenship rights as Americans in order to (2) urge blacks, on the pain of anticipated extermination, to abandon the United States and repatriate to Africa.

Garvey's political program left his followers confused and ultimately disillusioned. In order to drive them to the ancestral homeland he insisted that they could expect little in the way of redress in the United States. On the other hand the oppression suffered by his constituency required that he commit himself to a program of collective self-defense in the United States—with the clear implication, if

[74] *Ibid.*, II, 62, 119, 122, 132, 234; for a discussion of the racial doctrines of Mussolini's Fascism, cf. Gregor, *The Ideology of Fascism*, chap. 6.

we are to believe his hyperbolic characterizations, that social, political, and economic equality was a dream without substance. It soon became obvious that few blacks could or would repatriate to Africa. The fading dream of returning to the Homeland left blacks in this country with the hopeless prospect of remaining second-class citizens within the political trammels of the United States. After Garvey's arrest and deportation, the UNIA rapidly disintegrated to leave America's black population embittered and shorn of hope. Garvey left an ambiguous fascist heritage to American black nationalism—a heritage which was fully to resurface again only after the decline of the "civil rights movement" at the end of the sixties.

The Black Muslims

The same population elements that provided the base for the Garvey movement provided the support for Elijah Muhammad's "Nation of Islam." With the disappearance of Garvey from the political scene, an individual variously identified as F. Mohammad Ali, Wali Farrad, and W. D. Fard made his appearance in Detroit, which was alive with new black inmigrants from the South. The same inmigrants that provided the membership for revivalist and revitalist religions in the North—the dispossessed and displaced—provided the first members of Fard's black "Lost-Found Nation of Islam."

Fard's "Lost-Found Nation" became the black Nation of Islam of Elijah Muhammad—and the organization he founded is known, in our own time, as "The Black Muslims." The continuity shared by the Garvey movement and the Black Muslims is quite transparent. The older members of the Lost-Found Nation were for the most part ex-Garveyites, many of them conceiving Fard, and his "Prophet" Elijah Muhammad, the natural successors of the "prophet" Marcus Garvey. Muhammad, in fact, frequently referred to Garvey as a "fine Muslim," and called upon his followers to finish the work Garvey and his movement began. Malcolm Little, who was to become the most famous of the Muslims as Malcolm X, was the son of a Garveyite, Earl Little.[75]

While the theological, historical, and eschatological fancies of the black Muslims were more extravagant than the historical and programmatic commitments of Marcus Garvey, their character remained the same. The central theme around which the Black Muslim movement gravitates is "nationhood." The blacks of America are members of what Muslims call "the Lost-Found Nation of Islam," into which all blacks, irrespective of class, origin, or disposition, are to be drawn. National solidarity is conceived to be the psychological precondition for the rapid economic development of the "nation." The material prerequisite for black nation-building is a "separate geographical area" in North America to which the "Lost-Found Nation" can remove itself. These prerequisites and preconditions given, Elijah Muhammad promised to place blacks "on the same level with all other civilized and independent nations and peoples of this planet earth . . . ."

To create such a nation it was necessary to mobilize "masses" of blacks. The techniques, tactics, and style involved in the process, as well as the ultimate rationale which subtended them, are familiar. The masses of blacks were conceived so "deaf, dumb, and blind, mentally morally and spiritually . . ." that their mobilization required dedicated leaders who would direct their principal attention to the invocation of the young and organize them for "revolution."[76] It would be a revolution that would be "bloody" and "hostile" and which would "know no compromise," "overturning" and "destroying" "everything that gets in its way."

[75] C. Eric Lincoln, *The Black Muslims in America* (Boston: Beacon, 1961), chap. 1; Malcolm X, *The Autobiography of Malcolm X* (New York: Grove, 1964), pp. 1f.; E. U. Essien-Udom, *Black Nationalism: A Search for an Identity in America* (Chicago: University of Chicago, 1962), chap. 1.

[76] Malcolm X, *Autobiography*, pp. 199, 200f.

It would be led by revolutionaries who want "land so that [they] can set up [their] own nation, an independent nation."[77]

The membership of the Black Muslims was, in fact, composed largely of the young. They were mobilized in no small measure by the hyperbolic, and symbolic speech, the expressive imagery and the apocalyptic visions of an imminent Armageddon. The style of Muslim delivery, the fantastic susbtance of its eschatology, made it irrepressively anti-intellectual. Malcolm X, certainly one of the most, if not the most, gifted theoreticians of the movement, spoke of "intellectuals" as "useless." He is known to have had very little regard for black intellectuals.[78] He was committed to activism both by disposition and principle. The political style of the movement is familiar.

The organization of the "Nation" was and is rigidly hierarchical—with all authority concerning ideology, theology, programmatics, and strategy held exclusively by Elijah Muhammad, the "Messenger of Allah." While Muslims entertain the fiction of solidarist equality among all members of the Nation, it is obvious that the Messenger dominates the ministers of the Nation, the ministers, in turn, dominate the temples, and the captains of the temples, in turn, dominate the male membership, the Fruit of Islam. The women members of the Nation play a completely subordinate role. Malcolm X characterized their role as "to be weak."[79] The organizational characteristics of the movement are familiar.

Elijah Muhammad appoints all his ministers and those members who have any responsibilities to the Nation. Even those minor officials of the temples, initially appointed by ministers, must have their appointment confirmed by the

[77] A. Epps, *The Speeches of Malcolm X* (New York: Morrow, 1968), p. 68.

[78] Cf. Alex Haley, in Malcolm X, *Autobiography*, p. 405.

[79] For the organization of the Nation, cf. Essien-Udom, *Black Nationalism*, chap. 6; for Malcolm X's comments on women, see *Autobiography*, p. 228.

Messenger. The male membership of the temples is organized in paramilitary fashion, under the disciplined control of a captain, a first, second, and third lieutenants. The control is strict; and any failure to obey orders brings severe and summary punishment.[80] Even Malcolm X, independent, aggressive, and activist that he was, submitted meekly to the absolute controls exercised by the Messenger. Muhammad himself is revered as a charismatic genius with a reverence that has become standard for such movements.

Elijah Muhammad, like Garvey, advocated a developmental nationalism, predicated on a conviction that masses of oppressed mankind, led by a personalist and charismatic leadership employing paramilitary and disciplined organization, could win for their community a place in the sun. All the choreography of such movements was invoked during the Nation's period of maximum recruitment. Thousands of blacks were drawn to meetings characterized by expressive and evocative histrionics. Like Garvey, the Muslims entertained a collection of fantasies about the lost and glorious history of their African homeland. Like all nationalists, the Muslims harbor exalted conceptions of their past glories and anticipated destiny. The nationalism of the Nation is clearly traditional. "We want to build a nation that will be recognized as a nation," Muhammad has insisted, "that will be self-respecting and receive respect of the other nations of the earth."[81]

The fascism of the Black Muslims is an exacerbated Fascism. Like Garveyism, the fascism of the Muslims has degenerated into a racism that shares more than superficial kinship with the exacerbated fascism of Hitler's National Socialism. If the National Socialists entertained convictions about the mysteries of Nordic origins in the lost Atlantis, the Black Muslims talk of an "Original" black man who lived on Earth

[80] Cf. A. Barnette and E. Linn, "The Black Muslims are a Fraud," *Saturday Evening Post*, February 27, 1965.

[81] Elijah Muhammad, *Message to the Blackman in America* (Chicago: Muhammad Mosque no. 2, 1965), p. 169.

"sixty trillion years ago." The "so-called Negroes" of America are, according to the Muslim account, actually members of the "lost tribe" of Shabazz. They are, in fact, the "chosen" of the nonwhite peoples, good by nature, pious by innate disposition, the "cream" of the earth and the most beautiful of God's creatures. The whites, on the other hand, are abortions created six thousand years ago by a malicious black scientist named Yakub, who produced, through a controlled process of selection, a mentally and physically impaired, depigmented collection of "devils." Since that time the "white devils" he created have, under a dispensation from Allah, tested the mettle of the "chosen" by inflicting torments upon them. The period of trial is almost over and the supremacy of the select of Shabazz is imminent.

Given these convictions, it is not surprising that in a series of interviews conducted in the early sixties all Muslims queried responded to questions concerning their appraisal of Caucasians with the judgment that whites are innately inferior and "by nature, devils." Minister James 3X, by way of illustration, argued that whites were afflicted with an "inborn fear and hatred" of the black man generated by the white man's "feeling of inferiority." "The white man," he continued, "has discovered that he is weaker than the black man. His mental power is less than that of the black man—he has only six ounces of brain and the Original Man has seven-and-a-half ounces. . . . The white man's physical power is one-third less than that of the black man."[82]

The racism of the Black Muslims is more explicit, less muted, than was that of the Garvey movement. Garvey did insist, irrespective of his many qualifiers, that no race was inherently evil or inherently inferior. Only *after* his break with the Muslims, after he had experienced something akin to a religious and political conversion, could Malcolm X grant that "the white man is *not* inherently evil. . . ." As a Black Muslim his prevailing conviction, like the prevailing

[82] As quoted in Essien-Udom, *Black Nationalism*, p. 135; cf. Malcolm X, *Autobiography*, pp. 166f.

379

convictions of the Muslims in general, was that the whites, as a race, were irredeemably defective—physically and morally. The whites were "devils"—"without exceptions."[83]

The fact that Muslim racism is a reactive racism does not make it any the less pernicious. Every contact with whites is an occasion for misgivings and suspicion. Like the Garveyites, the Muslims anticipate an inevitable racial conflagration; and they expect that conflagration to destroy the white race. The destruction will be the fulfillment of prophecy. The whites, debased and subhuman creatures that they inherently are, will be exterminated by the judgment of Allah. Blacks will then find themselves in their "rightful" place, "at the top of civilization." In effect, man's social relations, his history, and his destiny are inextricably linked to his racial characteristics.

Beyond this racial eschatology (which bears remarkable resemblance to the inanities bruited about by the "Nordic societies" that prepared the way for the reception of Hitler's racial policies), the proposed Muslim solutions to America's racial problems are as complex and confusing as those articulated by Marcus Garvey. At one time it seemed as though the Muslims advocated a return to their "native land"— which was apparently in the Near East. In the official Muslim Ten Point Program, however, a demand is made for "a separate state or territory . . . either on this continent or elsewhere . . ." with the proviso that it be "fertile and minerally rich" and that it be supported by the United States government for at least twenty-five years. In 1959 Muhammad demanded "three, four, or more states" to be carved out of the continental United States. Yet elsewhere he insisted "We're not demanding territory in America. No, sir," he went on, "we're asking America only if they don't allow us to go back to our own people and to the country from which we came."[84]

[83] Epps, *Speeches of Malcolm X*, p. 182; Malcolm X, *Autobiography*, p. 377; cf. *ibid.*, pp. 245, 271. L. Lomax, *When the Word is Given* (New York: World, 1963), pp. 62f.

[84] As cited, T. Draper, *The Rediscovery of Black Nationalism* (New

It is most difficult, as a consequence, to identify either the land which is to be the basis of their nationhood or the policy or policies calculated to obtain it. All that the Black Muslims have succeeded in doing is to develop all the trappings of nationhood—a flag, a sort of defense establishment, a program of "national development," and a political leadership class. Barring divine intervention, there is little prospect that the Muslims can obtain a land that would provide the material basis of nationhood. In the interim Muslims are commited to a belief system that makes any contact between blacks and whites fraught with anxieties and inevitable illwill. If Muslims are convinced that "the white man was created a devil, to bring chaos upon the earth . . . ,"[85] any contact with whites must produce almost intolerable tensions. Contacts between the races have always been enormously sensitive—the conviction that one or the other race is inherently evil, invincibly perverse, can only make such interaction the occasion for self-fulfilling prophecies of doom.

The Muslim solution has been consistently to "separate the slaves from their slave master. . . . Complete separation; not only physical separation, but moral separation . . . ."[86] But since such separation is an unlikely prospect for the foreseeable future, Malcolm X, as a Black Muslim, offered an alternative, interim program in which "the American black man should be focusing his every effort toward building his own businesses and decent homes for himself. As other ethnic groups have done, let the black people, wherever possible, however possible, patronize their own kind, hire their own kind, and start in these ways to build up the black race's ability to do for itself. That's the only way the

York: Viking, 1970), pp. 80f.; cf. Epps, *Speeches of Malcolm X*, pp. 123, 126, 130f.

[85] Malcolm X, *Autobiography*, p. 206.

[86] Malcolm X, in K. Clark, *The Negro Protest* (Boston: Beacon, 1963), pp. 28f.; cf. Malcolm X, *Autobiography*, pp. 248f.; "Malcolm X's Speech at Queens College," in Lomax, *When the Word is Given*, pp. 175f.

American black man is ever going to get respect. . . . The black man in America has to lift up his own sense of values." And elsewhere Malcolm suggested that "the black man should control the politics of his own community."[87]

But if any or all of the minimal program proves feasible it would imply that the black man in America, in self-segregated enclaves, *could* obtain his own businesses, enjoy decent housing, and earn respect. If, on the other hand, the intrinsic evil of the "white devils" precludes the prospect of *any* success, the minimal policy stands condemned as a hopeless political strategy.

In effect, the Black Muslims entertained a maximal program that involved a complete physical separation of blacks and whites predicated on the sure conviction that *no* racial accommodation was possible. At the same time, they entertained a minimal program whose feasibility rested on a conviction that *some* kind of accommodation was possible. At best the minimal strategy conjures up an inescapable vision of political violence as an intrinsic necessity. If the white man is created a devil and is inherently evil, black enclaves, created in conformity with the minimal program, could only exist in an uneasy state of siege until the maximal program is effected. Although Black Muslims insisted that they did not advocate violence, their belief system concerning the inherent traits of the white man makes "defensive violence" a predictable certainty.

The implicit recognition that such political violence is inescapable has led Muslims to seek allies outside the confines of the United States. They have assiduously sought (with no appreciable response) the support of their "millions" of "Muslim brothers" in Africa, the Near East, and Asia. Their numerical and material inferiority, conjoined with their dark vision of inevitable racial strife, has made the nationalism of the Black Muslims unrealistically dependent on "international" support. The fact that their "white enemy" constitutes an overwhelming majority in North America, and possesses all but a monopoly on the instruments of coercion,

[87] Malcolm X, *Autobiography*, pp. 278f., 318f.

drove the Muslims to seek allies elsewhere. It is clear that the search for international allies is not the consequence of any "Marxist" considerations—that is to say, the Muslims do not seek out Marxists, or Marxist-Leninists, to support their "liberation." The Muslims, for example, were quick to charge the Soviet Union with "racism." Indeed, if *all* whites are tainted with intrinsic evil, there is no reason to believe that white Marxists would be any less afflicted. Given these premises, the Muslims have sought allies among the "nonwhite peoples"—the selective criteria are, once again, racial. Malcolm X insisted that "we see again that not ideologies, but race, and color, is what binds human beings. Is it accidental that as Red Chinese visit Africa and Asian countries, Russia and America draw steadily closer to each other?"[88] In fact when Fidel Castro made overtures to Malcolm X on the occasion of his visit to Harlem, every effort was made by Muslims to redefine Castro as a "black man."[89] Black nationalists have traditionally been non-Marxists, if not explicitly anti-Marxist. They would characteristically rather "gravitate toward any nation of colored people engaged in combat with the Caucasian devil."[90]

The species traits of black nationalism are relatively clear. Black nationalists of whatever faction tend to be massmobilizing revolutionaries whose political strategy invariably involves a hierarchically organized political elite making expressive populist appeals. The leadership is invariably charismatic and messianic. Mobilization is predicated on a pervasive consciousness of kind rather than any class appeal. The organization conceives of itself as a vanguard, a revolutionary catalyst that acts as a "wick" that ignites a "powder keg." The black nationalist goal is the creation of a "grand nation" that will achieve its rightful place at the "top of civilization." That achievement will involve disciplined sacrifice in a massive developmental program in order to offset

[88] *Ibid.*, pp. 274, 278, 289; cf. Epps, *Speeches of Malcolm X*, pp. 123f.
[89] Lincoln, *Black Muslims*, p. 18.
[90] Essien-Udom, *Black Nationalism*, pp. 292f.

the disabilities of the past caused by the oppression inflicted by the privileged. Perhaps the most succinct and responsible characterization of the Black Muslims is provided by Archie Epps' analysis of Malcolm X as a Black Muslim spokesman. "In the end," Epps argues, "black nationalist strategy was authoritarian. . . . Malcolm X's conception of society was based on two laws of the jungle: (1) the conflict between natural enemies and (2) the survival of the fittest." To define the political "reality" for masses of men, Malcolm employed condensed imagery and extended metaphor—the noncognitive style featured by such leaders. He employed "poetized logic," vast and unqualified generalizations. His discussions were filled with allusions to "foxes" and "wolves," to "snakes" and "jungle beasts" that inhabited the bestiary that was the contemporary world. Given such images, the consequence was a commitment to romanticized and purifying violence.[91] Such romanticism invokes the postures of masculine protest, the paramilitary organization, the rummaging about among the "arts of self-defense," the military titles and the language of positional and guerrilla warfare that have become endemic to black nationalist variants of Fascism.

The fact is that black nationalism in general and the Black Muslims in particular constitute a nonviable variant of fascism. It is nonviable largely because its fascism is exacerbated—its nationalism has in some cases clearly degenerated into racism and as a consequence becomes politically unrealistic. The suggestion that the "nonwhite" peoples of the world could or would rally to support effectively black revolution in the United States is hardly convincing. Whether those nonwhite peoples are members of the orthodox Moslem communities of the Near East, or the Chinese communists, there is no evidence whatsoever that any support they provide black nationalists will be anything more substantial than words. Mao Tse-tung may indeed voice his "support" for the "black man's liberation struggle," but it is

[91] A. Epps, *Speeches of Malcolm X*, pp. 43, 49, 60ff., 91, 107.

unlikely that under any foreseeable circumstances black Americans can expect anything more than words of encouragement from the Chinese. Members of the African community may, indeed, bring up the plight of black Americans before the General Assembly of the United Nations, but the record of General Assembly debates and the attendant resolutions does not inspire confidence in their political substance.

The radicalism that has found expression in the nationalism of Garvey and Muhammad has been a despairing and nonviable fascism. A movement with mass-mobilizing aspirations, it has never been able to mobilize masses in sufficient numbers to effect its revolution. Garvey's inflated membership figures were the product of dreams rather than reality. In their own time, the actual membership of the Black Muslims probably never exceeded fifteen thousand full-fledged members—and, at best, fifty thousand hangers-on. At one point Malcolm X referred to forty thousand members and at another fifteen thousand members. The latter figure seems to be the most accurate; and that number marks the peak of Muslim recruitment. The organization was very fragile and with the alienation of Malcolm X its membership has apparently eroded.

Black nationalism has been, for all intents and revolutionary purposes, a mass-mobilizing movement without masses. It has also been a nationalism without a nation. Its "nation" has been at various times, "somewhere in Asia," in Africa, in North America and sometimes no more than self-segregated enclaves in the United States. At its worst black nationalism has not been nationalistic at all—its nationalism has degenerated into a form of reactive racism which defined its friends and enemies largely, if not exclusively, in terms of racial criteria. As a consequence one hundred and eighty million whites, no matter how liberal or sincere any might be, were inevitably identified as real or potential enemies. Malcolm X, while still a minister of Muhammad, insisted that he didn't know a single white man that was not a "devil." The Muslims taught that all whites, "without exceptions" were "intrinsically evil."[92] Nor did the black Muslims successfully avoid the blandishments of anti-Semitism. Malcolm X, as a Black Muslim, frequently reiterated the thesis that Jews were a special class of white oppressors. They were the whites most intimately associated with the exploitation of blacks in the ghettoes; they were, furthermore, the whites who gulled blacks into "nonviolent" strategies. Jews, Malcolm frequently reminded his audiences, provided the principal leadership for the NAACP.

"A lot of the Jews have a guilty conscience when you mention exploitation," Malcolm insisted, "because they realize that they control ninety percent of the businesses in every Negro community from the Atlantic to the Pacific. . . ." He argued that "Jews who have been guilty of exploiting the black people in this country, economically, civically, and otherwise, hid behind—hide their guilt by accusing the Honorable Elijah Muhammad of being anti-Semitic . . . ." He insisted that a Jew always manages to "think Jew." The Jews "sap the very life blood of the so-called Negroes," he went on, "to maintain the state of Israel, its armies and its continued aggression against our brothers in the East."[93]

Muslims, in general, like the Garveyites before them, conceive the Jews as a subset of enemies categorized within the broader class of the "white enemy." That does not make their anti-Jewish generalizations any less irresponsible, or any less pernicious.

The anti-Semitism of Mussolini's paradigmatic Fascism, latent for fifteen years in Italy, reasserted itself in the anti-Jewish legislation of 1938. Clearly the decision to impose restrictions on the Jews was a consequence of Mussolini's peculiar political opportunism, but the capacity to entertain political anti-Semitism seems endemic to nationalism once it becomes exacerbated. Mussolini's rapprochement with

[92] Malcolm X, *Autobiography*, p. 160.
[93] Clark, *The Negro Protest*, p. 25, 31; Lomax, *When the Word is Given*, p. 201; Malcolm X, *Autobiography*, p. 286; Lincoln, *Black Muslims*, p. 166.

Hitler, his overtures to the Moslems of the Near East, dictated his exploitation of anti-Semitism. The Black Muslim appeal to their "brothers" in the East, their antipathy to all whites, provoke similar postures among black nationalists.[94]

All these disabilities conjoined create circumstances which invariably restrict the recruitment potential of black nationalist movements. Their philosophy is manifestly desperate and despairing. They promise action and activity—their rhetoric is suasive and expressive—but their immediate and long-range prospects of success are, at best, minimal. They attract the most disaffected and displaced. While their displays strike resonances in the long-suffering black community, their political strategy is calculated to produce defeat, their organizational tactics singularly fragile and given to internecine factionalism. Their ideology alienates the best elements of the black community. At best they can serve as auxiliaries in the struggle to ameliorate the life circumstances of blacks in America. Even in that capacity black nationalism produces results which are counterproductive with respect to its own political advantage. If black nationalists are successful in mounting sufficient threat to compel the white to pay ransom to the black community—in the effort to purchase peace—any amelioration of the black man's lot reduces the political potential of black nationalism. The black nationalists become "tools" of Negro moderates who use the threats of black nationalism to wring concessions from whites. The burden of increasing the ante in the direct confrontation with whites falls on the black nationalists; their black political opponents are the beneficiaries; and the political mortality of black nationalists can be expected to increase. They are compelled by the logic of the circumstances to make more and more outrageous and "nonnegotiable demands"—and run all the attendant risks—to someone else's political benefit. The leadership of black nationalist groups are more and more frequently either sacrificed to the security forces of the "enemy community" or

[94] Malcolm X, *By Any Means Necessary* (New York: Pathfinder, 1970), pp. 116f., 152, 159f.

consumed in their own conspiratorial, almost psychopathic, violence.

With seriously restricted recruitment potential (restricted largely to the very young, the very alienated—what they themselves choose to call the "lumpenproletariat"), occupied in what has now become a very high risk strategy, black nationalists are giving more and more evidence of not having anywhere to go. Malcolm X, during the last months of his life, made public display of the disintegration that has begun to set in among black nationalists.

After his break with the Black Muslims, Malcolm abandoned almost all the critical convictions that constituted the content of black nationalism. At one point, in response to queries, he even admitted that he had *no* economic or political program that might resolve "the complex problems" that beset blacks in the United States. He rejected, with some qualification, the notion of an "independent black state in the United States." But if he rejected separatism, he continued to reject integration. He rejected racism in principle, but he could give few convincing suggestions as to how blacks might effectively ally themselves with whites. The fact is that Malcolm admitted just before his assassination that he would be "hard pressed" to articulate an "overall philosophy." During the last few months before his assassination he invoked the expression "black nationalism" less and less frequently. It is hard to tell what Malcolm X had become after his break with the Black Muslims—but it is reasonably clear that his black nationalism had dissipated itself in frustration.

American Radicals and Marxism

Whatever becomes of black nationalism, and whatever transformations beset the student radicals, it is fairly evident that Marxism will play little part in the belief systems they generate or entertain. The Black Panthers, for example, will advocate "picking up the gun" and attribute the injunction to "Chairman Mao"; but the invocation to that kind of "revolutionary violence" has precious little to do with classical Marxism or Leninism. It has far more affinity with the *squadrismo* of Fascism, or the street warfare of National Socialist Brownshirts. Black radicals may well read Frantz Fanon's paean to violence—the violence that "creates the New Man"—but they will find the rationale for therapeutic violence not in Marx or Lenin, but in Sorel and Mussolini. Black radicals have given every indication of being essentially unconcerned with Marx or Marxism. Malcolm X admitted he knew little of Marx; but he did insist that he knew of no "socialist system," managed by whites, in which the black man was accorded equal place. Black nationalists, irrespective of Marxist claims that socialism resolves the racial question, have voiced strenuous objections to the "racism" of the Soviet Union and Castro's Cuba. Eldridge Cleaver, and some of his exiled and factional Black Panthers, have been disillusioned by the "racial solution" offered by Castro's "socialism." As a consequence, it seems fair to conclude that, whatever "socialism" black nationalists allude to, it will have little affinity with Marxism. Malcolm X, for example, while he rejected capitalism, refused to be identified as a "communist" or a "socialist"—although he showed manifest admiration for the "religious (and anti-Marxist) socialism" of Nasser's Egypt.[95]

Black radicals, whatever their persuasion, have shown little disposition to take Marxism seriously. They will affect its slogans and some of its speech patterns, but there is little Marxist substance in that. Harold Cruse, perhaps the most sophisticated among them, has overtly rejected Marxism as an orientation appropriate to the black struggle. He has stated flatly, "As Western Marxism had no adequate revolutionary theory for the colonies, American Marxists have no adequate theory for the Negro." He candidly refers to the

[95] *Ibid.*, pp. 20, 126; Malcolm X, *Malcolm X Speaks* (New York: Grove, 1965), pp. 126, 179; J. Clytus, *Black Man in Red Cuba* (Coral Gables: Univ. of Miami, 1970); L. Lockwood, "Introduction" to *Conversation with Eldridge Cleaver* (New York: McGraw-Hill, 1970), pp. 16-21.

"dead-end politics of American Marxism, which has lost its relevance to the realities of Negro existence." There is a tendency to reject proletarian socialism for a form of national, if not racial socialism. Even after he had abandoned the nationalism of the "Nation of Islam" Malcolm X remarked that "revolution" could not be made with "working class whites." He insisted that "the lineup" in future struggles would be "based on race." Cruse had added that the black man's "national boundaries are the color of his skin, his racial characteristics." Similarly, in a response to a query, Stokely Carmichael recently maintained that "While prior to the twentieth century the major contradiction was one of class, in this century the contradiction of race becomes important."[96]

Black radicals will probably formulate a program of "racial socialism," a reactive and exacerbated fascism, essentially non-Marxist, if not anti-Marxist, in character. It will probably continue to be expressive, generational, activist, voluntarist, and committed to romantic notions of the therapeutic value of violence. Black radical organizations will probably continue to be fragile, enjoying but minimal recruitment potential, afflicted with a superabundance of charismatic and messianic leaders. Black radicals, in the traditional fascist mode, will continue to speak, as does Earl Anthony, of their leaders as "almost sacred." Their organizations will, in all probability, remain hierarchical with the leadership identified by military title: "field marshal," "captain," "lieutenant," and so forth. The membership will continue to be young and politically unsophisticated—for, as Anthony admits, the very young "are the most impressionable and most easily disciplined and directed." This succeeds, black radicals continue, in "[keeping] power and

[96] H. Cruse, *Rebellion or Revolution?* (New York: Morrow, 1968), pp. 77, 73, 78; Malcolm X, *By Any Means Necessary*, pp. 12f.; as quoted, *San Francisco Sunday Examiner and Chronicle*, March 1, 1970, p. 5. Cf. H. Cruse, *The Crisis of the Negro Intellectual* (New York: Morrow, 1967), pp. 372, 381; *Rebellion or Revolution?*, pp. 107, 109, 117.

control in the hands of the leadership." They will talk of the "cleansing force" of violence and invoke the now familiar choreography of uniforms, slogans, symbols, and hyperbolic speech. They will continue to walk around "with their black leather jackets worn loosely draped across both shoulders— a style imitative of the leather-coated German officers of World War II." They will continue to talk of "the masses . . . constantly looking for a guide, a Messiah, to liberate them from the hands of the oppressor. The vanguard party must exemplify the characteristics of worthy leadership." They will continue to insist that the vanguard party must be "activist" and "raise the consciousness of the masses"— that one must somehow reach "the instinctive man. . . ."

The latter can be accomplished, for instance, through "revolutionary art" characterized by radical blacks in the following fashion:

This is revolutionary art—pigs lying in alley ways of the colony dead with their eyes gouged out—autopsy showing cause of death: They fail to see that majority rules. Pictures we draw show them choking to death from their inhuman ways—these are the kinds of pictures revolutionary artists draw—.

The Viet Cong stabbing him in his brain—black people taking the hearts of the enemy and hanging the hearts on the wall (put one more notch on our knife) skin them alive and make rugs out of them—

We must draw pictures of Southern cracker Wallace with cancer of the mouth that he got from his dead witch's uterus.[97]

The style and the content are familiar. Given the low recruitment potential and marginal success of such radical movements, they will become increasingly exacerbated. Fascism, so enflamed, has in the past degenerated into the racial

[97] Cf. E. Anthony, *Picking Up the Gun* (New York: Dial, 1970), pp. 25, 88f., 90, 2; P. S. Foner, ed., *The Black Panthers Speak* (New York: Lippincott, 1970), pp. 44, 42f., 27, 18.

socialism of Hitler's variant of radicalism. There is little like-lihood, of course, that such black movements could ever seriously threaten the larger community in the foreseeable future. They are in all probability more of a threat to their immediate host community—the ghetto itself. Such move-ments are extremely volatile—and the present is a time of great confusion. Whether they can overcome the disabilities that have traditionally afflicted black nationalism awaits to be seen. In any event, whatever the outcome, the movement will take on the traits of an exacerbated fascism in style and content or cease to have any political significance whatever.

The Marxism of white student radicals, on the other hand, is no more substantial—nor is there much prospect that stu-dent radicals will become any more Marxist in the future. While Marxist scholarship and Marxist-orientated intellec-tuals will be long with us, rooted in a respectable and inter-esting intellectual tradition, student radicals will be less and less disposed to take them or their traditions seriously.

There are by now some clear indications that student radicalism has exhausted its recruitment potential. Mem-bership in radical student groups has probably already peaked. The major radical student organizations such as S.D.S. have split into factions and their membership either eroded or driven, by frustration and unrealistic strategies, into terrorism. Random acts of terrorism, episodic bombings, kidnappings, the diversion of aircraft in flight and assassina-tions mark, for a movement without broad-based popular support, a final desperate strategy. By their own admission incapable of generating mass support, alienated from blacks, disposed to "go it alone," the New Left radicals have, in effect, abandoned Marxism, faulted their infantile fascism, and descended to the depths of anarcho-terrorism. The macabre fascination some student radicals have manifested for the "urban guerrilla" fantasies of Carlos Marighella, for instance, is their certification of bankruptcy. Marighella en-joins "urban guerrillas" to undertake terrorism executed "with the greatest cold bloodedness . . . ," to be carried out largely by students whom, he cynically characterizes, as "being politically crude and coarse . . . ."[98]

Marxism, even Marxism-Leninism and Trotskyism, has traditionally opposed such acts of individual violence. George Novack, as a knowledgeable Marxist, quite correctly identifies terrorism as "anti-Marxist," "anti-democratic and elitist" because of its reliance upon conspiratorial methods of "a tiny minority"—the product of "subjectivism and impatience, of frustration and desperation."[99] Fascists, in turn, abjured terrorism unless it was supported by a broad-based popular sentiment—and even then it had to be surgically employed.

The radical student movement has begun to display the clinical features of disintegration. As the tactics become more and more reprehensible and hazardous, fewer and fewer students are likely to be attracted to the cult of the "guerrilla poet." The few that are attracted will tend to be more and more clearly sociopathic—and one doesn't build a revolutionary vanguard—whether Marxist or neofascist—with lunatics.

Nonregime radicalism, growing out of real problems that afflict the advanced industrial countries, manifests itself, at its best, as an adolescent and/or nonviable fascism—at its worst it degenerates into a confusion of racial fascism or anarcho-terrorism. It will probably produce much heart-ache, probably repression of considerable magnitude—and will leave all the problems unresolved. The problems to which students and blacks address themselves deserve something better.

[98] C. Marighella, *Minimanual of the Urban Guerrilla* (Berkeley: Long Time Comin', 1970), pp. 34, 44.

[99] G. Novack, "Marxism versus Neo-Anarchist Terrorism," *International Socialist Review* (June 1970), p. 15.

CHAPTER NINE

Conclusions

Growing anarchy in the Third World would very likely involve racist and nationalist passions. At the very least, this would create major pockets of disruption and chaos in the world . . . . Another threat, less overt but no less basic, confronts liberal democracy. More directly linked to the impact of technology, it involves the gradual appearance of a more controlled and directed society. Such a society would be dominated by an elite whose claim to political power would rest on allegedly superior scientific know-how. Unhindered by the restraints of traditional liberal values, this elite would not hesitate to achieve its political ends by using the latest modern techniques for influencing public behavior and keeping society under close surveillance and control . . . . Persisting social crisis, the emergence of a charismatic personality, and the exploitation of mass media to obtain public confidence would be the stepping-stones in the piecemeal transformation of the United States into a highly controlled society.[1]

Z. Brzezinski

THERE can be little doubt that the remaining years of the twentieth century will be years of violent and stressful political change. What has been suggested here, in broad and discursive fashion, is that the major expressions of revolutionary politics in the remainder of the twentieth century will most likely evince at least some of the species-traits of fascism. The efforts undertaken to identify revolutionary politics in our time as "socialist" or "Marxist" have been

[1] Z. Brzezinski, *Between Two Ages: America's Role in the Technetronic Era* (New York: Viking, 1970), pp. 52f, 252f.

singularly unpersuasive. Karl Marx would have found very little in the political culture and political institutions of Cuba, China, or Russia that he could identify as Marxist. We know, on the other hand, that Mussolini found much in Stalin's Russia that bore a significant resemblance to the political system he, Mussolini, had created in Italy. Mussolini insisted that our time would be characterized by the prevalence of political systems that were mass-mobilizing, nationalist, statist, autarchic, integralist, and militarist—organized behind the leadership of charismatic political "heroes" who, using the agencies of the unitary party, would mobilize essentially "classless" masses to the cause of *national* rehabilitation and rebirth—to capture or recapture real or fancied glory.

Karl Marx and Friedrich Engels had an entirely different vision of our century. They conceived it a century of proletarian revolution, a century in which the "contradictions" which attend intensive capital investment and advanced industrial development would produce irrepressible conflict between social classes. They conceived their revolution to be a function of industrial maturity—manifesting itself in the advanced industrial nations. They saw nationalism gradually diminishing in political significance as early as the middle of the nineteenth century, and they anticipated a decline in the role of "heroes" in the working out of history. If they conceived a special prerevolutionary or postrevolutionary role for the political party, they never made that conviction explicit. They seemed to conceive their revolution as the essentially spontaneous response of an economic class to the obvious disabilities that afflicted the prevailing, and increasingly nonviable, economic system.

It seems reasonably clear that Mussolini, having the advantage of a quarter-century, more adequately anticipated the political features of our century than did Marx or Engels. He saw twentieth-century revolution more in terms of mass mobilization than in terms of economic determinants—and leadership more in terms of personal qualities than in terms of the representation of economic forces.

The Fascism of the Underdeveloped Nations

The most obvious feature of revolution in the twentieth century is its prevalence in "underdeveloped" communities —that is to say, those social systems characterized by an essentially agrarian economy, a low capital investment index, low per capita productivity, and low productivity per man hour. In effect, revolution, both social and political, has come to those social systems least capable of generating or supporting the kind of "socialism" or "communism" anticipated by Karl Marx and Friedrich Engels. For all the "dialectical" reasoning that attempts to obscure this transparent fact, it is obvious that political events have disconfirmed Marx's prognostications. Contemporary revolution is not the by-product of industrial maturity, economic concentration and the political maturity of the proletariat—it seems to be the result of real and relative deprivation, protracted collective humiliation, population pressures, and the fragility and maladaptation of traditional political and social forms in a period of rapid economic innovation. In such circumstances large segments of the population are displaced, their security threatened, aspirations kindled. Societies are awakened from a torpor that had, in some cases, lasted for centuries. Communities aspire to status, place, and security; and "development" has become the term that refers to the entire complex process. Political analysts and historians speak of "economic development" and an ideally correlative process, "political modernization." These processes are calculated to lift underdeveloped countries to a stage of economic maturity that permits them to provide for their needs, compete in the contemporary world, and effectively defend their national interests against real or fancied "imperialist" powers.

A number of economists and political analysts have attempted to identify the conditions governing economic development and the attendant political modernization. While the catalogue of conditions varies with each author, almost all emphasize "national integration," the generation of a sense of nationality that reduces the salience of parochial

396

interests—those clan, tribal, religious, or regional preoccupations that obstruct collective purpose and dissipate collective energies. Many analysts focus on the reordering of political priorities—the fostering, for example, of a disposition to delay gratification in order to provide for capital accumulation in the service of "social overhead," the construction of adequate road, rail, communications, and educational systems necessary for sustained economic growth and development. Frequently this reordering of priorities necessitates extensive "land reform" to redirect income from those who are disposed to consume into the hands of those who are disposed to invest. Very often this can be accomplished only at the cost of violent revolution, peasant uprisings, and civil war directed by the "declassed urban intelligentsia"—the "revolutionary modernizers." Furthermore, developmental processes seem to require a postrevolutionary abatement of intrasystemic violence and disorder—tight control over the means of coercion—as well as a centralized agency for resource allocation. All of this is conducted in a situation of high emotional tension. There is a cry for discipline, sacrifice, and dedication. The postrevolutionary transit from a basically, or largely, agrarian society to the level of economic maturity is marked by considerable individual and collective discipline and emphatic sacrifice. The compensations in such an exacting environment tend to be psychological—"moral"—rather than economic. One sacrifices and is disciplined in the service of "the revolution," the "fatherland," or the "Leader."

In the world of underdeveloped countries, pluralistic aspirations and parliamentary strategies seem to have a low survival potential. Authoritarian and hierarchical political dispositions seem to more and more characterize the Third World. The "one-party state" seems to be an increasingly pervasive feature of these communities in the throes of systemic change. More and more frequently "charismatic" leaders gear the volatile sentiments of masses to the services of nationalist and developmental political programs. More and more frequently the entire political system is sustained by a rationale (or a rationalization, if one will) that is identified as a special political truth: "Arab" or "African" "socialism" —"Marxism-Leninism" of "Maoism"—"Nkrumahism" or "Guided Democracy." The pervasive similarities between all these systems have suggested to a number of analysts that we are dealing with movements sharing a family or generic relationship.[2] The claim that has been discursively argued in the pages of this exposition is that paradigmatic Fascism, the Fascism of Benito Mussolini, most fully exemplifies these family or generic traits.

In this sense a careful scrutiny of Fascism as an ideological system is far more instructive if one is to appreciate something of the political and social goals and institutions of modern mass-mobilizing movements than is the Marxism of Marx and Engels. Where classical Marxism can only provide a tortured and implausible rationale for the totalitarianism of Stalinism, Maoism, or Castroism, the logic of the Fascist argument is its straightforward justification.

This is not to say, of course, that all mass-mobilizing movements and the regimes they create are identical—any more than all the races and populations that constitute *homo sapiens* are identical. What is suggested is that a reasonably specific family of movements, and the regimes they produce when successful, share a set of reasonably specific traits best exemplified in paradigmatic Fascism. Implicit in Fascism's earliest formulations was the intention of creating a totalitarian political system, an "integrated" social order in which all men, all classes, and all productive categories, would be marshaled to the nationalistic and developmental "ideal purposes" of the authoritarian state under the aegis of a charismatic "Leader." However faulted the clear intentions of Mussolini's Fascism may have been by a complex set of political and historical circumstances, Fascism *did* attempt to construct a modernizing developmental and totalitarian system whose overt features included a one-party

[2] Cf. R. C. Tucker, "Towards a Comparative Politics of Movement Regimes," *American Political Science Review*, 55, 2 (June 1961), 281-89.

state, a party regularly subject to purging, the invocation of political criteria to establish moral or "revolutionary" rectitude, an economic system calculated to control consumption in order to increase the sum of disposal investment or "productive" capital, extensive bureaucratic control of productive processes, controlled information flow, a militarization of the community, systematic inculcation of a relatively specific ideology, a disposition to appeal to violence not only to resolve immediate practical problems but to foster the moral qualities of the ideal "revolutionary" as well.

Since the termination of the Second World War many of the economically underdeveloped nations of the world have attempted to negotiate the distance between economic and industrial backwardness to maturity. The problems that attend the process, the tensions which it generates, the institutional innovations which are the precondition and the consequence of the entire complex sequence, conspire to produce analogues, in varying degrees of intensity and differential similarity, of Mussolini's Fascism.

If Italy at the turn of the twentieth century was a "new nation" only recently unified, still riven by parochial and regional loyalties, largely agrarian in character, without an effective communications, transportation, and educational system, beset by corruption and political factionalism, and reduced to marginal importance in international affairs, the "new nations" that have made their appearance after 1945 have been similarly characterized. The difference between the Italy of the turn of the century and the "new nations" of the mid-twentieth century lies in the order of magnitude that distinguishes them on the scale of "newness," parochialism, underdevelopment, corruption, and international inferiority. Nonetheless, the effort to resolve the problems that characterize their circumstances has produced political systems, and political persuasions that subtend them, that share surprising similarities with the political system and the political persuasion that manifested themselves in Fascist Italy.

The "unitary," "integralist," and "ideological" party has become a commonplace fixture in such political environ-

399

ments. Single-party authoritarian regimes in the Middle East, Asia, Africa, and Latin America advertise the possession of a totalistic ideology, "Arab Socialism," the "Thought of Mao Tse-tung," "African Socialism" and some one or another variant of "Marxism-Leninism." "Charismatic" leaders seem to be regularly associated with such regimes. Such leaders come in a variety of styles: they may be "saviors" like Kwame Nkrumah, or "Great Helmsmen" like Mao, or "Maximum Leaders" like Castro. Press censorship and restricted information flow invariably accompany such systems, and militarization and bureaucratization seem to be equally invariable accompaniments.

Fascism not only prefigured such systems but provided their rationale as well. While "Marxists" continued to speak of the "proletariat," "democracy," and "internationalism," Fascism made the case for the mass-mobilizing authoritarianism, elitism, and nationalism that seem endemic to rapidly developing economic and political systems. The notion of the sole or unitary party was anticipated in the "totalitarianism" of Gentile's political philosophy. By the mid-thirties Fascist handbooks contained justificatory arguments in support of a single, hierarchically constituted party led by a "charismatic" leader—while the Soviet Union was still attempting to persuade the world that Stalin's Russia was the "most democratic" social and political system mankind had ever known.

Fascist theoreticians were the first to anticipate the spread of the totalitarian persuasion. As early as the mid-thirties, for example, Mihail Manoilescu was attempting an analysis of the unitary party—the backbone of totalitarian regimes —that recognized that such a political institution could, in fact, make its appearance in a variety of "cultural, political, and racial" environments—that the "political climate of our time favored and fostered its appearance and growth." He went on to suggest that the future would see the world-wide diffusion of the unitary party state. He argued that economic needs (of unspecified magnitude) and threats to national integrity or independence might well move a community to produce the analogue of the unitary party and the hierarchically constituted authoritarian state.[3] Manoilescu conceived the twentieth century to be the century not of Marxist anarchosyndicalism, but of the unitary party and the "organic" and "collectivistic" political order of which it was both the creator and the instrument.

If, in fact, the unitary party state was at least in part the consequence of delayed or thwarted industrialization and modernization—and if threats to national security and independence tend to generate political responses analogous to those which have characterized the Fascist persuasion—we can expect more and more communities to assume "fascistic" traits. Almost all commentators on the developmental problems which face the underdeveloped countries have alluded to the special disabilities suffered by those countries in the last half of the twentieth century. Almost all have concerned themselves with the problems that are the consequence of rapid industrial development in communities suffering significant population pressure. Rapidly increasing populations mean lower per capita incomes and a rate of consumption that reduces the potential for savings and productive investment. "Revolutionary" governments under such circumstances are faced with a constellation of problems—maintaining at least minimum subsistence levels while at the same time generating, collecting, and effectively allocating scarce investment capital. All of which suggests agencies of interest management, the provision of noneconomic incentives, the maintenance of "revolutionary" commitment among populations living on marginal subsistence yet expected to perform at maximum productive levels. The one-party state, the charismatic leader, the "ideologized" political culture, the histrionics and choreography of "radical" politics, all seem to flow naturally from such circumstances and the effort to meet them effectively.

Population pressure was, of course, one of the central concerns of paradigmatic Fascism. The problem of "living space

[3] M. Manoilescu, *Die einzige Partei* (Berlin: Stollberg, 1941), pp. 12f.

(*spazio vitale*)"[4] was a principal preoccupation. Like many Third World communities, Fascist Italy's development was impeded by rapid population increments, but the Fascists were ill-disposed to attempt to curtail the prevailing rate of growth. The competitive disadvantage this produced for Fascist Italy, the demand for more adequate resources to increase the support capability of the Italian peninsula, the increasing controls exercised over consumption and prices, the subsequent necessity to insulate the Italian economy from more favored economies, all led to the appearance of institutional features with which we are all reasonably familiar.

Given the prevailing rates of population growth in Africa, Asia, and Latin America, it would not be unreasonable to expect the nationalist contest for space and for resources in those areas to become increasingly exacerbated. Recourse to arms would seem to be a predictable eventuality—particularly in those areas of the world in which population growth is now outstripping the support potential of the land itself. The effort to meet the challenge of economic development and political modernization under conditions of high population density suggest that more and more of the elements of Fascism will recommend themselves to communities in protracted crisis. The recruitment, mobilization, and control strategies necessary for mounting regional struggles and providing the industrial base required to sustain such struggles in the last half of the twentieth century augur the development of political systems that share precious little affinity with anything anticipated by classical Marxism, but which will probably look more and more like one or another form of fascism.

Where such struggles become particularly vicious and taxing, one can even expect some form of racism to manifest itself—to produce a variant of the exacerbated fascism that makes racism a technique for maintaining high emotional salience, commitment, and dedication. If it is the case that

---

[4] Cf. D. Soprano, *Spazio vitale* (Milan: Corbaccio, 1942); L. Mainardi, *Nazionalità e spazi vitali* (Rome: Cremonese, 1941).

there are fascisms of various degrees of malevolence, the form that might well accompany struggles for living space in South Africa, Latin America, and parts of Asia might very well develop into racial fascisms not far removed, in terms of potential horror, from that which laid waste to Europe during the Second World War.[5] Harrison Salisbury, for example, has suggested that the conflict that looms over the Sino-Soviet border is largely the consequence of China's seemingly irreducible rate of population growth. China has indicated an interest in a "China irredenta" of about five and a half million square kilometers—land now under Russian dominance—in which millions of Chinese could be effectively settled. The most responsible estimates of China's population growth indicate that China's population is expanding at a rate of twenty million persons per year. The population density of Central Asia, of Mongolia and eastern Siberia (the land now in contention) is, by way of contrast, among the lowest in the world. Moreover, the maritime provinces of Siberia are rich farming areas.[6] As the contest becomes more and more sanguinary, it becomes fairly obvious that the lines being drawn become more and more racial in character. Khrushchev is reported to have referred to the "Yellow Peril" and to the danger from "Oriental hordes" in the course of his discussion of Sino-Soviet relations. Russia has, in fact, charged the Chinese with "playing upon the national and even racial prejudices of the Asian and African peoples."[7] The possibility that the nationalism and militarism that animates Asian radicalism might become the vehicle for an ugly racism cannot be completely dismissed.

[5] Ronald Segal has suggested something like that in his *The Race War* (New York: Viking, 1966).

[6] H. E. Salisbury, *War Between Russia and China* (New York: Norton, 1969), chap. ix. Cf. G. Borgstrom, *The Hungry Planet* (New York: Macmillan, 1967), chap. vii, and A. Kruchinin and V. Olgin, *Territorial Claims of Mao Tse-tung* (Moscow: Novosti, n.d.).

[7] *The Polemic on the General Line of the International Communist Movement* (Peking: Foreign Languages Press, 1965), pp. 212, 214; cf. N. Barrymaine, *The Time Bomb: Today's China from the Inside* (New York: Taplinger, 1971), Part Three.

That even "Marxist" and "socialist" systems should begin to display such a curious syndrome of traits has provoked serious misgivings among contemporary "revolutionary Marxists." Recently Leonid Brezhnev has insisted that Maoism is not, in fact, Marxist at all. Maoism, he has maintained, has "mounted an attack on the principles of scientific communism." Moreover, China has most "unsocialist" "Great Power aspirations" which include, among other things, aggressive territorial demands on her neighbors. To pursue its "messianic" course, Maoism, according to Brezhnev, has "militarized" China and advocates war as the ultimate strategy for world revolution.[8]

A. Kozharov, amplifying Brezhnev's analysis, alludes to the emphatic nationalism that enflames Maoist enthusiasms as well as the "cult of personality" that renders it so "un-Marxist." Maoism, furthermore, is "subjectivist and adventurist." Under the command of an "infallible Leader," the "will" of masses is mobilized. Those who resist such mobilization are "enemies of the people." Kozharov insists that all of this is quite alien to Marxism.[9]

Similar kinds of judgments emanate from the German Democratic Republic. An editorial from *Einheit*, the principal theoretical journal of East Germany's "Marxists," insists that Maoism is a "non-Marxist . . . petty bourgeois nationalistic philosophy." Maoism is the product of men inured to an economically primitive environment. The Chinese population, almost exclusively peasant in character, is particularly susceptible to the "extreme voluntarism" and "wild nationalism" that typify petit bourgeois social thought. Maoism, the editorial continues, has substituted "voluntarism for historical materialism" and conceives "history not as a history of the class struggle, but as a struggle between rival nations" in which a "decisive role" is assigned to revolutionary war. Maoism is a "fusion of nationalism with Great Power chauvinism and the theory of violence." Maoism's

[8] L. I. Brezhnev, "Introduction," in V. I. Krivtsov, ed., *Maoism Through the Eyes of Communists* (Moscow: Progress, 1970), pp. 8-10.

[9] A. Kozharov, "Maoism: Policy and 'Theory'," *ibid.*, pp, 21f., 27.

clear intention, according to *Einheit,* is to "dominate the world."[10]

For the editorialist of the Soviet *Kommunist,* Maoism is a petit bourgeois nationalism predicated on a theory of violence, a bureaucratic despotism supported by a pervasive militarism. Under this despotism the working class has been "deprived of the possibility of defending [its] interests" and "trade unions have been abolished."[11] To which Kozharov adds, the "former capitalists and feudal lords . . . continue to receive large sums of money as interest on nationalized enterprises and hold responsible posts in the economy and in the state apparatus."[12]

If one draws together all these characterizations, one does not have to be too astute to arrive at the same conclusions drawn by the "Marxist-Leninist Organization of Britain" and the "Marxist-Leninist Organization of the U.S.A.," which argue that what we are contending with when we deal with Maoism is a "miltary-fascist dictatorship" supported by "fanatical young fascists"—the Red Guards.[13]

Needless to say, any number of other "Marxists" have, as we have seen, made similar judgments concerning the "Marxism" of the Soviet regime. By the late sixties Maoists, in their turn, began to refer consistently to the Russian regime as one composed of "Soviet revisionist fascist brigands" who advocate "social-fascism." The Soviet Union has, for Maoists, become a "fascist state."[14]

Most of this is, of course, simple abuse. Behind the rhet-

---

[10] "Thought of Mao Tse-tung versus Marxism," an editorial from *Einheit, ibid.,* pp. 34f., 40f., 46.

[11] "The Situation in China and the CPC at the Present Stage," an editorial in *Kommunist, ibid.,* pp. 69f.

[12] Kozharov, "Maoism . . . ," *ibid.,* p. 27.

[13] "The Situation in the People's Republic of China: Report of the Central Committee of the Marxist-Leninist Organization of Britain," *Proletariat, 1,* 2 (August-September 1970), 29, 49.

[14] Cf. M. Waters, *Maoism in the U.S.: A Critical History of the Progressive Labor Party* (New York: Merit, 1969), p. 10, and Chiao Jung-wen, "New and Old Czars are Jackals from the same Lair," in *Studies in Comparative Communism, 2,* 3-4 (July-October 1969), 210f.

oric, however, is the substance that makes these "Marxist" judgments worthy of serious concern. Systems like those generated in postrevolutionary Russia and post-World War II China do seem to display a great many fascist features— certainly more fascist than "Marxist" traits—and "revolutionary Marxists" have finally begun to appreciate that fact. What we have suggested is that the circumstances which attend industrialization and modernization and increasing competition for space and resources has produced a disposition, not only among "Marxist" but among a large number of innovating political systems that can best be characterized as "fascistoid." The fascist persuasion seems to have a marked relevance for a variety of aspiring revolutionary movements.

If one turns one's attention to Africa, it becomes clear that the demands of rapid economic development, population pressure, the presence on the southern tip of the continent of non-Negroes, the existence of a racial fault that cuts across North Africa dividing Arabs and blacks, conjoined with the pervasive sense of status deprivation that afflicts the new nations of the continent, might very easily give rise to, or has given rise to, modern analogues of the ugliest of prewar fascist movements.

The nature of current problems in Africa and the real possibility of a protracted crisis of almost incalculable magnitude turn on the fact that famine haunts the continent. If high-yield grains and rice have made some impact in Asia (the so-called "green revolution"), the same cannot be said of the "Dark Continent." The overall productivity of food has simply failed to keep pace with population growth on the African continent. Since the First World War the per capita productivity of African peasant labor has apparently declined by about twenty percent.[15] During the same period the African continent has been balkanized into what are

[15] Cf. R. Dumont and B. Rosier, *The Hungry Future* (New York: Praeger, 1969), R. Dumont, *False Start in Africa* (New York: Praeger, 1969).

406

essentially nonviable political entities. With exceptions such as Nigeria, the Congo, and Egypt, Africa is composed of what Leonard Barnes has called "ungovernable mini-states," all afflicted with retarded economic development, animated by a grievous sense of humiliation and resentment, enflamed by dangerous racial sensitivities, and suffering intense population pressure.

During the last century the standard of living enjoyed by the advanced industrial nations of North America and Europe has left that of Africa very far behind. The industrialized nations, composed of (at best estimate) thirty percent of the world's population, enjoy about eighty percent of the world's welfare benefits. And the distance between the per capita income enjoyed by Americans and Europeans and that suffered by Africans is apparently increasing rather than decreasing. One can only speculate on the degree of frustration that will mount in the African states over the next two or three decades. A protracted crisis of the magnitude suggested, enflamed by racial animosities, charged with resentment and an irrepressible sense of humiliation, is the natural environment for the development of one or another more virulent form of fascism. Stanislav Andreski was not the first, for example, to suggest that "African socialism furnishes the justification for the attempts to despoil and drive out the Indian traders . . . just as National Socialism provided the perfect formula for anti-Semitism in central Europe, because the Jews (like the Indians in East Africa) could be condemned from a nationalistic point of view as aliens, and from a socialist standpoint as capitalists. In Zanzibar racialist socialism provided the slogans for exterminating the Arab. . . ."[16]

Whether or not racism becomes a constituent part of Africa's "radical" politics, it is fairly clear that the developmental systems produced by the efforts to industrialize the "Dark Continent" have already given evidence of the essentially

[16] S. Andreski, *The African Predicament* (New York: Atherton, 1968), pp. 201f.

fascist, rather than Marxist, character.[17] African socialism and Arab socialism share far more species traits with paradigmatic Fascism than they do with the political system anticipated by Marx and Engels. Such systems could not even be characterized as "Leninist," if we take Lenin's intentions to be those expressed in his *State and Revolution*. In *State and Revolution*, Lenin spoke of an essentially democratic political system characterized by universal suffrage, a restricted mandate for elected representatives, the recall by petition of public officials, and finally, the voluntary association of productive communes. Lenin anticipated an anarchosyndicalist system in which there would, in fact, be no state. Whatever African and Arab socialisms have produced, they have not produced the fulfillment of either Marx's or Lenin's vision of the "New Society." They have, on the other hand, produced political systems that share impressive affinities with that produced during the twenty years of Fascist rule in Italy.

Those African systems disposed to rapid change that do not degenerate into simple military dictatorships or old-fashioned despotisms seem destined to approximate one or another form of fascism. A number of commentators have alluded to the prospect. Angelo del Boca and Mario Giovana have recently lamented,

> The choice of one national party, the adoption of certain typically fascist methods and the installation of authoritarian regimes might well prove to be only transitory. . . . At the moment, however, the danger of fascism undoubtedly exists in Africa . . . .[18]

Similarly, Aldo Garosci has written:

> [In the new regimes that have sprung up in Africa] "Socialism," "Communism" and "Fascism," which elsewhere are separated by a host of traditions and sociological fac-

[17] Cf. A. J. Gregor, "African Socialism, Socialism and Fascism," *Review of Politics*, 29, 3 (July 1967).

[18] A. del Boca and M. Giovana, *Fascism Today: A World Survey* (New York: Pantheon, 1969), pp. 396f.

tors, are perilously close to one another. Where there is no real working class movement, but only a mass of peasants and urban workers controlled by charismatic groups or leaders of middle-class origin, where autarchy, the one-party system and the effort towards industrialization are based on the well-defined privileges of groups who blackmail and manoeuvre the technicians, the forces of production and the intellectual elites, can we really speak of Socialism or Communism, or of a national or popular democracy, or should we not just call it Fascism?[19]

Guy Hunter sees the prospects of development in Africa characterized by what might best be identified as a "benign fascism," that is to say, "a system which emphasizes participation at the point where it is real and personal, and which controls the necessary bureaucracy, not by representation which so easily loses reality, but through a pervasive Party animated by a single ideal."[20]

Historically, of course, European fascisms came to power with the passive or active, episodic or protracted assistance of nonfascist allies. In underdeveloped areas such as Africa, on the other hand, declassed intellectuals pursuing a fascist program frequently need not compromise their policies in order to accommodate nonfascist elements. Their programs become "egalitarian," but with provision for the "traditional hierarchical elements of African society." The unitary party mobilizes a political following behind myths and symbols, and the party leader becomes the "embodiment of the essential values" of the people. The prevailing sentiment is nationalist—at critical times racist—and the overall commitment is to interclass collaboration in the service of rapid industrial development.[21] The entire undertaking is associated with the posturing and the masculine protest that became a familiar political style in the interwar years in Europe.

[19] As cited, *ibid.*, p. 427.

[20] G. Hunter, *Modernizing Peasant Societies* (New York: Oxford, 1969), p. 286.

[21] Cf. *ibid.*, chap. ix.

Much the same account could be provided for Latin America. Georg Borgstrom's judgment represents competent opinion on the future of the continent: "Latin America is swiftly developing into the new witches' cauldron of our generation, much more explosive than ever the hungry millions of teeming Asia or the tribal peoples of Africa, involved in nationalistic ravings and agitation for freedom."[22] Arthur Whitaker and David Jordan have alluded to the increasing role of nationalism and statism in Latin America—allusions that suggest something about the character of the revolutionary movements the last quarter of the twentieth century will bring with it.[23] While such movements will probably employ Marxist locutions, it is reasonably clear that their programmatic commitments will be more fascist than Marxist. Ché Guevara's formal allies in Argentina were Peronistas. As has been indicated, theoreticians of Latin American revolutionary movements have indicated an intimate affinity between the "new" radicalism and the fascist movements of Vargas and Peron.

Gino Germani's account of Peron's revolutionary fascism is instructive.[24] If Peron was, in fact, a fascist—and Castroism has found in Peronism a natural ally—one can anticipate a radicalism in Latin America that will manifest more and more of the features of paradigmatic Fascism. Peron sought support among the disenfranchised; he was opposed by those fellow officers who maintained connections with the land-owning aristocracy and big business. Just as the most effective opponents of Mussolini's Social Republic of Salò were the members of the land-holding aristocracy, the monarchy and big business, the opposition to Peronism was composed of the aggressive elements of the privileged classes—a phenomenon that the Castroites, Ché Guevara and Regis Debray among them, came to recognize. Andreski has indi-

[22] Borgstrom, *The Hungry Planet*, pp. 270f.

[23] A. P. Whitaker and D. C. Jordan, *Nationalism in Contemporary Latin America* (New York: Free Press, 1966), chaps. ix, x.

[24] G. Germani, "Fascism and Class," in S. J. Woolf, ed., *The Nature of Fascism* (New York: Random House, 1969), pp. 65-96.

cated that "Peron's *justicialismo* incorporated elements of both extremes of the . . . political spectrum." Peron's support came essentially from the *descamisados*, the "shirtless" working class Argentinians.[25] The most radical *descamisados*, Jorge Ricardo Masetti among them, ultimately joined in the Guevara-inspired guerrilla revolutionaries—making the union of political "left" and "right" in Latin America a historic political reality.

Given the nature of the political and social crises that afflict Latin America, Brzezinski has suggested that "In Latin America the more extreme reforms may be more reminiscent of Peronism and fascism than of communism."[26] Countries beset by delayed industrialization, stressful population pressures, an irrepressible anti-imperialist (anti-North American) animus, enflamed by nationalism, and suffering collective status deprivation, will tend to adopt and adapt some variant of classical Fascism. The problems facing Latin America are those that Fascism attempted to resolve. They are not Marxist problems. Classical Marxism was a system that developed in response to the real or fancied problems of the industrial nations of the nineteenth century. Fascism, on the other hand, was the first systematic and radical attempt to resolve the problems of status-deprived nations of the twentieth century. Mussolini addressed himself to nationalistic anti-imperialism, to the problem of capital formation and the organization of national productive enterprise, to a resolution of demographic and resource concerns, and in so doing he was addressing himself to the problems of the twentieth century.

When Mary Matossian attempted a synoptic description of the "ideologies of delayed industrialization,"[27] she produced, in fact, a stenographic rendering of the ideology of

[25] S. Andreski, *Parasitism and Subversion: The Case of Latin America* (New York: Schocken, 1969), pp. 223-31.

[26] Brzezinski, *Between Two Ages*, p. 279.

[27] M. Matossian, "Ideologies of Delayed Industrialization: Some Tensions and Ambiguities," in J. Kautsky, *Political Change in Underdeveloped Countries* (New York: Wiley, 1962), pp. 252-64.

411

paradigmatic Fascism. The ideologies Matossian identifies with "delayed" industrialization resonate with the same concerns central to the Fascism that developed in Italy during the second decade of our century. Since that time more and more radical political movements have adopted the style and content of Mussolini's *Partito Nazionale Fascista*.

Recently Ludovico Garruccio has suggested that "the charismatic leaders of nations in the process of development have sought recourse to the fascist model . . . . Fascist Italy, in fact, offers an instructive paradigm of nations undertaking industrialization."[28] Societies in transition have utilized analogues of the political institutions and the political rationale that first made their manifest appearance in Fascist Italy. More than that, developing nations have sought to instill, among their constituencies, fascist moral sentiments. In their attempt to control volatile emotions, unleashed by rapid and dislocating change, they have made regular appeal to the essentially military virtues of courage, sacrifice, obedience, and loyalty. Mussolini's "citizen-militiaman" has become the model for developing societies. Once again the hero "half-soldier and half-monk" conjured up by José Antonio, the "worker-soldier" of Ernst Jünger, and the "warrior youth" of Robert Brasillach, have become the models for revolutionary youth throughout the underdeveloped world. These have been, and are, fascist models. Marx never conceived his "new men" in the guise of warriors.

In our own time youth movements impelled by explosive sentiments, employing the histrionics and choreography of mass mobilization, fascinated by charismatic heroes, have supplied host organizations with the energy and the enthusiasm for revolution in various parts of the globe. Myth, symbol, and armed conflict have again surfaced as political forms. The unitary party has become one of the most common vehicles of national and revolutionary aspirations, suppression of opposition a universal commonplace, censorship and indoctrination an expected function of government.

---

[28] L. Garruccio, *L'industrializzazione tra nazionalismo e rivoluzione* (Bologna: Mulino, 1969), pp. 50f.

Fascism was the first unequivocal expression of this new persuasion in politics. Mussolini's Fascism provided not only the style and the institutions but the rationale for the radical politics of the twentieth century. However various their specific features, the common content and the common style of the radicalisms of our time mark them as species of the same political genus.

The Fascism of Developed Nations

Most of the radicalisms we have surveyed have been produced in nations that would, on the basis of a variety of indices, be characterized as "underdeveloped." Ludovico Garruccio has made a case for Fascism and its variants as a political persuasion appropriate—functional—for a polity negotiating the transit from the stage of economic "take-off," that period in which economic development becomes self-sustained, through the "drive to maturity," that period during which the nation achieves relative industrial sophistication.

Garruccio's arguments are very persuasive. The preconditions of take-off, the radical shift in economic and political priorities, the sacrifice and discipline necessary for a sustained drive to maturity are the stuff of which radical mass-mobilizing movements are made. The one insistent problem that bedevils this kind of analysis of generic fascism is the historic experience with National Socialist Germany—one of the most impressive of the fascisms of the twentieth century. Both Matossian and Garruccio, conceiving fascism as an ideology of delayed industrialization, have registered something like puzzlement concerning the interpretation of the political radicalism of National Socialism. By whatever indices one selects, it would appear that Germany at the time of Hitler's advent to power was an industrially mature nation. Although it had succeeded to political unification relatively late, by the middle of the thirties it had surpassed France on almost every economic indicator. It was, in fact, this consideration which suggested to Marxist-Leninists that

413

"fascism" was a product of "late capitalism (*Spätkapitalismus*)."

The effort to associate fascism, in its various forms, exclusively with a specific period of economic development has never, as a consequence, been absolutely convincing. One or another form of fascism has appeared in political communities at various stages of economic and industrial maturity. The association of fascism with generic "mass movements," as "mass movements . . . captured by totalitarian cadres . . . ,"[29] is, on the other hand, more suggestive and defensible and less restrictive. Rather than a "class" or "economic" phenomenon, generic fascism has more persuasively been associated with the availability of mobilizable masses, masses composed of individuals who enjoy no strong community or class ties, who are "detached" and "anomic" as a consequence of protracted crises. Such an analysis of fascism conceives it to be the consequence of *crisis politics*, in a political environment that affords a mass-mobilizing movement mobilizable human resources of whatever class provenience.

It seems intuitively clear that a society threatened with protracted crisis—in which masses are collected in urban concentrations that tend to undermine primary group identifications and loosen voluntary associations—might very well (whether that society is industrialized or not) provide the preconditions for the advent of an aggressive totalitarian movement with its charismatic leaders and its surrogate community in the form of the unitary party. José Ortega y Gasset early maintained that the demographic expansion of Europe over the last century had provided the recruitable masses for just such "barbaric" political parties.[30] Ortega y Gasset's lamentation—his assessment of the consequences of mass intervention in politics—is not, of course, applicable only to Europe. The entire globe has endured an increase

[29] W. Kornhauser, *The Politics of Mass Society* (New York: Free Press, 1959), p. 59.

[30] J. Ortega y Gasset, *The Revolt of the Masses* (New York: Norton, 1932), chap. iv.

in population unparalleled in history. The doubling time of the world's population has been reduced to something like forty or forty-five years. "Masses," whether urban or not, have come, and will continue, to characterize the twentieth century. Inmigrant populations, displaced by industrialization or the rapid urbanization that attends industrial maturity, tend to provide the "atomized" and "alienated" individuals who constitute the population base for mass mobilizing movements. "Mass society," Kornhauser suggests, "is highly vulnerable to totalitarian movements and regimes."[31]

Because the rate of population growth is almost three percent in various parts of the globe, "masses" have become available in both the developed and the underdeveloped portions of our world. As it happens some technological innovation, selective "modernization," may make its appearance in underdeveloped areas—producing a declining death rate, a burgeoning population and urbanization—making displaced masses available for political mobilization. In industrially advanced environments, technologically facilitated access to available and recruitable masses is a consequence of "technetronic" sophistication itself.

The breakdown of traditional society—the precondition for economic take-off—massive inmigration as a consequence of the drive for industrial maturity, and rapid urbanization as a consequence of industrial maturity with the attendant erosion of role associations and stable interpersonal patterns of behavior, all conduce to the generation of politically accessible "masses." The youthfulness of such contemporary masses renders them more amenable to mobilization. The radical mass-mobilizing movements of our century have been characteristically youthful. Their style has been, again characteristically, youthful. In populations in which mobilizing elites have access to large numbers of dislocated young people—young people who find themselves in interstitial and ill-defined roles, threatened by personal and collective insecurity, driven by goal aspirations whose

[31] Kornhauser, *Politics of Mass Society*, p. 33.

415

fulfillment requires massive and systemic social change—some of the necessary conditions for political mass mobilization clearly obtain. Radical movements, movements directed toward the accomplishment of systemic change—anti-liberal and anti-parliamentarian in character—have been expressive and volatile movements of the young and the disaffected. Animated by a sense of real or fancied deprivation, a sense of real or fancied frustration, the young and the dislocated can be rendered eminently recruitable by a sustained crisis. The nature of that crisis in the twentieth century has ranged from a lost war to a protracted military conflict, from economic catastrophe to international humiliation. We have no assurance that we have catalogued most, much less all, of the possible necessary and/or sufficient conditions that produce successful mass-mobilizing radical movements, but we can be reasonably certain that some such conditions will obtain throughout the remainder of our century.

Some of those conditions are characteristic of underdeveloped communities. But it is also true—the historic case of National Socialist Germany has made that abundantly clear—that the conditions for a mass-mobilizing, radical movement can manifest themselves, perhaps with less frequency, in an industrially advanced environment as well. Modernization produces the dislocations, the status threats, the aspirations and the disaffections that increase the probability of successful mass mobilization. There is, furthermore, some reason to believe that the complex problems that have begun to accrue around advanced industrial systems can produce protracted systemic crisis.

Protracted, humiliating, and costly "limited wars" have created tensions in the United States. Massive pollution problems are beginning to tax the ingenuity and patience of urban populations. Recently inmigrant, newly urbanized masses, shorn of traditional loyalties and patterns of interpersonal behavior, faced with massive threats to status and survival as well, are, as has already been suggested, eminently mobilizable. Universities are producing inordinate numbers of "alienated" intellectuals, symbol manipulators, gifted with schooled talents that make them a candidate cadre for mass-mobilizing activities.

Perhaps more significant is that the United States, as the most advanced industrial nation in the world, utilizes (or will shortly utilize) about fifty percent of the world's resources. The standard of living of about five or six percent of the world's population is sustained by the availability of large quantities of the world's disposable resources. Should the modernizing radical movements that have invested large parts of the Third World actually succeed in even moderate industrialization, the United States can perhaps expect corresponding reduction in available resources—and a subsequent threat to a standard of living North Americans have learned to consider a birthright.

Should international relations continue to produce only embarrassment, humiliation, and nuclear threat for North Americans, and should access to available resources be restricted—particularly at a time when, for the first time, large segments of the North American population find themselves at the doorstep of the "American Dream"—the consequences might well be incalculable. This status and welfare threat, conjoined with the realization on the part of strategic elites in our society that a massive program of environmental and population control is necessary if we are to survive, might very well produce a mass-mobilizing movement sharing many of the species traits of paradigmatic Fascism.

Fascism's demand for "committees of competence" to govern Italy's industrial system might find its analogue in the demand that governance, in a postindustrial United States, be exercised by a specially trained elite. Recently Zbigniew Brzezinski has suggested that North America has entered the "technetronic" age—an age in which society is more and more shaped culturally, psychologically, socially, and economically by sophisticated technology and electronics. The tutelary, pedagogical, and bureaucratic responsibilities

417

which Fascism assumed in order to negotiate the transit to economic maturity might well find their analogue in the requirements generated by the operation of a complex technetronic postindustrial society.

In a world in which "global ghettoes" can be anticipated, in which incredibly large numbers of people will be maintained at marginal subsistence levels, in which militarism becomes a style of life for emerging nations, all the fascist arguments concerning "living space" have immediate relevance not only for underdeveloped but for postindustrial societies as well. The fascist concerns for an insulated and autarchic economic system—the self-contained and viable "ethnarchic community" characterized by reduced consumer consumption, discipline in the face of a hostile external world, sacrifice in the service of the national community—may all prove eminently relevant for the United States in the last quarter of the twentieth century.

The possibility of the resurfacing of fascist themes in continental North America is entertained by a number of commentators. Jacques Ellul has made us all painfully aware of the possibilities. Given the geometric rate of increase in the cost of supplying and maintaining a complex postindustrial society—given the requirements of regional and continental planning implied not only in population and environmental control but global defensive capability as well—a centralized and hierarchical fascist model immediately suggests itself.

"Whatever the area of interest," Ellul has insisted, "problems are raised by technology which demand technical solutions but which are of such magnitude that they cannot be solved by private enterprise: for example, pollution of water supplies and of the urban atmosphere. . . . Only rigorous and authoritarian measures of general control can solve these problems if they are to be solved at all. That is to say, appeal to dictatorial state action is indispensable. . . . The state takes on increasingly extended and numerous activities. It considers itself the ordainer and preceptor of

418

the nation."[32] This invokes a fascist rather than a Marxist image.

Ellul is well aware that these developments signal the irrelevance of classical Marxism. He indicates that for classical socialism "the suppression of the state" was a necessary condition for the liberation of man. The anticipated development of the entrepreneurial, pedagogical, tutelary, and totalitarian state is a fascist, and not a Marxist, eventuality. The organization of the Soviet state, for example, as a consequence and in Ellul's judgment, satisfies fascist, and not Marxist, commitments.[33]

Brzezinski, in turn, has spoken of tendencies evident in the United States as productive of a "technological managerialism." Such a system might well result from "persisting social crisis, the emergence of a charismatic personality, and the exploitation of mass media . . ." which could transform the United States into a "highly controlled society."[34] Conjoined with a political strategy that invokes masses, such an authoritarian managerialism could be no better described than the fascism of an industrially mature society.

These suggestions are, of course, highly reminiscent of James Burnham's intimations concerning the "managerial revolution."[35] Burnham suggested, as did Mussolini, that the affinities that united "Stalinism (communism), Nazism (fascism) and New Dealism [which Burnham considered an 'embryonic managerial ideology']" were far more significant than their differences. Mussolini argued that Stalinism and Roosevelt's New Deal attempted to provide some of the same political strategies to the resolution of contemporary problems that Fascism had anticipated.[36] Both Burnham

[32] J. Ellul, *The Technological Society* (New York: Random House, 1964), p. 237.

[33] *Ibid.*, p. 245f.; cf. pp. 289-91.

[34] Brzezinski, *Between Two Ages*, p. 253.

[35] J. Burnham, *The Managerial Revolution* (New York: John Day, 1941), chap. xiii.

[36] Cf. Mussolini, "Che cosa vuole l'America?" *Opera*, xxvi, 300-302.

and Mussolini conceived Roosevelt's "New Deal" to be something less than a mature ideology—the first tentative moves in the direction of a sophisticated mass-mobilizing, technologically oriented, and elitist belief system. The implication seems irrepressible that the tendencies that first manifested themselves in the New Deal might resurface, as a consequence of protracted crisis, as a true mass-mobilizing, totalitarian movement.

In the recent past, student radicals and the "new left" have legitimatized a political style calculated to be maximally serviceable to an American variant of fascism. The content of that prospective fascism would, of course, be dictated, not by student fancies, but by the range and magnitude of the national and international problems the last quarter of the twentieth century will bring in its train. Rather than an adolescent fascism—a fascism which commits itself to the nationalism of underdeveloped countries and seeks its mobilizable masses among the peasantry of the Third World—the fascism of industrially mature communities would mobilize the disgruntled urban petit bourgeoisie, the "conservative" working classes, the marginal agricultural classes, the half-educated and the youthful "intellectuals" so abundant in a "society of masses." One can conceive such a movement as the analogue of Hitler's National Socialist movement—with or without its racism. Such a movement, in the effort to resolve problems of unprecedented challenge and complexity, might well exploit the hyperbolic and symbolic speech, the political style, symbols, salutes, and mass demonstrations made legitimate by the student and "new left" radicals. The political violence made commonplace by the "new left" politics of the sixties might serve its political strategy eminently well. A mass-mobilizing political movement prepared to attempt a radical solution to national problems, invoking the fears and aspirations of the "silent majority" of Americans, could easily manipulate the political style of student and "new left" radicalism not only to suppress or absorb student and/or "new left" radicals but to mobilize hitherto apathetic masses. An American

420

fascist movement, when suppression of student or minority dissidence is not its purpose, might well become the carrier movement for student and minority radicals—just as Fascism became the carrier movement for Futurism.

We have, of course, only the vaguest intimation of how mass mobilization in the United States might proceed. It is possible, for example, that an American fascism might mobilize sentiment around the symbols of racial identification. Under crisis conditions—serious urban guerrilla warfare, for instance, conjoined with real or imagined external threat—the black minority in America might very well become the object of organized enmity and political discrimination. Identified in the minds of many "middle Americans" with "revolutionary anarchy" and conceived a "fifth column" in the service of Third World revolutionary movements, blacks, afflicted with high social visibility, would make ideal scapegoats for a mass-mobilizing radical movement. Furthermore, David Apter not long ago suggested that the United States is becoming increasingly bifurcated—with American society increasingly dominated by a "small but powerful group of intellectually participant citizens, trained, educated and sophisticated" to the exclusion of others who are "reduced in stature" because they were "scientifically illiterate."[37] These "illiterates" become increasingly superfluous—and blacks are disproportionately represented among their number. Black performance norms (for whatever reason) still remain approximately one standard deviation (15 I.Q. points) below white performance norms. A malevolent mass-mobilizing movement might very well ememploy such considerations as a rationale for systematic discrimination. There are any number of ominous indicators that suggest that the United States might very well develop into a racially riven society that might make recourse to some form of racial fascism.

A form of racial fascism that exploited racial sentiments of high emotional salience might well feature other traits

[37] D. Apter, "Ideology and Discontent," in D. Apter, ed., *Ideology and Discontent* (New York: Free Press, 1964), p. 31.

that historic fascisms have evinced. Gordon Rattray Taylor has suggested, for example, that population problems in the advanced industrial communities could easily generate direct government control over not only the quantity of offspring but their quality as well. "It is virtually certain," he has suggested,

> that [our] total failure to face the biological realities created by our own scientific advances will cause such disaster that there will be a sudden reversal of [the policy that conceives marriage an "unlimited franchise to procreate"]. And once the right to bear children comes under regulation, the use of those powers to improve the genetic stock rather than to degrade it could follow relatively easily.[38]

In effect, a fascism possessing familiar racial and eugenic overtones is, according to Taylor, a distinct possibility.

On the other hand, the possibility of a national fascism involving a policy of racial accommodaton that took the form of parallel communities—self-segregated black and white communities sharing a common national loyalty—is another conceivable variant. Black nationalism in the United States, given its half-articulated belief system, has (more regularly than the "new left" likes to recall) been prepared to make common cause with American "racists." Marcus Garvey worked closely with the Ku Klux Klan and the Anglo-Saxon Clubs. The Black Muslims entertained rapprochement with the American Nazi Party, and Malcolm X insisted that he had more confidence in the honesty and integrity of avowed racists than of any "liberal." More recently Stokely Carmichael insisted that Hitler was one of the "great political leaders" of the twentieth century.

Under appropriate conditions of stress, it is conceivable that a mass-mobilizing movement, organizing itself into "White" and "Black" legions, might foster the development

[38] G. R. Taylor, *The Biological Time Bomb* (New York: World, 1968), p. 180.

of self-governing but racially segregated communities *in situ* in the United States. Such vertically segregated communities would provide blacks upward mobility without threatening the security of the surrounding white communities. It is conceivable that given a "black nationalist" disposition, such an accommodation might win substantial black support. Should such a strategy be made attractive to the mobilized white majority, all that would be required for its initial political persuasiveness is the availability and high visibility of a reasonably large number of blacks that would identify themselves with the program.

While all this is admittedly highly speculative, any number of variations could conceivably be played on fascist themes in an industrially advanced society. Such societies, possessed of mobile and dislocated populations, in some cases suffering incredible population densities, and with highly volatile student populations, could easily lapse into the style and content of one or another variant of fascism. In one manner or another a number of commentators has suggested that advanced technology renders minoritarian and authoritarian control a high-order probability. Ellul, for one, has suggested that the development of sophisticated technological controls has generated a pragmatic and activist disposition among denizens of advanced industrial societies that constitutes the precondition for radical collectivist, voluntarist, and elitist movements that could only be best characterized as variants of fascism.

Fascism, Mass-Mobilizing Movements, and Political Analysis

When an informal discipline such as political science or history finds itself faced by the kinds of curiosities with which we have dealt, an attempt is made to bring order into the confusion by redefining some critical terms and by generating a new conceptual schema that might house all the subject elements. Hopefully, the proffered definitions and the new conceptual formulations reveal a transparent order that reduces the apparent confusions and dissipates the sense of paradox that attends the discussion.[39]

Unhappily, although a number of commentators has offered analytic schemata designed to house some of the considerations with which we have dealt, we are still a long way from possessing a compelling analysis. Carl Friedrich and Zbigniew Brzezinski have suggested that the analysis of radical political movements in the twentieth century might be effectively undertaken by analytically distinguishing between two genera: autocracy and heterocracy.[40] Under the genus *autocracy* one classifies a variety of forms of political rule characterized by the governance of a ruler who is not responsible to anyone else for his actions. Among the species of autocracies is one of particular significance for the twentieth century: *totalitarianism*. Totalitarian rule is a species of autocratic rule distinguished from others by certain distinctive traits. Totalitarian regimes are autocracies minimally characterized by the possession of (1) a reasonably specific official ideology based upon a radical rejection of liberal and parliamentary persuasions, (2) a unitary mass movement of solidarity, hierarchically organized under the authoritarian leadership of a charismatic leader and a directive and tutelary elite, (3) a technologically conditioned near-monopoly of the means of communication and coercion, and (4) centralized direction, under bureaucratized control, of the entire economy.

Upon such a construal, fascist and communist regimes are subspecies of one and the same species. They are construed to be "basically alike, or at any rate more nearly like each other than like any other system of government, including earlier forms of autocracy."[41] They differ, of course,

---

[39] Cf. A. J. Gregor, *An Introduction to Metapolitics* (New York: Free Press, 1971), chap. 5, particularly pp. 131ff.

[40] C. J. Friedrich and Z. K. Brzezinski, *Totalitarian Dictatorship and Autocracy* (New York: Praeger, 1962), chap. 1.

[41] *Ibid.*, p. 5.

in a variey of ways, but their similarities, for the purposes of *analysis*, are more fundamental than their differences.

If we recognize the differences that characterize the various totalitarianisms of our time—differences in ideological persuasion, the employment of political terror, recruitment base, and overall rate and degree of effectiveness—the shared similarities afford a handle on comprehensive interpretation. For the purposes of *time conditioned* and *specific explanation*, on the other hand, subsets of descriptive and theoretic empirical generalizations would have to be invoked with which the proposed conceptual schema could not be immediately concerned. If one aspires to predict the course of development of systems like that which characterized Fascist Italy, or which now characterize Maoist China, knowing that these systems are both "totalitarian" would be a necessary, but only preliminary, intelligence. In order to begin to generalize, to collect comparative data, one must generate sorting criteria that identify discriminable categories. The concept "totalitarianism" is a category in which we can store, and readily retrieve, pieces of information otherwise neglected. Moreover, such categories *do* suggest *low level generalizations* that support equally *low level*, but plausible, *predictions*. We, in effect and for example, expect "totalitarian" systems to maintain their "revolutionary integrity" by regular purges. We also expect such systems, irrespective of what is said in the heat of controversy, to create and maintain an elaborate bureaucratic infrastructure. We have come to expect such eventualities largely because the concept "totalitarian" is the product of the historic experience of the past half-century. To decide to call a system "totalitarian" means that we have made a guarded knowledge claim that the subject system is possessed now, or in the determinate future will be possessed, of some reasonably specific traits.

Should such "experimental" or "provisional" naming prove to have empirical utility, analysts proceed to pursue similarities and explore differences. One of the differences frequently referred to in the literature of "totalitarianism" is that of "ideological" incompatibility. Friedrich and Brzezinski distinguish between the "communist" and "fascist" subspecies of totalitarianisms in terms of their "proclaimed purposes and intentions." We have here considered, in some considerable detail, just how different those "proclaimed purposes and intentions" might in fact be. When F. L. Carsten, for example, attempted to characterize synoptically "fascist" movements he identified the following traits as specific and "distinguishing": In his judgment fascist systems were (1) "strongly nationalist and violently anti-communist and anti-Marxist"; (2) they were anti-liberal, authoritarian and anticipated a political order organized under the aegis of a single party; (3) the unitary parties that animated the regimes were "strongly elitist" and "military in character"; (4) such movements were animated by a "powerful myth," a myth of the nation and/or the race and, "above all, the myth of the 'Leader'"; and finally, (5) such movement appealed to all social groups—the only exclusions were "profiteers, the parasites, the financial gangsters, the ruling cliques, the rapacious capitalists, [and] the reactionary landowners."[42]

If one reviews such a seriatim list of distinguishing traits one finds it difficult to identify the differences that mark off "fascist" from "communist" political systems. Surely now that mutual charges of "Great Power chauvinism" and "mad nationalism" have been directed against the Soviet Union by "Marxist" China, and against China by the "Marxist" Soviet Union, it is doubtful whether "nationalism" is a species-defining trait. Moreover, since the Soviet Union has identified Maoism as an "anti-Marxist" and "anti-communist" "petit bourgeois" ideology, it is doubtful whether one can invest any assurance in such a feature as species discriminating. The Soviet Union, similarly, would appear to be no less "anti-Marxist" than Mao's China or Castro's Cuba. All such systems are equally anti-liberal, authoritarian, and informed

[42] F. L. Carsten, *The Rise of Fascism* (Berkeley: University of California, 1967), pp. 230-32.

by hierarchically organized one-party states. The unitary parties have all been elitist and military in disposition and character. They are all infused by "powerful myths," not the least of which is the "myth" of the charismatic leader: Stalin the "universal genius," Mao the "never setting Red Sun," Castro the "telluric force." All have attempted to mobilize *all* population elements with the exclusion of the "profiteers, the parasites, the financial gangsters, the ruling cliques, the rapacious capitalists [and] the reactionary landowners."

In substance, whatever distinctions there are between "fascist" and "communist" movements in terms of "ideological" commitments—they are singularly superficial. The "Marxism" of "communist" movements has long since dissolved into a collection of simple turns of speech lacking any significant Marxist substance.

Whatever distinctions there are between "fascist" and "communist" hegemonic movements, "ideology" seems to provide singularly insubstantial differentiae. The class origins of the leaders of the respective movements seem equally undiscriminating. The leaders of all radical movements derive from manifestly petit bourgeois and bourgeois provenance. Lenin was the son of a petty noble; Mao the son of a "rich" peasant; Hitler was the son of a petty state official; Mussolini was the son of a small property owner and a schoolteacher. The cadre of such movements come, characteristically, from equally bourgeois backgrounds.

Distinctions based upon respective "social" or recruitment bases seem more promising. "Fascist" movements tend to recruit among the petit bourgeoisie while "communist" movements appeal to working masses. Once again the distinctions must be drawn with care. For Marx and Engels, the peasantry constituted a section of the petit bourgeoisie. If "fascist" movements recruit petit bourgeois elements, and the peasantry is numbered among the petit bourgeoisie, then one has *prima facie* difficulty in distinguishing between the recruitment bases of "fascism" and "communism." "Communist" movements have never, for instance, made a successful revolution with the urban proletariat. The Chinese revolution was undertaken with the support of the peasantry; the Cuban revolution was (according to Ché Guevara) a "peasant-guerrilla" movement; even the Russian revolution could hardly be characterized as a proletarian revolution.

A more profitable distinction seems to be in terms of *urban* petit bourgeois recruitment as distinguished from *rural* petit bourgeois recruitment. The most prominent movements characterized as "fascist" in the past have been those that have recruited largely among the semi-urbanized and urbanized petit bourgeoisie. With the exception of some unsuccessful "fascist" movements, such as Codraneu's "Iron Guard," such movements have been made up of these elements.

The distinction between totalitarian movements would seem to reside not in any serious ideological differences, but, at least in part, in differences in their respective recruitment bases. All such movements we have considered have been essentially mass-mobilizing developmental dictatorships under single-party auspices. Their ideological persuasions have, in substance, been remarkably similar. Whatever distinctions there are between mass-mobilizing movements seem to turn on the stage of industrial maturity they inhabit at the time they undertake their "renovating" revolution. Some of these revolutions have taken place while the subject community was at the *preindustrial* stage; others while the subject community had just negotiated the self-sustaining "*take-off*" phase; still others, to which we have only alluded, have suffered their radicalism after they had attained *industrial maturity*. Whatever distinctions are to be found in the respective recruitment bases of the various radical movements probably turn, in large part, on the stage of economic development at which the "revolution" finds them.[43]

The fact seems to be that the mass-mobilizing movements of our time recruit *whatever* population elements are avail-

[43] Cf. L. Garruccio's interesting discussion, "Le tre età del fascismo," *Il Mulino*, 213 (January-February 1971), 53-73.

able. It would seem to be fairly obvious that at various stages of economic development different population elements become mobilizable. At no time is such mobilization based on any *serious* Marxist criteria. Mobilizable masses become "proletarianized," for example, either by fighting in the hills or by being inculcated with the "thought" of one or another "leader." In the last analysis *anyone*, any member of *any* class or population category, is a potential "revolutionary." All that is necessary is the development of the requisite "consciousness." In this sense the ultimate logic governing recruitment is shared by both "fascist" and "communist" mass-mobilizing movements.

The intentions that animate most such movements seem to be essentially developmental.[44] Those who characterize themselves "Marxist revolutionaries" identify the cardinal tasks of the "socialist" revolution as "economic development with the main emphasis on socialist industrialization . . . and mechanization of agriculture; the launching of a genuinely cultural revolution with the purpose of raising the educational and ideological level of the people and reorganizing science and art on a Marxist-Leninist basis; and raising the people's standard of living."[45]

These cardinal tasks are no less the tasks assumed by Mussolini's Fascism. They are not specifically "Marxist" or "socialist" tasks. Most of the mass-mobilizing movements prominent in the twentieth century have been similarly developmental in intention. When not specifically developmental, as was the case with National Socialist Germany, their aspirations—the rapid expansion of industrial capacity to meet Germany's defensive and aggressive requirements—produced an environment sharing many affinities with that which typifies retarded or renovating economies undergoing revolutionary development.

Whatever the case, it would seem that we are dealing

[44] In this regard, cf. John H. Kautsky, *Communism and the Politics of Development* (New York: Wiley, 1968).

[45] Kozharov, ed., "Maoism . . . ," in *Maoism Through the Eyes of Communists*, p. 31.

with a class of mass-mobilizing movements under single-party auspices that aspire to the creation of a totalitarian political order. Such movements seem to be novel products of the twentieth century and seem to involve some of the technological developments characteristic of our time (rapid mobility, all but instantaneous communication over long distances, instruments of coercion capable of controlling large populations, among others) as well as the availability of mobilizable masses. In general such movements set developmental tasks for themselves—at least this seems to have been the case during the critical years between the First World War and the present. This does not mean, of course, that other tasks and other crises might not generate similar movements in industrially sophisticated environments.

Of all the movements that have made an appearance since the First World War, only Fascism represents these developments with clarity. However more successful other movements have been in meeting the goals they have set themselves, it was Fascism that most clearly identified the tasks, the strategies, and provided the animating persuasion for the radical movements of our time.

From Marxism to Fascism

Having inherited an intellectual tradition born during the interwar years, most political analysts have continued to insist that the radicalism of our time is rooted in Marxist soil. In a certain sense that is true. Mussolini's Fascism grew out of the intellectual patrimony funded by classical Marxism. The first Fascists were, in fact, responding to problems unresolved by the extensively formalized social and political convictions of Marx and Engels. Men such as A. O. Olivetti, Sergio Panunzio, and Roberto Michels were Marxists before they became Fascists.

Michels, whose thought has received international attention, was originally a radical socialist—a convinced Marxist. Under the impact of the events at the turn of the century, Michels began an intellectual development which led him into the Fascist ranks.[46] He not only anticipated and contributed to the articulation of the rationale of Fascism, he provided descriptive characterization of its development and, after its advent to power, elaborated upon its central themes.[47] His lectures on political sociology, delivered in Rome in 1927, provide a catalogue of Fascist themes. The central themes revolved around the motivation, mobilization, and organization of masses. Problems of collective psychology, the political and social roles of strategic and functional elites, the nature of organizations and their capacity to integrate hierarchically individuals and groups, are matters which occupied Michels' attention.

Michels' intellectual trajectory characterized that of Fascism in general. The problems to which Michels responded were the problems which Marx and Engels had left without resolve—problems that plagued not only revolutionary intellectuals but political actors as well. They were problems that were to continue to agitate revolutionaries throughout the remainder of the century. The generation of "revolutionary consciousness" remained as much of a problem for Lenin as it has for Mao and for Castro. The effort to "instill" in nonrevolutionary masses an appropriate "consciousness" has produced "thought reform" in Maoist China, sloganeering in the Soviet Union and Castro's Cuba, as well as Regis Debray's rather quaint conviction that "proletarian consciousness" is generated when one joins in the systematic violence of guerrilla bands. Moreover, Michels' insistence

[46] Cf. F. Pfetsch, *"Die Entwicklung zum faschistischen Führestaat in der politischen Philosophie von Robert Michels"* (Doctoral Dissertation, Ruprecht Karl University, Heidelberg, 1964).

[47] The most interesting of Michels works in these regards include "Psychologie der antikapitalistischen Massenbewegungen," in *Grundriss der Sozialökonomik*, 9, 1 (1934), 241-359; *Patriotismus: Prolegomena zu einer soziologischen Analyse* (Munich: Duncker & Humblot, 1929), and *Studi sulla democrazia e sull'autorità* (Florence: Sansoni, 1933).

that nationalism provides, in the twentieth century, special advantage in the mobilization of masses has found its confirmation in Chinese and Cuban nationalism.

In effect, the "new radicalism" that made its appearance after the Second World War has followed, albeit belatedly, the same course pursued by Fascist social thought after the end of the first world conflict. Less and less emphasis has been, and is being, placed on the "objective" conditions governing mass mobilization and revolution. More and more frequently the "subjective" conditions—the individual and collective disposition to make revolution—are invoked. As a consequence Fascist themes appear more and more frequently in radical literature. Activism, voluntarism, the recourse to political violence, not only for tactical or strategic purposes but in order to obtain some putative psychological or moral benefits as well, are now all indispensable components of radical and revolutionary belief systems. All these accretions signal the distance radical thought has traversed in the three-quarters of a century since the death of Engels and the crisis of classical Marxism. Michels is more relevant to radical politics than Marx; Mussolini shares more similarities with Castro than Castro does with Lenin. The Yippies and the Futurists have more affinities to each other than either has to anything in the tradition of classical Marxism. The structure, the institutions, and the functioning of Stalin's state apparatus find more analogues in Mussolini's corporative state than anywhere in Marx's plan for the dictatorship of the proletariat. Finally, and in point of fact, Fascist thinkers, before the termination of the Second World War, had embarked on the anguished discussion of "alienation," "existential commitments," and "humanism" that has come to characterize the more tortured radicals of our time.[48] As a consequence, the radicals who preoccupy them-

[48] Cf. for example, G. S. Spinetti, *Fascismo e libertà* (Padua: CEDAM, 1941); V. A. Bellezza, *L'esistenzialismo positivo di Giovanni Gentile* (Florence: Sansoni, 1954); U. Spirito, *Giovanni Gentile* (Florence: Sansoni, 1969); V. Vettori, ed., *Giovanni Gentile*. (Florence: La Fenice, 1954).

selves with the "moral issues," with "existential concerns," and with a "new humanism" share more features with the philosophic lucubrations of Fascist neo-idealism than they do with any vital tradition in Marxism.

English-speaking political analysts have so thoroughly neglected Fascist thought that they have contented themselves with a collection of superficial and pedestrian judgments concerning "Fascism's anti-intellectualism" and its "lack of any serious sociological or political content." Actually, the men who contributed to the articulation of Fascist ideology included some of the most notable in contemporary European intellectual history. Fascists borrowed extensively from the thought of Vilfredo Pareto, Gaetano Mosca and Max Weber. Roberto Michels and Corrado Gini, certainly important figures in twentieth-century social thought, were numbered among the members of the Fascist Party itself. Giovanni Gentile, easily one of the more interesting social and political philosophers of the twentieth century, died in its service.

Whatever the case, however competent or incompetent, interesting or uninteresting, elaborate or simplistic Fascist thought was, it was, at least in significant measure, a response to problems inherited from classical Marxism that at that time beset, and that continue to beset, the nations of the modern world. Innocent of any familiarity with the rationale produced by Fascism, many radical thinkers have reproduced its content—more have simply simulated its style. Radicalism's affinities with paradigmatic Fascism have become so palpable that recognition of their relationship has become fairly commonplace. Not only have social scientists such as William Kornhauser analyzed their similarities in terms of the politics of mass society, and economic theorists such as Ludovico Garruccio related those similarities to the preconditions and conditions governing stages of economic growth, but Richard Lowenthal has recently traced the advent, among "left-wing" radicals, of fascist style.[49]

[49] R. Lowenthal, "Unreason and Revolution," *Encounter, 33,* 5 (November 1969), 22-34.

Tracing the initial departures from Marx's historicist and rationalist persuasion to V. I. Lenin, Lowenthal catalogues the species traits of contemporary radicalism: voluntarism, activism, a fascination with romantic violence, a commitment to the primacy of politics and war, all conjoined with a preoccupation with "heroes"—men who embody the unitary will of the people and whose personal qualities "insure" the "people's victory."

In a curious and certainly unanticipated manner, Mussolini, in insisting that the twentieth century would be the century of fascism, appears to have been prescient. The twentieth century seems destined to suffer fascism in one or another form in one or another political community. Whether underdeveloped communities strain to mobilize men and resources, or developed communities seek to manage the complexities of a postindustrial society, the availability and effectiveness of a now familiar collection of choreographic, histrionic, intellectual, and political strategies urge themselves upon political actors.

A Selected Bibliography

The following publications are offered as a supplement to those specifically cited in the footnotes. The publications (by-and-large secondary sources) which appear in both places are those which have served in a critical way in formulating the central theses of this book. The publications herein cited vary in quality, but all contributed to the preparation of the manuscript. The publications are divided into subheadings by chapter except those which have served as primary source references.

PRIMARY SOURCE REFERENCES

Castro, Fidel. *The Selected Works of Fidel Castro.* 3 volumes. Cambridge, Mass.: MIT Press, 1971.

Guevara, Ernesto "Ché." *Obras completas.* 4 volumes. Buenos Aires: Editorial del Plata, 1968–.

Lenin, V. I. *Collected Works.* 45 volumes. Moscow: Progress, 1960–1970.

Mao Tse-tung. *Selected Works.* 4 volumes. Peking: Foreign Languages, 1967.

Martí, José. *Obras completas.* 24 volumes. Havana: Editorial Nacional de Cuba, 1963–.

Marx, Karl, and Engels, Friedrich. *Werke.* 39 volumes. Berlin: Dietz, 1961–1968.

Mussolini, Benito. *Opera omnia.* 36 volumes. Florence: La fenice, 1951–1963.

Stalin, J. V. *Works.* 13 volumes. Moscow: Foreign Languages, 1952–1955.

CHAPTER ONE

Andics, Hellmut. *Rule of Terror: Russia under Lenin and Stalin.* Translated by Alexander Lieven. New York: Holt, Rinehart and Winston, 1969.

Azrael, Jeremy R. *Managerial Power and Soviet Politics.* Cambridge: Harvard, 1966.

Black, C. E. *The Dynamics of Modernization.* New York: Harper, 1967.

Burnham, James. *The Managerial Revolution.* New York: John Day, 1941.

Conquest, Robert. *The Great Terror.* New York: Macmillan, 1968.

Dallin, Alexander and Breslauer, George W. *Political Terror in Communist Systems.* Stanford: Stanford University Press, 1970.

Davis, Horace B. *Nationalism and Socialism.* New York: Monthly Review, 1967.

Deutscher, Isaac. *Ironies of History: Essays on Contemporary Communism.* New York: Oxford University Press, 1966.

Garruccio, Ludovico. *L'industrializzazione tra nazionalismo e rivoluzione: le ideologie politiche dei paesi in via di sviluppo.* Bologna: Mulino, 1969.

Heilbroner, Robert L. *Between Capitalism and Socialism.* New York: Random House, 1970.

Holt, Robert T. and Turner, John E. *The Political Basis of Economic Development.* Princeton: D. Van Nostrand, 1966.

Jobet, Julio C. *Los fundamentos del marxismo.* Mexico City: Diogenes, 1971.

Johnson, Harry G. (Editor). *Economic Nationalism in Old and New States.* London: George Allen & Unwin, 1968.

Kautsky, John H. *Political Change in Underdeveloped Countries: Nationalism and Communism.* New York: John Wiley & Sons, 1962.

Kofler, Leo. *Stalinismus und Bürokratie.* Berlin: Luchterhand, 1970.

Laqueur, Walter. *The Fate of the Revolution: Interpretations of Soviet History.* New York: Macmillan, 1967.

Lemberg, Eugen. *Nationalismus.* 2 volumes. Munich: Rowohlt, 1964.

Lichtheim, George. *Imperialism.* New York: Praeger, 1971.

Manoilesco, Mihail. *Le siècle du corporatisme*. Paris: Felix Alcan, 1938.

Moore, Stanley. *Three Tactics: The Background in Marx*. New York: Monthly Review, 1963.

Procacci, Giuliano (Editor). *La "rivoluzione permanente" e il socialismo in un paese solo, 1924–1926*. Rome: Riuniti, 1963.

Rizzi, Bruno. *La lezione dello stalinismo*. Rome: Opere nuove, 1962.

Rostow, Walt W. *The Stages of Economic Growth*. New York: Cambridge University Press, 1969.

Schapiro, Leonard. *Totalitarianism*. New York: Praeger, 1972.

Spilimbergo, Jorge E. *La revolucion nacional en Marx*. Buenos Aires: Coyoacan, 1961.

Stalin, Joseph. *Problems of Leninism*. Moscow: Foreign Languages, ·n.d.

Trotsky, Leon. *The Revolution Betrayed*. Translated by Max Eastman. Garden City, N.Y.: Doubleday, Doran, 1937.

Tucker, Robert C. *The Marxian Revolutionary Idea*. New York: Norton, 1969.

von der Mehden, Fred R. *Politics of the Developing Nations*. Englewood Cliffs, N.J.: Prentice-Hall, 1964.

Ward, Barbara. *Nationalism and Ideology*. New York: Norton, 1966.

Chapter Two

Adams, H. P. *Karl Marx in his Earlier Writings*. London: George Allen & Unwin, 1940.

Avineri, Shlomo. *The Social and Political Thought of Karl Marx*. New York: Cambridge University Press, 1968.

Axelos, Kostas. *Marx penseur de la technique*. Paris: Editions de Minuit, 1960.

Barion, Jakob. *Hegel und die marxistische Staatslehre*. Bonn: Bouvier, 1963.

Bollnow, Hermann. "Engels Auffassung von Revolution und Entwicklung in seinen 'Grundsätzen des Kommunismus.'" In Iring Fetscher (Editor). *Marxismusstudien.* First Series. Tübingen: Mohr, 1954.

Breuer, Karl H. *Der junge Marx: Sein Weg zum Kommunismus.* Cologne: Luthe, 1954.

Calvez, Jean-Yves. *La pensée de Karl Marx.* Paris: Editions du Seuil, 1956.

Cornu, Auguste. *Karl Marx: Die ökonomisch-philosphischen Manuskripte.* Berlin: Akademie, 1955.

Fleischer, Helmut. *Marx und Engels.* Munich: Alber, 1970.

Gregor, A. James. *A Survey of Marxism.* New York: Random House, 1965.

Livergood, Norman D. *Activity in Marx's Philosophy.* The Hague: Nijhoff, 1967.

McLellan, David. *Marx Before Marxism.* New York: Harper and Row, 1970.

Mende, Georg. *Karl Marx' Entwicklung vom revolutionären Demokraten zum Kommunisten.* Berlin: Dietz, 1960.

Meszaros, Istvan. *Marx's Theory of Alienation.* New York: Harper and Row, 1970.

Mondolfo, Rodolfo. *El humanismo de Marx.* Buenos Aires: Fondo de Cultura Economica, 1964.

———. *Marx y Marxismo.* Buenos Aires: Fondo de Cultura Economica, 1960.

Oiserman, T. I. *Die Entstehung der marxistischen Philosophie.* Translated from the Russian by Erich Salewski. Berlin: Dietz, 1965.

———. *Die Entfremdung als historische Kategorie.* Translated from the Russian by Siegfried Wollgast. Berlin: Dietz, 1965.

Ollman, Bertell. *Alienation: Marx's Conception of Man in Capitalist Society.* New York: Cambridge University Press, 1971.

Röhr, Heinz. *Pseudoreligiöse Motive in den Frühschriften von Karl Marx.* Tübingen: Mohr, 1962.

Rosenberg, D. I. *Die Entwicklung der ökonomischen Lehre von Marx und Engels in den vierziger Jahren des 19.*

Jahrhunderts. Translated from the Russian by Wilhelm Fickenscher. Berlin: Dietz, 1958.

Ryazanoff, D. *The Communist Manifesto of Karl Marx and Friedrich Engels Edited, with an Introduction, Explanatory Notes and Appendices.* Translated by Eden and Cedar Paul. New York: Russell & Russell, 1963.

Thier, Erich. *Das Menschenbild des jungen Marx.* Göttingen: Bendenhoeck & Ruprecht, 1961.

Tucker, Robert. *Philosophy and Myth in Karl Marx.* New York: Cambridge University Press, 1961.

Ullrich, H. *Der junge Engels.* 2 volumes. Berlin: DVW, 1961, 1966.

Venable, Vernon. *Human Nature: The Marxian View.* New York: Knopf, 1945.

CHAPTER THREE

Boudin, Louis B. *The Theoretical System of Karl Marx.* Chicago: Kerr, 1907.

Cunow, Heinrich. *Die Marxsche Geschichts-, Gesellschafts- und Staatstheorie.* 2 volumes. Berlin: Vorwärts, 1920.

Gottheil, Fred M. *Marx's Economic Predictions.* Evanston: Northwest University Press, 1966.

Hammacher, Emil. *Das philosophisch-ökonomische System des Marxismus.* Leipzig: Duncker & Humblot, 1909.

Kautsky, Karl. *Die materialistische Geschichtsauffassung.* 2 volumes. Berlin: Dietz, 1929.

———. *The Economic Doctrines of Karl Marx.* Translated by H. J. Stenning. New York: Macmillan, 1936.

Rosdolsky, Roman. *Zur Entstehungsgeschichte des Marxschen "Kapital."* 2 volumes. Vienna: Europa Verlag, 1968.

Untermann, Ernest. *Marxian Economics.* Chicago: Kerr, 1927.

Wolfson, Murray. *A Reappraisal of Marxian Economics.* Baltimore: Penguin, 1964.

Wygodski, Witali S. *Die Geschichte einer grossen Entdeckung.* Translated from the Russian by Horst Friedrich and Horst Richter. Berlin: Verlag Die Wirtschaft, 1965.

CHAPTER FOUR

Adler, Max. *Lehrbuch der Materialistischen Geschichtsauffassung.* 2 volumes. Berlin: Laubsche Verlagsbuchhandlung, 1930.

——. *Die Staatsauffassung des Marxismus.* Darmstadt: Wissenschaftliche Buchgesellschaft, 1964.

Bernstein, Eduard. *Der Sozialismus einst und jetzt.* Berlin: Dietz, 1923.

——. *Die Voraussetzungen des Sozialismus und die Aufgaben der Sozialdemokratie.* Stuttgart: Dietz, 1899.

Biermann, W. E. *Die Weltanschauung des Marxismus.* Leipzig: Roth & Schunke, 1908.

Bukharin, Nikolai. *Imperialism and World Economy.* New York: Fertig, 1966.

Daniels, Robert Vincent. *The Conscience of the Revolution: Communist Opposition in Soviet Russia.* New York: Simon and Schuster, 1969.

Gay, Peter. *The Dilemma of Democratic Socialism: Eduard Bernstein's Challenge to Marx.* New York: Collier, 1962.

Gorki, Maxim. *Lenin y el Mujic: Reflexiones sobre la Crueldad Rusa.* Translated from the Russian by Pedro Pellicena. Madrid: Oriente, 1928.

——. *Untimely Thoughts.* Translated from the Russian by H. Ermolaev. New York: Eriksson, 1968.

Hilferding, Rudolf. *Das Finanzkapital.* Berlin: Dietz, 1955.

Hobson, J. A. *Imperialism.* Ann Arbor: University of Michigan, 1967.

Kautsky, Karl. *The Class Struggle.* Translated by William E. Bohn. New York: Norton, 1971.

——. *The Dictatorship of the Proletariat.* Translated by H. J. Stenning. Ann Arbor: University of Michigan, 1964.

——. *Ethik und materialistische Geschichtsauffassung.* Stuttgart: Dietz, 1919.

——. *Gegen die Diktatur.* Berlin: Litfass, n.d.

——. *Die Soziale Revolution.* Berlin: Vorwärts, 1904.

——. *Terrorismus und Kommunismus.* Berlin: Verlag Neues Vaterland, 1919.

———— and Bruno Schoenlank. *Grundsätze und Forderungen der Sozialdemokratie.* Berlin: Vorwärts, 1905.

Kemp, Tom. *Theories of Imperialism.* London: Dobson, 1967.

Labriola, Antonio. *Essays on the Materialistic Conception of History.* Translated by Charles H. Kerr. Chicago: Kerr, 1904.

————. *Socialism and Philosophy.* Translated by Ernst Untermann. Chicago: Kerr, 1934.

Luxemburg, Rosa. *The Accumulation of Capital.* Translated by Agnes Schwarzschild. London: Routledge and Kegan Paul, 1951.

————. *The Russian Revolution and Leninism or Marxism.* Ann Arbor: University of Michigan Press, 1961.

Masaryk, Thomas G. *Philosophischen und sociologischen Grundlagen des Marxismus.* Vienna: Konegen, 1899.

Serge, Victor. *From Lenin to Stalin.* New York: Pioneer, 1937.

Sombart, Werner. *Grundlagen und Kritik des Sozialismus.* 2 volumes. Berlin: Askanischer Verlag, 1919.

————. *Der proletarische Sozialismus.* 2 volumes. Jena: Fischer, 1924.

————. *Sozialismus und soziale Bewegung im neunzehnten Jahrhundert.* Jena: Fischer, 1897.

Sorel, Georges. "The Decomposition of Marxism." In Irving Louis Horowitz. *Radicalism and the Revolt Against Reason.* New York: Humanities, 1961.

————. *Les polémiques pur l'interprétation du Marxisme: Bernstein & Kautsky.* Paris: Giard & Brière, 1900.

————. *Saggi di critica del Marxismo.* Milan: Sandron, 1903.

Untermann, Ernst. *Die logischen Mängel des engeren Marxismus.* Munich: Verlag der dietzgenschen Philosophie, 1910.

Woltmann, Ludwig. *Der historische Materialismus.* Düsseldorf: 1900.

Ziegenfuss, Werner. *Lenin: Soziologie und revolutionäre*

441

Aktion im politischen Geschehen. Berlin: De Gruyter, 1948.

CHAPTER FIVE

Arcari, Paola Maria. *Socialismo e democrazia nel pensero di Vilfredo Pareto.* Rome: Volpe, 1966.

Bonomi, Ivanoe. *Dal socialismo al fascismo.* Rome: Formiggini, 1924.

Borkenau, Franz. "Zur Soziologie des Faschismus." In Ernst Nolte (Editor). *Theorien über den Faschismus.* Berlin: Kiepenheuer & Witsch, 1967.

Corradini, Enrico. *Discorsi politici* (1902–1923). Florence: Vallecchi, 1923.

———. *La unità e la potenza delle nazioni.* Florence: Vallecchi, 1912.

———. *La vita nazionale.* Florence: Lumachi, 1907.

Gregor, A. James. *The Ideology of Fascism.* New York: Free Press, 1969.

———. *Interpretations of Fascism.* New York: General Learning, 1974.

Joll, James. *Three Intellectuals in Politics: Blum, Rathenau, Marinetti.* New York: Harper and Row, 1960.

Le Bon, Gustave. *The Crowd: A Study of the Popular Mind.* London: Benn, 1952.

Marinetti, Filippo, *Futurismo e fascismo.* Foligno: Campitelli, 1924.

———. *La grande Milano tradizionale e futurista.* Verona: Mondadori, 1969.

———. *Teoria e invenzione futurista.* Verona: Mondadori, 1968.

Melis, Renato (Editor). *Sindacalisti italani.* Rome: Volpe, 1964.

Michels, Robert. *First Lectures in Political Sociology.* Translated by Alfred De Grazia. New York: Harper and Row, 1949.

———. *Italien von heute.* Zurich: Füssli, 1930.

————. *Political Parties.* Translated by Eden and Cedar Paul, New York: Dover, 1959.

————. *Sozialismus und Faschismus in Italien.* 2 volumes. Munich: Meyer & Jessen, 1925.

Mosca, Gaetano. *Elementi di scienza politica.* 5th edition. 2 volumes. Bari: Laterza, 1953.

Nanni, Torquato. *Bolscevismo e fascismo al lume della critica marxista.* Bologna: Cappelli, 1924.

Olivetti, Angiolo Oliviero. *Il sindacalismo come filosofia e come politica.* Milan: Alpes, 1924.

Pareto, Vilfredo. *Corso di economia politica.* 2 volumes. Turin: Einaudi, 1949.

————. *Manuale di economia politica.* Milan: Libreria, 1919.

————. *Les systèmes socialistes.* 2 volumes. Paris: Giard & Brière, 1902.

————. *Trasformazioni della democrazia.* Rocca San Casciano: Cappelli, 1964.

————. *Trattato di sociologia generale.* 2nd edition. 2 volumes. Milan: Communità, 1964.

Pfetsch, Frank. *Die Entwicklung zum faschistischen Füherstaat in der politischen Philosophie von Robert Michels.* Heidelberg: Ruprecht-Karl Universität, 1964.

Schuler, Erwin. *Pareto's Marx-Kritik.* Tübingen: Becht, 1938.

Scrivo, Luigi (Editor). *Sintesi del futurismo: storia e documenti.* Rome: Bulzoni, 1968.

Vajda, Mihaly. "The Rise of Fascism in Italy and Germany." *Telos,* No. 12 (Summer, 1972).

Zimei, Artemisia. *Marinetti: narratore, sintetic, dinamico di guerre e amori.* Rome: Le stanze del libro, 1941.

CHAPTER SIX

Buchanan, Keith. *The Transformation of the Chinese Earth.* New York: Praeger, 1970.

Elegant, Robert S. *Mao's Great Revolution.* New York: World, 1971.

Galli, Giorgio. *La tigre di carta e il drago scarlatto: il pensiero di Mao Tse-tung e l'Occidente.* Bologna: Mulino, 1970.

Huang Sung-K'ang. *Li Ta-chao and the Impact of Marxism on Modern Chinese Thinking.* Paris: Mouton, 1965.

Isaacs, Harold R. *The Tragedy of the Chinese Revolution.* Stanford: Stanford University Press, 1961.

Johnson, Chalmers A. *Peasant Nationalism and Communist Power.* Stanford: Stanford University Press, 1962.

Karol, K. S. *China: The Other Communism.* New York: Hill and Wang, 1967.

Konstantinov, F. V., Sladkovsky, M. I. and Georgiyev, V. G. (Editors). *A Critique of Mao Tse-tung's Theoretical Conceptions.* Moscow: Progress, 1972.

Krivtsov, V. I. (Editor). *Maoism Through the Eyes of Communists.* Moscow: Progress, 1970.

Leibson, Boris. *Petty-Bourgeois Revolutionism.* Moscow: Progress, 1970.

Lewis, John Wilson (Editor). *Party Leadership and Revolutionary Power in China.* New York: Cambridge University Press, 1970.

Li Yu-ning. *The Introduction of Socialism into China.* New York: Columbia University Press, 1971.

Ling, Ken. *The Revenge of Heaven.* New York: Ballantine, 1972.

Lowe, Donald M. *The Function of "China" in Marx, Lenin and Mao.* Berkeley: University of California Press, 1966.

Malukhin, A. *Militarism—Backbone of Maoism.* Moscow: Novosti, 1970.

Masi, Edoarda. "Mao's Thought and the European Left." *Socialist Revolution,* 1, No. 4 (July-August, 1970).

Mehnert, Klaus (Editor). *Maos zweite Revolution.* Stuttgart: Deutsche Verlags-Anstalt, 1966.

Meisner, Maurice. *Li Ta-chao and the Origins of Chinese Marxism.* Cambridge: Harvard University Press, 1967.

Oksenberg, Michel (Editor). *China's Developmental Experience.* New York: Praeger, 1973.

Peng Shu-Tse and Peng Pi-lan. *The Chinese Revolution.* Three Parts. New York: Socialist Workers Party, 1972.

Schram, Stuart. *Mao Tse-tung.* Baltimore: Penguin, 1966.

Sladknovsky, M. I. (Editor). *Developments in China.* Moscow: Progress, 1968.

————, Kovalov, Y. F., and Sidikhmenov, V. Y. (Editors). *Leninism and Modern China's Problems.* Moscow: Progress, 1972.

Snow, Edgar. *Red Star over China.* New York: Random House, 1938.

Urban, George (Editor). *The "Miracles" of Chairman Mao.* Los Angeles: Nash, 1971.

Wakeman, Frederic. *History and Will: Philosophical Perspectives of Mao Tse-tung's Thought.* Berkeley: University of California Press, 1973.

"The Situation in the People's Republic of China." *Proletariat, 1,* No. 2 (August-September, 1970).

CHAPTER SEVEN

Conte Agüero, Luis. *Fidel Castro, Vida y Obra.* Havana: Lex, 1959.

Dalton, Roque. *¿Revolución en la revolucion? y la critica de derecha.* Havana: Casa de las Americas, 1970.

Draper, Theodore. *Castro's Revolution: Myths and Realities.* New York: Praeger, 1962.

————. *Castroism: Theory and Practice.* New York: Praeger, 1962.

Estrada, Ezequiel Martinez. *Martí: el héroe y su acción revolucionaria.* Mexico, D. F.: Siglo XXI, 1966.

Fagen, Richard R. *The Transformation of Political Culture in Cuba.* Stanford: Stanford University Press, 1969.

Halperin, Maurice. *The Rise and Decline of Fidel Castro.* Berkeley: University of California Press, 1972.

Huberman, Leo and Sweezy, Paul M. (Editors). *Regis Debray and the Latin American Revolution.* New York: Monthly Review, 1968.

James, Daniel. *Ché Guevara*. New York: Stein and Day, 1969.

Karol, K. S. *Guerrillas in Power: The Course of the Cuban Revolution*. New York: Hill and Wang, 1970.

O'Connor, James. *The Origins of Socialism in Cuba*. Ithaca: Cornell University Press, 1970.

Petit, Antoine G. *Castro, Debray contre le Marxisme-Léninisme*. Paris: Laffont, 1968.

Pierini, Franco, *"Ché" Guevara*. Milan: Longanesi, 1968.

Retamar, Roberto Fernandes. *Lectura de Martí*. Mexico, D. F.: Editorial Nuestro Tiempo, 1972.

Sinclair, Andrew. *Ché Guevara*. New York: Viking, 1970.

Tutino, Saverio. *L'Ottobre Cubano*. Turin: Einaudi, 1968.

Chapter Eight

Anthony, Earl. *Picking up the Gun: A Report on the Black Panthers*. New York: Dial, 1970.

Backhaus, Giorgio (Editor). *"Kursbuck": l'opposizione extraparlamentare*. Venice: Mondadori, 1969.

Bergmann, Uwe; Dutschke, Rudi; Lefevre, Wolfgang; and Rabehl, Bernd. *Die Rebellion der studenten oder die neue Opposition*. Hamburg: Rowohlt, 1968.

Bracy, John H. Jr.: Meier, August; and Rudwick, Elliott (Editors). *Black Nationalism in America*. New York: Bobbs-Merrill, 1970.

Chertoff, Mordecai (Editor). *The New Left and the Jews*. New York: Pitman, 1971.

Cleage, Albert and Breitman, George. "Myths About Malcolm X: Two Views." *International Socialist Review, 28*, No. 5 (September-October, 1967).

Cleaver, Eldridge. *On the Ideology of the Black Panther Party*. San Francisco: Black Panther Party, n.d.

Cronon, Edmund David. *Black Moses: The Story of Marcus Garvey and the Universal Negro Improvement Association*. Madison: University of Wisconsin, 1955.

Cruse, Harold. *Rebellion or Revolution*. New York: Morrow, 1967.

————. *The Crisis of the Negro Intellectual.* New York: Morrow, 1967.

Draper, Theodore. *The Rediscovery of Black Nationalism.* New York: Viking, 1969.

Edwards, Adolph. *Marcus Garvey.* London: New Beacon, 1967.

Essien-Udom, E. U. *Black Nationalism.* Chicago: University of Chicago Press, 1962.

Foner, Philip S. (Editor). *The Black Panthers Speak.* New York: Lippincott, 1970.

Garvey, Jacques A. *Garvey and Garveyism.* Kingston: United, 1963.

Green, Gil. *The New Radicalism: Anarchist or Marxist?* New York: International, 1971.

Habermas, Jürgen (Editor). *Antworten auf Herbert Marcuse.* Frankfurt: Suhrkamp, 1968.

Hoffman, Abbie. *Woodstock Nation.* New York: Random House, 1969.

Lincoln, C. Eric. *The Black Muslims in America.* Boston: Beacon Press, 1961.

Lomax, Louis E. *When the Word is Given . . .* New York: World, 1963.

MacIntyre, Alasdair. *Herbert Marcuse: An Exposition and a Polemic.* New York: Viking, 1970.

Marks, Robert W. *The Meaning of Marcuse.* New York: Ballantine, 1970.

Moore, Chuck (Editor). *I Was a Black Panther.* Garden City, N.Y.: Doubleday, 1970.

Perlini, T. *Che cosa ha veramente detto Marcuse.* Rome: Ubaldini, 1968.

Schanche, Don A. *The Panther Paradox: A Liberal's Dilemma.* New York: Paperback, 1970.

Schoeps, H. J. and Dannenmann, C. *Die rebellischen Studenten: Elite der Demokratie oder Vorhut eines linken Faschismus?* Munich: Bechtle, 1968.

Vincent, Theodore G. *Black Power and the Garvey Movement.* San Francisco: Ramparts, 1972.

Chapter Nine

Almond, Gabriel A., and Coleman, James S. (Editors). *The Politics of the Developing Areas.* Princeton: Princeton University Press, 1960.

Bauer, P. T. "The Economics of Resentment: Colonialism and Underdevelopment." *Journal of Contemporary History,* 4, No. 1 (1969).

Brzezinski, Zbigniew. *Between Two Ages: America's Role in the Technotronic Era.* New York: Viking, 1970.

Deutsch, Karl W., and Foltz, William J. (Editors). *Nation-Building.* New York: Atherton, 1966.

Doob, Leonard W. *Patriotism and Nationalism: Their Psychological Foundation.* New Haven: Yale University Press, 1964.

Ellul, Jacques. *The Technological Society.* Translated by John Wilkinson. New York: Random House, 1964.

Friedrich, Carl J. "Die Macht der Negation und das Verhängnis totaler Ideologie." In *Atlantische Begegnungen: eine Freundesgabe für Arnold Bergsträsser.* Freiburg: Rombach, 1964.

Geertz, Clifford (Editor). *Old Societies and New States: The Quest for Modernity in Asia and Africa.* New York: Free Press, 1963.

Gregor, A. James. *Contemporary Radical Ideologies: Totalitarian Thought in the Twentieth Century.* New York: Random House, 1968.

———. "African Socialism, Socialism and Fascism: An Appraisal," *Review of Politics,* 29 (July, 1967).

Kohn, Hans. *The Age of Nationalism: The First Era of Global History.* New York: Harper, 1962.

———, and Sokolsky, W. *African Nationalism in the Twentieth Century.* Princeton, N.J.: D. Van Nostrand, 1965.

Marshall, Byron K. *Capitalism and Nationalism in Prewar Japan: The Ideology of the Business Elite, 1868–1941.* Stanford: Stanford University Press, 1967.

Minogue, K. R. *Nationalism.* New York: Basic Books, 1967.

Organskii, A.F.K. *The Stages of Political Development.* New York: Knopf, 1965.

Plebe, Armando. *Quel che non ha capito Carlo Marx.* Milan: Rusconi, 1972.

Segal, Ronald. *The Race War.* New York: Viking, 1966.

Smith, Anthony D. *Theories of Nationalism.* New York: Harper and Row, 1971.

Snyder, Louis L. *The Dynamics of Nationalism: Readings in its Meaning and Development.* Princeton: D. Van Nostrand, 1964.

Symmons-Symonolewicz, Konstantin. *Nationalist Movements: A Comparative View.* Meadville, Pa.: Maplewood, 1970.

Wilson, George M. *Radical Nationalist in Japan: Kita Ikki, 1883-1937.* Cambridge: Harvard University Press, 1969.

Index

451

Marx, 137; and lack of theoretical consciousness among guerrillas, 302; and land reform, 281; and leadership, 283; Marxism of, 261, 298; and Marxism-Leninism, 260f, 274, 283f, 293, 296, 297, 303f; mass mobilization and vanguard leadership, 284; Matthews on, 285, 295; and Mussolini, 266, 284f, 294-296, 310, 315-317, 321n; as nationalist, 283; and non-communist character of his revolution, 260f; as non-Marxist, 260f, 262, 265, 283; opposed to dictatorship, 284; and Peronism, 261, 310; and personalism, 274, 285; as petty-bourgeois, 283; and productionism, 317; as "putschist," 283; revolution compared with Fascism, 274, 316f; and revolutionary nationalism, 275, 310; and student radicals, 328; thought of, 297; and totalitarianism, 290, 319; and the United States, 290; and voluntarism, 295; and working class support, 316

Castro, Raul, 282; on Castro's knowledge of Marx, 297

Chai, W., 253n

charismatic or exceptional leader, 134, 258f, 394, 397; as arbiter of ideological truth, 258; Castro as, 295, 296f, 301, 400, 427; Debray on, 314; in developing countries, 412; Fascism and, 246; as fascistic, 354, 400; Garvey as, 372; Guevara as, 301; Mao as, 297, 400, 427; and mobilized masses, 15, 141, 185, 362; Mussolini as, 230, 233, 245; Nkrumah as, 400; and party purge, 236, 246, 258; Stalin as, 427; and Third World, 353; and totalitarian movements, 414; and totalitarianism, 424; and unitary party, 23, 187; as "universal genius," 236, 246, 258

Chernyshevsky, Nicholas, 110, 202n; influence on Lenin, 197, 199; on the "New Man," 201; *What Is to Be Done?* 110, 199; on will, 201

Chiao Jung-wen, 405n

Chile, 286

China, 4, 12f, 15, 114f, 237f, 242, 244f, 261, 286, 395; and its historical boundaries, 20; Sino-Soviet dispute, 403

Mao's China, 224; elitism and Nationalism in, 227; and fascistic features, 406, 426; and Great Cultural Revolution, 236-238; and guerrilla heroes, 20; as hierarchical, 358; and industrial development, 19; mass mobilization in, 264; as moralistic, 19; and population problems, 403; as radical, 19; socialization in, 319; as totalitarian, 420

Chou Yang, 237

Clark, Kenneth, 381n, 386n

Cleaver, Eldridge, 389

Clough, R. T., 155n

Clytus, J., 389n

Codreanu, Corneliu, 428

Cohn-Bendit, Daniel, 349, 349n, 356, 356n

communism: Chinese, 224f, and nationalism, 225; and fascism, 17, 408, 424, 426f; as an intellectual ideology, 23; of Marx and Engels, 396; of underdeveloped countries, 133f

Communist Party, as "bourgeois" for Debray, 308; as bureaucratic, 315, 356

of China, 221, 225, 258; Central Committee of, 238; domes-

Hoffman, Abbie, 324n, 332, 333n,
334n, 335n, 336n; on Marxism,
335f; on mass manipulation,
334; and myth, 333; and na-
tionalism, 359; and Sorel, 333;
and Yippies, 332
Holland, 95
Hook, Sidney, 72n
Hopei, 239
Horkheimer, Max, 322
Horowitz, Irving L., 314n, 319n
Hoselitz, Bert F., 116n, 117n
Hsu Kuang-ping, 254, 254n
Huberman, Leo, 314n
Hunter, Guy, 409, 409n
Hyndman, H. M., 120

India, 115
intellectuals, alienated, 417;
contemporary radicals and, 207;
declassed, 8, 202, 208, 409;
and developmental systems,
397; displaced, 15, 174; as
elitists, 23, 174; as ideologists,
187; as leaders of Cuban revolution, 305; Li and, 207-209;
Malcolm X on, 377; military, 23;
and nationalism in China, 225;
and socialism in Cuba, 262;
urban, 23
Israel, 386
Italy, 12f, 102, 104f, 160, 166,
176f, 245, 268-272, 286; and
economic development, 18,
266f; Fascism and economic
development of, 266f
Fascist, 195, 317, 399;
mass-mobilization in, 264; and
military models, 20; population
pressure in, 401f; racial legislation in, 386; as totalitarian, 424
as a "new nation," 399;
as proletarian nation, 17, 176-
179, 267; proletarian, lack of
class consciousness in, 18;
students in, 325f

Jacobs, Paul, 328, 328n, 330,
330n, 331, 331n
James, Daniel, 282n, 314n
James 3X, 379
Japan, students in, 325f, 327
Johnson, Chalmers A., 225, 225n
Joll, James, 155n, 173n
Jordan, David, 410, 410n
Julien, Claude, 262n
Jünger, Ernst, 412
Justicialismo, 411. See also Peron

Kamenev, Lev, 235, 237
Kamenka, Eugene, 42n
Kammari, M. D., 121n
Kang Chao, 250n
Kang Sheng, 239
Kansu, 241
Kautsky, John, 8n, 223n, 337,
337n, 429n
Kautsky, Karl, 62n, 112, 121n;
as anti-nationalist, 121
Kemalism, 7
Kemp, Tom, 124n
Keniston, Kenneth, 328n, 330,
330n; and style of radical stu-
dents, 330f
Kennan, George, 321n
Kerr, Charles H., 102n
Khrushchev, Nikita, 403
Kiangsi, 241
Kiangsu, 239
Kirk, Russell, 325n; on student
radicals as "left-wing fascists,"
325
Klein, A., 329n
Konstantinov, F. V., 210n
Kornhauser, William, 186n, 414n,
415n, 433
Kozharov, A., 404n, 405n, 429n
Krivtsov, V. I., 404n
Kropotkin, Peter, 329
Kruchinin, A., 403n
Krupskaya, Nadezhda, 199, 199n
Kommunist, 405
Kugelmann, Ludwig, 72, 72n

Mussolini, Benito (*cont.*)
lems, 168, 170; as nationalist, 226, 411; compared with nationalists, 151f, 170f; and "New Deal," 420; and "New Man," 147, 270f; influence of Oriani on, 203-205, 247; influence of Pareto on, 143-146, 203, 247; and Pareto's "theory of elites," 145; and control of his Party, 231-233, 245, 248, 293; as petty-bourgeois, 427; as pragmatic, 266; and productive relations, 108; as productivist, 178; and problem of non-revolutionary proletariat, 205; and Italy as proletarian nation, 176, 308; and racism, 373f; and revolution, 110; and ancient Rome, 15; and sentiments as motives for action, 143f, 147; and Social Republic of, compared to Castroism, 410, compared to Peronism, 410; and socialism, 311-313; and socialization, 313; influence of Sorel on, 143, 203, 247, 343; and Stalin as "crypto-fascist," 185; and Stalinism, 419; and syndicalists, 139f; and totalitarianism, 255; and violence, 148f, 152, 270f, 343, 345; and voluntarism, 105, 108, 205, 246; and lack of working class support, 316; and World War I, 168-171, 270

Napolitano, Tomaso, 184n
Nasser, Gamal Abdel, 7, 20; and civilization of Pharaohs, 15; and fascist contacts, 355
Nasti, A., 184
nation, agrarian, 219; as object of allegiance, 167; bourgeois, 220; capitalist, 130, 133, 195, 218; Garvey and Negro, 366; industrial, 219, 322f, and student rad-

icals, 322f; Lost-Found, 375f; Marx and, 50; Mussolini and the concept of, 171; plutocratic, 12, 133, 187, 195, 220, and Fascist ideology, 16, 133, 217, 222
proletarian, 133, 187, 195, 220; China as, 318; Fascists and the, 222, 352; Italy as, 176f, 217, 219; Mussolini and Italy as, 176; and student radicals, 351, 355
socialist, 130, 133, 221; and control by unitary party, 257
Nation of Islam, 375. *See* Black Muslims
National Association for the Advancement of Colored People, 369, 386
National Socialism, 8, 14, 373; and Black Panthers, 389; and Party of Hitler, 258; and racism of Black Muslims, 378
nationalism, 7, 12, 248; of African States, 350; of Arab States, 350
black, 14, 360, 383; as developmental, 383; as fascist, 384, 392; ideology of, 387; and Malcolm X, 388; and National Socialism, 391f; as non-Marxist, 388f; and racism, 422; and violence, 388
and Bolshevism, 349; in Castro's Cuba, 264, 350-352, 431; Chinese, 351f, 431; and communism, 23, 309; and development, 12, 20; Engels on, 395; and Fascism, 349; and Futurism, 349; of Garvey, 363-365; Gentile on, 272; and ideology of Castro, 310, 349; and international class struggle, 226; Lenin on, 128; Lenin and Marxist, 218; of Mao, 225f, 350, 403, 431; of Martí, 265; Marx on,

Plekhanov, Georgi, 112; on consciousness, 101; Lenin on, 199; influence on Lenin, 102
Portugal, 273
Prezzolini, Giuseppe, 173, 173n, 185; on similarities between Marxism-Leninism and Fascism, 185
proletarian, proletariat, 12, 89; bourgeoisified, 91, 307f; Castro and, 284; class in Marx, 50, 53f, 227, 228; lack of class consciousness, in Italy and Russia, 18; class consciousness 'of, according to Debray, 307; according to Lenin, 107-109; according to Marx, 72, 80f, 87-94, 305f, 341; according to Mussolini, 107f; according to syndicalists, 107-109; as concept in the work of Marx, 44, 308; and consciousness, 196, 207, 209, 220f; Cuba's, 305; Debray on, 307; definition of, according to Castro, 297, according to Debray, 308, according to Fascists, 308, according to Maoists, 308f, according to radicals, 23; and emiseration in Marx, 43, 69, 71f; Engels on, 79, 341; and Fascism, 16; German, in World War I, 168; international, 121, 167; Lenin on, 122; "Mao's thought" defines, 242; Marx on, increase of, 30, 54, 69-71; internationalism of, 51, 112; as majority of population, 55, 80f; revolution and nation, 50, 395; spontaneous organization of, 55; victory of, 33f; and mass mobilization, 142; nation, 12, 351f, Italy as, 176f; and student radicals, 355; and the nation, 168; and national

liberation, 117f; nationalism, 177; revolution for Debray, 305; problem of non-revolutionary, 87, 94, 153, 173, 177, 209, Debray on, 307; Marcuse on, 338; Mills on, 338; and New Left 355; socialism rejected by black radicals, 390; urban, and communist movements, 428; and vanguard, 107, 196, 308; world historical, 129, 196
Puchetti, A. C., 143n

Quaglio, C., 211n

Rebehl, Bernd, 349, 349n, 351, 351n
Radek, Karl, 235, 246
Rader, Dodson, 324n, 350, 350n; I Ain't Marchin' Anymore, 350
radicalism, 23; as an amalgam, 21; contemporary, 25; definition of, 22; "left" and "right" wing, 16-18; Maoism as, 23; political ideologies of, 16; similarities between, 15, 22
radicals, black, 389, 390; Fascists as, 16; in Italy, 166; as Marxists, 167; their movements as fascist, 412; and their regimes, 19; radicals, 19; student, as anti-authoritarian, 355f; and anti-intellectualism, 329, 331, 333; and Castroism, 328; and classical Marxism, 328; and factionalism, 327; as generational phenomenon, 328; ideology of, 323; and irrationalism, 334; as "left-wing" fascism, 324f, 354; and Leninism, 328; and Maoism, 328; and Marxism, 323, 392; and the use of myth, 332f; and surrogate nationalism, 350f, 359; and proletarian nations, 351, 354; and problem of

Smith, R. F., 275n
Snow, Edgar, 205n, 253
Social Democratic Party, of
  England, 120; of Germany, 95,
  168, 306; of Russia, 86, 200
socialism, Fascist, 313; international, 217; Marxian, 18; and
  nationalism, 167; non-Marxist,
  15; Stalin's, 12
Socialist Party of Italy, 86;
  Mussolini as leader of, 105
Sombart, Werner, 97n
Soprano, Domenico, 402n
Sorel, Georges, 103f, 104n, 108n,
  146, 152f, 166, 177, 323; "Apology for Violence," 147; and
  Black Panthers, 389; on Corradini, 152; influence on Fascist
  squadristi, 302; influence on
  Hoffman, 333; and masses and
  mobilization, 104, 148; influence on Mussolini, 145, 152,
  343; and myths, 148; and nationalism, 119f; and problem of
  non-revolutionary proletariat,
  141; and Italian syndicalists,
  107, 150, 166; on violence, 343
South Africa, 403
Soviet Union, 24, 93, 137, 192,
  212, 273, 290, see also Russia;
  and domestication of Bolshevik
  Party, 234f; and its historic
  boundaries, 20; and Cuba, 292f,
  317-319; as fascist, 17, 131-134,
  136-138, 356, 405, 426; and
  military industries, 19; nationalism in, 130f; as racist, 383,
  389; and "All-Peoples State,"
  226f; and student radicals, 356
Spain, Falangist, 273
Spinetti, G. Silvano, 432n
Spirito, Ugo, 432n
Spock, Benjamin, 322
squadristi, 302; and Black
  Panthers, 389
Stalin, Joseph, 6, 86, 191n, 192n,

194, 210n, 212f, 235n, 238,
  246; as anti-nationalist, 121;
  and domestication of Bolshevik
  Party, 131, 234f, 248, 293;
  and bureaucracy, 245; and "routinized charisma," 258; Concerning Marxism in Linguistics,
  212; and his Constitution, 246;
  and Russian creativity, 15; and
  development, 18, 131, 192; and
  Fascism, 86, 132; and similarities with Fascism, 134; as
  genius, 130, 212f, 236; on ideas
  and life conditions, 93; on the
  role of exceptional leaders, 191f;
  and Marxism, 17, 136, 184, 246;
  Mussolini on, 132, 185; and
  Party as control agency, 235;
  and reforms of 1935-1936, 184;
  and the Soviet State, 191f; and
  state socialism, 191
Stalinism, 22; and bureaucratic
  collectivism, 132; as developmental dictatorship, 194; and
  Fascism, 131f, 183f, Ardemagni
  on, 184, Borkenau on, 193,
  Burnham on, 419n, Fromm on,
  193f, Halevy on, 186, Mussolini
  on, 185, 395, 432, Reich on,
  193f, Rizzi on, 193, Trotsky on,
  194
Stirner, Max, 356
Stone, N. I., 27n
Students for a Democratic Soci-
  ety, 326f, 329, 392
Suarez, A., 284n, 285n, 319n
Sukarno, Achmed, 20, 355
Sun Yat-sen, 7
Sweezy, Paul, 314n
Syndicalists, and elitism, 107-
  109; and Fascism, 16, 312;
  Italian, 107-109

"take-off," 9-11, 14, 413, 428
Tasca, Angelo, 174, 174n
Taylor, Gordon R., 422, 422n

LIBRARY OF CONGRESS CATALOGING IN PUBLICATION DATA

Gregor, A. James
The Fascist persuasion in radical politics.
Includes bibliographical references.
1. Fascism.   2. Radicalism.   3. Socialism.
I. Title.
JC481.G686   320.5'33   73-2463
ISBN 0-691-07556-5